During his remarkable career, David Hill has been chairman then managing director of the Australian Broadcasting Corporation; chairman of the Australian Football Association; chief executive and director of the State Rail Authority; chairman of Sydney Water Corporation; a fellow of the Sydney University Senate; and chairman of CREATE (an organisation representing Australian children in institutional care).

He has held a number of other executive appointments and committee chair positions in the areas of sport, transport, international radio broadcasting, international news providers, politics, fiscal management and city parks.

David came from England to Australia in 1959 under the Fairbridge Farm School Child Migrant scheme. He left school at 15, then returned to complete his Master's degree in economics while working as an economics tutor at Sydney University.

After graduating in 2006 in classical archaeology from the University of Sydney, David became an honorary associate at the university in the departments of archaeology and classics and ancient history. He is also a visiting fellow at the University of New South Wales. Since 2011 he has been the manager of an archaeological study of the ancient Greek city of Troizen. He has for many years been a leading figure in the international campaign to have the Parthenon sculptures returned from the British Museum to Greece.

David is the author of the bestsellers *The Forgotten Children* (2006), *1788* (2008), *The Gold Rush* (2009), *The Great Race* (2011) and *The Making of Australia* (2014).

Also by David Hill

The Special Relationship

Australia and the Monarchy

David Hill

WILLIAM HEINEMANN: AUSTRALIA

A William Heinemann book
Published by Random House Australia Pty Ltd
Level 3, 100 Pacific Highway, North Sydney NSW 2060
www.penguin.com.au

Penguin
Random House
Australia

First published by William Heinemann in 2015
This edition published in 2016

National Library of Australia
Cataloguing-in-Publication entry

Hill, David, 1946– author
Special Relationship, The/David Hill

ISBN 978 0 85798 755 6 (paperback)

Monarchy – Australia – History
Monarchy – Australia – Public opinion
Australia – Politics and government – History

321.870994

Cover images: Rob Griffith Pool, Getty Images (front); National Museum of Australia (back)
Cover design by Nada Backovic
Internal design by Post Pre-press, Australia
Typeset in Sabon by Post Pre-press, Australia
Printed in Australia by Griffin Press, an accredited ISO AS/NZS 14001:2004
Environmental Management System printer

CONTENTS

HOUSE OF SAXE-COBURG & GOTHA 1840–1917 and HOUSE OF WINDSOR 1917–Present Day

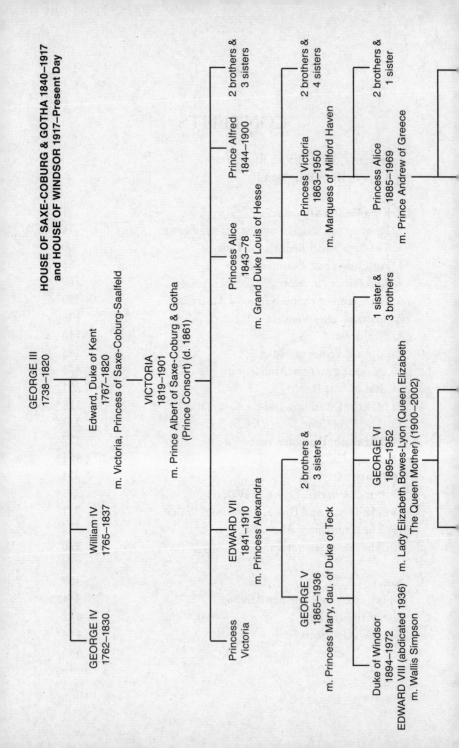

GEORGE III
1738–1820

GEORGE IV
1762–1830

William IV
1765–1837

Edward, Duke of Kent
1767–1820
m. Victoria, Princess of Saxe-Coburg-Saalfeld

VICTORIA
1819–1901
m. Prince Albert of Saxe-Coburg & Gotha
(Prince Consort) (d. 1861)

Princess Alice
1843–78
m. Grand Duke Louis of Hesse

Prince Alfred
1844–1900

2 brothers &
3 sisters

Princess Victoria
1863–1950
m. Marquess of Milford Haven

2 brothers &
4 sisters

Princess Alice
1885–1969
m. Prince Andrew of Greece

2 brothers &
1 sister

Princess
Victoria

EDWARD VII
1841–1910
m. Princess Alexandra

2 brothers &
3 sisters

GEORGE V
1865–1936
m. Princess Mary, dau. of Duke of Teck

GEORGE VI
1895–1952
m. Lady Elizabeth Bowes-Lyon (Queen Elizabeth
The Queen Mother) (1900–2002)

1 sister &
3 brothers

Duke of Windsor
1894–1972
EDWARD VIII (abdicated 1936)
m. Wallis Simpson

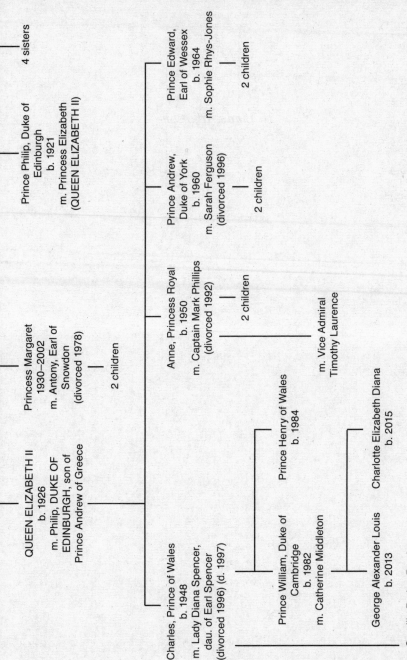

To Linda Atkinson

I

KING GEORGE III

I am, therefore, commanded to signify to your Lordships His Majesty's pleasure that you do forthwith take such measures as may be necessary for providing a proper number of vessels for the conveyance of 750 convicts to Botany Bay.

THE SPECIAL RELATIONSHIP BETWEEN the British royal family and Australia began when British explorer and naval captain James Cook claimed possession of the east coast of the great south land in 1770 in the name of King George III.

George III had ascended the throne on 25 October 1760 aged twenty-two, the third monarch from the German House of Hanover. The Hanoverians had been called on to provide the British monarch when Queen Anne, the last of the House of Stuart, died without any surviving children and was succeeded by her second cousin, George I, in 1714. George III was the first of the kings of the House of Hanover to be born in England and to speak English as his first language.

He became king on the death of his grandfather, George II; his father having died nine years earlier in 1751.

As a young man George was given a broad education. He was the first monarch to study science and to be seriously interested in the subject. Later he would assemble one of the most comprehensive collections of eighteenth-century scientific and astronomical equipment, which is now in London's Science Museum. A year after becoming king he married Princess Charlotte of Mecklenburg-Strelitz, whom he first met on their wedding day. Despite an arranged marriage the couple enjoyed a happy union, and, unlike his grandfather and his son, George III did not take a mistress. He and his wife had fifteen children, nine boys and six girls.

During his long reign King George oversaw the British victory over France in 1763 in the Seven Years War, which made Great Britain the dominant European power, ruling in India and North America, until many of Britain's American colonies were lost in the American War of Independence. Yet, despite reigning over a vast empire for sixty years, King George spent almost all of his life living in the south of England, devoted to his family, farming and the study of science.

Captain Cook had sailed from England in 1768 on the first of his three great voyages to the Pacific, visiting Tahiti to witness the transit of Venus in 1769 – an astronomical event that was used to measure the distance between the earth and other planets. Cook was ordered to then sail westward in search of the great south land. He became the second European explorer after Dutchman Abel Tasman in 1642 to reach New Zealand, and took six months to navigate its coast and confirm it consisted of two major islands. He then headed west, and at 6 am on 19 April 1770 his second lieutenant, Zachary Hicks, sighted the land that Cook would name New South Wales.

Cook decided to 'follow the direction of the coast northward'.[1] Ten days into the journey his ship, the HMS *Endeavour*, entered a large bay, which became known as Botany Bay. There the botanist Joseph Banks and his team collected hundreds of plants and seeds. Cook and his crew stayed a week in the bay, giving the British enough time to collect fresh water and wood before heading north. Of course, they could have no inkling that their countrymen would later choose Botany Bay as the location for Britain's first settlement in this vast land.

Towards the northern tip of Australia, the *Endeavour* was badly damaged when it hit the edge of the Great Barrier Reef. After several weeks of repairs Cook sailed on, and at the very top of the east coast he successfully navigated his way through the Torres Strait. He landed on a small island he named Possession Island and claimed the entire coast of Australia for King George III on 22 August 1770:

> Notwithstanding I had in the Name of His Majesty taken possession of several places upon this coast I now once more hoisted English Colours and in the Name of His Majesty King George the Third took possession of the whole Eastern Coast from the above Latitude down to this place by the Name of New South Wales together with all the Bays, Harbours, Rivers and Islands situate upon the said coast after which we fired three Volleys of small Arms which were answered by the like number from the Ship.[2]

Cook's mapping of more than 3000 kilometres of Australia's east coast set in train the long, fraught process of British colonisation of the great south land. In 1779, almost ten years after his visit, Joseph Banks recommended to a House of Commons enquiry that surplus British convicts be sent to Botany Bay. Seven years later, and after many complaints of overburdened prisons and hulks in Great Britain, King George III authorised the establishment of a British convict settlement in his most recent overseas territorial possession: New South Wales.

> The several gaols and places of confinement of felons in this kingdom being so crowded a state that the greatest danger is to be apprehended . . . His Majesty, desirous of preventing by every possible means the ill consequences . . . has been pleased to signify . . . his royal commands that measures should immediately be pursued for sending out of this kingdom such convicts . . . His Majesty has thought it advisable to fix upon Botany Bay.[3]

And so began the organisation of the largest overseas migration the world had ever seen. The detailed planning was also authorised by King George:

> I am, therefore, commanded to signify to your Lordships His Majesty's pleasure that you do forthwith take such measures as may be necessary for providing a proper number of vessels for the conveyance of 750 convicts to Botany Bay, together with such provisions, necessaries and implements for agriculture as may be necessary for their use after their arrival.[4]

At the time of the decision to form this British settlement, the king was forty-eight years old, in the twenty-fifth year of his long reign and by all accounts in good health. He was quick to involve himself in all the major decisions to establish the colony, including the detailed preparation of the First Fleet and the welfare of the settlement in its first years. He was one of the last British monarchs to be so directly involved in the day-to-day decisions of his governments, and it was during his long reign that there began a shift towards the power of parliament and the rise of governance by a cabinet of politicians. Surviving documents indicate the king appraised himself of such detail as 'bedding for each of the convicts' and 'surgical instruments and medicines' as well as signing the commissions for all the senior officers appointed to take the convicts to Botany Bay, including fleet commander and colony's governor Captain Arthur Phillip and chief surgeon John White.[5] In addition, King George defined the limits to the governors' powers in the new colony, which included control over currency, powers over the marines, fortifications, the authority to 'pardon and reprieve', meting out discipline, making laws for the colony, the establishment of criminal trials and courts, and punishment and executions.

At a meeting with his senior government ministers at the court of St James on 20 April 1787, the king authorised the area of what would later be known as Australia that would become part of his empire.[6] By the end of the eighteenth century Britain had lost the American colonies but it still held most of Canada and a number of possessions in Africa and India. Over the next century it would add large tracts of territory in Africa, Asia and the Pacific, including the former colonies of the Portuguese, French and the Dutch. The new colony in Australia included the 3000 kilometres of the east coast claimed on the king's behalf by Captain Cook seventeen years before, and extended further south to include the island of Van Diemen's Land, which had been discovered by Abel Tasman in 1642 and claimed by him for Holland. King George also wanted for Britain the area from the east coast 'to the westward as far as the one hundred and thirty-fifth degree east latitude, reckoning from the meridian of Greenwich', which is roughly equal to drawing a line down the centre of the Australian continent and claiming all the land to the right. [7] At the time, the British had seen none of this land other than Cook's survey of some of the coast, though parts of it had been explored and charted – and some of it claimed for Holland – by the Dutch in earlier centuries.

The First Fleet of convicts left Portsmouth on 13 May 1787 to build the first European settlement in Australia. Their voyage lasted eight months, with 1500 crowded onto eleven small ships, along with what was hoped to be enough food for two years, and tools and equipment to build a new life at Botany Bay. In addition to the 800 male and female convicts, there were nearly 300 marines, officers, officials, wives and children, and several hundred in the ships' crews. Only two ships in the fleet were naval. The remainder were chartered from private operators and were returned to private merchant shipping after they had dropped off their cargo.

After departing from England the fleet stopped at Tenerife, Rio de Janeiro and Cape Town for water and fresh supplies. At both Rio and Cape Town the crews took aboard seeds and seedlings to plant once they reached Australia, and about 500 farm animals, including cows, horses, chickens, geese, ducks and pigs. During the voyage Phillip and his chief surgeon adopted an enlightened policy of regularly cleaning the convict quarters and allowing prisoners to exercise each day on deck. They also supplemented the dreary diet of salted meat and dry ship's biscuit with fresh fruit when they were able to buy some in the ports along the way.

The passage of the First Fleet was a remarkable success. All the ships survived the journey and even though the fleet was split in the Southern Ocean, they all arrived in Botany Bay within forty hours of each other between 18 and 20 January 1788. Only forty-eight people died during the voyage, a fraction of the losses on the second and some subsequent fleets.

The white settlers met local Aboriginal people on their first day on land. Captain Arthur Phillip's instructions, signed by King George III, ordered that the British find a harmonious way of dealing with native inhabitants and that any violence towards them be punished:

> You are to endeavour by every possible means to open an intercourse with the natives, and to conciliate their affections, enjoining all our subjects to live in amity and kindness with them. And if our subjects shall wantonly destroy them, or give any unnecessary interruption . . . it is our will and pleasure that you do cause such offenders to be brought to punishment according to the degree of the offence.[8]

Armed with these strict orders, and having been told that the Indigenous inhabitants should be 'treated with every mark of friendship', the newcomers thought at first that perhaps there would indeed be peace between them and the locals.[9] However, relations between the new settlers and the Aboriginal people from the start were characterised by a mutual incomprehension that gradually worsened. The first encounters were friendly enough, but soon there were more and more incidents of violence as the settlers increasingly deprived the locals of their traditional lands and sources of food. Not only this, but in April 1789, more than a year after the arrival of the First Fleet, there was an outbreak of smallpox during which some estimate as much as half the local Aboriginal population died.[10]

The establishment of the new convict colony was a struggle. Within a few days, Botany Bay was deemed unsuitable for settlement due to its poor soil and inadequate supply of fresh water, and Phillip hastily chose a bay in Port

Jackson, twelve kilometres to the north, which he named Sydney Cove. Some of the animals that had been brought aboard at Cape Town had died before the ships reached New South Wales, and others ambled into the dense bush and were lost. The first planted crops were almost a total failure, with enough grain harvest to support the settlement for only a few weeks; Phillip's very first dispatch from Sydney to England, four months after arriving in the new colony, warned the British that more supplies must be sent:

> The great labour in clearing the ground will not permit more than eight acres sown this year with wheat and barley. At the same time the immense number of ants and field mice will render our crops very uncertain. Part of the livestock brought from the Cape, small as it was, has been lost and our resource in fish is also uncertain.[11]

When the letter reached England early the following year, colonial secretary Lord Sydney wrote immediately to the British Admiralty to say that King George III had authorised the urgent dispatch of a supply ship to relieve the colony, and for additional supplies to be sent, as Phillip had asked.

> The letters which have been received from Captain Phillip, governor of New South Wales, representing that a great part of the provisions sent out with him . . . had been expended, and that there is an immediate occasion for a further supply, together with certain articles of clothing, tools, implements for agriculture, medicines etc. . . . His Majesty has given orders that one of his ships of war of two decks . . . shall forthwith be got ready to carry out the said provisions and stores.[12]

Within a month the admiralty had responded by appointing Lieutenant Edward Riou as captain of the HMS *Guardian*, which would ferry fresh supplies to New South Wales. The king, having taken a strong interest in the welfare of the First Fleet, was across many of the details of the *Guardian*'s preparation – he even made sure that the ship was modified according to the request of Joseph Banks: the eminent botanist had suggested that in addition to sending food and other provisions, a shed should be built on the *Guardian*'s quarterdeck for trees and plants that could be transplanted in Sydney.

> Having laid before the king a letter from Joseph Banks proposing that a small coach may be erected on the quarterdeck of the Guardian, for the purpose of conveying to Port Jackson, in pots of earth, such plants and trees as will be useful in food or physique . . . I am commanded to signify to your Lordships His Majesty's pleasure . . . that you do give orders that it may be immediately erected.[13]

In September 1789 the *Guardian* sailed from Portsmouth with more than 900 tonnes of supplies, including a large amount of grain, vegetables, herbs, fruit and livestock, including sheep, horses, cattle, goats, rabbits and poultry. Riou made good time sailing and reached the Cape of Good Hope on 24 November. However, a month later, on Christmas Eve, when the *Guardian* was deep in the Southern Ocean and more than 1000 kilometres south-east of the Cape, it smashed into an iceberg. About half the crew managed to board the five small lifeboats, but four of these were subsequently lost. The fifth was rescued two weeks later by a French ship, about 400 kilometres off the east coast of Natal.

Meanwhile, Captain Riou and the remaining sixty-one crew who had stayed on the waterlogged *Guardian* managed not to sink by continually pumping out water from the stricken ship. Two months later they were seen south of Madagascar by a passing Dutch vessel, which helped tow the half-sunken *Guardian* back to Cape Town.

Over the next few months a number of British ships in the second fleet of convicts bound for Australia called in at Cape Town and took with them what could be salvaged from the *Guardian* for the now starving colony in Sydney. Their arrival in June 1790, and the supplies they brought, saved the First Fleet's settlement.

King George III maintained a strong personal interest in the welfare of the colony after his first bout of mental illness in the British summer of 1788. Although it has never been conclusively proven, it is believed the king suffered for much of his adult life a genetic disorder called porphyria, when a build-up of natural chemicals in the body afflicts the nervous system. Symptoms of the increasingly disabling disease include severe pains in the abdomen, chest, limbs and back; also mental problems such as confusion, hallucinations, disorientation and paranoia.

Given the king's mental illness, the House of Commons had passed the Regency Bill in February 1789, authorising his eldest son and heir, 26-year-old George, the Prince of Wales, who did not have a good relationship with his father, to act as regent. But before the House of Lords could pass the bill, the king recovered. For some years after this he appeared to function normally and continued to take a strong personal interest in the affairs of the new colony in Australia. In June 1792 colonial secretary Henry Dundas wrote to tell Governor Arthur Phillip that the king had read all of the first sixteen dispatches sent back from Sydney to various British government officials:

I have received and have the honour of laying before His Majesty your letters of the numbers and dates mentioned in the margin [delivered by the ships] *Waaksamheyd* and the *Supply* tender, which, notwithstanding the different periods they set out [for England] arrived at the same instant.[14]

Just as King George III took a direct interest in the fortunes of the First Fleet, the new colonists took a strong interest in their monarch. When the last ship of the First Fleet, the navy ship *Supply*, finally left Sydney to return to London in November 1791, it carried on board the first live kangaroo taken to England as a gift for the king; and two years later, when word finally reached the Sydney settlement that the king had recovered from his first bout of serious illness, seventeen of the most senior officers, including judge David Collins, chaplain Richard Johnson and John White, sent a message of sympathy:

> We, His Majesty's most dutiful and loyal subjects, the officers of the civil and Military Establishments of New South Wales, filled with the deepest sense of gratitude for the mercies of Almighty God in restoring our most Gracious Sovereign to health from a dangerous and afflicting sickness, most humbly beg to approach your Excellency with our sincere and heart-felt congratulations on that happy and distinguished event, and to declare our unshaken loyalty and attachment to His Majesty's person and government.[15]

'Loyalty to the Motherland' was ingrained in the officers of the First Fleet, and from the beginning of white settlement of Australia, the structure of local colonial society reflected that of Britain, from the largely British hereditary ruling class down to the subservient lower orders.

By 1810, the colony was under the command of a new governor, Lachlan Macquarie, after two years of turmoil that had seen the overthrow of his predecessor, Captain

William Bligh. Macquarie was a visionary who defied the model of the rigid British class system and offered former convicts the prospect of social acceptance and government jobs, moves that ultimately put him out of step and out of favour with his London superiors.

By now King George III was seventy-two years old and at the height of his popularity. But he was already virtually blind with cataracts and in pain from rheumatism, and his mental health was further diminished. The king was convinced his condition had been worsened by the stress caused by the loss in 1810 of his youngest and favourite daughter, Princess Amelia, who died aged only twenty-seven after several years of ill health. And so the following year he finally allowed himself to be subjugated to the *Regency Act* of 1811, after which the Prince of Wales was regent for the remainder of George III's life. Despite signs of a recovery in May 1811, the king never fully recovered his health, and from the end of 1811 was kept well away from the public eye at Windsor Castle until his death in 1820 aged eighty-one.

His son, George IV, became king at fifty-seven years of age. In stark contrast to his father, George IV lived an extravagant lifestyle, modelling himself as a leader not only in terms of his authority over the nation but in new styles of leisure, fashion and taste. While he had been regent during the last years of the Napoleonic Wars, his private spending had caused widespread resentment among the British ruling elite and, unlike his father, he took little interest in government and even less interest in Australia.

When he died only ten years later in 1830, he was succeeded by his younger brother, William, who was even less involved in the British government than George IV had been. He had no interest in the foreign policy of Great Britain, and certainly not in a place thousands of miles away.

After a short reign of only seven years, King William IV died in 1837 aged seventy-one.

His successor was his niece, and the granddaughter of King George III, Alexandrina Victoria, who ascended the throne on 20 June 1837 and would be a towering influence over Australia during her reign of sixty-three years.

2

FIGHTING FOR AND AGAINST
THE BRITISH CROWN

Together with other diverse false traitors ... armed and
arrayed in a warlike manner ... with guns, muskets, blunder-
busses, pistols, swords, bayonets, pikes, and other weapons,
being then unlawfully, maliciously and traitorously assembled and gathered wickedly, maliciously, and traitorously did
levy and make war against our said Lady the Queen ... and
did then maliciously and traitorously attempt and endeavour
by force and arms to subvert and destroy the constitution and
Government ... and deprive and depose our said Lady the
Queen of and from the style, honour, and kingly name of the
imperial crown of the said part of her dominions.

AFTER THE FIRST EUROPEAN colony of New South Wales
was founded in Sydney in 1788, other settlements were
progressively established that led to the formation of six
separate British colonies: New South Wales, Tasmania,

Victoria, South Australia, Queensland and Western Australia. The development of the Australian colonies was marked by a reverence to Queen Victoria. Two colonies – Victoria and Queensland – were named after her. In cities, towns and villages across the country there are still parks, mountains and rivers, towns, suburbs, streets, railway stations, public buildings, statues, schools, colleges and hospitals all named after Victoria. In Adelaide there is Victoria Square; in Perth, Victoria Park; in Melbourne, Victoria Dock, the Victoria Market and Queen's College; in Sydney, the Queen Victoria Building, Victoria Park and Queen's Square; and in Brisbane, Victoria Park.

Queen Victoria was the daughter of Prince Edward, Duke of Kent, who was the fourth son of King George III. She inherited the throne of Britain and its empire in 1837 because her father's three elder brothers had all died, leaving no legitimate, surviving children. Victoria was to become a revered figure in Australia, cementing the affections of Australians to the British Crown, ties that have remained for more than two centuries.

Victoria became queen less than a month after she turned eighteen. Two and a half years later she married her first cousin, Prince Albert, the German son of Ernst, Duke of Saxe-Coburg and Gotha, and took his name of Saxe-Coburg and Gotha, which would remain the British royal family name until the unpopularity of the Germans in World War I prompted it to be changed. Albert and Victoria's marriage was by all accounts a happy one and together they had nine children (five daughters and four sons) between November 1840 and April 1857. Albert was a source of great support for his wife as she took over the running of the royal household, estates and offices. When he died following a bout of typhoid fever in December 1861, Victoria sank into years of deep mourning. Over the next decade her popularity diminished as a result of her self-imposed isolation and withdrawal from public appearances, and it was not until she finally re-emerged in the early 1870s that her reputation recovered.

The first major threat to the sovereignty of Queen Victoria and the authority of British rule in her empire came after gold was found in Australia in 1851. The first discoveries were at Ophir in western New South Wales, but within a few months there were much bigger finds 1000 kilometres to the south in the new colony of Victoria, sparking a rush of prospectors from all over the world. Within five years the Australian population of less than half a million people had doubled, and by 1858 it exceeded one million.

From the beginning of the gold rush there were tensions on the goldfields of both New South Wales and Victoria between the diggers and the British authorities over a licence fee that had been set by authorities, which was thirty shillings a month and paid in advance – irrespective of whether the digger found any gold. The official justification for the fee was that Australia, as a British colony, belonged to the Crown, and therefore any gold found in the land was owned by the queen.

The setting of the licence fee encapsulated tensions between the ruling class and the lower orders that had been simmering in the colonies during Lachlan Macquarie's governorship and since, but its unpopularity didn't stem the rush to the goldfields, which left the upper echelons of Sydney and Melbourne society shocked as the lower orders raced off to try to make their fortune, leaving an inconvenient shortage of labourers and domestic servants:

> Hardly a man is content to remain where he is . . . you hear endless stories of ladies who have been used to large establishments, and giving parties, now obliged to give up all thoughts

of appearance, and open the doors even themselves . . . no servants are to be had, and many of the best and pleasant families literally driven out of the country because of it.[1]

The discovery of gold attracted to Australia thousands of men and women from a host of other countries who felt no allegiance to the British Crown and in many cases had no respect for British authority. This was particularly the case for Americans who had come over having won, seventy years earlier, their war of independence from the British. And many of the Irish who came saw immigration to the Australian goldfields as an escape from British oppression at home. Added to the mix were thousands from various other European countries that had experienced revolutions only a few years before in 1848. All were bound to fight any strictures placed on them in this new country.

Not only that, but diggers who had struggled to reach the goldfields from far away found life there hard enough even before paying a tax. For most, the fields meant limited food, high prices, rough accommodation, lack of women and family, tedium, fatigue and loneliness, all of which contributed to the resentment they felt towards the heavy-handed ways of the police who collected the fee. Even among the many British loyalists there was a view that the licence fee was too high. To add insult to injury, the licence was only valid for twenty-six working days – the diggers were not allowed to work on Sundays.

In June 1853 the Anti-Gold Licence Association was formed at Bendigo in Victoria, where more than 20,000 diggers from Ballarat, Bendigo, Castlemaine, Heathcote, Stawell and other sites signed what became known as the Bendigo Petition, which detailed the miners' grievances. The thirteen-metre-long petition was bound in green silk, taken to Melbourne and given to governor Sir Charles La

Trobe, who was moved to write to the colonial secretary in London, Sir George Grey, to warn him about what he called huge numbers of 'politically restless' immigrants who spoke of 'subverting the queen's authority and introducing a different order of things'.[2] By the end of the year thousands of miners had taken to wearing red ribbons in their hats to mark their opposition to the fee.

In June 1854, a new governor arrived to replace the retiring Sir Charles La Trobe as Queen Victoria's representative in Victoria. Forty-seven-year-old Sir Charles Hotham was an experienced colonial administrator; he sailed to Melbourne with his wife, Lady Jane Sarah, the daughter of Lord Bridport and a descendant of Horatio Nelson. The couple arrived in Melbourne on 22 June 1854 and were greeted with great pomp and ceremony, which disguised some of the deep-rooted resentment of the diggers on the goldfields. As the vice-regal pair crossed the Yarra River for the first time to enter the city, they passed under a banner with the words 'Victoria welcomes Victoria's choice'. Hotham recorded that:

> Immediately in front of me a band of 200 of the lowest orders forced their way into the procession and locked arm in arm, during the greater part of the road, sang 'Rule Britannia' and 'God Save the Queen'.[3]

Three months later he visited the goldfields of Bendigo, Ballarat and Castlemaine where, he reported in a letter back to London, he was thronged by thousands of diggers who 'burst forth shouts of loyalty to Her Majesty, and cries of attachment to the old country'.[4]

> Not less than 20,000 men assembled . . . by force they took the horses from my carriage, yoking themselves instead, and

18

dragged it into town. There were triumphant arches, flags, bands of music, vehicles gaily caparisoned, and a continued roar of cheering.[5]

Back in Melbourne, in October 1854 and a month after his trip to the fields, Hotham ordered a clampdown on the collection of miners' licences, and that rather than their occasional inspection there should be a systematic search across the goldfields twice a week. These stringent police hunts inflamed the miners and aggravated the already high tensions on the diggings, and on 11 November at a mass meeting at Bakery Hill, the Ballarat Reform League was established and a number of diggers elected to draw up a charter.

The charter was radical for its time, although all its principles were ultimately adopted into the Australian political system. It called for universal suffrage, the abolition of property ownership as a requisite for becoming a member of parliament, payment for MPs, voting by ballot and short-term parliaments. The diggers' charter also called for the abolition of the licence fee and reform of the administration of the goldfields. It threatened:

> If Queen Victoria continues to act upon the ill advice of dishonest ministers and insists upon indirectly dictating obnoxious laws for the colony . . . the Reform League will endeavour to supersede such royal prerogative by asserting that of the people, which is the most royal of all prerogatives, as the people are the only legitimate source of all political power.[6]

The Ballarat Times aptly described the Ballarat Reform League as a major development in the history of Australia:

> This League is not more and not less than the germ of Australian independence. No power on earth can restrain

the untied might and headlong strides for the freedom of the people of this country.[7]

The British government now feared that the actions of the diggers would lead to the formation of a rebel government in Victoria in which the power of the monarch might be taken by the people, vested in elected representatives.[8] Aware of the growing tensions on the diggings, Governor Hotham in mid-November sent 450 extra soldiers – two regiments of the British army – and police to the goldfields with orders 'to use force, whenever legally called upon to do so', without regard to the consequences.[9]

On Monday 27 November in Melbourne, Hotham agreed to meet with a deputation elected by the miners to discuss their concerns. The meeting went badly as the governor refused to release the diggers who had been arrested for burning down the Eureka Hotel the previous month, and made no other concessions to the miners' demands. The next day at Ballarat a gathering of around 10,000 diggers turned sour when they were told their deputation to the governor had come back empty-handed. A provocative motion was also passed,

> that this meeting, being convinced of the obnoxious licence fee is an imposition and an unjustifiable tax pledges itself to take immediate steps to abolish same by at once burning all their licences. That in the event of any party being arrested for having no licence, that the united people will, under all circumstances, defend and protect them.[10]

The diggers had thrown down the gauntlet to the authority of the Crown. They were threatening to fight if the authorities continued to police the mining licence.

The following day the local gold commissioner, Robert

Rede, who was the 'Crown writ small' on the diggings, ordered another licence hunt, but when the police reached the gravel pits they were stoned by the miners and forced to retreat. Rede reinforced the police with soldiers, which resulted in several gunshots being fired by both sides and a reading of the *Riot Act* to the diggers.

> Our sovereign lady the Queen chargeth and commandeth all persons being assembled immediately to disperse themselves and peaceably to depart to their habitations or to their lawful business, upon the pains being contained in the Act made in the first year of King George for preventing tumults and riotous assemblies. God Save the Queen.[11]

Rede then set the Crown on a collision course with the miners when he ordered the cancellation of all further mass meetings, including one that had been organised for the following Sunday. In a report to the colonial secretary, Rede made it clear that the issue was much bigger than the licence fee:

> The absolute necessity of putting down all meetings, public and private, I think must now be apparent for the abolition of the licence fee is merely a watchword. The whole affair is a strong democratic agitation by an armed mob. If the government will hold this and other goldfields it must at once crush this movement.[12]

Tensions on the goldfields continued to grow. On Thursday police fired on miners who could not produce licences and tried to get away. On Friday afternoon 1500 angry diggers hoisted the Southern Cross flag for the first time and swore their allegiance to it. The flag depicted five white stars on a blue background, and to many of these men it symbolised a new, purely Australian flag. It was said by some that these men wanted independence 'from the British yoke' and that 'a flag of insurrection' had been hoisted.[13] In the afternoon they began military 'drills' in a timber stockade they had built at nearby Eureka. There were about 150 armed diggers in the stockade when, in the early hours of Sunday morning, about 300 police and soldiers attacked. After an exchange of gunfire the outnumbered and outgunned miners were quickly overrun. During the fighting twenty-two miners and five soldiers were killed, scores were injured and more than 100 survivors were rounded up and arrested.

News of the attack on the diggers at Ballarat met with a mixed reception. Very quickly there were a number of public declarations of support for Queen Victoria and the actions taken by Hotham, including from the Melbourne Town Council and the colony's Legislative Council. However, there was also widespread criticism of Hotham and the government's actions. Two days after the attack, the Melbourne *Age* published an editorial that questioned the use of force against the miners:

> When peace shall lie once more regained, and there shall be time for deliberate judgment, the citizens will reckon with the government. Meantime, they will not pledge themselves to support it; and they will not organise themselves into bodies for the purpose of filling the place of that expensive military force, which should never have been sent out of Melbourne. [They] do not sympathise with the revolt, but neither do they sympathise with the injustice and coercion. [They] will not fight for the diggers nor will [they] fight for the government.[14]

Three days after the attack on the Eureka stockade, on 6 December a public meeting was called outside St Paul's church on Flinders Street in Melbourne. It attracted 6000 people but failed to pass the expected resolution in support of the government. The local press also expressed a lack of confidence in the government but reminded readers of the loyalty to Queen Victoria and her representative Hotham – and the political order that came with her:

> we are at the bottom loyal to our Sovereign, and respect her representative, but we have no confidence in the officials who rank below him, and who of late created the entire disturbance in the country, by ill-advised measures.[15]

The Eureka uprising and the crushing of the stockade fuelled calls for Australia's colonies to break away from the British monarchy and form a republic. According to an article in *The Age* eight weeks after Eureka, on 23 January 1855, by *The Empire*'s correspondent, the idea of a republic was now a serious consideration:

> The future independence of Australia is no longer a mere dream . . . but is a cherished dream of thousands in Victoria . . . The outbreak at Ballarat has, like a sudden flash of lightning, lighted darkness of the future, and prepared us some measure for those coming changes . . . The blood spilt will be the seed of free and noble thoughts and actions. Every great expression of political freedom and development of national independence in the world has received a bloody baptism . . . in Melbourne . . . the city . . . has manifested a sympathy with armed resistance to authority and with revolutionary and republican views . . . Independence is no longer the bugbear that it was, the idea we laughed at before we regard now with serious earnestness.[16]

Early in 1855, the thirteen men who were believed to be the ringleaders of the Eureka rebellion were tried. The charges against them made it clear they were seen to be trying to overthrow Queen Victoria herself:

> together with other diverse false traitors . . . armed and arrayed in a warlike manner . . . with guns, muskets, blunderbusses, pistols, swords, bayonets, pikes, and other weapons, being then unlawfully, maliciously and traitorously assembled and gathered wickedly, maliciously, and traitorously did levy and make war against our said Lady the Queen, within that part of her dominions called Victoria and did then maliciously and traitorously attempt and endeavour by force and arms to subvert and destroy the constitution and Government of the said part of her dominions as by law established, and deprive and depose our said Lady the Queen of and from the style, honour, and kingly name of the imperial crown of the said part of her dominions.[17]

There were more problems for the government when all these trials saw the accused acquitted. However, the passions that had been fuelled by the Eureka massacre were slowly abating, and in February there was a large public meeting in Melbourne's Temperance Hall to discuss: 'Is separation from the mother country practicable at the present time?'[18] Most of the speakers were against the idea of the colony severing its relations with the British Crown. The meeting was told republicanism was 'the purest form of government on earth', but that the colony of Victoria was not ready for independence. One speaker insisted independence was neither practicable nor desirable and another that the colonists were ungrateful to even consider it.

Hotham continued as governor of the colony of Victoria but in November 1855 he sent his resignation to London.

In the week before Christmas and in declining health, he caught a chill and died on New Year's Eve. Following his death the passions raised by Eureka further waned, and the most serious threat to the relationship between the Australian people and the British monarchy began to fade into history.

—

Over the next 100 years, Australians readily signed up in the name of the British monarchy to fight in the Crimean War, the New Zealand Māori wars, the Boer Wars, the Boxer Rebellion in China, World War I and World War II.

Australian colonists began enlisting to fight in the Crimean War as soon as news of Britain's declaration of war on Russia on 27 March 1854 reached Sydney by ship. The Crimean War had broken out when Russia defeated a weakened Ottoman (Turkish) Empire in late 1853 and established control of key territory along the Black Sea coast. Britain and other European powers had always felt threatened by the prospect of the Russians having naval access to the Mediterranean and issued an ultimatum that Russia ignored, resulting in the outbreak of war between Russia and an alliance of Britain, France, the Ottoman Empire and Sardinia.

A big public meeting in Sydney on 22 May 1854 supported a 'Loyal Address to Her Majesty' and expressed the 'hearty approval' and 'readiness to submit to the calamities' of fighting alongside Britain in the war.[19] When some locals expressed concerns about Australia's involvement, they were shouted down as being unpatriotic. Henry Parkes, who was at the beginning of a long parliamentary career in which he would become premier of New South Wales five times, publicly mocked them with the remark, 'What, are we no longer Englishmen?'[20] With this remark, Parkes summed up the feelings of many of the British population of this colony: they were loyal ultimately not to their new home but to their country of birth.

Immediately after hearing of the declaration of war in the Crimea, Australia was plunged into what *The Sydney Morning Herald* described as 'Russiaphobia'. Over the following months newspapers discussed quite seriously which city – Sydney or Melbourne – the Russians would invade first, and the chairman of Sydney's Defence Committee warned that Russian spies might already be in Australia, 'noting the defenceless state of our harbour'.[21] In July, the *Herald* headlined 'Russian designs on India and Australia' and suggested they had already assessed Sydney as a potential target:

> The Russian frigate *Dwina* [has] ventured so far south as to take a flying survey of the harbour of Sydney; and several vessels of the Russian squadron appear to have recently made a more deliberate examination of Singapore.[22]

Little is known about how many Australians went to the Crimea or how they fared during the war. It is known that some of the volunteers who went to fight in the cavalry, artillery and infantry were sworn in to British regiments at the site of Sydney Mint and that many had to find their own uniforms, horses and accoutrements.[23] After the battles of Balaclava and Inkerman, the Allies took the strategically important port of Sevastopol in 1855; and at the Treaty of Paris on 30 March 1856 peace was finally made when Britain succeeded in having Russia agree not to operate a navy in the Black Sea, and land was ceded both to the Russians and the Ottomans.

In the decade after Crimea, larger numbers of Australians joined the wars between the New Zealand Māori and the British colonists in New Zealand. Prompted by disputes over land purchases, the wars were initially fought by British forces against the locals, but as time went on they increasingly involved New Zealand colonial militia; and after more than a decade of intermittent fighting, the hostilities escalated in 1860 and the campaign became more vicious:

> During the last three weeks, several murders of settlers by insurgents, of a fiendish nature, have taken place. Their toma-hawks are more feared now than their muskets. Ambush and massacre are the order of the day.[24]

By early 1861 both sides had sustained hundreds of casualties. A truce was negotiated in March 1861; however, the hostilities flared again in 1863 with the Waikato War when the British forces, working with heavy artillery, systematically took possession of Māori land by driving off the inhabitants and laying waste to Māori villages and cultivations.

In August 1863 Australian newspapers were reporting that the British forces needed more men. According to the Melbourne *Argus*, 'Her Majesty's forces' of about 5000 men were 'very inadequate' because 'the native army of 7500 fighting men could be brought into the field against the Queen's troops'.[25] So nearly 2500 Australian colonist volunteers enlisted to fight, encouraged by the promise of land that would be confiscated from the Māori. Mainly from Victoria, New South Wales, Tasmania and Queensland, many volunteers were non-professional men looking for an alternative to the goldfields in Australia: 'diggers to policemen and brewer to butcher'.[26]

The Australian colonies supported their men going to fight for this far-flung corner of Victoria's empire. In New South Wales the colonial parliament agreed to 'support the war effort and Britain'[27] and *The Sydney Morning Herald* claimed it was important to 'support the homeland', citing 'the ascendancy of the British Race' as a very noble motivation for recruiting and fighting in New Zealand.[28] In Queensland the *Brisbane Courier* reported that:

> No sooner was it known, even in this distant and young colony, that volunteers were required to help our brothers in New Zealand, than numbers of young men showed themselves to be eager recruits – not on account of any ultimate benefits held out to them, but because they, in common with all Englishmen, felt it their duty to assist any ultimate benefits held out to countrymen.[29]

Large crowds of enthusiastic well-wishers turned out to cheer the first men to leave Sydney in August 1863 in scenes of 'novelty' and 'festivity' not previously seen in the colony.[30] The following month *The Argus* reported that a large and lively crowd had turned out at Melbourne's Spencer Street railway station to cheer more than 400 privates and four officers leaving for the port and shipment to the war.[31] Tasmania, with a population of less than 50,000 in 1863, could ill afford the exodus of men, but even it was able to accept the justification for the war.

The Australian venture into the war was not an overwhelming success. From the 2400 men who crossed the Tasman, over 300 deserted when they reached New Zealand, while others committed a number of offences and were discharged as unfit for military service. Before signing up to the war, the Australians had been promised three years' paid service in the army to be followed by the grant of fifty acres to each private and up to 400 acres to senior officers of land in New Zealand. However, a little over a year later, the Waikato War subsided, and by late 1864 the majority of the Australian colonial force found themselves without a wage or a means of earning a living in New Zealand.[32] The land that had been taken by force from the Māori people was eventually offered to the soldiers, but much of it was of poor quality for farming. By March 1865 over 1500 men were 'literally out of work' and 'stranded on a patch of land with no money with only military rations to live on'.[33]

By the mid-1860s and after some had fought in various inauspicious empire wars, most Australian colonists did not even know what Queen Victoria looked like, though she had been on the throne for nearly thirty years. However, their devotion was soon to be given a boost by the visit of her son Prince Alfred, on the first royal tour of Australia.

3

THE FIRST AUSTRALIAN
ROYAL TOUR

'Good God, I am shot . . . my back is broken.'

IN 1867 PRINCE ALFRED, Duke of Edinburgh, the fourth
child and the second son of Queen Victoria and Prince
Albert, was sent on a goodwill trip to Australia and a
number of other British colonies. He came for much the
same reason as each of the royal tours over the next 150
years: because the 'colonials . . . could be linked more
closely to the Crown if occasionally they saw more of
the royal family'.[1] During his visit to Australia perhaps
the most dramatic incident of any tour to the country
occurred – Prince Alfred narrowly survived an assassination attempt when he was shot at a picnic in a Sydney
park.

At the age of twelve and encouraged by his father, Prince
Alfred joined the Royal Navy. While it was not unusual for

boys of that age to go to sea, Queen Victoria is reported to have complained to a European relative that Prince Alfred was too young to be leaving the palace.[2] According to the queen, her younger son was very pleasant to be around and while staying at Windsor 'his dear face sheds sunshine all over the house'.[3] It has been suggested that part of the reason for the Prince Consort wanting his son in the navy was to remove him from the influence of his older brother, Edward, whose 'colourful social life' was already causing the royal family some consternation.[4]

In 1862, when the Bavarian-born King Otto of Greece was deposed, Prince Alfred was chosen by a Greek plebiscite to succeed him. After Greece had won its independence from the Ottoman Empire in a war spanning 1821–32, the powers of Britain, France and Russia had decided (without consulting Greece) at a conference in London in 1832 that the new country would be more stable if it became a constitutional monarchy. Since the Greeks had no history of monarchy and no royal lineage, the European powers arranged to impose Prince Otto, the second son of King Ludwig I of Bavaria, as the first in a line of kings for the new state.[5] But after his removal from the throne, at Queen Victoria's request the British government blocked plans for Prince Alfred to be named as his successor and, instead, Prince William of Denmark was chosen as King George I of the Hellenes.

Prince Alfred remained in the British navy, where he was promoted to midshipman, then lieutenant. In 1866 he was made Duke of Edinburgh and given the formal title of captain of the HMS *Galatea*, though he did not actually command the ship. By the time of his voyage to Australia, the prince had demonstrated competence as a sailor and had become a 'pleasant, personable young man'.[6]

The *Galatea* (from the Greek, meaning 'milky white') was launched in 1859 as part of the build-up of Britain's empire navy. It was a large warship – eighty-five metres long and weighing 4251 tonnes – and had a crew of 450 men. In 1866 it was refitted for Prince Alfred's world tour, and it sailed from Plymouth in January 1867. The captain and his crew received detailed directions for the Australian cruise in June at Gibraltar, but it was another month before the news was published in the Australian press: the telegraph linking Australia and Britain was still five years away, and it took around thirty days for the fastest post to travel through Europe by train to southern Italy, then by steamer across the Mediterranean and Red Sea and through the Indian Ocean to Australia.

The British government sent little exact information to the colonies other than to advise 'that Her Majesty's ship *Galatea*, under the command of His Royal Highness the Duke of Edinburgh, is about to proceed on service, and will probably visit the Colony under your government in the course of the present year'.[7] Despite not knowing exactly when the prince would reach Australia, every colonial capital began planning to celebrate Alfred's arrival, each trying to outdo its rivals with extravagant design and spending on decorations and entertainment.

The *Galatea* reached Australia three months later. After leaving the Mediterranean, it sailed to Madeira, then across the Atlantic to Rio de Janeiro and on to the tiny south Atlantic British colony on the remote island of Tristan da Cunha. By late August it had reached Cape Town, where the township was decked out in bunting for Alfred's arrival. After South Africa it had been scheduled to call in at Mauritius, but the visit was cancelled when reports reached Cape Town of a major outbreak of typhoid on the island.

As it sailed towards Australia, the *Galatea* was heading for Perth, but it was forced by a 'huge gale' to divert south, and to the disappointment of Western Australia, a visit to the colony was abandoned. Instead, the ship sailed on to Adelaide. South Australia was the only colony that had been established by free settlers rather than convicts. At the time of the prince's arrival it had a population of around 170,000 people, most of whom lived in Adelaide and the surrounding farming and mining communities.

On 29 October the ship was first seen off the coast of Adelaide, and the next day it anchored off Glenelg Pier, where a large crowd had already gathered. *The Adelaide Observer* told its readers the *Galatea* was 'one of the fastest and finest frigates in Her Majesty's service':

> She is beyond comparison the best representative of the British Navy that has visited these waters . . . She is a perfect model of naval architecture – a complete realisation of the old English ideal of an ocean queen.[8]

Among the first ashore were the young prince's equerries, thirty-five-year-old Lord Newry and the Honourable Eliot Yorke, who was a year younger. The role of equerry had originally been named for a senior attendant with responsibility for the horses of a person of senior rank, but the role had gradually shifted, and by Prince Alfred's time equerries assisted the member of the royal family with their official duties, including providing advice on protocol and announcing visitors and guests at formal audiences.

Newry and Yorke disembarked the ship before the prince, so on their way through Adelaide to reach Government House they were the first to see a number of giant decorated triumphal arches over the city streets. Such elaborate adornments would be a feature of every town and city the prince and his entourage visited over the next six months, and a regular feature of all royal tours to Australia for the next fifty years.

When the equerries arrived at Government House, they

discovered that the local reception committee had amassed a long list of official engagements for Alfred, despite his wish for a less formal tour. Overstuffed agendas, too many dignitaries and excessively long speeches were also to be a feature of almost every part of the prince's Australian visit – and of all royal tours that followed.

The next afternoon, 31 October, Prince Alfred became the first British royal to set foot on Australian soil when he stepped ashore at Glenelg Pier. The local press went overboard with excitement in reporting the event:

> The visit is the commencement of a new era in the history of the world . . . From today, the eyes of the world will be on Australia, as it welcomes its royal guest.[9]

The London *Times*, however, was less grandiloquent about the visit, reporting rather snootily that 'colonial life is sad and dull, and the excitement of a royal visit will be the more welcome for that'.[10]

The prince was greeted on a hot morning by the colony's governor, Sir Dominick Daly, the premier, Henry Ayers, about 300 parliamentarians and other dignitaries, and cheers from a very large crowd, which had been growing in size since early morning and taken every vantage point around the bay. As the prince came ashore, many in the crowd failed to recognise him: in an age before newspapers published photos, most of the locals had no idea what he looked like, and he was dressed sombrely instead of in the dazzling regal uniform many had expected.

Leaving the pier at Glenelg in a large horse-drawn coach, Prince Alfred received the first inkling of the tumultuous impact of his visit. Tens of thousands of people lined the route cheering and throwing whole bunches of flowers into the coach.

When he reached Adelaide Town Hall there was a huge cheering crowd of around 35,000 people, including about 4000 children, who sang 'God Save the Queen' to the prince. The British press noted another feature of British royal visits to Australia for the next century: that the Australians were even more excited about the monarchy than the British were at home. Reporting on the prince's first day in Adelaide, the *Pall Mall Gazette* told its readers that 'loyalty never went to such excesses at home'.[11]

Adelaide was lit up at night by 40,000 decorated gas illuminations on the city buildings, and huge bonfires burning along the waterfront and in the Adelaide Hills. However, not everyone who witnessed the spectacle was impressed. *The South Australian Register*'s correspondent wrote:

It is well known that they manage these things better in France and that even London now makes some attempt to conduct its illuminations in accordance with artistic designs. Why, then, should Australia, when a good opportunity presents itself, fritter away large means in a great number of little efforts? Of the other outdoor demonstrations the arrival of the prince in Adelaide was of course intended to be the chief, and nobody can say that the people who witnessed it did not thoroughly enjoy themselves. The Duke of Edinburgh had come, and that was enough. It must have occurred, however, to many people who stood in the smartly decorated street, with the brightest of blue skies above and swarms of gaily dressed people covering the fronts of all the houses, to exclaim 'God bless him!' as the prince passed by, that the procession – for a climate like this – had far too much of the English dinginess about it. In fact, had it not been for the red coats of the volunteers, together with the general outburst of joy, the line of carriages and the dusty followers on foot might have been taking part in the most melancholy instead

35

of the most cheerful of ceremonies. But this arose chiefly from the inevitable black coat and the chimney-pot hat which the Englishman takes with him to all climates and wears in all seasons. Nothing at the best of times will give such a costume a holiday appearance, and it is certainly not improved by being covered with a thin coating of dust and brought into contrast with surrounding sunshine, streets covered with flags, and balconies filled with ladies blooming like flowers.[12]

During his three weeks in South Australia, Prince Alfred laid the foundation stones for the Victoria Tower, the new Adelaide Post Office and Telegraph Station and the Prince Alfred College named after him. He attended banquets, balls, receptions, garden parties, picnics, church services, concerts and sporting events, including cricket matches between the crew of the *Galatea* and local South Australian teams.

There was a torch-lit procession and concert for him in, appropriately, Victoria Square, which included a German community choir dressed in traditional costumes singing a number of favourite German songs – Lutherans had been migrating to farm in South Australia from the late 1830s and pioneered the Australian wine industry in the Barossa Valley and the Adelaide Hills. After the concert the prince thanked them with a speech in German, reminding them that as the son of Prince Albert of Saxe-Coburg and Gotha, he was an 'heir to the German throne'.[13]

On one Saturday night the royal party went to the opera, but they were surprised to find more than half the theatre was empty: a local businessman had bought up most of the seats hoping to sell them at much higher prices but the Adelaide public would not pay the exorbitant amounts demanded.[14]

In the city's Botanic Gardens Alfred planted a tree and surprised his hosts by telling them that as children he and his brother had kept as pets kangaroos that had been brought back to Windsor Castle from Australia as gifts from various British naval captains.

Such was the enthusiasm generated by Prince Alfred's visit that a local Adelaide newspaper suggested the separate colonies should unite as one nation, with Prince Alfred as king:

> A federal union of the Australian colonies . . . is a distant event, unless an inducement like that now offered takes men's minds. We should attempt to obtain British approval to a federal union of these colonies under the leadership of the young Prince amongst us . . . whom they could crown King of Australia.[15]

After two weeks in Adelaide, the prince was taken to see some of the hinterland on South Australia's first rail line, which had opened only six years before. His party travelled more than eighty kilometres north to Kapunda, and in the Mount Lofty Ranges he went on a night shoot and bagged fifty-two possums. On a trip to the south of Adelaide to Lake Alexandrina, the prince for the first time met with local Aboriginal people and witnessed a corroboree in which around 400 Aboriginals danced for him:

> They were drawn up on the shore when His Royal Highness landed, and they gave him as hearty a cheer as he has yet heard in South Australia, or perhaps in any part of the world . . . His Royal Highness showed himself freely amongst them, and seemed both interested and amused by his first acquaintance with the South Australian natives. When some sort of order had been obtained, Pontoni, a native, attended by several of his tribe, advanced to the Prince and read to him clearly and distinctly the following address: 'To His Royal Highness

the Duke of Edinburgh, Your Royal Highness, We, who are young men belonging to all the Laki Tribes of Natives, are glad to tell you our joy at seeing you in this our country. Our old men show to Your Royal Highness the Corroboree, or as we call it, Ringbalin, such as our Fathers used to have before the white man came here.'[16]

The press reported that the night ended with some embarrassment when a local politician, Mr John Baker, tried to persuade the black girls to dance naked for the prince:

When the men [dancers] had pretty well exhausted themselves, two girls were induced to come forward and dance, but we cannot say this was a pleasing sight. The honourable Mr Baker asked the rest of the women to strip, and dance in the nude before His Royal Highness. This request must have been thoughtlessly made as it was received with disfavour by the black women and most of the white people present. We were told that one poor black girl indignantly asked 'What for black women do that when white women no do that?' . . . It was to say the least a mistake which we believe Mr Baker on reflection would be the first to acknowledge.[17]

The *Galatea* finally sailed from Adelaide for Melbourne on 21 November. As the prince prepared to leave, around 250 people from various musical societies and choirs assembled in front of Government House and sang a parting hymn, a copy of which was presented to Alfred in a silver casket.

—

The city of Melbourne that greeted Prince Alfred was one of the largest and most elegant cities in the southern hemisphere. Less than twenty years before it had been a small settlement of barely 30,000 people servicing farming communities across Victoria, but by 1867, sixteen years after gold had been discovered eighty kilometres north of Melbourne, it had a population of nearly a quarter of a million and for the remainder of the nineteenth century it was Australia's largest city.

Melbourne's centre boasted wide paved streets that were laid out in an orderly rectangular grid. A number of grand stone buildings had already been built and more were being planned or under construction, including the bluestone Carlton and United Brewery, the Menzies Hotel and the Mechanics' Institute. The vast city of tents from the early gold-rush days was increasingly being replaced by tidy brick and timber suburban housing.

For many weeks before the prince's arrival, a local organising committee had been busily preparing his reception. Throughout the city there were giant timber triumphal arches garnished with greenery and flowers. As in Adelaide, most of the buildings, shops and city parks had installed coloured gaslights for display at night during the royal visit. On Parliament House at the top of Collins Street, electric lights had been put in for the first time, which were flashed on and off regularly by an operator. The decorations were not to everyone's taste – the *Church Times* described them as 'almost Babylonian':

> The growing love of ostentations, extravagance and the growth of sensual gratification which is quite alarming, and which at present absorbs our rulers and leaders.[18]

As the *Galatea* sailed up Port Phillip, the ship's guns saluted and were answered by cheers, hoots and whistles from the hundreds of small boats out on the harbour to welcome the prince. After the royal party's experience of Adelaide, the prince's equerries had sought fewer formal events and long speeches, and requested more of an opportunity to move around and meet people. Because the prince intended to stay in Victoria for only a month, it was his wish that 'ample opportunity be afforded for a view of colonial scenery and colonial enterprise and colonial industry untrammeled by the ceremonials of State visits'.[19] Needless to say the request was largely ignored, and a seemingly endless succession of local mayors and other officials insisted on meeting and addressing the prince at every opportunity.

Despite the large crowds that poured in to Melbourne and especially to St Kilda Pier on Sunday 24 November, the prince did not appear even on the deck of the *Galatea*. But around 2 pm the following day, and as huge crowds crammed the waterfront and the roads leading into the city, he finally came ashore on a steam launch. Greeted by the Victorian colony's governor, Viscount Canterbury, Premier Sir James McCulloch, a choir singing three verses of 'God Save the Queen' and deafening cheers from the crowd, the prince boarded a horse-drawn coach for the eight-kilometre ride into Melbourne. The procession was stopped several times along the way by the crowds closing in on the road and by local politicians handing the prince bound 'declarations of loyalty', which Alfred passed on to his aides without opening or giving them more than a glance.

Crossing the Yarra River and passing the crowds that had climbed onto every possible vantage point, the prince was taken to the Town Hall, where he was loudly cheered. There he gave a short speech in which he thanked everyone on behalf of himself and his mother, Queen Victoria. He was then taken back across the Yarra to Government House for his first night in the city, made brilliant by bonfires, and gas and electric light shows. In the Fitzroy Gardens, giant flame pots illuminated the walks and lawns and Chinese lanterns and gas brackets hung in the trees.

During his stay in Melbourne, Prince Alfred laid the foundation stone of the new Town Hall, and attended receptions, parties and banquets and a special race meeting at Flemington Racecourse. While he was at a dinner in the Town Hall, singers from the local German community arrived carrying torches but were kept waiting while the lord mayor gave a lengthy speech. When he learned the singers were standing outside holding their torches, apparently Alfred leaned across to the mayor and said, 'Cut it short, Mr Mayor, the Germans are burning their fingers.' He then left the table and joined the singers and, speaking in German, told them that their 'presence in Australia would strengthen the bonds which bind our two great Teutonic nations'.[20]

In a gesture of charity, some of Melbourne's civic leaders and merchants organised a free banquet on the banks of the Yarra River so that poorer people would have the opportunity of meeting the prince. By 2.30 pm on 28 November a huge crowd was still waiting on a very hot day for the prince to arrive, and was becoming unruly. Alfred was warned by local officials not to attend the banquet for fear 'his person [would] be placed in jeopardy', and when the increasingly hungry and thirsty crowd was told the prince was not coming, they broke through the barriers to reach the food and drink.[21] *The Argus* described the scene as a 'bacchanalian picture of unbelievable horror set against the general background of struggling carnivora':

So large a crowd never assembled in Victoria before . . . here in the Zoological Gardens was one vast mass of human beings, variously estimated at from 60,000 to 100,000 . . . by one o'clock [they] were ready for the feast . . . there was nothing to do but wait for the prince to declare the banquette open. At twenty minutes to two . . . the crowd was already enormous, and increasing, and people too hungry to be nice. Still the prince did not come . . . At half past two the famished mob could hold out no longer, the long tables were rushed, and in a few seconds there was not a vestige of all the vast store of provisions.[22]

By early December the prince began touring the country-side outside Melbourne, including Pettavel vineyard in Geelong, where, 'to the delight of the locals', the royal party prolonged their stay before loading several cases of the wine onto their coach;[23] and Winchelsea, where Alfred officially opened a new bridge over the Barwon River.

He also travelled through Colac and some of Victoria's farming districts to Australia's largest inland settlement of Ballarat, by now the largest goldmining town in the world. The Eureka rebellion in Ballarat had taken place only thirteen years before, but at the time of Alfred's arrival there was no sign of any lingering resentment towards the prince, Queen Victoria or the institution of the British monarchy. In fact, when Alfred reached Ballarat on the dry, hot afternoon of 9 December, a crowd estimated at 100,000 repeatedly stopped his procession as the mass of people sprawled on the road, making his passage impossible. The arches that adorned the city rivalled those in Melbourne for size and colour, and a parade of a traditional paper dragons was organised by members of the local Chinese community who joined in an array of dazzling traditional costumes.

Over the next few days Alfred attended a ball, went to the horseraces and down a number of goldmines in both Ballarat and Bendigo, where he was given several small gold nuggets as gifts. The prince showed a keen interest in mining. While at the Ballarat Band of Hope mine he donned miners clothing and 'taking a miners pick chipped off pieces of quartz in the search of gold'. When they were deep underground, the mine manager sent up for several bottles of brandy and a supply of glasses to 'keep out the cold'.[24] A few days later, in the Latham and Watson mine in Bendigo, the prince again went underground and dined with the diggers on a selection of 'nuts, cheese and wine and champagne'.[25] At the Catherine Reef Company's Mine, 'the Royal Party with joyful alacrity selected a suitable garb ... the mouth of the mine was crowded with spectators ... eager to witness the various improvised dresses [to go underground] ... some were turbaned like the Turk, with large towels in lieu of hats'.[26]

On the evening the prince arrived at Bendigo, there was a torch-lit procession in which a firework was thrown from the crowd into the parade and a float caught fire, burning four young boys to death; then on the night that a ball was to be held in Alfred's honour, a gas lamp flared in the wooden hall built for the occasion and burned down. However, the show had to go on: rather than cancel the event, it was hastily transferred to the courthouse.

After a few more days on the goldfields, the royal party returned to Melbourne for Christmas. On Christmas Eve the prince attended a giant fancy-dress ball organised by the Melbourne City Council. The imaginative costumes included

> gods and goddesses, monarchs, monks, and mountebanks, queens, countesses and Cindarellas; the stately duchess and saucy vivandiere; the heros and heroines of all ages; the statesmen and literati; the clown and the rustic; the armed knight and the lady fair; flower girls innumerable; soldiers and sailors; Turks, Greeks and Circasians; the furred Russian and turbanned, Polish ladies, Spanish gitanas, Indian brigands and brigandese, courtiers, hunters, fishermen, and costermongers.[27]

The prince disappointed many when he appeared in his formal uniform and not in fancy dress, but appeared to enjoy himself and danced enthusiastically.

Alfred spent Christmas Day privately and quietly on the *Galatea*. On Boxing Day night he and his party arrived ashore late for a concert of Mendelssohn's *Cantata Athalie*. When the prince finally entered his box the conductor stopped the 400-strong choir so they could start again at the beginning with the playing of the National Anthem. But during the concert the prince 'appeared less than over-whelmed with interest, and on several occasions looked at his watch'.[28] Shortly after the interval he and his party rose and left early – before the performance of the 'Alfred March', which had been especially composed for the occasion.

On New Year's Day Alfred attended a military parade at Flemington Racecourse, then on 4 January the royal party travelled by train from Melbourne to Williamstown where right on schedule they boarded the *Galatea*. Referring to many earlier occasions when the prince and his party had arrived late for official engagements, one paper sardonically suggested that 'at least on his departure, the prince was punctual'.[29]

The South Australian Advertiser provided some interesting insights about the prince and his deportment in Victoria, as well as that of his party, a few days after his departure:

> It must ever be regretted that His Royal Highness was not accompanied by a sage and mature mentor. It was not to be expected that a young man of twenty-three should himself be equal to the extraordinary position in which the Duke here found himself. The second son of a monarch occupies a very uncertain position. As the probabilities of his being wanted to fill the throne diminish, so does the importance of the younger son . . . Coming here, he found himself invested with unusual importance . . . so loyal people paid him due respect, flunkies entrusted themselves upon him, and ladies adored him. On the whole, he got through pretty well. He might have done his work in a more business-like way, he might have visited

44

our charitable institutions . . . he might have lightened some sorrowful hearts. It was not his fault that he did not do those things, or any of them. The people entrusted with the duty of receiving him led him to suppose that he was to do nothing but revel and make merry.[30]

The following day's edition alleged that while the royal party were in Melbourne they engaged in some openly 'fast behaviour, including excessive drinking, gambling and visiting Melbourne's . . . brothels'.[31] The newspaper posed the question as to whether

the wise and experienced gentlemen of the Reception Committee . . . would like their sons at the age of twenty-three to be exposed to the dissipation and the temptation to which they have treated the queen's son during his six weeks' stay.[32]

As for the prince's companions, Lord Newry and the Honourable Eliot Yorke, the paper said that 'neither has elevated the youthful aristocracy of England in the estimation of colonists, and the prince had been much better destitute of their company'.[33] The paper described the prince as 'no snob; his frank manners and unassuming deportment have helped considerably to unprince him', but made the observation that 'royalty, to look well and be preserved, should be kept in a glass case seen only from a distance, and then surrounded with the trappings of state'.[34]

———

After clearing the heads of Port Phillip, the *Galatea* sailed south across the Bass Strait and on the afternoon of 6 January reached the long estuary of the Derwent River that led to Tasmania's capital of Hobart. Convict transportation had continued to Tasmania until 1853, some years after it had ended in New South Wales, and even when Prince Alfred arrived in early 1868 there were still convicts in gangs building the colony's roads.

When the *Galatea* came close to the harbour in Hobart it was surrounded by scores of small craft that had come out to welcome the prince. As with Adelaide and Melbourne, the city was decorated for Alfred's arrival with big decorated arches across the major streets. The largest was made of giant whale bones since Hobart had for many years been a major port for Southern Ocean whalers.

That evening Alfred came ashore for dinner at Government House with the Tasmanian governor, Colonel Sir Thomas Gore-Browne, before returning for the night to the *Galatea*. To celebrate his arrival, the locals lit large bonfires that night all along the hills behind Hobart and on the slopes of Mount Wellington.

The next day the prince took the customary ride through the city, laid the foundation stone for the building of the Hobart to Launceston railway, visited a soap factory, the Cascade brewery, a hospital and an orphanage; and in the evening attended a royal ball (where the *Galatea*'s band provided the music). On Saturday he watched a regatta on the Derwent, and was introduced to the last surviving Tasmanian Aboriginals, Truganini and King Billy (Lanney). According to the local newspaper the prince arrived at the regatta on horseback almost an hour late. King Billy and the 'old lady' Truganini were standing on the steps of the pavilion by the river, with their 'protector' and about twenty other local dignitaries, waiting to be 'presented' to the prince. After brief introductions the prince rode around the crowd, who 'cheered enthusiastically', watched some of the races and then rode back into town.[35]

Alfred and his entourage next headed north with the prince riding his own coach, escorted by a detachment of the colony's First Light Cavalry and about 100 local men for the 200-kilometre ride to Launceston. It had been raining heavily over the weekend in the north of Tasmania, and after the extreme heat of South Australia and Victoria the royal party enjoyed the moderate temperature, and the countryside, which reminded them of the southern counties of England. Nor did the weather discourage a large turnout of people to see the prince:

> the wet weather could not dampen the enthusiasm and the roads leading to Launceston were crammed with people at an early hour, all on their way to see the prince. Families who rarely ever leave their bush homes could not allow this event to pass without being present, with their children to see the son of Queen Victoria. This was the one idea actuating all; this was the grand motive which impelled nearly 20,000 people to assemble.[36]

Alfred was relatively casually dressed in 'cord breaches, knee boots, a serviceable coat and a "wide awake" hat' when he attended a civic reception in the centre of Launceston where 3000 schoolchildren 'on a specially built platform' sang 'God Save the Queen'.[37] He responded to the welcome by giving his by now regular short speech thanking the crowd on 'behalf of the queen':

> I have much satisfaction in thanking you for the cordial manner in which you have welcomed me . . . I also gratefully acknowledge, on behalf of the Queen, your expressions of devotion and loyalty for the Queen's throne and person . . . Nowhere has Her Majesty more devoted subjects than in Tasmania.[38]

After returning to Hobart, the royal party boarded the *Galatea* and sailed for five days in stormy weather north, across the Bass Strait and along the New South Wales coast up to Sydney, where the arrival of the prince was eagerly anticipated. Despite more heavy rain that morning, thousands of small boats crowded into Sydney Harbour, many of them charging spectators for a chance to catch an early glimpse of the prince. As the *Galatea* moved closer to anchoring, the visitors could see the foreshores were deep with crowds of people who had packed all the vantage points. At Circular Quay a great welcoming pavilion had been erected with a series of cupolas and a dome rising from the colonnaded structure. Outside, the walls were adorned with banners, shields and images of lions. As Alfred stepped ashore he was introduced to a large number of dignitaries, including the colonial governor, Lord Belmore, the premier, James Martin, and a host of local parliamentarians. The heavy rain stopped but many of the officials who had been waiting for some hours were drenched because of the 'ill-fitting carpentry' and leaking canvas roof.[39]

After the official welcome, Alfred was driven around Sydney and cheered by the thousands of people lining the streets, before being taken back to Government House in the Botanic Gardens, where that night he watched Sydney's spectacular illuminations, which *The Sydney Morning Herald* claimed outstripped all other Australian centres in the scope and size of the display:[40]

> The event attracted an immense number of spectators who thronged every available portion of the Domain. The illumi- nations . . . surpassed anything of the kind ever before seen in this hemisphere.[41]

The prince stayed at Government House for the duration of his visit to Sydney, and for the next few weeks he attended up to three or four events each day, including civic receptions, balls, church services, concerts, and visits to the Randwick horseraces, the Australian Museum, Sydney University (Australia's first) and a naval display on the harbour. He also visited Parramatta, the lower Blue Mountains and Windsor (west of Sydney, where Australian agriculture had first started following British settlement), and was taken by steamer to Newcastle, where a giant welcome arch had been made of the coal for which Newcastle had already become famous. The prince commented on the excellent wines from the nearby Hunter Valley vineyards.

At the end of the Sydney tour, Alfred had been scheduled to sail directly for New Zealand, but Queensland successfully lobbied for his itinerary to be changed so he could first visit Brisbane. Queensland had become a separate colony from New South Wales only nine years before, and was immensely proud to have been named after Prince Alfred's mother. The colony, which stretched nearly 3000 kilometres from the Tweed River in the south to Cape York in the north, had started with a population of a little more than 20,000 people; however, by the time of Prince Alfred's visit, its number had crept up to about 100,000 – due again to the discovery of gold only four months before, which would bring great prosperity to the colony.

Brisbane had had the least time of all the Australian cities and towns to prepare for the arrival of the prince, which the local press reported caused great confusion:

> The glorious uncertainty, which hangs over every aspect of the tour . . . even the time of the departure of the welcoming vessels [on Moreton Bay] has not been decided.[42]

It was yet again raining heavily when the royal party sailed into Moreton Bay, and Prince Alfred asked the captain to stand off the port until the next day. From the early hours of the following morning, large crowds filled the city and the banks of the Brisbane River. The city had done its best to hastily decorate the city, but the Brisbane Courier reported that the 'sadly drooping arches of pine and cypress curved over the roadways . . . gave a rather funereal air to the city'.[43]

Alfred's itinerary was much the same as it had been in the bigger colonial cities of Sydney and Melbourne, but on a smaller scale. On the first two days he completed the obligatory tour of Brisbane's main streets in a horse-drawn carriage, laid the foundation stone for the Brisbane Grammar School, attended an official luncheon and a parliamentary dinner and watched a fireworks display. As he had experienced in other cities, a local German choir came to sing for him while he was dining at Brisbane's Government House:

> During dinner at Government House in the evening, a torch-light procession of Germans arrived and serenaded the royal visitor with various selections from the vocal music of their fatherland. The Prince after dinner came out on the balcony and bowed his acknowledgements.[44]

At the request of the local colonial premier, Scottish-born farmer Sir Robert Mackenzie, Alfred agreed to a tour of south-west Queensland: the farming districts of the Darling Downs and the towns of Ipswich and Toowoomba. To reach Toowoomba by rail on a line that had been opened only the year before, the Queensland railway workshops had hastily prepared a royal carriage, since the young railway had no special rolling stock. A large part of the car made for Prince Alfred was open at the sides and with a canvas canopy so that people could see him standing on the rear of the train. The train had no sleeping berths and no provision for catering.

After travelling for about 160 kilometres through Ipswich and Toowoomba, and having a packed picnic lunch on the train, the royal party reached the railway siding near the tiny settlement of Jondaryan late in the evening. As there was no suitable accommodation anywhere nearby, a tiny timber shed had been built on the side of the single track for Prince Alfred's overnight stay. The little house had two rooms. One was a small sitting room furnished with some chairs and a dresser, a basin and a jug of water. The other was even smaller, with the bed intended for the prince taking up almost all the space. Nearby a large tent had been pitched where an evening meal was prepared and served.

The prince's entourage were not even offered beds. Some slept lying around a large campfire, others sitting in the lounge chairs of Alfred's carriage on the train, and some went to a local farm. It was probably the worst accommodation ever offered to a member of the royal family, and the prince reportedly made no attempt to hide his annoyance.[45] The following morning he was again upset when the necessary horses did not arrive to allow him to take part in a scheduled hunt:

> His Royal Highness was astir at daylight eager for the sport; but the promised horses were not forthcoming. It was said that they had got out of the paddock, but some slanderously asserted that the too liberal potations in the evening of those whose duty it was to see that they were brought caused the disappointment. His Royal Highness, though evidently vexed, made the best of it, and took a few shots at less noble quarry.[46]

The following night back in Brisbane was to be the last before the party returned to Sydney. A formal dinner had been planned with the premier and local government members, but the prince, no doubt heartily fed up after the trip to Jondaryan, sent one of his equerries to say that he would be dining alone in his suite.

Arriving back in Sydney on 3 March 1868, after a week in Queensland, a very tired Alfred asked for fewer engagements and functions until the *Galatea* was ready to sail for New Zealand in early April. His wish to be left alone was largely respected. He took time out to ride through the bushlands to the north of Sydney Harbour, and on a small steam launch explored the bays and estuaries of the beautiful Hawkesbury River to Sydney's north. However, the prince did agree to attend a grand picnic at beautiful Clontarf on Sydney's Middle Harbour, which had been organised for 12 March to raise funds for a sailor's retirement home.

The picnic lunch was well underway by the time Alfred and his party began the half-hour trip down the harbour, with the Royal Sydney Yacht Squadron providing a guard of honour of boats on either side of the prince's barge. At Clontarf, Alfred walked through the large crowd of about 1500 picnickers, who were in the process of eating a large quantity of oysters, lobsters and chicken and drinking almost 1200 magnums of champagne and nearly 800 bottles of beer, to join the governor, the premier and other officials who were having lunch in a large marquee.[47]

Shortly after lunch, as the prince was strolling across the grass, he was shot at close range. 'Good God, I am shot . . . my back is broken,' Alfred was heard to shout as he fell forward on his hands and knees.[48] The would-be assassin, an Irishman called Henry James O'Farrell, tried to fire again but was quickly overwhelmed by a coach-maker called William Vial, and O'Farrell's second shot missed the prince and went into the foot of George Thornton, one of the prince's hosts at the picnic.

The injured prince was hurriedly carried into the marquee, where his bloodied clothes were cut back from the wound. The bullet had entered his back, glanced off a rib and appeared to have become lodged somewhere in his abdomen. Now unconscious, he was wrapped in bandages and laid out on a stretcher made from planks of the picnic lunch tables that had been strapped together. As quickly as possible he was put on a steam ferry back to Sydney and up to Government House.

By now police constables had hold of O'Farrell and were having to ward off angry picnickers calling for his lynching. Scurrying down to the ferry to get their handcuffed prisoner back to Sydney and into custody, the police then had to stop the ferry crew from lynching O'Farrell as they jostled him aboard for the trip back.

The next day's edition of the *Herald* reported the city's outrage and mortification that such an event should have happened on its shores:

> A universal feeling of sorrow, shame, and rage pervades the community. The whole colony has been wounded in the person of its royal guest. A crime, which everyone will repudiate with horror, has shadowed our reputation . . . [anyone] who mingled with the awe-stricken crowd could not fail to be impressed with the universal exclamation of bitter sorrow that such a deed should have been perpetrated in New South Wales. The sentiments of loyalty, of hospitality, of national pride were touched to the quick. It was a generous shame, which felt a stain like a wound. The passion would have passed all restraining bounds if the guilty wretch had not been quickly and safely removed from the reach of the popular vengeance . . . [The people were] hungry for an immediate application of lynch law.[49]

At first there were grave fears that the young prince would die. In Sydney and later in the other colonial capitals, crowds gathered outside the newspaper offices and telegraph office to hear the latest news. Two days after the assassination attempt, the doctor from the *Galatea* successfully removed the bullet from Alfred's abdomen and cleaned the wound. Fortunately, it was clear that the bullet's progress had been impeded by the several layers of rubber at the crossover of the royal braces, so it had not penetrated as far as first thought. But now a nervous wait began to see if the wound would become infected. When it became clear that the prince would survive, and the news of his recovery reached Buckingham Palace, Queen Victoria observed that the attack on her son's life 'has, I am sure, only further aroused the loyalty of my Australian subjects, so heartily displayed in his reception'.[50]

While he lay recuperating in Government House, many people flocked to public meetings to condemn the attempt on his life. In Sydney on the day after the shooting, 20,000 people had attended a public meeting that saw an outpouring of patriotic fervour towards the British monarchy and the empire, as well as a great deal of anti-Irish and anti-Catholic sentiment.

O'Farrell, aged thirty-five, was tried at Sydney eighteen days after the shooting. The barrister with the thankless task of defending him was Butler Cole Aspinall, who had previously successfully defended the rebel leaders of the Eureka stockade. Aspinall sought to have O'Farrell found not guilty by reason of insanity, citing O'Farrell's history of mental illness and his recent release from an asylum. But it was in vain: O'Farrell was convicted and sentenced to death by Judge Alfred Cheeke, and was hanged on 21 April 1868 in Darlinghurst Gaol.

Henry Parkes, who was at the time the colonial secretary (the chief government representative in parliament), used the attempted assassination to his own political advantage by capitalising on the nearly hysterical public mood. Within a week he had introduced into the New South Wales parliament new legislation governing the laws of treason. Driven by Parkes and his premier, James Martin, the legislation passed through both houses of parliament in one day and was given assent the next day by the governor, Lord Belmore. It became an offence punishable by two years' jail to refuse to toast the queen's health or 'to use any language disrespectful of the Queen', or 'to write or publish any words disrespectful to Her Most Gracious Majesty'. But the laws, which had oppressive conditions that went beyond any legislation ever seen in New South Wales or in Britain, survived only two years before the conditions were repealed.

Immediately after the shooting a public subscription fund was established 'to raise a permanent and substantial monument in testimony of the heartfelt gratitude of the community at the recovery of HRH', and this eventually resulted in the building of Sydney's Royal Prince Alfred Hospital.

Three weeks after the shooting, the prince made his public reappearance. Escorted by a detachment of heavily armed troopers, he rode in a carriage in the early afternoon from Government House to Sydney Town Hall, with the streets 'crammed with crowds more demonstrative and emotional than any he had encountered in Australia'. He was taken through the city and then out for a drive into the suburbs and 'enjoyed the ride very much'.[51] It was the same when he went for a ride in his coach the following day:

Manifestations of loyalty and joy at his recovery met his eye on all sides. Never before was the city dressed out so prettily with flags, and the suburbs were all liberal in their display of bunting. Sydney was overjoyed to have their Prince back in their midst and most gratified at his reappearance in public.[52]

The following day it was announced the prince would be leaving Australia and heading home without going to New Zealand as originally planned. The night before he left, he was hosted at a lavish state banquet at Sydney Town Hall, and the next day he entertained local dignitaries on board the *Galatea* before it sailed away from Australian shores.

The general feeling in Australia was that the visit had been an outstanding success, apart from the unfortunate attempt on the prince's life. But in an account of the tour published after Alfred departed, local historian J. G. Knight said the schedule had been overly punishing for the young royal:

> Accepting as correct the general conclusion that no royal personage in any part of the world ever received a more enthusiastic welcome at the hands of the same number of people, it is to be feared that, in testifying our loyalty to a son of our beloved queen, we were somewhat prone to overtax the physical as well as mental endurance of our illustrious guest, and that the time left at the disposal of His Royal Highness was far too little for his own personal comfort.[53]

The ship had a stormy voyage around Cape Horn but safely reached the River Thames two months later, and the prince was reunited with his mother in August 1868. He had been away for about twenty months and had travelled further than any member of the British royal family before him.

Prince Alfred made two more visits to Australia but neither was anywhere near as eventful as the first great royal tour of 1867–68. In 1869, and again in the *Galatea*, he made the first visit of any royal to Western Australia, arriving in Fremantle in late January, and going on to Adelaide, Melbourne and Sydney, where he visited the newly built hospital that commemorated his narrow escape from death.

The following year he returned again, for a shorter trip to Sydney and then Melbourne, where he made another visit to Flemington to watch the 1870 Melbourne Cup.

Four years after his extensive voyages in the *Galatea*, Prince Alfred married Grand Duchess Maria Alexandrovna of Russia, the second daughter of Czar Alexander, on 23 January 1874. They had four daughters and a son, but the marriage was not happy, not least because of the prince's serial infidelities with celebrated courtesans in London, Paris and Malta, where he was posted as rear admiral, vice admiral and later admiral of the British Mediterranean fleet.

His only son, Prince Alfred Alexander, became entangled in a scandal involving his mistress and shot himself in a suicide attempt in January 1899, during his parents' twenty-fifth wedding anniversary celebrations. He briefly survived the shooting and was sent to Meran, a spa in the Italian South Tyrol, to recover, but died two weeks later.

Prince Alfred spent the last seven years of his life as the ruler of the tiny state of Saxe-Coburg and Gotha, the birthplace of his father, having assumed the title in 1893 on the death of his bachelor uncle, Duke Ernest II, who left no children.

Prince Alfred died aged fifty-five on 30 July 1900, six months before his mother, Queen Victoria. He reportedly died of throat cancer, though it was strongly rumoured he had actually contracted syphilis. He is buried just outside Coburg in the family's ducal cemetery in Germany.

Alfred was not only the first royal to visit Australia but he travelled great distances and saw more of Britain's far-flung empire than any other member of his family until his great-nephew Prince Edward, who would become King Edward VIII.

4

FOR QUEEN AND COUNTRY

Our loyalty? We ought to resent the bare idea that anything is needed to show our loyalty . . . If England were involved in a great war with a great Power . . . we ought to risk our last shilling and our last life.

FROM THE ARRIVAL OF the first convicts in 1788 until 1870, the Australian colonies were defended by regular British forces. The first settlement was protected by marines who sailed with the convict ships. In 1790 they were replaced by the specially recruited New South Wales Corps, which was recalled in 1810 following its members' involvement in widespread corruption and the overthrow of Governor William Bligh. The corps was replaced by the British 73rd (Perthshire) Regiment under the command of the new governor, Lachlan Macquarie. Altogether twenty-four British regiments were stationed in Australia before 1870. Most of their time was spent guarding convicts or suppressing the movements of the Aboriginal people. The most notable military action by the British forces was the attack on the goldminers' stockade at Eureka in Victoria in December 1854.

From 1870 each of the six colonies became responsible for raising and maintaining its own army and navy. Given their limited resources, the colonial infantry, cavalry and artillery were made up mostly of unpaid volunteer militia and a few paid regular soldiers. As there was no serious external threat to the colonies, the only action their forces saw was when they went off to join Britain's empire wars.

Throughout the nineteenth century the British Empire had continued to expand. With the defeat of Napoleonic France and the decline of the old European powers of Spain, Portugal and the Netherlands, Britain ruled supreme. In 1877 Queen Victoria took the title of Empress of India and increasingly became the matriarchal symbol of an all-conquering empire on which 'the sun never set', and which would readily use force on any occasion to protect its vast colonial interests.

The first assignment of Australia's own troops to fight in one of Britain's wars was in 1885 when the New South Wales Infantry Battalion went to fight Mahdist rebels in Sudan. In 1819 Sudan had been invaded by Egyptian forces, and from then was governed by an Egyptian administration. By the middle of the century, Britain had taken greater control over the affairs of Egypt. In the early 1880s the British-backed Egyptian regime in Sudan was being threatened by the followers of a Muslim cleric named Muhammad Ahmad, who called himself the Mahdi, 'guided one'. These 'Mahdists' wanted to overthrow Egyptian rule in Sudan. The Egyptian government sent an army south to crush the revolt but it was soundly defeated by the Mahdist forces, and General Charles Gordon, former governor of Sudan, was sent back to Khartoum to organise the evacuation of loyal troops and civilians. He arrived in February 1884; the city was soon under siege by the Mahdists but Gordon insisted on staying, hoping to repel the rebels. Realising his plight, the British sent an army to his aid in September 1884 under the leadership of General Garnet Wolseley but by the time Wolseley reached Khartoum, Gordon was dead. On 26 January 1885 an estimated 50,000 Mahdists had broken into Khartoum and killed the 4000 soldiers and civilians inside the city, including Gordon.

In February 1885 the news of Gordon's death reached Australia by telegraph, and within weeks the New South Wales colonial government had announced that it was sending troops in aid of the empire. It was seen as an historic occasion, a 'red-letter day' in the history of the colony: 'this colony, not yet a hundred years old, has put forth its claims forever to be recognised as an integral portion of the British Empire' proclaimed a New South Wales newspaper.[1]

In justifying the commitment of troops, the prominent politician Henry Parkes echoed his previous sentiments about the Crimean War when he told a public meeting that the colony 'was as loyal as England itself' and that its people wanted to 'make ourselves known . . . by the qualities by which Britons are distinguished':

> Our loyalty? We ought to resent the bare idea that anything is needed to show our loyalty; we are always loyal, and I go so far as this, that if England were involved in a great war with a great Power, if she were in a position of extremity, we ought to risk our last shilling and our last life.[2]

With only fifteen days to prepare, on 3 March the New South Wales contingent marched from Sydney's Victoria Barracks to board ship at Circular Quay. It included 522 infantry soldiers, 24 officers and an artillery battery of 212 men[3] carrying ten sixteen-pound guns.[4] On each soldier's helmet was a crest with an image of Queen Victoria's crown. At the time New South Wales dispatched the troops, the British had made no request for military help but had agreed to accept the New South Wales troops on the basis that they pay their own expenses and act under British command.[5] When, within weeks, the colonies of Victoria, South Australia and Queensland also offered to send soldiers, the British politely declined, citing the 'difficulties of transport and water' that 'made it very undesirable to accumulate during the summer months any larger force [in Sudan] than already settled'.[6]

The commitment of the force to a country few had heard of and a conflict few understood was widely popular because it was in support of Queen Victoria and her empire. On the day of the departure of the force, a public holiday was called and thousands came to cheer the troops as they marched to Sydney's Circular Quay, where they boarded the *Iberia* and the *Australasian* for the voyage across the Indian Ocean to north-east Africa.

Not only Sydney, but the whole country, appeared to be stirred by the departure of the troops for the Sudan on Tuesday . . . The streets were crowded from an early hour with those who arrived by the boats from Newcastle and other northern ports, and with the arrivals by train and steamer . . . The display of bunting in the streets on several previous occasions has been very liberal, but that of Tuesday was probably never surpassed . . . Although New South Wales has been hitherto a strictly non-combative colony, the present occasion proved that it could be 'on the military' quite as much as the most belligerent of nations . . . When the head of the procession was seen, a ringing cheer rent the air, and as the contingent passed each balcony or point where the crowds were collected, the cries of 'That's them,' accompanied by the clapping of hands and shouts of 'hooray,' were almost deafening. As the procession passed, the crowds on either side closed in and followed slowly in a densely packed mob to the Circular Quay.[7]

To help pay for the expedition, a Patriotic Fund was established, which attracted 'large contributions from all sources' from the public.[8] There were also generous donations to the soldiers, including 575 flasks of Johnnie Walker Highland whisky, 19 cases of 'best champagne', 2000 cigarettes and two boxes of smoking pipes, 20 cases of aromatic horse condiment, 20 cases of insecticide, 200 prayer books, 150 cases of fruit and a bottle of 'relish' for each soldier to ward off seasickness on the voyage.[9] Within two weeks of the announcement of the deployment, Sydney's leather goods manufacturer Alderson & Son had produced for the contingent 700 pairs of boots, 800 pairs of shoes with laces, 250 leggings, 40 saddles and bridles plus a number of revolver cases, belts and spare leather strapping.[10]

There was criticism of the venture. *The Bulletin* ridiculed the contingent before and after it returned. A local MP, the Scottish-born David Buchanan, told the New South Wales parliament that 'the whole country lashed into madness . . . while one glance of the sensible rational mind would at once reduce their commotion to an absurdity'.[11] Overwhelmingly, however, the public and the press dismissed such attacks as unpatriotic and cowardly:

> We feel contempt for the cowards who oppose this movement, and especially for the ignorance of those who would stop the departure of troops accepted by the people of England.[12]

The Australians landed at Sudan's Red Sea port of Suakin on 29 March 1885, where they joined a large force of British soldiers. In the six weeks they were in Sudan, the Australians never reached Khartoum, were only on the periphery of some local skirmishes and spent much of their time helping to build a local railway and burying the men killed in earlier fighting. By May the British government had decided to abandon the campaign, and the Australians sailed for home on 17 May.

Although returning comparatively unscathed, the Australian troops were welcomed as heroes by a jingoistic press, with the *Geelong Advertiser*'s praise a prime example: 'With the entire honour that we can pay them, the men unselfishly went forth to do battle for the motherland which was supposed for the moment to be in peril.'[13]

Arriving in Sydney on 19 June, the returning troops were held at North Head quarantine station for five days, where one of the soldiers died of typhoid. Five days later and dressed in their khaki uniforms, they marched to Victoria Barracks, leading a Sudanese donkey brought back by one of the soldiers. At the barracks, which had been built for British troops in the 1840s before being handed over to the local force in 1870, they stood in the pouring rain to hear speeches of thanks from the colonial governor, Lord Loftus, the premier, Alexander Stuart, and their commanding officer, Colonel Richardson.[14] Each of the soldiers was given a special medal that had an image of the veiled head of Queen Victoria, and the following month a citizens' banquet was given in honour of the Sudan contingent at Exhibition Hall, which was located in Prince Alfred Park and had been built in 1870 to commemorate the centenary of Captain Cook's landing at nearby Botany Bay.

—

Two years after the Sudan campaign, Australians had another opportunity to demonstrate their loyalty and love for Queen Victoria when she celebrated fifty years on the British throne. The Golden Jubilee celebrations in Australia on 20 and 21 June 1887 for the queen were the biggest festivities the country had ever seen. Throughout her long rule, Victoria had never visited the continent; indeed, she had never shown great interest in any of her colonial possessions. A minority in Australia would have known what she looked like from a scant number of photographs or portraits on the walls of senior officials' offices. Yet at the time of the Golden Jubilee, the reverence shown was almost religious in its fervour. In Melbourne there were the customary giant triumphal arches and magnificent displays of gas illuminations:

> Never did Melbourne present a more brilliant appearance than on the night of Tuesday June 21, under the bright and many coloured lights and illuminations by which all citizens gave viable expression of their loyalty . . . Such a display has never been made in Melbourne before, and it will probably be long ere we look on its like again.[15]

In the evening the city was closed to traffic as an estimated 50,000 crowded in to see the light show.[16] 'The streets from end to end were a moving river of people' and all of the city's major streets and buildings were adorned with 'fairy lamps, gas lights, Chinese lanterns and jets of coloured flame'.[17] On the larger buildings, including the Treasury, Parliament House, General Post Office, public library, railway station and Government House, hung giant glass portraits of Victoria wearing a crown lit from behind with coloured gaslights.

In Sydney there was a public holiday as business 'followed

the example of government offices and closed for the day', and an estimated 150,000 people came into the city for the new display of illuminations:

> In the evening the city was a perfect blaze of lights from the centre to the various outskirts. Immense crowds of people thronged all the principal streets . . . and George Street was so densely packed that all idea of making reasonable progress had to be abandoned.[18]

In Brisbane, 'immense crowds, grouped in hordes' crammed the city streets in the evening to watch the illuminations.[19] In South Australia, 'before eleven o'clock' the streets of Adelaide were 'filled to overflow',[20] an estimated crowd of 50,000 thronged and 'a genuine spirit of loyalty and heartiness pervades all classes of society'.[21] During the day thousands of children joined a procession from Victoria Square, and in the evening buildings were illuminated with images of Queen Victoria in 'stars and crowns'.[22]

In Western Australia, where the colonial population was only a little over 43,000 people, the celebrations focused on Perth. In the morning there was a public reception at Perth Town Hall followed by a sports carnival. In the evening there was a fancy-dress ball at the Town Hall and a jubilee ball at Government House, which was described as 'one of the largest, if not the largest, which has ever been given in the colony'.[23] Western Australia also celebrated the jubilee with the colony's governor either reducing the prison terms or releasing thirty-six local convicts. The remaining prisoners were given 'roast beef, plum pudding, hot potatoes, a double allowance of tea and sugar, a pint of beer each and some tobacco'.[24]

In Tasmania, the second-largest city of Launceston boasted that their celebrations were without equal. The

Launceston Examiner reported that the night-time illuminations resulted in an all-time record gas consumption and
would be a great 'memory for coming generations':

> The display of the last two nights in Launceston far surpasses
> that of the capital and has been unequalled in any town of
> similar size in the Australian colonies.[25]

The celebrations involved all churches, religions and
races across Australia. Catholic, Wesleyan and Anglican
churches, as well as Jewish and German communities, all
sent messages to Buckingham Palace expressing devotion
and loyalty.

In Nowra on the New South Wales south coast, where
800 schoolchildren marched in a local procession, *The
Shoalhaven Telegraph* claimed:

> In no part of Her Majesty's Colonial possessions was there a
> more sincere or general manifestation of loyalty to the person
> and character of our sovereign lady than in the Shoalhaven
> District.[26]

A week before, *The West Australian* had made the point: 'In
common with your Majesty's loyal and dutiful subjects we,
in the distant part of Your Majesty's dominions, humbly
desire to convey to Your Majesty our unabated loyalty.'[27]

Part of the saturation coverage of the jubilee in local
newspapers included the publishing of panegyric poems
submitted by enthusiastic readers:

> Though half the world between us lies,
> Yet near or far thy sons we are.
> The sharers of thy gain or loss –
> One race beneath divergent skies.

Joined by the bond of kindred ties –
That half beneath the Polar Star,
And this beneath the Southern Cross.
All hail, Victoria![28]

There was a note of discord to the celebrations in Sydney a few weeks before the jubilee celebrations. On 3 June 1887 a public meeting was held in Sydney's Town Hall to discuss how the funds that had been raised for the jubilee might be spent. According to *The Sydney Morning Herald*, the meeting was disrupted by a number of men describing 'themselves as democrats' who 'were strongly opposed to any celebrations whatsoever'.[29] The dissidents, most of whom wanted Australia to become a republic, passed a motion opposing a proposal to invite thousands of children to a grand jubilee fete. A further meeting was called a week later by supporters of the jubilee but was again disrupted and, in the resulting 'mayhem', the meeting was closed early by the mayor.[30]

The disrupted meetings were condemned in the New South Wales parliament, where members called for three cheers for Queen Victoria and burst into 'God Save the Queen' as they left the chamber. On 15 June a third meeting was called, which attracted more than 12,000 people, the largest ever held in Sydney, according to *The Sydney Morning Herald*, which said the meeting was 'held as a protest against the disloyalty of a paltry section of the community and the ruffianism which would deny the citizens the right to speak in their own halls'.[31] The anti-monarchists turned up again and were accused of chanting 'Mrs John Brown', a reference to scurrilous rumours that Queen Victoria's relationship with her trusted personal servant John Brown was more than a friendship.

Attending the meeting was Henry Parkes, who had

recently become the New South Wales premier for the fourth time, and up-and-coming political leader Edmund Barton, both of whom spoke strongly in favour of the jubilee. Parkes once more spoke of local loyalty to the British crown:

> Loyalty means something more than attachment to any royal person. It means the settled form of government under which we live. Barton spoke of the attachment of Australians to the British monarchy: we English folk are too much attached to our ancient monarchy . . . there are few institutions in this country which are so deeply rooted in the hearts of the people as the monarchy.[32]

The supporters of the monarchy easily outnumbered the republicans, and motions condemning the republicans and supporting the monarchy and the jubilee were overwhelmingly carried. At the jubilee celebrations a week later, there were no reports of any discordant voices.

5

TWO PRINCES IN AUSTRALIA

The growing unpopularity of Prince Albert Victor is giving
both the Queen and the Prince of Wales serious anxiety . . . he
is dense, apathetic, short-tempered and sulky . . . the young
princesses openly deride Victor's stolidity, and even George
must feel a certain amount of contempt for his older brother's
lack of savoir faire . . . The Queen makes no secret of her
disappointment at his repeated failures in public.

IN 1881 AUSTRALIA HOSTED seventeen-year-old Prince
Albert Victor, the eldest son of Prince Edward (later
King Edward VII) and the grandson of Queen Victoria.
Accompanying him to Australia was his fifteen-year-old
brother, Prince George Frederick Ernest Albert, who
would become King George V when Albert Victor died
of pneumonia. When the brothers visited Australia in
1881, Prince Albert held the title of Prince Albert Victor
of Wales, and his brother, Prince George of Wales.

Prince Albert was born in January 1864; George,

seventeen months later. When Albert was seven, his mother appointed a tutor for him, the Reverend John Neale Dalton. Dalton complained that Albert's mind was 'abnormally dormant' and advised the boy's father that Albert needed the stimulus of his brighter, younger brother in order to learn. So for six years the boys were educated together, and Prince Albert was continually outshone by George.[1]

In 1879 and after a great deal of discussion between Queen Victoria and her son Edward, Albert and George were sent on a three-year sea voyage, which would include a visit to a number of British colonies, including Australia. Edward believed a naval career would be good for the education of the princes, particularly Albert, who remained not as impressive or as robust as his younger brother: '[Edward] was determined to send his sons to sea . . . chiefly with a view to the mental and moral training that they would receive as midshipmen in Her Majesty's Navy'.[2] The tour was also an opportunity for the British Empire to show off its strength to its dominion colonies and the rest of the world.

The princes sailed on the HMS *Bacchante*, an 85-metre-long, 3692-tonne battleship powered by both sail and steam. The ship carried a crew of 450, which included some forty officers and fifteen midshipmen, including the two princes. Escorting the *Bacchante* were a number of other British Royal Navy warships, including the *Carysfort*, *Tourmaline, Inconstant, Cathay* and *Cleopatra*, with a combined crew of more than 1000 men. Travelling with the two young princes was their tutor, John Neale Dalton. Seven years after the voyage, Dalton published a two-volume account of the tour, *The Cruise of Her Majesty's Ship the* Bacchante, which was based on the voyage and private journals, letters and notebooks of the princes, and was dedicated to Queen Victoria by 'Her Majesty's affectionate and dutiful grandsons'.

The palace insisted that when the princes were on board the ship they were to be treated exactly the same as the other midshipmen and were to take 'their turn in all weathers, by day and night and at watch keeping and going aloft, at sail or drill, boat duty . . . and mess with the other midshipmen and cadets in the gunroom'.[3] However, the princes were given a large captain's cabin to share, which was fully furnished and fitted with two 'swinging cots' or beds suspended to allow for a more comfortable sleep with the rocking of the ship. Dalton had the adjoining cabin and almost always accompanied the princes when they went ashore in Australia.[4]

The squadron left Portsmouth on its long voyage in October 1879. Over the next three years the *Bacchante* sailed over 86,000 kilometres, 48,000 under sail and the remaining 38,000 under steam. In addition to spending three months in the Australian colonies, the tour included visits to America, Africa, Asia, the Falkland Islands, South Africa, Fiji, Singapore, Ceylon, Aden, Egypt, the Holy Land and Greece.

The flotilla sailed first to the Mediterranean in 1879 and then via Madeira and Tenerife on to a tour of the West Indies early in 1880, calling in at Port of Spain in Trinidad and Tobago, Grenada, St Vincent, Jamaica and Bermuda. Later in the year, the ships sailed back to Spithead, Portsmouth, and in October 1880, the *Bendigo Advertiser* reported that it had received via submarine cable a telegram saying:

> The squadron, with [the princes] aboard sailed from England today. The exact destination of the squadron has not transpired, but it is understood the vessels will remain away for some time on a prolonged cruise.[5]

The ships headed for the southern hemisphere, stopping at Montevideo in Uruguay, then the British-controlled Falkland Islands before sailing back across the Atlantic to South Africa. Their reception in Dutch-dominated Cape Town was relatively subdued compared with the rousing reception they would later receive in Australia. Dalton was unimpressed by the place:

> [South Africa] is no use to us for emigration, or for any other purpose, as it is; it may become in the hands of those who originally colonised it, and who have become passionately attached to its soil . . . The British race has the whole of the continents of America and of Australia for its overplus of population, and can well afford to stand on one side and let another branch of the Teutonic stock have this.[6]

After leaving the Cape the *Bacchante* sailed across the Indian Ocean and made its first call in Australia at the port of Albany on the south coast of Western Australia on Sunday 15 May 1881, a customary stop for ships sailing from England to Melbourne and Sydney. At the time Western Australia, which had been established as a colony by the British in 1829, had a population of only 31,000 people 'scattered over . . . her vast expanse, which stretches from the tropics to the Southern Ocean'.[7]

> An area of 1,000,000 square miles . . . nearly equal in size to British India, it is five times the size of France and eight times that of Great Britain and Ireland, and has a coast line of over three thousand miles long.[8]

Albany was a settlement of just a few hundred people spread along the coast and on nearby farms in and around King George III Sound, which was named by the English explorer George Vancouver almost 100 years before when he was on his way to explore the north-west of Canada in 1792. Because of the small local population, the royals were able to relax and enjoy themselves in a way they could not when they reached the bigger towns and cities further to the east.

On arriving in Albany the royal party was met with a message from Perth from the governor of Western Australia, Sir William Robertson, who asked if they were able to come to visit the colony's capital. However, the princes declined, saying it was too far and would take too long to divert there. In Albany they were able to receive their first news since they had left England – it came 'fresh every morning' on the telegraph that since 1872 had connected the major centres of Australia with the overland telegraph to Europe; and before the party left the town three weeks later, the two young princes sent a birthday telegram greeting to their grandmother, Queen Victoria, who had turned sixty-two on 24 May.[9]

On their first day ashore, Albert and George went to shoot quails before they spent their first night on Australian soil in a

> small shanty [that] consists of two rooms completely empty and with clean bare floors; each room has a large open fire-place and plenty of jarrah wood, a pile of which last is stacked in the veranda outside, so as to be conveniently handy for throwing on the fire all night through.[10]

The next day they were up early for a kangaroo hunt:

> We rode after the kangaroo through the bush, and soon put up a few, two of which, by the help of the dogs, we killed, and kept their pads, which we sent home to the Princess of Wales

by the next mail as those of the first kangaroos we have seen in their native land. We also caught an opossum which we found in the traditional position up a gum-tree. Returning at 11 A.M., had an excellent breakfast in the kitchen of the farmhouse, agreeing that no cream or milk, butter or eggs, bread or tea, we had ever tasted was half so good as those here set before us.[11]

On this second day they rode through the tiny township of Albany on horses requisitioned from the local police. Two days later Prince George played cricket 'watched by many of the colonists and a few aborigines' in a team made up of the *Bacchante*'s crew against a local Albany side. During the game the *Bacchante*'s band came ashore and played at the cricket field.[12] They attended a ball at the local courthouse, which had been 'simply but effectively decorated'. The princes 'danced nearly every dance'. Two days later the royals hosted a concert in the courthouse in town and invited the locals to a performance of 'the Snowdrop Minstrels (the *Bacchante*'s negro troupe)'.[13]

After three weeks the party left Albany for the 2500-kilometre voyage east to Adelaide, leaving the *Bacchante* for repairs to a damaged rudder; the princes were transferred to the escort ship *Cathay* for this next leg of their tour. On the way they sailed along the arid southern shores and past the Spencer Gulf, which had been named by the English explorer Matthew Flinders eighty years before in 1802 after the lord of the admiralty Earl Spencer, Princess Diana's great-great-great-grandfather. They also sailed passed Kangaroo Island, named by Flinders when the crew of the *Investigator* had shot hundreds of kangaroos there for their first fresh meat in many months.

Sailing up the Gulf St Vincent, Albert and George landed at Adelaide's Glenelg Pier on Sunday 12 June, where they were met by 'a great crowd of people, who were out for their Sunday afternoon'.[14] The local newspaper reported that the princes 'looked well and in good spirits', and the locals were eager to demonstrate their loyalty to the royal family:

> A very large crowd, numbering some thousands [with] trains on both lines being literally crammed with passengers. [The princes] were met by unmistakable evidence of loyalty . . . and afforded our people an opportunity of testifying how strong is the attachment felt for the old country.[15]

In describing the two young men, a local newspaper reiterated that Prince George was more impressive than his older brother:

> [Prince Albert] is, in both appearance and disposition, very much like his mother, being of slight make and apparently not very strong. He is said to exhibit a modest and tiring disposition and . . . owing to the entire absence of affection or condescension in his demeanour, he has never been able to exhibit the proverbial qualities of the British middy [midshipman] . . . His younger brother, Prince George . . . is of a somewhat different disposition, being fond of active exercise, and altogether of a very vivacious temperament. Being more robust in health and of a stronger build than his brother, he seems well adapted for the profession chosen for him.[16]

The royal party was impressed with how clean Adelaide was:

> Everything seemed like home but there was none of the squalor we see on the outskirts of Liverpool or Manchester,

75

and no poverty anywhere apparent . . . everywhere there is an all pervading look of cleanliness and freshness.[17]

As they were driven through the crowds to Government House, the princes heard 'the first cheers of a British crowd that have sounded in our ears for many a day',[18] and once the crowd realised which of the party the princes were, the 'throng pressed around Albert and George to shake their hand'.[19]

At the time of the visit, the colony of South Australia was almost the size of Western Australia because it still included what later became the Northern Territory, so it covered more than two million square kilometres and stretched from the Indian Ocean to the Southern Ocean. A 3000-kilometre railway was under construction from Adelaide to Darwin and already nearly 1000 kilometres had been built – even though the colony's population of 300,000 people (ten times that of Western Australia) was overwhelmingly concentrated in a small area to the south and around Adelaide.

Everywhere the princes travelled in the colony they were greeted with large, enthusiastic crowds:

After dinner, we went to the theatre . . . All the streets, it being a Saturday night, were filled with dense crowds, and there was much cheering. The enthusiasm of the people . . . is most hearty and thorough.[20]

At the end of their Adelaide stay and before leaving for Melbourne, Prince Albert told a crowd that they had been overwhelmed by the enthusiasm shown to the monarchy:

Though our stay in South Australia has of necessity been brief, we can assure you it has been a thoroughly enjoyable one. We have often heard of your wellbeing, and of your loyalty; we have now witnessed them both for ourselves.[21]

On 20 June the royals left Adelaide to travel 800 kilometres east overland by horse, coach and train, and all along the route they were greeted by more cheering crowds:

> Along the route small crowds and knots of people gathered by the roadside in watch for the coming Princes . . . At the doors of many a thatched cottage . . . groups of children were marshalled to see the royal progress, and infants were held up in their mothers' arms to look at what they could not understand.[22]

At Echunga crowds of people lined the streets to see them pass. At Macclesfield 'flags were flying from all the buildings . . . and the Highnesses were welcomed by hearty cheers', and at Strathalbyn 'the school children lined the streets and sang "God Save the Queen" before three cheers for the princes'.[23]

On 21 June the princes went on another kangaroo hunt before they reached Kingston and a special train took them to Lucindale, where children turned out in rows along the platform, and on to Penola, where the townspeople crowded the station to sing 'God Save the Queen'.[24] Across the border into the colony of Victoria, the party caught a Cobb & Co. stagecoach with a new 'four-in-hand'. Cobb & Co. had started operating fast passenger coach services in the early days of the gold rush in Victoria. The four-in-hand was a coach drawn by four horses with the reins rigged to allow the coach to be driven by a single driver. The horses were changed with a fresh team every twelve to twenty kilometres, which dramatically reduced journey times. By the time of the princes' visit, Cobb & Co. operated hundreds of daily coach services across a network of thousands of kilometres in Victoria, New South Wales, South Australia and Queensland.

As the royals approached Casterton 'the Oddfellows all came out in procession with their banners and band to play us in to town for lunch' and at Wannon the party changed horses just before dusk before reaching Hamilton where they planned to stay the night:

> As we approach Hamilton many bonfires were lit by the side of the road and a constant succession of rockets are let off, while crowds of people, some in waggonettes, and others on horseback, come out to meet the coach . . . [in town] all across the square the people are standing so thickly we can only at a very slow pace approach the hotel . . . Before dinner we go out on the balcony in front of the hotel where there is a vast amount of cheering for the queen.[25]

After sleeping the night at Hamilton they left at 8 am on a special train that had been provided by the colony of Victoria for the 300-kilometre trip into the city of Melbourne. When they stopped briefly at Ararat, about 200 kilometres from Melbourne, the boys in the town lined one side of the platform and the girls the other to sing, which the princes described as 'the best we have heard anywhere'.[26]

They arrived at Melbourne around 4 pm and were greeted by the colony's premier, Graham Berry, who had migrated to Victoria from Twickenham in the early days of the gold rush in 1852 and made a fortune as a grocer. On the ride in the coach up Melbourne's Collins and Swanston streets to Government House, 'both sides of the streets were lined with people who all seem very pleased and kept cheering away as loud as they could'.[27]

The princes stayed on the *Bacchante* while they were in Melbourne. They had not seen the ship since Albany but said that though they'd been away from it for fifteen days, they had 'thoroughly enjoyed' themselves.[28] The following day when they came ashore on a steam launch, 'a large number of persons collected at the town pier to witness the disembarkation . . . The princes were cheered by the spectators, and they responded by lifting their hats'.[29]

They said they were impressed by the great city of Melbourne, which 'rivals in appearance those of the older capitals of Europe . . . the magnificent Post Office, the gigantic Treasury, the University, the Parliament Houses, the Union and Melbourne Clubs, the City Hall . . . the Wool Exchange . . . the government Railways . . . all are Cyclopean in the architecture, all seem built to last forever'.[30] The princes were well aware that the discovery of gold had made the colony the fastest-growing in the British Empire:

> It was gold that made her, that brought the bone and the muscle and sinew that have built up so rapidly her prosperity; no single British colony has ever enjoyed prosperity so rapidly and so great as that which has fallen to Victoria.[31]

During their two weeks in the city they visited Melbourne Mint, the Botanic Gardens, the horseraces at Caulfield, were shown the armour of the bushranger Ned Kelly who had been hanged in Melbourne Gaol the previous November, and Prince Albert laid the foundation stone for the building of the Melbourne Cricket Ground.

On 29 June they went by special train to the goldfields and were 'welcomed by about 15,000 people' as they were taken by carriage up Ballarat's Lydiard Street.[32] According to the princes, 'the crowds were simply enormous, the broad streets were thick with them . . . and they were all cheering and waving hats and handkerchiefs'.[33] After touring the goldmines they were taken down to see an underground mine, in a small cage elevator, each carrying a lighted candle:

All of a sudden we come upon a flash of light, the cage comes to a standstill, at the 420-foot level, and we get out into a cavernous chamber hollowed in the rock, where we have to drink in champagne to the health of the manager and success to the mine. At the same time the men sing the National Anthem in musical chorus the echo of which goes resounding along the galleries . . . re-entering the cage we are soon wound to the surface and come out once more into daylight, where we find a photographer ready to shoot us at once, in miners' clothes just as we are. We signed our names in the book, and find that the Duke of Edinburgh visited the same mine.[34]

In the afternoon they were driven back to the railway station and the 'streets were still thronged with thousands of people, who cheered just as heartily in the dusk of the evening as they had done in the morning'.[35]

Back in Melbourne, the following day they were invited to a ball in their honour attended by more than 2000 guests. In welcoming them the governor, Lord Normanby, told the royals

that he had resided now for many years in British colonies, and whatever their other characteristics might be, he could answer for their loyalty and affection for the Queen, and their love for the old country, and that Australia had given full proof that England may rely on the devotion of her loyal people on this side of the world.[36]

And on 4 July, towards the end of their visit, the city's lord mayor assured the princes:

no part of the British Empire is more loyal and devoted . . . towards the throne and the person of our most gracious sovereign than in this city, the capital of the colony which is honoured with Her Majesty's name.[37]

On behalf of the princes, Albert responded in kind:

When the Queen hears from us of the loyal sentiments you have this day expressed towards the Crown of Great Britain it will be a fresh assurance to Her Majesty that in the southern hemisphere the Queen has no more true or faithful subjects than the people of Victoria.[38]

Before leaving Melbourne, Albert and George attended a concert, remarking 'the whole thing was most successful, the music good and well performed, and the people bright and pleasant', and journeyed by train to Sandhurst in Melbourne's south-east, where they were welcomed by a 'brilliant and enthusiastic crowd . . . a most enthusiastic reception, we never saw anything equal to it'.[39]

As a parting gift at Government House on 6 July, the princes were given a gift of a rug made from the skins of platypuses, which Albert noted was a

queer looking little animal . . . becoming rarer every year in Australia now . . . He is quite a survival of ancient days; he has a duck's bill, the body of a large water rat, and webbed feet.

—

After two hectic weeks, the princes finally left Melbourne on 8 July. The *Bacchante* was still experiencing rudder trouble so they transferred to another of the Royal Navy escort ships, the *Inconstant*, for the five-day, 1000-kilometre voyage to Sydney. The party had intended visiting Tasmania but to the disappointment of the island colony, the plan was abandoned when the royals said they had insufficient time.[40]

A surprising incident took place while they were sailing along the New South Wales coast. The princes in their log claimed to have seen the legendary ghost ship the *Flying Dutchman*, which from the later eighteenth century was believed by many seafarers to be real:

> At 4 am the *Flying Dutchman* crossed our bows. A strange red light as of a phantom ship all aglow, in the midst of which light of the masts, spars and sails of a large brig 200 yards distant stood out in strong relief as she came up on the port bow. The lookout man on the forecastle reported her as close on the port bow, where also the officer of the watch from the bridge clearly saw her, as did the quarter deck midshipman, who was sent forward at once to the forecastle; but on arrival there was no vestige, nor any sign whatsoever of any . . . Ship . . . the night being clear and the sea calm. Thirteen persons altogether saw her.[41]

In contrast to their arrival scenes in Melbourne and Adelaide, the disembarkation in Sydney on 13 July was relatively quiet. After anchoring in the harbour they were landed in the early afternoon, where the public was excluded at Farm Cove, and walked up to Sydney Government House.

By now, New South Wales had a population of three-quarters of a million people and while Victoria's population had earlier overtaken it during the gold rush, New South Wales was growing faster and was expected to become the largest colony again within a few years. The princes were greeted by huge crowds as they were taken around the city. That evening they attended a mayoral ball with 2000 guests held in the giant Exhibition Hall. A local newspaper described the ball as the grandest event in the colony's history:

Entering the ball-room, the scene was a resplendent one . . . drapery hung from the ceiling. Festoons of shrubs and flowers hung from the upper bannisters along the whole of the building . . . Flags and banners from every nation – Britain being prominent – were suspended from every available spot, while all the side space was occupied by drapery streamers of every colour . . . the ball-room was brilliantly lighted, there being gasoliers at short distances, and rows of gas lamps off variously coloured globes . . . and near these huge mirrors . . . in the centre a fountain played upon a magnificent collection of shrubs, pot plants, and bouquets, specially collected from the Botanical Gardens.[42]

Over the next seven days the princes were shown the highlights of Sydney, including the Botanic Gardens, the Town Hall, the Art Gallery, St Andrew's Cathedral, St Mary's Cathedral and the Australian Museum. They were impressed by the giant Post Office building, which had been opened in Martin Place in 1874, and 'admired it more each time' they passed it. At Sydney University they saw the Great Hall and were told that 'women are admitted equally with men to all the privileges of the university'.[43] At the southern end of the city they were surprised at seeing so many Chinese people, who had come in large numbers to the gold rushes in the 1850s before all the colonies began introducing laws to stem Chinese migration. Indeed, after a dinner at Government House, they recorded:

Sir Arthur Kennedy told us several anecdotes about the Chinese. He was once governor at Hong-Kong, and is now at Brisbane; he says that he and Miss Kennedy and her maid are the only Europeans he allows in his house, everyone else is a Chinaman. He also spoke about the uselessness of attempting to keep out the Chinese immigration to Australia; they will come, and the only thing to be done is to deal wisely with them. (They appear, however, to meet with a cold reception wherever they go).[44]

The royal party was also impressed by the colony's military, who they believed were of a higher standard than the British soldiers they had replaced in 1870:

> Nor is it any exaggeration to state that in respect to physique, education and intelligence, the noncommissioned officers and gunners, not only equal, but probably surpass any three batteries in the imperial service. The standards of discipline and efficiency is in all respects a very high one.[45]

Albert and George appear to have enjoyed Sydney and said that whenever they were recognised in the streets the people 'were very hearty and demonstrative, cheering suddenly, their faces all lit up with attachment to England'.[46] After seven days in the city, on 20 July they left on a special train from Central Station to the Blue Mountains and visited Parramatta, Blacktown, Penrith, Blackheath, Mount Victoria and the coal centre at Lithgow ('the Sheffield of Australia', as the princes noted it was called).[47] They were due to attend a Freemasons Ball with 1500 guests in Sydney later that evening but arrived back late 'and too tired', so did not attend.[48]

Before leaving Sydney, Prince Albert ceremonially laid the foundation stone for a statue of Queen Victoria outside St James' church at the top of Macquarie Street; the statue was unveiled seven years later as the centrepiece of Australia's centenary celebrations in 1888.

On 10 August and after almost a month, they finally left the city, which they described as the 'most beautiful city of the queen's dominions', for the next leg of the tour to Queensland.[49] As they sailed out of Sydney Harbour they recorded that the crowds lining the shores were the largest they had ever seen.

It took six days of sailing to cover the 1000 kilometres to reach Brisbane, the capital of Queensland, whose population by now was around 220,000 people. Just before dusk they entered Moreton Bay and as darkness fell and they were transferred to a steam ferry for the journey up the Brisbane River to Government House, the locals lined the river banks and lit bonfires and fireworks all the way up.[50]

In a message on their arrival, the local colonial parliament assured the royals that Queenslanders were as loyal to the British monarchy as the other colonies:

> We, Her Majesty's loyal and dutiful subjects . . . beg to approach Your Royal Highnesses with earnest assurances of our loyalty and devotion to the throne and person of her most gracious Majesty the Queen, and to congratulate Your Royal Highnesses on your safe arrival in this colony.[51]

The next day was made a public holiday and most shops and businesses were closed, while thousands of people went down to see the *Bacchante* and the other ships of the squadron, which were all open for the public to visit.

After a visit of only three days in Queensland, the royals ended their Australian tour, setting off on the journey home to England via Fiji. As the squadron began the voyage, a large 'number of excursion steamers filled with passengers accompanied the navy ships out of Moreton Bay'.[52]

The British were pleased with their visit and relieved that only 108 navy crew members out of a fleet total of 1700 had deserted while the ships were in Australian waters.

> Considering the many inducements that are open to the colonies to the bluejackets for bettering himself, and the readiness

with which he can get an engagement upcountry on account of his handiness and general usefulness, this was perhaps no worse than we might have expected.[53]

The three months of the Australian royal tour had been an outstanding success from the viewpoint of both the Australians and the British. According to Prince Albert, the Australian leg had been the most successful of the entire three-year voyage:

> During the whole quarter of the year that we have spent in Australia from the time we landed in Albany, we have enjoyed ourselves more than at any other place since we left England, everybody has been so kind and so hospitable. As the shores of Australia recede from our view we are conscious of very mingled feelings. We are glad that it has been our happy privilege to visit there; we are sorry that they are not better known to our fellow countrymen in Great Britain . . . After England, Australia will always occupy the warmest corner of our hearts . . . What is ours is theirs, and what is theirs is ours. As our past history is theirs, so may their future be bound up with ours from generation to generation. We are united to them not merely by the ordinary bonds of friendly intercourse which may exist between alien nations, but by the ties of kindred, by the ties of a common language and literature, by ties of common interests and common institutions, and by ties of common allegiance to one sovereign and one law.[54]

On returning to England, George remained in the navy and nineteen-year-old Albert went to Cambridge University, where he showed little intellectual curiosity, was excused from sitting exams and eventually awarded an honorary degree. In 1884 he spent some time at Heidelberg University learning to speak German and after returning to England joined the 10th Hussars. He was dogged by scandal and rumours of homosexuality and relationships with unsuitable women, and by the mid-1880s was attracting criticism from his grandmother, the queen, his father and his brothers and sisters. The concerns of the royal family were being reported in the newspapers in Australia:

> The growing unpopularity of Prince Albert Victor is giving both the Queen and the Prince of Wales serious anxiety . . . he is dense, apathetic, short-tempered and sulky . . . the young princesses openly deride Victor's stolidity, and even George must feel a certain amount of contempt for his older brother's lack of savoir faire . . . The Queen makes no secret of her disappointment at his repeated failures in public.[55]

There were also remarks about the prince's bad manners in public:

> Victor's utter inability to string together half a dozen sentences coherently seems inexplicable . . . at several public dinners His Royal Highness has given great offence by chatting loudly to his neighbour while speeches were going on.[56]

Three years later, in July 1889, when Prince Albert was twenty-five years of age, he was linked with a gay brothel in London's Fitzrovia district. In what became known as 'the Cleveland Street Scandal', the London police had raided the brothel and:

> According to the newspapers 'the name of Prince Albert Victor, the eldest son of the Prince of Wales, has been mentioned in connection with the disgraceful affair'.[57]

He was sent to India on a seven-month voyage a few months later to avoid the trial and the press coverage. But only two years later he was implicated in another scandal: the suicide of a chorus girl, which was reported in the English and then the Australian papers:

Romantic Suicide of a Chorus Girl

> The newspapers hint that Miss Lydia Manton, the chorus girl at the Gaiety Theatre London, who recently committed suicide, was the recipient of attentions from the Duke of Clarence and Avondale, eldest son of the Prince of Wales, though she was the nominal mistress of Lord Charles Montague, who gave evidence at the inquest. The affair is causing a profound sensation.[58]

Several attempts were made to marry off the increasingly embarrassing Albert, or Eddy, as he was known in the royal circles. The first was to eighteen-year-old German Princess Alix of Hesse (Alexandra Feodorovna), who was also a grandchild of Queen Victoria. But the young princess did not accept Albert's proposal. In 1890 he was to marry Princess Hélène of the deposed Orléans royal family of France, but her family blocked her conversion from Catholicism that would have been necessary for her to marry into the British monarchy. Finally, 24-year-old Princess Mary of Teck, of mixed British and German royalty, agreed to marry Albert Victor. The royal wedding was planned for February 1892 but a month before Prince Albert developed pneumonia and, despite the best medical attention, he died on 14 January 1892.

His father wrote to Queen Victoria in abject grief, saying, 'Gladly would I have given my life for his', and his younger brother George wrote:

how deeply I did love him and I remember with pain nearly every hard word & little quarrel I ever had with him & I long to ask his forgiveness, but, alas, it is too late now.[59]

The royal family was devastated by the tragedy, but when Albert died a major problem for the monarchy had been averted. The more impressive Prince George was now second in line to the throne. He married his deceased brother's fiancée, Princess Mary, in July 1893 and seventeen years later, after the death of his father, Prince George became King George V. King George and Queen Mary had four children, including two British kings: Edward, who would briefly become King Edward VIII before abdicating, and his younger brother, who would take the crown as King George VI.

6

THE CREATION OF THE NATION
OF AUSTRALIA

The nation would be called the Commonwealth of Australia.
The queen (and her heirs and successors) would be the
head of state, with the governor-general her representative
in Australia, who would give assent to bills passed by the
national parliament before they could become law.

WHEN THE SIX COLONIES of New South Wales, Victoria,
South Australia, Western Australia, Queensland and
Tasmania were discussing whether to unite to become
the nation of Australia in 1901, the rumblings of the
fighting at Eureka were long past and there was never any
serious suggestion that a newly formed nation would be
a republic, as the United States had become more than a
century earlier. There was no question that the new nation
would remain a colony of the British Empire, with Queen
Victoria as its head of state.

As the six colonies grew throughout the second half of the nineteenth century, they met more frequently to discuss issues of mutual concern such as postal services, telegraph, rail and coach services and lighthouses. In 1886 the Federal Council was formed but New South Wales refused to join it, which made it impractical as a forum for seriously discussing federation.

The first real spark that led to the colonies talking in earnest about uniting as a nation arose from a speech made by Premier Henry Parkes in the northern New South Wales town of Tenterfield; it became known as the 'Tenterfield Oration'. At the time the colourful Parkes was a veteran politician serving his fifth term as premier of New South Wales. He had been born in England in humble circumstances and migrated to Australia in 1839, where he became a formidable public figure. He married three times and fathered seventeen children – and, it was claimed, had sired others outside his marriages. When his first wife, Clarinda, died in 1888, Parkes had already had two of the five children he would have with his second wife, Eleanor. When Eleanor died in 1895, eighty-year-old Parkes married for the third time, to his 23-year-old housekeeper, Julia Lynch.

Delivering the 'oration' at the Tenterfield School of Arts Hall on 24 October 1889, Parkes told his listeners that the time had come for the 'creation on this Australian continent of an Australian government and an Australian parliament':

Australia [now has] a population of three and a half millions, and the Americans numbered only between three and four millions when they formed the great commonwealth of the United States. The numbers were about the same, and surely what Americans have done by war, the Australians can bring about in peace.[1]

Parkes called for 'leading men from all the colonies' to meet at a constitution convention:

> This convention will have to devise the constitution which will be necessary for the bringing into existence a federal government with a federal parliament for the conduct of this great national undertaking . . . I believe . . . that the time has come . . . and all the great national questions . . . will be disposed of by a fully authorised constitutional authority.[2]

The other colonial premiers were initially sceptical of Parkes's suggestion because in past years New South Wales had stalled these discussions. Nonetheless, the premiers of Victoria, Tasmania, South Australia and Queensland agreed to meet with Parkes early the following year at the Victorian colonial parliament in Melbourne. Their host in February 1890 was the Victorian premier Duncan Gillies, and the others present were Parkes, Queensland's Sir Samuel Griffith and South Australia's John Cockburn. Tasmania sent its colonial secretary, Bolton Stafford Bird, and its attorney-general, Andrew Inglis Clark. Western Australia did not participate in the conference but sent Sir James Lee Steere as an observer. New Zealand sent its colonial secretary, Captain William Russell, and the veteran political leader Sir John Hall. The New Zealanders had been invited because Parkes proposed the inclusion of New Zealand in a nation to be called Australasia.

During the seven sitting days of the meetings, discussion focused on whether a national union was appropriate and how it might be achieved. On the fifth day, Captain William Russell explained why his country did not want to be part of a united Australasia. He said New Zealand was different in many ways from Australia, and argued the white settlement of New Zealand had been far better handled and that they did not want Australian involvement in relations with their indigenous peoples.

> Not only have the settlers had to struggle against the forces of nature, but against a proud, indomitable, and courageous race of aborigines . . . Their right to their lands was recognised from the first . . . instead of confiscating it we admitted their claim to its full possession, administration and disposal . . . one of the important questions in New Zealand politics for many years to come must be that of native administration, and were we to hand over that question to a federal parliament – to an elected body, mostly Australians, that cares nothing and knows nothing about native administration . . . the advance of civilisation would be enormously delayed.[3]

Russell concluded by asking Parkes to change Australasia to Australia – and so ended the brief involvement of New Zealand in the creation of the nation of Australia.

On the last day of the conference, Parkes secured a historic breakthrough, with the passing of a resolution calling for the colonies to unite, which was forwarded to Queen Victoria.

> To the Queen's Most Excellent Majesty.
>
> May it Please Your Majesty. We Your Majesty's loyal and dutiful subjects, the Members of the Conference assembled in Melbourne to consider the question of creating for Australia one federal government . . . desire to approach Your Most Gracious Majesty with renewed expressions of our devoted attachment to Your Majesty's throne and Person . . . We most respectfully inform Your Majesty that . . . we have unanimously agreed . . .
>
> That, in the opinion of this conference, the best interests

and the present and future prosperity of the Australasian colonies will be promoted by an early union under the Crown.[4]

The serious business began in Sydney early the following year, in March 1891, to draft a constitution for a united states of Australia; amid the euphoria and optimism of the moment, few delegates would have any inkling that it would take another ten years of oscillation, obstruction and political skullduggery for the new nation of Australia to be inaugurated.

The Constitutional Convention took place at the New South Wales colonial parliament and was hosted by an ageing Parkes, whom *The Sydney Morning Herald* described as looking 'faded and weary, [he] fails to give the impression of revered force which his peculiar bearing has hitherto always strongly conveyed'.[5]

The convention was the most impressive gathering ever of senior colonial figures in Australia. The forty-six delegates from New South Wales, Victoria, South Australia and Tasmania had been elected by each of their parliaments. Twelve were either premiers or former premiers, nine were lawyers, including four Queen's Counsels, and nine were knighted. Many of the delegates would dominate the federation process over the next ten years and play leading roles in the early days of the first Australian governments.

Accompanying Parkes and among the New South Wales delegation was Edmund Barton, who would later take over from Parkes as the unofficial leader of the Australian federation movement and become Australia's first prime minister. Barton's love of the good life and the time he spent at his club had earned him the nickname of 'Toby Tosspot' by *The Bulletin* magazine. The other delegates included South Australia's premier 'Honest Tom' Playford and Charles Kingston, who would later replace Playford and become a leading player in the federation story. The Queensland team included its premier and lawyer Sir Samuel Griffith, who would play a vital role in the final constitution, and Tasmania sent Andrew Inglis Clark, who turned up at the convention with an already drafted constitution. Clark's draft contained many features of the American constitution that would be adopted for Australia, including a national senate with equal representatives from each state. It was in Sydney at the 1891 convention that Western Australia made its first full appearance in the nation-building process. The delegation was led by Premier John Forrest, a giant of a man and already a well-known explorer.

The conference discussed such matters as the rights of the colonies, or states as they would become. Also dominant was the argument for free trade and the abolition of interstate tariffs and about the powers of the national parliament, the executive, the judiciary and national defence. The meetings stretched over more than a month, and on the last day, after the delegates had finally agreed on the wording for the constitution, Parkes proclaimed it would 'be remembered as long as Australia and the English language existed'. The meetings finally ended 'with three vigorous cheers . . . for the Queen'.[6]

The nation would be called the Commonwealth of Australia. The queen (and her heirs and successors) would be the head of state with the governor-general her representative in Australia, who would give assent to bills passed by the national parliament before they could become law. The colonies would become states. There would be two houses of parliament: one popular, which would be called the House of Representatives; the other, the Senate, to consist of an equal number of representatives from each of the colonies. The final preamble of the Australian constitution agreed on at the convention made clear the pre-eminent role of Queen Victoria and the British Crown in the future nation:

> Whereas the Australian colonies . . . have . . . agreed to unite under the Crown of the United Kingdom of Great Britain . . . it is expedient to make provision for the admission into the Commonwealth of other Australasian colonies and possessions of Her Majesty: Be it therefore enacted by the Queen's most Excellent Majesty . . .

At the conclusion of the Sydney convention all the delegates agreed to take the constitution back to their colonies for ratification and then to the people for a referendum so they could have the final say on the formation of the new nation. Only Premier John Forrest made it clear before leaving Sydney that Western Australia was unlikely to join – the vast colony with a population of just over 50,000 people felt 'distrust, disinterest and hostility'[7] towards federation and saw little advantage in ceding powers to a national government based thousands of kilometres away. It also feared the loss of local colonial tariffs and that its fledgling industries would be swamped by larger and more established competitors in the east.[8]

Opposition to federation in New South Wales also continued unabated. Three months after the Sydney convention, in June 1891 Parkes's position was further weakened when he faced an election. He was returned to office but with a reduced majority and dependent on the support of the emerging Labor Party members, who were more focused on social and industrial change than federation. Then, in October 1891, and now seventy-six years old, tired and in ill health, Parkes resigned as premier and the federation bill languished.

The Victorians did keep their promise, and the constitution bill was passed in both their houses of parliament,
but was then effectively shelved as the colony waited for
New South Wales to provide a lead, which didn't come.
Queensland, South Australia and Tasmania were 'ready for
action' but also 'paralysed by the uncertain action of New
South Wales'.[9]

The issue languished for more than two years, until
a renewed push came not from the politicians or parliaments but from the people and specifically from 'federation
leagues', which were essentially democratic conferences of
citizens. In late 1894, recently elected New South Wales
premier George Reid agreed to raise federation with his
colleagues from the other colonies. Reid had previously
been a strong opponent of the idea, but was cynical enough
to see the tide of public opinion was turning in its favour.

Early the following year, at Reid's instigation, the
premiers met in the 'gentlemen only' Tasmania Club in
Hobart to hammer out a course to federation. At 10.30 pm
on 29 January 1895, Reid appeared at the front door of
the club and from the top of the steps read out a statement
to the assembled press. It said that the premiers agreed to
federation, but this time the delegates to draft the constitution would be chosen by holding public elections in each
colony.

The fifty delegates – from New South Wales, Victoria,
South Australia, Western Australia and Tasmania – met
in Adelaide to write the new national constitution on
22 March 1897. Queensland did not attend as its parliament could not agree on the enabling legislation. Edmund
Barton from New South Wales was elected 'leader of the
convention' and was asked to chair the meeting.

The Adelaide convention worked effectively for twenty-
five days and had a new draft constitution outline just

at the point when the meeting was suspended so the premiers and many of the delegates could sail to London for the Diamond Jubilee celebrations of Queen Victoria on 20 June 1897. The 78-year-old monarch was celebrating a reign of sixty years, during which time the British Empire had become the greatest power the world had ever seen. The previous year, Victoria had surpassed her grandfather George III to become the longest-reigning monarch in British history.

In England, the Australian colonial premiers joined other leaders of the empire's dominions and representatives of the European monarchies for celebrations and a procession through London. Ten minutes ahead of Queen Victoria, each premier was drawn by four richly caparisoned horses and escorted by a contingent of their own colony's troops, from Buckingham Palace to St Paul's Cathedral. *The Age* reported that:

> In the second [carriage] were Mr Reid (New South Wales), Sir George and Lady Turner (Victoria). In the third were Mr Seddon (New Zealand) and Sir Hugh Nelson (Queensland) . . . in the seventh carriage were Sir John and Lady Forrest (West Australia) . . . The colonial troops here were greeted by cries from the crowd of 'Bravo Canada!' 'Good old Australia!' and 'Cooee!' Everyone was struck with the splendid horsemanship and fine physique of the colonial troops, whose appearance was greeted with thunderous applause from the East End to the West End of London.[10]

The premiers were caught up in the swirl of the pomp and ceremony of the great British Empire at its zenith. The Australian colonial press was effusive about the celebrations and the reception given to the colonial representatives:

> Words cannot adequately describe the celebration. The good
> old queen had a magnificent reception all along the line of the
> procession. Next to the queen the most enthusiastic greetings
> were given to the colonial premiers and the colonial troops.[11]

The day after the jubilee, the Australian premiers and their
wives were introduced to Her Majesty at Buckingham Palace
by the British colonial secretary, Joseph Chamberlain,
where, according to one Australian press report of the
event, 'the queen showed marked attention to the premiers
who she specially addressed'.[12] Among the other highlights
of the jubilee was a banquet for the premiers at Mansion
House, which was attended by the British prime minister,
the Marquess of Salisbury (who had visited Australia in the
early days of the gold rushes), and many other senior British
leaders.

Queen Victoria's Diamond Jubilee was, of course, also
celebrated in Australia. The festivities were reminiscent
of the Golden Jubilee celebrations, though this time there
was also a public holiday in almost every town and city
across the country. Sydney's Randwick Racecourse held a
special program that included the running of the Queen's
Stakes, Jubilee Cup, Diamond Handicap, Commemorative
Handicap and the Victorian Handicap.[13] At Wagga Wagga
in New South Wales there was a jubilee procession from the
railway station to the showground, which was followed by
a sports carnival.[14]

In South Australia, farmers proposed to send 20,000
carcasses of mutton and 500 carcasses of beef 'to London
to feed the poor of the city during the festival'[15] and similar
offers were made by farmers in Victoria and New South
Wales.[16] At suburban Norwood near Adelaide there was a
jubilee ball, where all of the local aldermen were presented
with a jubilee medal, and at nearby Mount Lofty the

foundation stone was laid for the building of the Queen Victoria Children's Convalescent Home.[17]

In Victoria, the city of Bendigo purchased an expensive portrait of Queen Victoria to be exhibited in the local public gallery.[18] In suburban Brunswick, the streets were decked with 'flags by day' and 'loyal illuminations by night'.[19] In rural Healesville, sixty-five kilometres north-east of Melbourne, 500 people turned out for a parade and the planting of a number of trees that were named after each of Queen Victoria's children.[20] At Echuca, in the north of the state, more than 1000 local children formed the jubilee parade 'with flags and bannerettes waving'.[21]

In Western Australia, the locals at Albany decided to build a bandstand on Sterling Terrace to commemorate the jubilee, while at Bunbury a new square called Queen Victoria Square was created by fencing off the centre of the town and planting trees there.[22] Sixteen prisoners were released from Western Australian jails and another twenty-five recommended for pardons as an 'act of clemency on the occasion of the queen's record reign'.[23]

In Tasmania, bell ringers 'ushered in Jubilee day with a merry peal at midnight'. At New Town in Hobart, thirty occidental flame trees were planted to form the Queen's Walk and the Hobart *Mercury* newspaper reported that it had to publish double the normal number of papers for its special jubilee edition.[24]

In Queensland, the town of Laidley, west of Brisbane, held a jubilee sports carnival with thirty events and 'hundreds of participants'.[25] In Rockhampton, a foundation stone was laid for a new Town Hall and the locals held a carnival that the local newspaper proudly proclaimed as 'the most brilliant display of the kind ever seen'.[26]

—

After the celebrations in London, the colony's leaders returned home and resumed the task of finalising the Australian constitution. Finally, on Saturday 12 March 1898, a draft was finished. Almost exactly ten years after Sir Henry Parkes's Tenterfield oration and 'under conditions of great nervous exhaustion and irritability' there existed an agreed constitution of the Australian Commonwealth.[27]

Three months later, New South Wales, Victoria, South Australia and Tasmania took the new constitution to be voted on by the people. Queensland and Western Australia were still dragging behind: in Queensland, there remained an absence of enthusiasm or any sizeable groundswell of support for national union; in Western Australia, the conservative political leadership remained convinced federation would be more harmful than beneficial to the economy.

In Victoria, South Australia and Tasmania, the 'Yes' vote was overwhelming. On election night in Melbourne, huge crowds gathered to witness the outcome of the poll. A highlight of the evening was the projection of lighted images onto a big screen, which was on top of the tally board. When Queen Victoria's picture was shown, 'the national anthem was sung from 30,000 throats, and was followed by round after round of cheering'.[28]

The poll did not go so well in New South Wales. Things had got off to a bad start in the Sydney campaign when Premier George Reid addressed a huge crowd at the Town Hall. He spoke for over two hours, going through the proposed constitution section by section. Rather surprisingly, considering he had pledged previously to use every influence to recommend it to the people, he began to highlight what he thought were its flaws:

> I cannot take up this bill with enthusiasm. I see serious blots in it which have put a severe strain on me . . . Because a great

nation's worth is, great as an Australian union is . . . in a continent as free as this, we ought to have, I admit, a more democratic constitution.[29]

Reid's mixed message was to prove a major problem in New South Wales, where the colony's parliament had stipulated that there needed to be 80,000 'Yes' votes. At the forefront of the opponents of the constitution was the Anti-Convention Bill League, which claimed the constitution was undemocratic and would mean the 'birth of minority rule in Australia'.[30] In their campaign for the 'No' vote they highlighted that each colony, or state as they would become known, would have the same number of senators, irrespective of their population:

> Seven hundred thousand people in three smaller states [South Australia, Tasmania – and Western Australia if they joined] will possess between them eighteen Senators, while two million and a half in the two larger states will be represented by only twelve senators.[31]

On election night 71,595, or 52 per cent, voted 'Yes' – more than 8000 votes too few for the bill to be passed. Much of the blame was rightly sheeted home to George Reid, who had gained the nickname of 'Yes-No' for his duplicity.

Under great pressure to salvage something from the mess, Reid telegraphed the other premiers and suggested they meet. Rather than abandon federation altogether, they agreed to, in Melbourne in January 1899. The premiers of New South Wales, Victoria, South Australia and Tasmania were joined by the new Queensland premier, James Dickson, whose inclusion was something of a surprise.

Although resentful of New South Wales's obduracy, the premiers of the other colonies realised they needed to make some concessions that Reid could take back to the voters of New South Wales. It was finally agreed that the site of the new national capital would be in New South Wales – provided it was at least 160 kilometres from Sydney. Because there had been a change to the bill, all the colonies had to go back to another referendum. This time, on 20 June 1899, there was a bigger turnout of voters and in New South Wales 107,420, or more than 56 per cent, voted 'Yes'. The 'Yes' vote increased in Victoria, South Australia and Tasmania above the level of the previous referenda. In Queensland, where they were holding their first vote, the 'Yes' campaign also won the day with 55 per cent of the vote.

Finally, with Western Australia still sitting on the sidelines, the other five colonies could progress to a national union. But Australia was of course still a British territory and unless it followed the American example of a Declaration of Independence, a law allowing the colonies to unite as a nation had to be first passed by the British parliament and assented to by Queen Victoria. Britain supported a united Australia because it would strengthen the British Empire's territories in the southern hemisphere. However, the British needed to be satisfied with the nature of the proposed Australian federation.

In January 1900 the five colonies decided who would go to London to negotiate Australian nationhood with the British. New South Wales chose Edmund Barton; Victoria, Alfred Deakin; South Australia, Charles Kingston; and Queensland, James Dickson. Tasmania opted for its former premier Philip Fysh because he was already in England, having become the colony's agent-general in London.

Negotiations with British colonial secretary Joseph Chamberlain began in March 1900 and continued for two months. The biggest disagreement the two parties had was over section 74 of the constitution which, according to the British, gave too much power to the new High Court of Australia as the highest court of appeal over the British Privy Council. The Australians spent weeks lobbying in London to avoid being made to keep the Privy Council as their court of appeal. At first they had little success: Chamberlain was at the time extremely powerful in Britain, and the country was riding a wave of enormous confidence regarding its empire. It seemed unlikely that the British would be persuaded by this group of colonials from thousands of miles away to make such a concession. The Australian delegates found Chamberlain 'iron-willed'; equally, however, most of them stubbornly refused to entertain the idea of changing their hard-won constitution. For his part Chamberlain described the colonials as 'some of the stoutest negotiators he had met in his life'.[32]

Finally, on 20 May 1900 both sides agreed to rewrite section 74 so that each could claim a partial victory. On 9 July Queen Victoria signed the *Commonwealth of Australia Constitution Act*, which allowed for the nation of Australia to come into being on the following 1 January.

After signing the act, Queen Victoria made a gift to the new nation of the pen, inkstand and table she had used to sign the document at Windsor Castle. The table, made of brass and ebony, was used at the Commonwealth of Australia inauguration ceremony in Centennial Park in Sydney on 1 January 1901 and is now kept in Parliament House in Canberra.

Signing the nation of Australia into existence was one of the last of Queen Victoria's great acts before she died only six months later. When she had become queen sixty-three years earlier, Australia had been a tiny place with a population of barely 130,000 people, living mainly in only two colonies, New South Wales and Tasmania. By the end of her reign the country had blossomed into a federation of six states with a combined population of almost four million. And despite the decades of tumultuous change during the Victorian era, Australians entered the twentieth century still deeply attached and committed to the British monarchy.

7

AUSTRALIA AFTER VICTORIA

The loss of Her Majesty . . . makes every unit of the nation stricken today with a grief which could not be felt in any other part of the world for any other sovereign.

BEFORE THE NEW NATION of Australia could start business, it needed an interim government until its first election. The man with the responsibility of picking the caretaker government was Queen Victoria's representative in the country: the nation's first governor-general John Adrian Louis Hope, the forty-year-old seventh Earl of Hopetoun.

The aristocratic Hopetoun was no stranger to Australia – he had been the governor of Victoria for more than five years from 1889. Born in Scotland, he was very much a product of the British establishment: educated at Eton and Sandhurst Military College, he was noted during his term as Victorian governor for his passion for hunting and horseriding, as well as for the unusual habit of powdering his hair. When he returned to Australia on

15 December 1900, he brought with him the same pomp as he had to Victoria the decade before. His staff included a private secretary, an assistant private secretary, a military secretary, an aide-de-camp, a house steward, twenty house servants and thirteen stable hands for his thirty horses.[1]

His appointment was well received in the colonies. New South Wales premier Sir William Lyne telegraphed London saying Hopetoun was 'eminently fitted for the position'.[2] South Australia's Sir Frederick Holder wired to say the appointment 'will be in every way pleasing' to the Australians; Queensland's Sir Robert Philp said Hopetoun would 'make a very good governor-general'; and Victoria's Sir George Turner declared that 'the Imperial government could not have made a happier choice'.[3]

Hopetoun had only two weeks to appoint a government before the planned inauguration of the nation on New Year's Day 1901. Three days after reaching Sydney he met with Sir William Lyne and, without consulting anyone else, invited him to form the first national government. The public and the press expressed 'blank surprise'.[4] Just about everyone had expected Edmund Barton, the undisputed leader of the federation movement, to be invited. Not only that, but Lyne had been one of the most outspoken opponents of federation, actively campaigning against nationhood.

For several days Lyne tried unsuccessfully to persuade various prominent politicians and other state premiers to join his government but none would agree, and on Christmas Eve he was forced to advise the governor-general he could not form a government. To everyone's relief, Hopetoun then turned to Edmund Barton, upon whom, in the words of *The West Australian*, 'no one could the honour have been more justly bestowed'.[5] His appointment was universally endorsed and by New Year's Eve he had managed to form Australia's first government, only hours before its inauguration.

The inauguration ceremony took place in Sydney's Centennial Park on New Year's Day. A giant procession set off at 10.30 am: floats, horse-drawn carriages, cavalry, marching soldiers, police, firefighters, stockmen, trade unions, church leaders, the senators from Sydney University, representatives of foreign governments and the premiers and officials from the other Australian states. An estimated 250,000 people lined the route, which started near Sydney Harbour in the Domain and wound its way along Macquarie Street through the city to Centennial Park.

In the park, a large white timber pavilion had been built for the occasion. After Lord Hopetoun was sworn in as governor-general, he read out a message from Queen Victoria that was recited simultaneously in the capitals of the other colonies by the local colonial governors, who were being sworn in as the new state governors:

> The Queen commands me to express through you to the people of Australia Her Majesty's heartfelt interest in the inauguration of the Commonwealth, and her earnest wish that under Divine Providence it may ensure the increased prosperity and well-being of her loyal and beloved subjects in Australia.[6]

The official program of celebrations in Sydney stretched over eight days and included athletics, cycling and swimming carnivals, a Highland gathering at the Sydney Cricket Ground, a giant trade unions parade, a military tattoo, a military church parade, a series of official banquets and the usual fireworks displays.

But the euphoria surrounding the founding of the British Empire's newest country was short-lived, because three weeks after Barton's inauguration, Queen Victoria was dead. She died at Osborne House on the Isle of Wight on Tuesday 22 January. At around midday she had regained consciousness for the first time in several days and called for her pet Pomeranian dog, which she had reportedly 'fondled for a minute'. She then 'talked a little' to two of her grandchildren, Princess Louise and Princess Beatrice, relapsed into unconsciousness and was pronounced dead at around 6.30 pm.[7] She was eighty-one years old and had been on the throne longer than any other British monarch. During this time she and her subjects had witnessed the elevation of Britain to foremost among the nations of the world. Her name would be given to an era and become the symbolic representation of the prestige and power of her kingdom.

Despite her lack of interest in Australia, the impact of her death and the outpouring of sorrow in the new nation were profound. On receiving the news by telegraph, each state hoisted down its flags to half-mast, and government offices, banks and private offices closed their doors and rolled down their blinds.[8] All organised entertainment was suspended and most shops were closed.[9]

The news of Victoria's death dominated the press in Australia as it did in Britain, and indeed throughout the world. Local newspapers editorialised that support for Queen Victoria was universal in Australia. The *Camperdown Chronicle* proclaimed that all people, whether 'socialist, Tory, Liberal, Quaker or Papist', were unanimous in their admiration and respect for the queen.[10] Even the socialist Wagga *Worker*, which opposed the monarchy 'as do all who are supporters of majority rule', said that Victoria was 'blameless' and had done 'her duty according to her necessarily limited ideas'.[11]

New South Wales's *Worker* described how, 'throughout

the length and breadth of Australia there was universal gloom.'[12] *The Argus* said:

> There is no need to write long panegyrics in her praise. Her deeds, her virtues, live in her people's hearts; nor is there need to tell her people's sorrow at her passing away. That sorrow is too real, too deep and true for words. The nation mourns its loss in silence that speaks more effectually than wailings loud and dismal.[13]

The Sydney Morning Herald wrote that Queen Victoria had given the people of the British Empire 'political, industrial, and civil liberty, tempered justice with mercy in administration of the country's laws, enfranchised the masses'.[14] It said she had become 'the synonym of the State, the personification of the patriotic and loyal sentiment, and the symbol of their pride of race'. In Adelaide *The South Australian Register* reported that 'signs of mourning met the eye at every turn . . . and there was scarcely a business establishment without one or more shutters up or black drapery'.[15] And in Perth *The West Australian* recorded 'the instinctive feeling of gloom and depression'.[16]

Throughout the country special memorial services were arranged. In Victoria, overflowing crowds attended a service at Port Melbourne's Town Hall; the bell at St James' Church in Dandenong tolled continually each evening, 'with mournful regularity, which had the effect of vividly reminding townspeople of the sad event'.[17] In Melbourne, a special meeting of the local council in Brunswick was called to send messages of sympathy to Buckingham Palace,[18] a party at Narre Warren to celebrate the return of two local soldiers from the Boer War was postponed and a euchre card night at the Richmond Oddfellows Club was cancelled.[19]

In Sydney's Methodist Hall, Queen Victoria was

compared to King David and described as 'God's greatest gift to the nation during the past century',[20] while in the small New South Wales country town of Molong all four churches overflowed with mourners attending special services. The people of Bowral sent their 'deepest sympathy' for the 'irreparable loss of our beloved Sovereign',[21] and a scheduled concert of the Mittagong brass band was abandoned.[22] A message was sent from a synagogue in Sydney from Jewish residents 'profoundly deploring the death of Her Most Gracious Majesty' and the synagogue's ark, pulpit, reading desk and pillars were draped in black.[23]

In Tasmania, 'all the churches, chapels and places of worship' held services where 'special anthems and hymns were sung'.[24] In western Queensland, 'the largest congregation that ever attended a divine service was present' at St Paul's Anglican Church in Roma.[25]

Speaking on behalf of the new nation of Australia, Edmund Barton said that the loss of Queen Victoria 'makes every unit of the nation stricken today with a grief which could not be felt in any other part of the world for any other sovereign'.[26]

Before Victoria's death, it had been understood that her son Edward, the Prince of Wales, would visit Australia in May 1901 to open the country's new national parliament. However, now that Edward was king, the task was given to his thirty-five-year-old son George, the Duke of Cornwall and York, who had of course come out as a young man in 1881 with his older brother Albert. This time George would be accompanied by his wife, Mary.

According to Australian news reports, the decision to send the duke to open the new parliament was made by King Edward, who said that Queen Victoria had wanted it that way:

My Mother assented to the Duke of York opening the first Parliament. Though the separation from my son at present cannot be otherwise than deeply painful, I still desire to give effect to the late Queen's wishes, as evidencing Her interest and my own in all that concerns the welfare of my subjects beyond the seas. I have therefore decided that the visit shall not be abandoned but shall be extended to New Zealand and Canada.[27]

George and Mary had been married for eight years by now. George was devoted to his wife, writing to her every day they were apart and, unlike his father, never taking a mistress.

The duke and duchess left Portsmouth for Australia on 16 March 1901. They sailed on HMS *Ophir,* which had operated as a regular passenger service between London and Australia before being chartered from its owners, the Orient Steam Navigation Company, for the royal tour. At 142 metres in length the *Ophir* was even larger than the royal yacht *Britannia*, built fifty years later.[28] In addition to visiting Australia, the royal couple would also call in at other British possessions including Malta, Ceylon, South Africa, New Zealand and Canada during their five-month trip.

The Sydney *Daily Telegraph* predicted the tour would be 'one of the most lavish undertaken by the monarchy'.[29] The hire of the ship *Ophir* cost £70,000 'and the cost of fitting her up has been no less than £56,000 and the cost of coal for the entire tour was £2500'; and at every stop on the tour of South Australia, Victoria, New South Wales, Queensland and Western Australia, there would be expensive decorations, pageants, ceremonies and demonstrations.[30]

The royal couple would also be travelling with the largest aristocratic entourage ever seen in Australia.[31] The

head of household was a former governor of Madras, Lord
Wenlock, whose brother, Sir Arthur Lawley, was at the time
the governor of Western Australia. The duke's private secretary was Sir Arthur Bigge, who had been private secretary
to Queen Victoria during the later years of her reign. Bigge
handled the personal affairs of the duke, while Sir John
Anderson of the Colonial Office was the private secretary
for official business.

The duke's equerries were Commander Sir Charles Cust,
who had served as his equerry for nine years already, and an
army officer, the Honourable Derek Keppel, who worked in
the royal household for nearly forty years until the death
of King George in 1936. The aides-de-camp included
Commander Bryan Godfrey Fausett of the Royal Navy,
Major James Henry Bor of the Royal Marines, Captain
Viscount Henry Crichton of the Royal Horse Guards,
retired cavalry officer Sir William Wentworth-Fitzwilliam,
and a former household cavalry officer, the Duke of
Roxburghe, who was a cousin of Winston Churchill. The
role of the aide-de-camp was, like the equerry, to attend
to all the needs of the duke, but he also provided friendship and company for him while horseriding and hunting.
Another aide-de-camp was an Australian – a member of
the Queensland Permanent Artillery, Lieutenant Colonel
John Joseph Byron. Byron was born in Ireland, migrated
to Australia and joined the Queensland Defence Force.
In 1899 he fought in the Boer War, was wounded in the
leg, mentioned in dispatches and awarded the Order of St
Michael and St George medal in February 1901 shortly
before the royal tour.[32] Also in the royal party was the
duchess's younger brother, Eton-educated Prince Alexander
of Teck. Australians were told he was 'a fine specimen of
the young British officer, tall and well set up [and] with
the swarthy complexion of a Spaniard'.[33] In addition, there

were three ladies-in-waiting for the duchess: Lady Mary Lygon, Lady Katherine Coke and the wife of the duke's equerry Derek Keppel.

While the reason for the tour was ostensibly to open Australia's first national parliament, another aim, as it was for all royal tours, was 'to draw the empire more together by creating a personal interest in the sovereign'.[34] During the tour the duke would also hand out specially minted medals and say thank you to the Australian troops who had fought alongside the British in the recent Boer War. The Boer War in southern Africa had followed years of hostilities between the British colonies in the south and the independent republics of the Dutch-Afrikaner settlers in the north. In 1899 all six Australian colonies had raised contingents to fight as part of the British Empire against the Afrikaners. After federation in 1901 they were the first troops to fight overseas for the nation of Australia. In a drawn-out and bitter struggle that lasted until 1902, about 16,000 Australians went to the war. Of these 282 died in action or from wounds, another 286 died from diseases, 38 from accidents or unknown causes and 6 were awarded the Victoria Cross.[35]

Before the arrival of the royal couple, a number of Australian newspapers published a portrait of Prince George that described the transformation of the carefree teenager who had visited Australia twenty years before into a more world-weary young man:

There must be many thousands of Australians who remember George . . . Duke of Cornwall and York, as a merry bright-eyed boy of fourteen [sic], who won his way into the hearts of colonists wherever the *Bacchante* put into port by his frank and unaffected manner, his ready laughter, his exuberant boyish enjoyment of everything he did. The boy has grown into a grave and serious man. Australians can scarcely fail to be impressed with the change . . . An almost oppressive sense of his responsibilities in life have marked him for their own. The sailor-boy has become lost in the prince, the youth full of fun and a spirit of mischief has become a man to whom life is a serious business.[36]

The official opening of the first Australian national parliament was to take place in Melbourne on 9 May. It would be another decade before the site of Canberra was chosen for the nation's new capital, and not until 1927 that construction of a new national parliament building was completed. In the meantime, the recently elected national parliamentarians would meet in the Victorian parliament in Melbourne. Since the inauguration of the nation on New Year's Day, the first federal elections for the new parliament had been held on 29 and 30 March, when thirty-six senators and seventy-five members of the House of Representatives were elected, including Edmund Barton, who was confirmed as prime minister. Sydney had the honour of being the city in which the first governor-general was sworn in, but Melbourne would open and host the first Commonwealth parliament.

When the *Ophir* sailed into Melbourne on Monday 6 May, Prince George became the first member of the British royal family to visit Australia twice. The press was impressed by the royal couple. The duke, according to the Sydney *Daily Telegraph*, was 'extremely pleasant faced and good natured' and the duchess simply 'captivated everybody' and was apparently 'one of those women whose photographs don't do them justice'.[37]

After being welcomed at St Kilda, the couple were driven past 'a sea of humanity like a swollen stream seven miles long' into Melbourne.[38]

The streets of Melbourne were lined with half a million spectators, many of whom had bought tickets to sit in wooden stands erected two or three stories high. People spilled from every window, step and vantage-point, waving flags and cheering. Thirty-five thousand schoolchildren waved union jacks and sang 'God Save the King' and 'God Bless the Prince of Wales' from the slopes of the Domain.[39]

A reporter for *The Sydney Morning Herald* who watched the procession from the roof of Parliament House wrote of dense masses of people along every thoroughfare, packed so closely that the streets as far as the eye could see were rolling billows of humanity, unceasing in motion and capped by a flying spray of flags and handkerchiefs.[40]

Travelling with the royals during their tour was the English author William Maxwell, who said he had never seen such crowds in England or anywhere else as he did in Melbourne:

> I have seen many royal progresses, but never have I seen one more hearty and spontaneous than that of the multitude of well-dressed men, women, and children who thronged the streets daily for nearly two weeks.[41]

At noon on Thursday 9 May, the Royal Exhibition Building hosted the opening of the parliament in a 'lavish ceremony' attended by 12,000 invited guests – Prime Minister Barton wanted the ceremony with the duke and duchess to be as inclusive as possible, and no other public building could hold that number of people. *The Argus* described the memorable day:

> The atmosphere was radiant and illuminated the vast spaces of the building and the great sea of faces with a bright Australian

glow. A sight never to be forgotten was the assemblage which, in perfect order but with exalted feeling, awaited the arrival of the Duke and Duchess in the great avenues which branch out from beneath the vast dome of the Exhibition Building.[42]

As it turned out, the date of opening the Australian parliament would be repeated twice. Twenty-six years later, on 9 May 1927, the son of the duke and duchess, who would later become King George VI, opened the first national parliament building in Canberra. Then, sixty years after that, the granddaughter of the duke and duchess, Queen Elizabeth II, officially opened the modern national parliament in Canberra on 9 May 1988.

At the opening in Melbourne, the clerk of the new parliament began by reading the Royal Patent in which His Majesty King Edward VII, 'trusting in the discretion of our son', gave the prince full power to hold a parliament:

> This done, His Royal Highness, standing with covered head, delivered the message from the throne. The first Parliament of the Commonwealth was declared to be opened. From the great company rose a mighty cheer; guns thundered in the crowded streets, and the princess, touching an electric button, flashed the message to every village over which, from every school in the State of Victoria, floated, next instant, the Union Jack.[43]

The ceremony was recorded in a vast and magnificent painting by the well-known Australian artist Tom Roberts. Titled *The Opening of the First Parliament of the Commonwealth of Australia by His Royal Highness the Duke of Cornwall and York, 9 May 1901*, the painting measures 5.65 metres across and is 3.6 metres tall. It later became known as 'the big picture' and was painted on three separate pieces of canvas that were stitched together. When Roberts was commissioned to paint the work of art, he was contracted to include the

> correct representations of the Duke and Duchess of York, the Governor-General, the governors of each of the states, the members of both Federal Houses of Parliament, and distinguished guests to the number of not less than 250.[44]

To compile accurate portraits of the key participants, he travelled extensively within Australia and to England to produce individual portraits in oil and pencil. He even asked his subjects for what he called 'measurements' to ensure he was able to reproduce their likeness with great accuracy: age, height, weight, hat size and even place of birth. In all, the picture included 269 separate portraits.

Prior to the opening, Roberts chose his vantage point to record the event, and later explained how on the day of the ceremony he climbed up the inside walls of the Exhibition Building to sketch the outline of the key people in the hall:

> I went to the hall of the Exhibition Building, and without getting seats, walked quietly at the very back, and climbing up some rails, I was able to see that immense gathering of people from Australia, and from so many parts of the world. It was very solemn and great. The heads on the floor looked like a landscape.[45]

As he hoped, the giant painting includes some remarkable detail. Anyone in it who is well-known is instantly recognisable, with a black armband worn in recognition of the death of Queen Victoria four months before. In the picture Roberts also honoured Henry Parkes, the 'Father of Federation', by including a rendition of his portrait, even though it was not hanging on the day of the ceremony.

Roberts started the painting in a room provided at the Exhibition Building. Then sometime after the ceremony, he took the painting to London to complete. He did so two and a half years later, in November 1903, but after it was finished the painting was not exhibited in Australia. Instead, it was presented to King Edward VII and remained in England for more than half a century. It was hung in St James's Palace until 1957, when Queen Elizabeth II agreed to return the painting to Australia on permanent loan. It was thought to be too large to hang in the first Canberra Parliament House, and for many years it languished in storage, only occasionally being put on public display, including for some years in Canberra's High Court building. Since 1988 it has been given a permanent home in the main foyer of the new Parliament House at the very heart of the building.

The 1901 opening was described by *The Argus* as 'marked by the splendour and solemn impressiveness that befitted its historic importance':

> By the hand of royalty, in the presence of the greatest concourse of people that Australia has seen in one building, and with splendid pomp and ceremonial, the legislative machinery of the Commonwealth was yesterday set in motion.[46]

But not everyone was happy that a member of Britain's hereditary monarchy had opened Australia's parliament. *The Bulletin* magazine would no doubt have voiced the frustrations of anyone with republican tendencies when it expressed the opinion that the duke had nothing of merit to offer the occasion:

The opening of the first Parliament of all Australia was an event large enough to stand alone. It wanted no tawdry trappings, no small accidental prince, no flags, no lank flapping frills and gaily coloured rags to make it memorable . . . Amid the circumstances which attended the union of a continent and the beginning of a nation there moved though a thin undersized man who has never done anything save be born, and grow up, and get married and exist by breathing regularly and be the son of his father who did the same things. And in the public eye he was, apparently, about three quarters of the pageant. The men who made the Commonwealth were eclipsed . . . by the man who has made nothing of any importance.[47]

The parochial local newspaper *The Argus* did not shy away from hyperbole in its report, describing Melbourne's celebrations and the decorations as 'never . . . paralleled in the previous history of Australia'.[48] Every night the city was illuminated with coloured light displays and every day bands played in the streets. The events included a giant Chinese procession, a parade of mounted Australian stockmen, torch-lit processions and a reception for the royal couple at Government House, which was followed by a great fireworks display. The local press reported that when the duke arrived at the reception he 'appeared much less nervous than when he first arrived, and looked wonderfully well in a black frock coat and silk hat'. But it was the duchess who captured most attention:

As Her Royal Highness entered the ballroom at Government House on Wednesday night on the occasion of the reception, there was no mistaking the meaning of the deferential hum which rose at sight of her. Very beautiful she looked, and not a person present but felt a pride in the presence of a future Queen . . . Her personality demands attention, and keeps it . . . she wore a gleaming black jetted petticoat, under a polonaise of richest embossed satin, with cut jet passementerie trimming. Her bodice was of closely jetted net, fitting with little fullness. Her jewels were exquisite. A coronet of diamonds surrounding amethysts was worn in the hair, a deep collar of diamonds being also worn, while a collarette of amethysts and diamonds was set below it. On her bodice she wore a diamond dragon, while diamond ornaments mingled with certain orders.[49]

Over the next few days, Prince George and Princess Mary were taken to a special horseracing carnival at Flemington, a public reception at Melbourne Town Hall, to the university to confer degrees, to attend a giant schools fete at the Exhibition Oval, to watch naval manoeuvres, a military tattoo, and to a military parade, where the duke handed out medals to Boer War veterans. On Tuesday 14 May at the Exhibition Hall, the duke and duchess gave the signal for the simultaneous hoisting of the 'Grand Old Flag' (the Union Jack) at every school throughout the country. Towards the end of the Victorian leg of the tour, the royal couple visited Hobsons Bay and the goldmining centre of Ballarat, where the duke had been twenty years before with Prince Albert.

Only on the last day of their ten-day visit were the pair given a break when Prince George went privately into the country with a shooting party. Dressed in a shooting outfit of 'grey knickerbockers, stout boots and a grey Alpine hat', the duke went hunting in Sale. There were twenty-one 'gentlemen' in the hunting party and on the way to the hunt, *The Sydney Mail* explained, the duke and duchess were introduced to two local Aboriginal men – 'representatives of a dying race', who 'cordially greeted the Duke'. Without missing a beat, the paper continued:

A splendid day's sport . . . The quail were plentiful, though being scattered a wide area had to be covered. The duke was in good form, and showed that he was a crack shot . . . After an hour's shooting the party rested, and had a smoke under a tree. Shooting was then resumed, and when the party stopped for luncheon a count was made, and it was found that 120½ brace of quail had been shot.[50]

—

On 16 May the royal party left Melbourne by train for the next leg of their tour – Brisbane via Sydney – and the *Ophir* was sent by sea to meet them. The train on which they travelled was a luxury carriage that had been built in the Eveleigh railway workshops in Sydney just in time for the visit. It was the most luxurious railway carriage ever built in Australia and is said to have reflected

the importance of the role of the British monarch in the government of the Commonwealth of Australia at the point of Federation and also in the social order and customs of the period.[51]

The royal carriage was internally divided into three sleeping suites, a dining room, galley and attendants' quarters as well as an observation room for an unrestricted view of the surrounding countryside. It was furnished with a number of lounge chairs, a bookcase, writing cabinet and cellarette in polished oak. The master bedroom and two auxiliary bedrooms were fitted with brass bedsteads, mirrored dressing tables, built-in wardrobes, fans, heaters, and en suite toilet and shower facilities. The dining room featured a carved oak sideboard with matching dinner wagon, and a table and six dining chairs. The interior decoration included over 300 individually hand-carved timber panels of polished

English oak and Australian cedar depicting botanical speci-
mens of New South Wales and fluted pilasters; and there
were etched glass panels featuring Australian flora, fine
carpets, gold-tinted velvets, silk drapes, the best Morocco
leather and upholstery as well as hundreds of gold-plated
items such as coat hooks and light switch covers. The ornate
ceilings were cream-coloured stamped zinc panels inset
with the royal coat of arms. After being used by the duke
and duchess in 1901, the carriage was subsequently used
by a number of royal visitors to Australia, including Queen
Elizabeth II and Prince Philip, for the next sixty years.

The Australian newspapers told their readers that the
grand train was big enough for the entire royal entourage:

> The royal train is a complete hotel. All meals are prepared
> on board by an experienced staff, and this involves a great
> deal of work, in as much as the party has been gradually
> increasing in numbers, in addition to the royal visitors and
> staff there are members of the household and servants – and
> eleven detectives – on board, and then there are the Pressmen
> and the railway and other officials, which brings the total
> number of passengers to about seventy.[52]

The train ride took three days from Albury on the Victoria–
New South Wales border to Sydney, then north-west to
the Queensland border town of Wallangarra. From the
Queensland border they travelled on the narrow-gauge
rail east through Toowoomba and Ipswich to Brisbane.
William Maxwell said the rail trip was a much better idea
than sailing up the coast on the *Ophir*:

> The prince and princess saw much more of the country from
> the train than they could have done from the deck of the
> *Ophir*, while many outlying districts had an opportunity of

sharing the national welcome. Their Royal Highnesses had a glimpse of that famous country known as the Darling Downs, which the botanist and explorer, Allan Cunningham, discovered in 1827.[53]

The duke and duchess were happy to travel overland as Prince George was well known for suffering seasickness. Indeed, the duke was so pleased with the journey that he sent a message to the New South Wales railway commissioner telling him that the overland train to the New South Wales border was 'the most comfortable one he had ever travelled in during his life'.[54] Apparently the fact that such a luxury train was available had 'astonished the royal visitors and their suite'.[55]

An estimated 100,000 people had lined the route of the royal procession when the duke and duchess reached Brisbane. During their four-day stay in Queensland, they attended a military parade of 15,000 troops, where the duke handed out 320 more medals won in the Boer War, met the public at the Exhibition Hall attended by 32,000 people, laid the foundation stone for the new Anglican cathedral in Brisbane, visited the horseraces, attended an agricultural show and watched the now almost obligatory fireworks display. When they were taken to see an Aboriginal corroboree, the duke was quoted as saying that they were 'the finest made coloured men he had met since leaving home'.[56] Before leaving Queensland for Sydney, Prince George said he and Princess Mary appreciated the 'beautiful manner' in which the city had been decorated and noted 'the great strides made by Brisbane' since his last visit twenty years before.[57]

They re-boarded the luxury train to head back to New South Wales but alighted at Broken Bay, north of Sydney, where the state governor, premier and a large contingent of officials welcomed them and saw them aboard the *Ophir*, which had sailed up from Melbourne to meet them.

In Sydney on 27 May a public holiday had been declared, and a huge crowd gathered to cheer the royals after they landed in Sydney Harbour and strolled around the Domain. Their ten-day schedule in New South Wales was every bit as hectic as it had been in Melbourne. On the second day more than 100,000 people turned out to see the duke inspect troops and hand out more Boer War medals in Centennial Park. On the days that followed, the duke and duchess watched naval manoeuvres, planted trees, visited the new Art Gallery of New South Wales and the prestigious Sydney Church of England Girls Grammar School that had opened six years before, laid the foundation stone for the Queen Victoria Memorial Pavilions at Royal Prince Alfred Hospital, attended a concert at Sydney Town Hall and went to Sydney University where the duke was conferred with an honorary degree.

Princess Mary with her ladies-in-waiting visited Katoomba in the Blue Mountains, and Prince George went on another hunting expedition by special train, this time for three days to Yanco, 560 kilometres south-west of Sydney. The royal hunting party, which included the governor-general, Lord Hopetoun, was not very successful. It had been a very dry season and the game was so scarce that the duke took to 'shooting cockatoos . . . a black swan and a few ducks'.[58]

On 6 June the duke and duchess sailed on the *Ophir* for a ten-day visit to New Zealand, before sailing back across the Tasman Sea to Hobart, where they stayed for two days. Despite the small population and the briefness of the visit, the newspapers reported that no more cordial welcome was given the duke and the duchess on their tour 'than they received from the inhabitants of Tasmania'.[59]

South Australia was the penultimate stop on the tour. By now the people of Adelaide felt that they could not reasonably compete with the elaborate decorations that had decked the city of Melbourne for the opening of the new national parliament, and the local newspaper expressed some doubt that Adelaide could, or should, go to the expense of trying to match the larger cities:

> Frankly, South Australians cannot reasonably hope to compete with the Victorians in the directions which have been indicated from day to day in the messages of our correspondents . . . Before the duke and the duchess can reach Adelaide they will be weary of the sight of triumphal arches and other conventional creations in the way of street adornment; and, though the people as well as the royal visitors have to be considered, the erection of arches is an expense which might with advantage be avoided. Apart from their evanescent character, these things cause the streets to be littered with unsightly stuff for days or weeks before and after their completion and to make them of adequate proportions in such wide thoroughfares as King William Street would be a costly undertaking; and in a few days they would be nothing more than mere lumber and rubbish, which would impress nobody and commemorate nothing.

The newspaper suggested South Australians could still express 'signs of joy' at the royal visit by 'originality of design' and 'resourcefulness'. It called on the local government to consider 'a comparatively inexpensive and yet finely effective scheme of decoration and illumination' of the city's main buildings and suggested the best decorations were the cheaper 'greenery and coloured drapings . . . festooned along and across the streets'.[60]

When the duke and duchess landed at Port Adelaide

early on the Tuesday afternoon of 9 July, more than 1000 pigeons were released as the couple were driven through large crowds to Government House. A local paper said:

> the procession, which lasted an hour, was a sight never to be forgotten. Bands were playing and there were 1200 school children carrying tiny Union Jacks and a bouquet of flowers while singing. It was estimated that there were from 130,000 to 150,000 people in the streets of Adelaide during the progress of the procession.[61]

During the six-day stay, they visited the children's hospital, were serenaded by the Adelaide German community Liedertafel, watched a football match, saw a children's parade at Adelaide Oval, yet another fireworks display, laid a foundation stone at the Queen Victoria Maternity Home, opened the knave of St Peter's Cathedral and attended a huge garden party at Government House. The duke also laid the foundation stone of a fallen soldiers' memorial, attended a military tattoo, reviewed the local troops and handed out more Boer War medals.

After leaving Adelaide for Perth and the last stop of the tour, the *Ophir* encountered rough weather and high seas across the Great Australian Bight and along the Western Australia coast. Arriving into Fremantle late on the evening of Sunday 21 July, the royals were taken on a special train into Perth, where they arrived at Government House close to midnight.

At the time of the royal visit in 1901, the entire population of the vast state of Western Australia was less than 200,000 people but still more than six times bigger than the mere 32,000 twenty years before when Prince George had last visited. The tour of Perth began the next morning with a procession through Perth and a reception and dinner at Government House that evening. Over the next four days the duke and duchess attended a special service in St George's Cathedral, where the duke unveiled a memorial in brass in honour of the fallen soldiers in the Boer War and presented more medals. Other events included visits to the Perth Mint, the national gallery, the public library and the zoo, a parade of 8000 local schoolchildren, a garden party and the renaming of Perth Park to Kings Park to mark the accession of King Edward VII to the throne.

On 26 July, and after two and a half months in Australia and New Zealand, the duke and duchess boarded the *Ophir* for the voyage back to England via South Africa. From the point of view of both the Australians and the British royal family, the tour had been another outstanding success, and the royal pair could return home reassured that the Crown seemed to have emerged undamaged by the passing of Queen Victoria. In fact, as he said in his farewell speech, Prince George believed the relationship between Australians and the monarchy was stronger than ever:

> I am proud to have been entrusted by the king with that mission, in accordance with the wish of my beloved grandmother, and to have had the honour of presiding at the inauguration of the first parliament of this newly constituted federation . . . We leave with many regrets, mitigated, however, by the hope that while we have gained new friendships and goodwill, something may also have been achieved towards the strengthening and welding together of the empire through the sympathy and interest which have been displayed in our journey, both at home and in the colonies.[62]

The Australian newspapers were equally enthusiastic about how the people were touched by the British throne, and the presence of the duke and duchess:

The royal visit is ended, and the *Ophir* and her attendant cruisers are speeding across seas towards another portion of the British dominions. On the political side the visit to the Australasian communities was a perfect success. It is now a wholly bright page of history. The heir to the throne and his consort performed their arduous part with a dignity never spoiled by offensive aloofness, and with unfailing courtesy and geniality . . . The presence of the visitors evoked a magnificent expression of Australasian loyalty to the throne, flag, and empire. It was a happy wish of Queen Victoria endorsed both before, and after her death by her son, to send the prince who, in the natural course of things, may yet wear the crown, to open the first parliament of the Commonwealth. It was the highest compliment that the Imperial Islands could pay to the federated states . . . For the rest the visit was one which established 'touch' between the throne and the people. It was as if the throne came to these far southern communities because they could not go to the throne . . . The visit created an opportunity for the loyal sentiment of the Commonwealth . . . to show itself proudly and joyously, and in all its strength and spontaneity.[63]

The tour of 1901 marked the successful transition by Australia from the Victorian era to the Edwardian. Before returning to England, Prince George thanked Australia for the 'happy and eventful months' of his tour and said he hoped his father, King Edward VII, might 'personally visit all the important provinces of the Empire'.[64] However, King Edward died in 1910 without having had the opportunity to do so, and then Australia, along with many other countries, was plunged into the horrors of World War I.

8

WORLD WAR I

Australia will stand beside the mother country to help and
defend her to our last man and our last shilling.

WHEN THE BOSNIAN SERB Gavrilo Princip shot Austrian
Crown Prince Franz Ferdinand in Sarajevo on 28 June 1914,
few could have imagined that within weeks, Australia, a
great distance away in terms not only of miles but of culture
and nationhood, would be dragged into a conflict involving
more than forty countries; and that more than 60,000
Australians would die in the war that followed.

Britain declared war on Germany on 4 August 1914
and the very next day Australian prime minister Joseph
Cook announced: 'When the empire is at war, so also is
Australia.' The government was supported in its hasty decision by the Labor opposition, whose leader, Scottish-born
Andrew Fisher, made it clear Australia would stand beside
the mother country to help and defend her to, as he characterised it, her last man and her last shilling.

Even before Australia had declared war and when there was intense speculation that the breaking out of hostilities was inevitable, newspapers were reporting that 'considerable enthusiasm and activity' reigned about the prospect of war. For several weeks before the general mobilisation, many local military officers were recalling officers who were on leave.[1]

Prime Minister Cook offered Britain 20,000 men to fight at any destination decided on by the British. The following day, 6 August, London cabled its acceptance of the force and asked that it be sent as soon as possible. Recruitment offices opened four days later and by the end of 1914 over 50,000 volunteers had been accepted into the Australian military.

Australia's decision to send troops to Great Britain's aid was supported throughout the country:

> The decision of the Commonwealth Government to send an expeditionary force of 20,000 men to aid Great Britain in the war in Europe was received with manifestations of approval among all sections of the community. The offer has been accepted, and this second stage has been followed by further enthusiasm and a rush of applications for enrolment.[2]

According to the newspapers, the 'patriotic fervour' continued 'unabated' as young men across Australia rushed to enlist to fight with the Allied forces in a war on the other side of the world that they knew little about, other than that it was for king and country. At the time, over 90 per cent of Australians had British ancestry and most thought themselves 'Australian-British', bound by the thread of kinship and proud to be a junior partner in the empire.[3]

The first Australian expedition sent to fight overseas left Sydney only a fortnight after war was declared, to attack German-occupied territories in Papua New Guinea. Germany had colonised sections of Papua New Guinea from 1884 and was already using the area as a base for radio communications with its warships operating in the South Pacific. On 11 September 1914 a 25-man force of Australian reservists successfully attacked and took the German radio station at Bita Paka in New Guinea. During the fighting six Australians were killed, while a German officer and thirty locally recruited German police were also shot. Two days later at Toma, the local German garrison of forty German and local recruits surrendered.

Meanwhile, back in Australia large numbers of volunteers were being recruited into the recently established Australian Imperial Force to go and fight in Europe under British command. By November 1914, the first convoy of ten transports, with escorts of Australian and British transports, left Albany in Western Australia:

> It was a very proud day for Australia . . . Australia and New Zealand troops are going to assist the motherland in the great struggle for supremacy . . . on Wednesday afternoon the whole thirty-six ships lined up in four divisions; crowded with khaki-clad brave young men all in good spirits and eager to get to the front. Everyone was filled with greatest enthusiasm and [Albany] gave one the appearance of a miniature Portsmouth when the men-of-war were in the harbour, and the soldiers and sailors were seen parading the streets of the town in thousands.[4]

The Australians were to complete their training in British-controlled Egypt before being sent to the trenches in France. However, at the end of October, the Ottoman (Turkish) Empire had entered the war on Germany's side and in November British first lord of the admiralty Winston

Churchill presented his plan for the Allies to attack Turkey's Gallipoli Peninsula. Churchill's initial plan was for a naval attack on the Dardanelles, but when this failed he decided to land Allied ground troops. This decision would, of course, seal the fate of the thousands of Australians and New Zealanders who had so enthusiastically gone off to fight.

Meanwhile, at the end of 1914, the newspapers were congratulating Australia's outstanding commitment to facing Britain's enemies, and so quickly pledging undying support for the mother country, whatever the cost:

> Australia has done her part magnificently, and her grand response in men, ships and food sent, we are told, through the people of the Homeland, who naturally were solemnly sensed with the seriousness of the struggle . . . There can be no going back now! It is war to the bitter finish now between Australia and Germany, just the same as it is between England and Germany. And Australia must win. There can be no question of how far or how much it must cost. There can be no limit . . . Until victory is ours no citizen of the Empire is justified in saying, 'We have done enough.'[5]

The troops sent to Turkey to fight on the ground included many Australians, who had been training in Egypt, near Cairo. On 25 April 1915 – which would later became Anzac Day – they landed at what is now known as Anzac Cove to try to push back and then break through Turkish lines.

The Gallipoli campaign was a disastrous failure. After the original landings on 25 April, the fighting, which lasted for the next eight months, yielded no significant territorial gain. The peninsula could not be captured, none of the objectives of the plan were achieved and both the Turkish and the Allied losses were staggeringly high. Finally, in December 1915, the Allies abandoned the campaign and withdrew. On each side more than 50,000 men had been killed and over 100,000 wounded. More than 8000 of those killed and 20,000 of those wounded were Australian.[6] Many Australians were awarded medals for gallantry; nine won the Victoria Cross.

After Gallipoli, most of the surviving diggers were taken back to Egypt, where they were joined by new recruits from Australia for more training before being sent to the Western Front. In March 1916 the process of shipping the Australian infantry to England began, in preparation for them being sent to France. Most of the Australian cavalry stayed in the Middle East to fight the Turks and the Arabs, who were still threatening British-controlled Egypt.

Many of the Australians based in England were camped on Salisbury Plain in Wiltshire, in the west country near Stonehenge, and in April and May 1917 they were inspected by King George V, along with their mascot, a live kangaroo, which in footage of the inspection can clearly be seen quietly standing watching the king's parade in front of the troops.[7] After the inspections, the king wrote to the troops:

I am very glad to have had an opportunity of inspecting the various training units of the Australian Imperial Force, and I wish to express my satisfaction with the appearance of the fine body of men on parade to-day.

You will, I know, acquit yourselves with credit when the time comes to reinforce those splendid Australian divisions at the front, whose deeds and fighting qualities have won the highest praise.

Do not forget your kinsmen, who have willingly given their lives for the Empire.

Emulate their example, and so preserve the proud record made by them in the Great War.[8]

While most Australians spent the greatest part of the war in France, many were committed to other theatres. At the outbreak of hostilities in 1914, Australia placed its newly formed navy under the control of the British Admiralty. At the time the Royal Australian Navy had 3800 personnel and sixteen ships, including the battle cruiser HMAS *Australia*, two light cruisers, the *Melbourne* and *Sydney*, three destroyers and two submarines. During the war the Australian ships saw action with British ships in the Pacific and Indian oceans as well as the Atlantic Ocean and the North Sea.

The first squadron of the Australian Flying Corps initially went to the Middle East in 1916 flying British-made biplanes, and the other three squadrons were in France from 1917. Over the course of the war more than 500 Australians flew planes and another 2000 provided the ground crew, administration and logistical support for the corps.

Of the army, those who were sent to France after Gallipoli were not part of the terrible bloodbath that was the first day of the Battle of the Somme on 1 July 1916, but were three weeks later at the nearby Battle of Fromelles, where on 19 July 1916, in what has been described as the worst single day in Australian history, more than 5000 men from the Australian 5th Division were lost.[9] A week later, on 27 July, the Australian 1st Division lost more than 5000 men during the assault on Pozières, with the 2nd Division losing a further 7000 in the next two attacks.[10] On 4 August yet another 6300 men from various divisions of the Australian Anzac Corps were lost during the attack on Mouquet Farm.[11]

By the time the Australians were withdrawn from the front to be relieved by Canadian troops in September 1916, they had lost in excess of 23,000 men, all of whom had been killed, wounded or gone missing in forty-eight days of fighting. The Australian Imperial Force had more casualties in eight weeks on the Somme than in eight months on Gallipoli.

The following year, between March and May, at the Battle of Bullecourt, the Australians were part of the successful capture of sections of the German Hindenburg Line, but at the cost of another 7482 men. In June 1917 the Australians launched an assault on the German lines at Messines, Flanders, and suffered a further 6800 casualties, including Major General Holmes, who was hit in the chest by an exploding German artillery shell while surveying the battlefield with the New South Wales premier, William Holman. Holmes was the most senior ranked Australian to be killed on the Western Front.

From September to November the Australians were heavily involved in the Battle of Ypres. During torrential rain they were ordered in heavy mud to attack Poelcappelle and Passchendaele and over the eight weeks of fighting suffered 38,000 casualties.

In the final year of the war, all five Australian divisions were involved in fighting the German Spring Offensive, which launched on 21 March 1918 and lasted with varying degrees of intensity for nearly five months. On 8 August the great Allied offensive began, taking into battle twenty divisions, including all five from Australia. By now the Australians were stretched. The huge casualties and the limited number of replacements available resulted in three battalions being disbanded to reinforce other units. But eventually, the Allies drove the Germans back. During what became known as the Hundred Days Offensive, the territory taken by the Germans was retaken by the Allies, the Hindenburg Line collapsed and in November 1918 the war was finally ended.

—

Prince George was crowned king in May 1910, after the death of his father, King Edward VII. In July 1917, by royal proclamation, King George V changed the name of the British royal family from Saxe-Coburg and Gotha to Windsor. The German name had become problematic for the monarchy at the outbreak of the war, and things came to a head when a German plane named the *Gotha* began bombing London in March 1917. The king's decision was widely praised in Australia. The Mount Gambier *Border Watch* newspaper said it would 'afford gratification throughout the empire'.[12] *The Australasian* described it as 'most sensible'[13] and *The Queenslander* said the king had 'in the most emphatic way possible' got rid of the 'utter abomination of a German family name'.[14] The Hobart *Mercury* wrote of the 'universal satisfaction' felt throughout Australia:

> It marks the illumination from our monarchical association of an influence which from the first has been utterly alien to the English spirit and which is now hateful not only to us of the British Empire but to all the free people everywhere . . . Henceforth [it] will be known as the House of Windsor. No title can be more fitting.[15]

Australia had been changing German-named towns since the outbreak of the war. In New South Wales the southern town of Germanton was changed to Holbrook in 1915, and in the central west the district of German's Hill was changed to Lister in 1916. In Queensland more than a dozen names were changed, including the inner Townsville suburb of German Gardens, which was changed to Belgium Gardens, and the suburb of Cramzow at Logan City, which was changed to Carbrook. Stegelitz, which was a centre of German farming on Queensland's Gold Coast from the late nineteenth century, had its name changed to Woongoolba in June 1916. In Tasmania, the town of Bismarck that had been established by German farmers from 1870 became Collinsvale. In Western Australia the town of Heidelberg, thirty kilometres east of Perth, was changed to Bickley. In Victoria the western town of Tarrington had been known as Hochkirch until it was changed in 1918.

In South Australia more than fifty places had their names changed during the war. The Germans had been a major source of immigration from 1838 and had spread out through the territory as they became the pioneers of much of Australia's wine industry. Buchfelde, near Adelaide, was renamed Loos after the great battle in France in 1915, the Adelaide suburb of Blumberg became Birdwood, and the small town of Grunthal became Verdun after the great battle in 1917.

Approximately 7000 German nationals, as well as some Australians who had German parents, were imprisoned, or 'interned', in Australia.[16] The largest camp in New South Wales was at Holsworthy in the south-west of Sydney. The other New South Wales camps were in the remote west of the state at Bourke, and at the old Berrima Gaol in the Southern Highlands, which was reopened in 1914, as was the old prison at Trial Bay on the Macleay River. In Victoria there was an internment camp at Langwarrin on the Mornington Peninsula, and in the Australian Capital Territory one was set up on the Molonglo River. In Western Australia there were camps on Rottnest Island and Garden Island. In Queensland there was a camp at Brisbane's Enoggera, and in Tasmania on Bruny Island. In South Australia there were small camps at Fort Largs and Port Adelaide. The internment camps were like prisons, but with 'ingenuity, industry and determination' the internees created 'cafes, clubs, newspapers, an array of small businesses, theatres, tennis courts, vegetable gardens, laundries, athletic demonstrations and even boat building and regattas'.[17]

—

Australia paid a very high price for its loyalty to the British Empire during the Great War. Of the 331,000 men who enlisted and served overseas, at the end of the war 92,000 Australians remained in France, 60,000 were in Britain and around 17,000 were in Egypt or elsewhere in the Middle East, all waiting for shipment home. Altogether more than 60,000 had been killed, 155,000 wounded and 4000 taken as prisoners of war.[18] Of all the British dominions, Australia suffered the highest rate of casualties for the number of men that went overseas to fight: 64.98 per cent, compared to 59.01 per cent in New Zealand, and 49.74 per cent in Canada.[19]

Thousands of Australian women also volunteered during the war, working in Australia and overseas as cooks, nurses, drivers, interpreters, munitions workers and skilled farm workers. Australian nurses served in Egypt, France, Greece and India, often in trying conditions or close to the front, where they were exposed to shelling and aerial bombardment.

At the end of the Great War, Australia was able for the first time to represent itself on the international stage. At the Paris Peace Conference held at Versailles in 1919, Australia had its own seat at the table, rather than being represented by the British delegation, which was led by Prime Minister Lloyd George. Initially, the push by the dominions to be allowed to participate on their own was opposed by the British and the Americans, who feared separate dominion representation would mean additional votes at the conference for Britain. However, Canada, Australia and India had each lost more men during the war than the powerful United States, and their case was ultimately agreed to by Lloyd George.

The win by the dominions, in large part due to the persistence of Australian prime minister Billy Hughes,[20] was enthusiastically embraced by the Australian newspapers:

> [Australia] has been given a place in the conference of nations; the great world has recognised her right to mould her future as she pleases. That is what the Australian forces have done not only in France, Gallipoli, and Palestine, but in Mesopotamia, in Persia, in Russia, and on the seas.[21]

After the conference, where Australia sought and was granted control of the former German colonies of Papua and New Guinea, Hughes argued that Australia could no longer rely on Britain and in future would need to do more to stand up for itself:

> The decision the Peace Conference has established is beyond all question that we are now a nation. We have earned our place among the nations of the world. We are still proud and happy to be part of the great British Empire . . . There was a day when we could go to England, but that day has gone. Every Australian must get that firmly in his mind. We must work out our own salvation.[22]

Australia came out of World War I keen for more independence from Britain. But this did not mean the nation wanted to distance itself from the British monarchy. If anything, the attachment of Australia to the king and the royal family had been strengthened by the experience of war.

The popularity of King George V in Australia had been enhanced in 1917 when he had changed the name of the royal family to Windsor, and he had also made a number of personal concessions that went down well. For the duration of the war Balmoral Castle was closed, shooting at Sandringham was curtailed, meals at the palace were plain and frugal, and the king gave up alcohol.[23] With his wife, Queen Mary, he sought to set an example of dutiful and patriotic encouragement by wearing military uniforms and making hundreds of visits to the Allied troops, including Australians, both in England and on the Western Front. In France while inspecting troops he was thrown from his horse and fractured his pelvis, an injury that would leave him in some discomfort for the rest of his life. The Australian press was generous in its acknowledgement of the work of the king and queen:

> King George's work has been done throughout in such a quiet and unassuming way that he has so far received much less appreciation and credit than he deserves. There are few accessible places on the war fronts, either by land or sea, which His Majesty has not visited in person, stimulating his sailors and soldiers by his presence, applauding and rewarding their valour, consoling with their sufferings and commiserating with their bereavements. Her Majesty the Queen has been indefatigable in good works, and, as all England know, the wounded in the hospitals, the nurses in the wards, the workers of many classes and degrees behind the lines, have been cheered and consoled by the gracious presence and kindly words of Queen Mary and of the King himself. The King's personal work has been thoroughly well done, and his knowledge today of the conditions under which his subjects live and work, are governed and provided for, is more complete and thorough, probably, than that possessed by any previous king.[24]

Australians were also impressed that the king's sons became part of the British military effort. The Prince of Wales, later King Edward VIII, served as a non-combatant officer on the Western Front. In France he met Australian diggers, who taught him to play two-up, which stood him in good stead when he visited Australia after the war in 1920. The king's second-eldest son, Albert, who became King George VI on the abdication of Edward, fought with the Royal Navy. The twenty-year-old was on HMS *Collingwood* at the Battle of Jutland off the coast of Denmark at the end of May 1916, the largest naval battle of the war, in which both sides had heavy losses. Albert was the only sovereign to have seen action in battle since King William IV. King George V's two younger sons also enrolled for military service. Prince Henry went at nineteen years of age to the Royal Military College at Sandhurst, and Prince George went to naval college at the age of thirteen in 1915, first at Osborne and later at Dartmouth.

World War I was devastating for Australia, as it was for so much of the world. From a population of 4.9 million in 1914, almost half a million men and women had volunteered: 15 per cent of them died and 36 per cent were wounded or became prisoners of war. In postwar Australia there were fewer men, and many of the wives with husbands who returned from the war found them traumatised and unable to readjust to civilian life. War widows were forced to become breadwinners, and the government struggled to find meaningful employment for returned diggers.

Barely eighteen months after the war ended, the 25-year-old son of King George V, Crown Prince Edward, was sent south to say thank you to all those who had sacrificed and suffered during the war, and to reconnect the British monarchy with its Australian subjects, in another enormously successful royal tour.

9

EDWARD, PRINCE OF WALES

The prince shows unnerving judgment in choosing 'pretty girls who are good dancers' but one cannot help thinking that the queen mother, sighing as mothers do sigh, would rather that her son choose 'good girls who are pretty dancers'.

BY THE END OF the war the monarchies in Russia, Germany and Austria-Hungary had collapsed. In Russia the February Revolution of 1917 had deposed the czar and installed the Bolshevik regime; by 1919 the German and the Austro-Hungarian empires had also seen their emperors and ruling kings and dukes abdicating to be replaced by republics. Inevitably, this provoked fears in Britain about support growing in its dominions for communism and republicanism. The British government, with the king's agreement, decided that the close relationship between Australia and the British monarchy should be bolstered by a visit from Prince Edward, the eldest son of King George V.

British prime minister David Lloyd George argued strongly for the prince to visit, saying that 'the appearance of the popular Prince of Wales . . . might do more to calm the discord than half a dozen solemn Imperial Conferences'.[1] The Australian press also saw the prince's proposed tour as a force of empire unity. The Adelaide *Mail* editorialised that:

> The crown of England is democratic to its core. It was its union of hearts with the people that saved it from the revolutionary blast, which wrecked the German, Russian and Austro-Hungarian dynasties. Moreover, the relationship has been cemented . . . by the activities of the prince . . . This is not the light task that some may imagine it to be. There are evil influences at work; the Bolshevist is abroad, the republican spirit is being fanned at home and in the dominions . . . the visit of the prince will help to combat these disruptive forces and tighten the bond between the throne and the [Australian] people.[2]

Prince Edward did not want to go, having been on visits to Canada and the USA the year before. According to Lady Lloyd George:

> He is very sick at having to go off on another tour, and when I said it was hard luck, said: 'Well, you tell the PM that.' He evidently thinks D [David Lloyd George] is largely responsible for it.[3]

In Lady Lloyd George's diary, however, she says it was the king who had told Edward he must go, whatever the views of the prime minister.

> I don't care whether the Prime Minister wants you to go or not. I wish you to go and you are going.[4]

King George V keenly believed that Edward's tour of the dominions would allow his son and heir to become 'better acquainted with the people of the empire' and to thank the colonies for the great sacrifice they had made during the war. Edward later described his role on royal tours in simpler terms:

> I was not charged with negotiating treaties with foreign governments or with promoting high imperial policy to the Dominions. Primarily my job was to make myself pleasant, mingle with the war veterans, show myself to the school children, attend native [dances], cater to official social demands, and in various ways remind my father's subjects of the kindly benefits attaching to the ties of Empire.[5]

At the time of the royal visit Australia had the most militant work force and labour movement of all the British colonies, as well as strong republican sentiment in some quarters. The country faced serious postwar economic problems and industrial unrest, and in the months before the visit the government had made itself unpopular by pushing through pay increases for members of parliament. Billy Hughes was the Australian prime minister. Though some felt his vision for Australia was a narrow one, he was a brilliant and pragmatic politician. His biographer Malcolm Booker said his 'gift lay in knowing what people wanted, and in articulating their desires in a way that won him their support'.[6]

Before his tour to Australia, Edward first visited the West Indies, the Pacific and New Zealand; later, he made a separate tour of India, Burma and Japan. He had already toured the United States in 1919, where he was given a 'hysterical welcome', and Canada, and these were good dress rehearsals for the subsequent Australasian tour.

Edward was born in Richmond Park on the outskirts

of London on 23 June 1894, the last decade of the rule of his great-grandmother, Queen Victoria. Christened Edward Albert Christian George Andrew Patrick David, the young prince was privately tutored with his brother Prince Albert ('Bertie'), who was eighteen months younger. Edward did not enjoy a good relationship with Bertie. They might have been closer, together enduring as they did a childhood dominated by a stern, disciplinary father and an often chilly, distant mother – a relationship that was 'at best formal and often acrimonious'[7] – but an uneasy rivalry developed out of their very different temperaments: Edward was charismatic, naturally athletic and confident; Bertie, in all aspects, was nervy, slow to learn and bad-tempered. Years later Edward said that what saved him from the wrath of their authoritarian father was that however poorly he performed, Bertie could always be trusted to do worse.[8]

In 1907, at the age of thirteen, Edward entered Osborne Naval College; in 1910 his father became King George V and sixteen-year-old Edward became the Prince of Wales and next in line to the throne. During World War I the prince visited the front line as often as he could while remaining protected from the risk of capture or death. This made him popular with veterans of the conflict, including Australian soldiers, whom he saw with his father at Pozières in August 1916.

On the eve of the Australian tour and now twenty-five years old, Edward was a feted celebrity at home and overseas. He was one of the world's most sought-after personalities, and had been extensively photographed and filmed on his visit to Canada and the United States the previous year, his image appearing in newspapers and on newsreels throughout the world. He seemed the epitome of glamour – an eligible, good-looking prince who liked the high life.

At the time of the tour he was deeply involved in an affair with a married woman, Freda Dudley Ward. Born Winifred (Freda) May Birkin, she had married aristocrat Dudley Ward in 1913 when she was eighteen and they had two young daughters. Freda began an affair with Prince Edward in London in 1918; at the same time, Freda's best friend, an Australian woman named Sheila Chisholm, was having an affair with Edward's younger brother, Prince Albert. With Freda, as he would later with his great love Wallis Simpson, Edward behaved very much like a little boy lost who needed mothering. While he was happy to be away from his parents, he dreaded being away from Freda and over more than ten years wrote her more than 2000 letters. In surviving letters (Edward wrote one or two letters a day to Freda when they were apart) he made it clear he did not want to go on the tour of Australia without her. On his earlier visit to Canada he had tried unsuccessfully to persuade her to accompany him, or at least meet him there. By the time he visited Australia, and despite numerous affairs with other women while on the tour, he was expressing great insecurity while away from Ward:

> Freddie Darling,
> Sweetheart; you just can't think what a huge comfort it was for your little David just to hear your divine little voice [on the telephone] . . . I'm terribly lonely tonight my Freddie Darling and it maddens me to be away from you . . . It seems all wrong somehow when we love each other as much as we do.[9]

———

Edward and his entourage sailed out to Australia on the HMS *Renown*: with its sister ship the *Repulse*. The two were the world's fastest and biggest warships. Launched in

1916, the *Renown* did not see active service during World War I and was converted for royal tours after the war. It was a massive vessel – more than 24,000 tonnes in weight, 230 metres long and nearly 30 metres wide – and was armed with six 38-millimetre guns and seventeen 102-millimetre guns. It carried more than 1200 officers and men, including the admiralty's 'finest band of forty-four players'.[10]

The prince's private apartment was the 'size of an admiral's quarters', with a sitting room, dining room and bedroom.[11] For entertaining, it was fitted out with an electric piano the prince had been given as a gift when he had visited America the previous year, and a new automatic gramophone. Some of the ship's guns were removed so that a much larger area of the deckhouse could be converted into entertaining space that included a promenade deck, squash court, cinema and dance floor.

Among Edward's entourage was his younger cousin, Lord Louis Mountbatten. Nineteen-year-old Mountbatten was considered by his superiors to be capable and hardworking, but according to his biographer he was 'not particularly brilliant; indeed he had the reputation of being something of a plodder'.[12] Mountbatten had been Prince Louis of Battenberg until 1917 when British royalty dropped their German titles and he became known by the anglicised version of his name. Sub-lieutenant Mountbatten served on the escorts of anti-submarine boats at the end of World War I and after the war studied at Cambridge University. He was said to have worked hard at getting the role of the prince's companion on the tour; his biographer describes how he 'began to pull every string that might secure him a place in the party'.[13] Later, Mountbatten wrote to the prince that 'I nearly jumped out of my skin for you . . . this, I need hardly say, was the chance of a lifetime'.[14] On the tour Mountbatten and the prince spent a great deal of time partying together. Australian journalist Keith Murdoch described Mountbatten as 'the prince's little chum', while Edward wrote to his mother that he'd had 'to sit on' his younger, enthusiastic cousin once or twice.[15]

Also accompanying Edward was his private secretary Godfrey Thomas, who had been appointed to the post the year before at the relatively young age of thirty. Thomas was the son of a brigadier-general and had been educated at Harrow before joining the British Diplomatic Service in 1919. Edward's father, King George V, questioned the wisdom of the appointment, given that the two men were close friend. It was thought that a stronger personality than Thomas might be better at curbing some of the prince's excesses. But Edward insisted on the appointment, saying Thomas was 'my greatest friend and the man I can trust and who really understands me'.[16] Also travelling on the Australian tour were the commander of the *Renown*, Admiral Sir Lionel Halsey, and Edward's equerries, Captain Dudley North, Captain Lord Claud Hamilton and Captain Sir Piers 'Joey' Legh.

When Prince Edward left London by train for Portsmouth on 16 March 1920, at the beginning of what would be a seven-month trip away, the king, the queen, the queen mother and other members of the royal family gathered at Victoria Station to say goodbye, and dense crowds lined the route between Buckingham Palace and Victoria Station to cheer the prince and other members of the royal family.[17] Arriving at Portsmouth to board the *Renown*, the prince was greeted by a large gathering of naval and military notables and as he boarded the ship 'faced a battery of cameras'.[18]

The *Renown* reached Carlisle Bay in Barbados nine days later. The following morning the prince officially landed and was greeted, wrote Mountbatten in his diary, by 'crowds of niggers . . . shrieking remarks such as "Tank de

Lord I've seen my King . . . and God bless de King".[19] After the West Indies the *Renown* sailed via the Panama Canal into the Pacific and to Honolulu, where the prince met veterans of World War I, then on to Fiji. On the morning of 24 April 1920 the *Renown* arrived in Auckland, New Zealand, and over the next four days the prince and his entourage travelled overland to Palmerston North, down to Wellington then across the Marlborough Sounds to Nelson, Christchurch, Invercargill and Dunedin.

From the south island, the *Renown* picked them up for the voyage to Australia. The tour began in Melbourne and from the moment the prince arrived he was given a punishing itinerary by his hosts. Buckingham Palace had already issued instructions that the prince was not to be made to attend any ceremonies before 10 am, and that three and a half days a week were to be kept free to allow him to rest.[20] However, these instructions were ignored in every state and territory, leading the commander of the *Renown*, Admiral Halsey, to complain at the start of the tour when he saw the proposed itinerary that he did 'not believe any human being could go through all of what was proposed'. During the tour the prince exacerbated the demanding schedule by regularly cavorting and dancing until the early hours of the morning at parties after the end of the evening's official proceedings.[21]

On the afternoon of Wednesday 26 May an estimated quarter of a million people lined Melbourne's streets to see the prince as he drove into the city.[22] The *Renown* had anchored in Port Phillip and the prince was brought on the paddle steamer *Hygeia* to St Kilda. Waiting to take the royal party were two sumptuous carriages followed by a number of smaller horse-drawn carriages and a fleet of cars for the large contingent of press, who were 'looking incongruous and out of place', commented Mountbatten in his diary.[23]

Prime Minister Billy Hughes rode in the second carriage and the Labor opposition leader in the fifth. Mountbatten described how each endured boos and cheers, depending on which part of Melbourne's suburbs they were driving through.

The twelve-kilometre parade took more than an hour because of the crowds, which had to be kept back by 'police, troops and barriers'.[24] Mountbatten had good reason, it seemed, to complain about a newspaper article published that day in Melbourne referring to 'the unpunctual prince', remarking in his diary that the delays were beyond the control of the royal party.[25]

On the first night at Government House there was an official dinner followed by a ball that finished at around 1 am. The music for the dancing was provided by the band from the *Renown*, 'much to the disgust of the Musician's Trade Union', said Mountbatten in his diary, 'who . . . entered a protest against the use of the ship's band ashore'.[26]

The next morning the prince had the first of many meetings with veterans of World War I, and bestowed a number of Victoria Crosses. About 1000 people attended the ceremony, 'nearly all of whom appeared in top hats'.[27] Edward expressed his admiration for the men from Australia and the other British colonies who had fought and died:

> I can never speak too strongly and too often of the great debt that the empire owes to its soldiers and sailors who fought and won the Great War . . . I want all ex-servicemen in every part of the empire . . . to remember me as an old comrade in arms, one who wants them always to look on him as a comrade in spirit.[28]

That evening the prince was driven to the Victorian parliament 'through a most enthusiastic mob' to address both the national Senate and House of Representatives, since the Victorian parliament was still playing host to the national one, and would do so for seven more years.[29]

> Tremendous crowds promenaded streets and viewed the decorations. The prince was expected to pass through the city on his way to parliament shortly before 7 o'clock, and large throngs gathered to greet him. The welcome of the parliament was impressive, but the welcome of the people was even more so.[30]

Edward ordered that no mounted police accompany him as he left parliament, and great crowds pushed around him; several men who jumped on the car trying to shake hands had to be speedily knocked off by orderlies. The prince later complained that within three days he was being physically manhandled by the overenthusiastic crowds:

> The 'touching mania', one of the most remarkable phenomenon connected with my travel, took the form of mass impulse to prod some part of the Prince of Wales . . . I can still hear the shrill, excited cry, 'I touched him'. If I were out of reach, then a blow to the head with a folded newspaper appeared to satisfy the impulse.[31]

Admiral Halsey wrote during the tour in a letter home that '[T]he people, in their excitement, throw all sorts of things into the car, and they do hurt – bunches of flowers are all right but when it comes to chocolate bars and fruit and parcels of all sorts it gets very dangerous – even coins are thrown which hurt horribly sometimes.'[32]

On Friday 28 May Edward met the public at the Exhibition Building. More than 20,000 people filed past him for two hours at the rate of 170 a minute, with over 100 reported as fainting and three taken to hospital. After the weekend, spent at Prime Minister Billy Hughes's country home in Sassafras, Edward officiated at a march-past of 1000 sailors, to commemorate the anniversary of the Battle of Jutland.

In the afternoon the prince was taken to the famous Melbourne Cricket Ground (MCG) and sat in the stand for which Prince Albert had laid the foundation stone in 1881. Below him thousands of schoolchildren had formed a giant map of Australia. Shortly before his arrival, the West Bendigo branch of the Australian Labor Party had passed a resolution calling on its members to prevent their children from taking part in the royal parades. Despite fear of discord before the tour, the Labor Party was careful not to offend or show any disrespect to the prince:

> That . . . members . . . take no active part in celebrating the occasion of the Prince of Wales's visit, and they refuse to allow their children to be taken from school for the purposes proposed . . . while it is not acting through any feeling of disrespect towards the visitor, the League nevertheless discerned it the duty of every democratic and progressive organisation or institution to refrain from pandering to the tool of the capitalistic system.[33]

But at the MCG that day children were out in force:

> This afternoon the prince adventured into fairyland – the fairyland of children. The fairground was the great arena of the Melbourne Cricket Ground . . . When the prince arrived he found confronting him an enormous outline map of Australia, with the words 'OUR PRINCE' printed right across it. The outline was a living one, composed of thousands of boys and girls . . . when the figure of the prince, dressed in

grey appeared in the stand there sounded a cheer . . . from 6000 children's throats.[34]

On Tuesday 1 June Edward was taken by train to settlements outside Melbourne. He travelled in the luxurious Victorian state governor's carriage, which had an observation balcony at one end, two grand bedrooms, a dining room, kitchen, two large bathrooms (each with a full-length bath) and accommodation for other support staff. At Geelong the crowds were so large the prince's staff joined hands with the police to keep them back, and at Colac hundreds of returned soldiers queued to shake Edward's hand. By now he was regularly shaking with his left hand to give his right hand a rest.

At Ballarat he met more veterans at a lunch at the Grand Hotel, then donned some brown miners overalls and descended more than 350 metres below the surface into an underground goldmine, just as his father and uncle had done in 1881. Later, at Kyneton, there was a tussle between Prime Minister Hughes and the Victorian premier, Harry Lawson, as both of them felt they had the right to introduce the prince to the local mayor:

> The honour fell to Mr Hughes, or anyway, he walked quicker than Mr Lawson, for it was him that did the presenting . . . as Hughes is exceedingly deaf he probably thought that he was being cheered as well.[35]

Back in Melbourne the rounds of official events continued and the prince kept burning the candle at both ends by regularly carousing until the early hours. Little of this was reported in the papers, but it was widely known in official circles that regularly two or three girls were invited to late-night parties.[36]

The next stop was Sydney, and even before Prince Edward arrived, the local newspapers were commenting on how exhausted he was looking, assuming it was down to his overloaded program:

It is to be hoped that Sydney will take warning by Melbourne's success in putting the prince out of action and refrain from the senseless and inhuman treatment given him here. On the day of his arrival the prince was palpably exhausted . . . He was quite past smiling once but although looking ill and worn, he faced a ball at Government House and struggled through a mass of people who refused to allow him even breathing space. He bowed his head and shook hands over 2000 times before he was allowed to join a rough and tumble of athletics called by courtesy dancing . . . the unhappy guest was overloaded with a programme grotesque in length, and the appalling selfishness of the people who were determined to see him.[37]

According to press reports, the crowds in Sydney were so large as to be 'something the prince had never seen before':

From an early hour, people began to pour into the city from every quarter. Trains, trams, ferryboats, motor cars, and every conceivable description of conveyance discharging their living freight. It was a gay and joyous throng . . . the fore-shores of the harbour were thick with people.[38]

Edward was initially able to avoid the crowds because he was landed at the Man o' War steps in the present-day Botanic Gardens, which connected with the private gardens of Sydney's Government House. However, he complained to Freda Ward that when he reached the house he was kept there for two hours of official introductions:

I landed at 10.00 A.M. & had 2 terribly pompous and trying hours official decorating & receiving 70 addresses and shaking hands at this bloody house; I could have killed Davidson the Governor [Sir Walter Davidson, governor of New South Wales] & the staff as he was too impossible & irritating for words!![39]

He had lunch at the Royal Randwick Racecourse, where he met with Sheila Chisholm's father. He described him to Freda:

He's such a sweet old man as you would say angel & I know you would like him as much as I do & he's just crazy about little Shellie & was so grateful for all the news of her that I could give him . . . Of course he's heard of you sweetie tho I didn't like to say much about Loughie [Lord Loughborough, Shellie's husband] particularly as Shellie seems to write home & say she is happy with him!! But then we know she isn't always quite quite truthful even to YOU is she darling so how can one exactly expect her to be to her family tho I hope she's more sincere with hers than I am with mine, what!![40]

Later that evening a party was organised, with girls invited for the prince and his entourage. Edward told Freda that he'd enjoyed the dancing but complained about the band:

I've just escaped from a terrible official party here & they are still dancing down below as I can hear – the band that was produced tho can't play and have never heard of jazz!![41]

He said that they partied at Government House until as late as 3 am on each of the next five nights. On several nights of this stay in Sydney, the prince had a favourite dancing partner, Mollee Little, whom a newspaper gossip column suggested was 'not quite unknown to the prince before he arrived in Australia'.[42] The prince wrote of Miss Little, whom he'd managed to get invited to one of the gatherings, to Freda, saying:

the only saving clause was that I managed to get Molly Little asked . . . The 'Dame' [Governor Davidson's wife] had heard that Miss Little & I were mutual friends of Shellie's & knowing that she was attractive & could dance guessed that I wld dance a lot with her if she came. And just to spite the old beta I've spent most of the evening with M.L. & we've had such a marvellous talk about Shellie & I think she's so sweet; not pretty but quite attractive & such a soft sympathetic little voice & she's such a link somehow tho. a very indirect one with YOU sweetheart.[43]

Edward told Freda he'd managed to have a good time, despite the governor and his wife, Sir Walter and Lady Margaret Davidson, whom he complained were 'pompous boobs' who 'tried to make it all as official & pompous and serious as possible'.[44]

At the time the local newspapers only hinted at the prince's heavy drinking, partying and womanising, though in one of the few franker stories, Keith Murdoch observed in Melbourne's *Herald* that:

The prince shows unnerving judgment in choosing 'pretty girls who are good dancers' but one cannot help thinking that the queen mother, sighing as mothers do sigh, would rather that her son choose 'good girls who are pretty dancers'.[45]

On Friday 18 June Edward made his first big public appearance at Sydney Town Hall, where thousands were waiting in the streets to be ushered past the prince at a rate of

250 a minute – not enough time for more than a glance, though 'practically everyone' was able to get a close view of the prince, said Mountbatten in his diaries.[46] Edward confided to Freda that he felt like a 'relic' and had had little chance to see the city of Sydney.

> I had 3 hard hours at the Town Hall this morning & thousands of people streamed past me and I felt more like a model or a relic . . . than ever!! But there were huge & dense enthusiastic crowds outside & it was really très emouvant the people here are far less rough than they were in Melbourne & I'm really having a far easier time here & the program is reasonable tho strenuous!! Of course I haven't really seen anything of the city yet except a few crowded streets and the harbour.[47]

On both Saturday and Sunday nights, half a dozen girls were discreetly invited to dine and to party into the early hours of the morning.[48]

It was not until after Edward had abdicated the throne more than fifteen years later to marry Wallis Simpson that many of the accounts of the playboy prince were made public. Sir Alan 'Tommy' Lascelles, who served various members of the royal family at Buckingham Palace as private secretary from the 1920s to the 1950s, joined the prince's staff in 1920 and worked for Edward until the abdication. He was not on the Australian trip but travelled elsewhere with Edward and in 1943 wrote in his diary that he had discussed the prince's behaviour with the then British prime minister Stanley Baldwin as early as 1927:

> I saw him [the prince] . . . often as near drunk as doesn't matter; I travelled twice across Canada with him . . . I probably knew him as well as any man did . . . I felt in such despair about him that I sought a secret colloquy with

Stanley Baldwin and told him directly that in my considered opinion the heir apparent, in his unbridled pursuit of wine and women, and of whatever selfish whim occupied him at the moment, was going rapidly to the devil and unless he mended his ways, would soon become no fit wearer of the British Crown.[49]

At the end of a tour of Canada with Edward in 1927, Lascelles described him as 'vulgar and selfish'. He later argued that Edward's irresponsible behaviour as an adult was because his 'normal mental development stopped dead when he reached adolescence' and 'his mental, moral and aesthetic development . . . remained that of a boy of seventeen'.[50]

Leaving Sydney the following Monday morning, the party went by train and car for nearly 300 kilometres to the site of Canberra. It had taken ten years after federation for agreement to be reached on Canberra as the location of the capital, and at the time of the prince's visit very little of the new city had been built. So remote was the place, with only a few 'homesteads of unpretentious features',[51] that some in the royal party thought they would be unable to find it and feared 'HRH [would] never arrive as a result'.[52] Edward was the first of many members of the British royal family to visit Canberra, but he stayed only for the day. His younger brother Albert later officially opened the first parliament building in Canberra in 1927, and Queen Elizabeth II opened the modern building in 1988.

For the 1920 visit, a royal camp was pitched at the foot of Kurrajong Hill, the site of the parliament, and Edward unveiled the foundation stone of the new city before 300–400 officials, many having come from Melbourne and Sydney for the occasion. A crowd lined the route to the site of the official event:

Small Union Jacks lined the avenue to the marquee where the luncheon was held. Near the top of the hill was an arch with a blue and gold background. The arch, which was artistically draped with greenery, bore the words: 'Capital Hill' was effectively decorated. The seat reserved for His Royal Highness was surmounted by a blue and gold dome – the prince's colours. At the rear of the prince was a huge Union Jack. The poles were prettily decorated with red, white, and blue ribbon, and from the dome there radiated, long lines of flags – the Union Jack and the Australian – and streamers of red, white and blue. On the prince's table the vases, which contained choice narcissus blooms, were draped with blue . . . The marquee was transformed into a thing of beauty and was every way worthy of the great occasion.[53]

At the time alcohol was banned in the Australian capital territory (prohibition was in force in the ACT from 1911 till 1928), but it did not stop the flow of drinks, and 'champagne corks could be heard popping from miles off' in the government marquee.[54]

Back in Sydney Edward, sounding unimpressed with his visit to Canberra, told Freda Ward that he had called for yet another party, at which he danced a great deal:

22nd June (2.00 A.M.) I got back from the up country trip at 10.30 P.M. beloved but was enticed to a party . . . it was a good jazz band [and dance] floor and I wanted some exercise after a ghastly political sort of day in the new federal district . . . called Canberra which is the site of the new Commonwealth capital!!

The following day he attended a lunch at the Town Hall for wounded sailors and soldiers, for which 'unprecedented crowds' turned up and gave Edward a 'great ovation'.[55] That afternoon he watched a parade of about 10,000 returned servicemen in Centennial Park, where the royal party were surprised at the lack of discipline of the Australian troops while the prince inspected them, the 'men, lounging about, talking as they felt inclined'.[56]

On 23 June he was taken by the premier, John Storey, and his senior Labor government colleagues on a boat ride along the beautiful Hawkesbury River north of Sydney. Edward did not attempt to disguise his political conservatism when he told Freda Ward that it was possibly the worst day of the tour so far:

> we've had almost the worst day of the whole trip certainly the most jarring to the nerves as we've had to spend 5 hours in a steam boat on the Hawkesbury River with the NSW Labour premier & 10 of his Labour government!! Their scheme was to get poor little me all to themselves & more or less interview me & as the whole crowd are Bolschies one had to be frightfully careful!! However as they made one an excuse for an oyster & champagne orgy at lunch on board & all of them got toxy except Storey the premier there wasn't much serious interviews about them tho & some of them struck out some nasty little bolschie ironies at the Admiral & me which hurt & then they began singing!! Oo! oo! oo! oo! What we went thru this afternoon mon amour . . .[57]

The following day at the Sydney Cricket Ground 8000 children formed a giant crest of the Prince Wales's heraldic feathers, underneath which they spelled out the words 'Many Happy Returns' because it was Edward's twenty-sixth birthday.

After two more days of public appearances, and having endured a number of 'hot air' speeches by local dignitaries, on Friday 25 June the prince boarded the *Renown* for the next leg of the tour. It was 7.15 pm but, despite the darkness, large crowds lined the shore and cheered as the motor launch shoved off from the Man o' War steps.

The *Renown* made heavy weather of the journey through rough seas in the Great Australian Bight and reached the port of Albany on the southern coast of Western Australia late in the afternoon of 30 June, where the party was taken immediately to the railway station for the 400-kilometre overnight train journey to Perth. Louis Mountbatten complained that the local dignitaries who met the prince had been told to come in travelling clothes but 'were all in pot hats', and that the sleeping compartments in the specially constructed royal train coach for the prince had only curtains rather than doors.

Arriving at Perth the next morning, the party was met by the 'the usual bigwigs' and 'tumultuous cheering from a large crowd which had collected', said Mountbatten.[58] The scene was captured by an excited Perth newspaper:

On Thursday morning people old and young were astir very early in the metropolitan districts. It was the morning of the prince's arrival . . . This sight itself was something that Perth residents very seldom see . . . The royal visitor was to arrive at the Central Station, and naturally positions of vantage had to be secured in good time. There was a steady stream of citizens by train and tram from the suburbs. Glorious sunshine after weeks of cloudy skies and torrents of rain prevailed for the arrival of the young representative of the British Crown, and our people from the coast and country regions congregated in thousands in the main thoroughfare of the capital in the happiest of moods to greet and do honour to the prince. The royal train pulled into the Central Station punctually to time . . . As the heir to the British throne stepped to the dais erected in front of the station a rousing cheer from the spectators in the immediate vicinity rent the air, and then followed the National Anthem. The scene was a gay one. 2000 schoolchildren accommodated on a stand facing the entrance to the station were garlanded in such manner as to present a bright and attractive color picture of red, white and blue, added to by the uniforms of the military and naval guards of honour and general decorations.[59]

John Curtin, a leading figure of the Australian Labor Party in Western Australia, and later prime minister, objected to the British throne being used as 'propaganda' for 'an imperial reconstruction of the postwar world'. Curtin had been a staunch anti-conscriptionist during the war and had even been jailed for a few days in 1916 for failing to enlist. He argued the prince should never have been put into the position of being a 'missioner for doubtful causes' by advocating the continuation of the British Empire after the war.[60]

Perth in 1920 was a small, isolated and deeply provincial, conservative city, and during Edward's stay Mountbatten recounted how the prince shocked his more staid lunch guests when he lit up a cigarette at the table:

Immediately after the king's health had been drunk, HRH not unnaturally, lit up a cigarette, which quite scandalised some of the dear ladies present, who had never heard of a 'gentleman' smoking at his luncheon, and were nearly prostrated with horror when informed that in England ladies not infrequently join the gentlemen with a cigarette.[61]

The royal tour in Western Australia was also punctuated by drama when, during a visit to the southern coastal town of Bunbury, the train on which the prince and his party were travelling derailed and a number of carriages, including the royal one, were overturned, throwing the prince's four-post bed 'the entire breadth of the coach':

A Very Narrow Escape

A most alarming accident happened to the royal train to-day at 2.15 pm when ten miles from Bridgetown when the royal car at the end of the train and the ministers car next to it left the rails and ploughed along the track for 200 yards and finally toppled over a low embankment. A third carriage also left the track but did not topple . . . The royal car was dragged a little way before the train stopped. The prince and other occupants of the carriage were imprisoned for ten minutes. Colonel Peck climbed on top of the overturned royal car, and with other helpers, pulled the prince up through the side window of the wrecked car . . . The prince's appearance was hailed with load cheers. He was absolutely unhurt, and when first seen by rescuers was calmly smoking a cigar and talking to Admiral Halsey.[62]

Later Edward joked, 'Well, anyway, at least we have done something which was not on the official program.'[63]

After eight days in Perth the tour headed by train to the goldfields at Coolgardie and Kalgoorlie, over 500 kilometres to the east. Great crowds once more lined Perth's streets as 'HRH departed and cheered and shouted "come back again" at the station'.[64] The royal party felt there was an element of 'red rag' to being sent to the goldfields of Western Australia: the workers were unionised, voted predominantly for the Labor Party and many were anti-monarchists. Nevertheless, as the local newspaper boasted, these men also had stood by the British Empire during World War I: at the outbreak of war, Coolgardie had made a list of their eligible men and three months later a list of men who had enlisted, and these are said to have exactly tallied.[65]

His Royal Highness the Prince of Wales will make his first acquaintance with the eastern goldfields and receive a right royal welcome from the loyal population of this section of Western Australia to-day. The major portion of the famous 11th Battalion, whose men were the first to land on the shores of Gallipoli, was recruited from this district. Soldiers who have brought equal lustre upon Australia by their deeds on the fields of France, Flanders, Syria and Palestine were also enlisted here.[66]

There were, as expected, some gestures of protests at the prince's visit. The Australian Workers Union in Kalgoorlie called on parents to prevent their children from going to see the prince and a proposed concert for the prince at nearby Boulder was cancelled by the local union. But none of this could dampen the general sense of enthusiasm for the visit, and it was splashed over the front page of the local newspapers.

THE PRINCE REACHES THE GOLDFIELDS
WONDERFUL SCENES OF ENTHUSIASM
FROM COOLGARDIE TO BOULDER
THIRTY THOUSAND CHEERING PEOPLE

A magnificent spectacle was provided to the royal guest. Outside the Kalgoorlie Station the central position was occupied by a dais from which the civic reception took place. Behind the surrounding barriers were great crowds and on the right an immense choir of children welcomed the prince with national airs to the accompaniment of the Kalgoorlie Band.[67]

Next, the royal party boarded a train for a journey that ran in almost a straight line for more than 1600 kilometres across the desert country of the Nullarbor Plain to Port Augusta in South Australia (which, as Mountbatten pointed out, was 'the same distance as London to Algiers').[68] About halfway across the desert and shortly before reaching the tiny railway town of Cook, the party stopped to witness a traditional dance, or corroboree, staged by local Aboriginal men and women. The prince admired their legs, which he joked to those present were ever thinner than his, but was far more offensive when he wrote to his lover Freda Ward: 'They are the most revolting form of living creatures I've ever seen. They are the lowest form of human beings & are the nearest thing to monkeys.'[69]

On Monday 12 July the train reached the outskirts of Adelaide, and the royal party transferred to four large English-made Crossley cars for the thirty-kilometre ride past large crowds into the city, which at the time, as Mountbatten wrote in his diary, was 'several times as big as Perth . . . though only a third the size of Melbourne or Sydney'.[70]

> South Australia outdid its own fine record to day, when the prince arrived here, after passing through the rich wheat country to the north, where the townships of Peterborough, Terowie, and Gawler put up wonderful receptions. The entire population of the province appeared to be assembled to welcome His Royal Highness at the railway station. After inspecting the fine looking guards of honour, the prince entered a motor car, and the procession began through a sea of people . . . The route of the procession was three miles long, and traversed the principal streets of the city, which were decorated, and lined the entire distance ten deep with cheering crowds.[71]

On the first night in Adelaide there was a dinner at Government House followed by an official reception, which finished around 10.30 pm. After the guests had left, the prince held a party with about two dozen people, including some local girls. There, said Mountbatten, 'everyone went mad, including the prince' and danced till two in the morning.[72]

The next morning Edward was driven through Adelaide's streets, with the crowds held back by barriers, to Jubilee Oval for a Boy Scouts demonstration before he went to the Austral Gardens to meet war veterans. While shaking hands with the maimed soldiers who were sitting in the front row, the prince became impatient with the crush of the ever-present cameras. By two in the afternoon the party was at Adelaide's Victoria Park Racecourse, where after betting on and watching the first race, they enjoyed 'a magnificent spread' of lunch at Tattersalls and drank 'an endless supply of champagne'.[73] The royal party had been told the Adelaide people were quieter and less emotional than those in other Australian cities but they found the racing crowd 'cheered and yelled' more than any other city they had visited.[74]

The local Adelaide press reported the visit as the colony's biggest event and one that would cement Australia to Britain:

The visit of the prince is one of the greatest events of our history. During his few short weeks in Australia . . . he has done more to tighten the bonds between the people [of Australia] and the throne than will be accomplished by any other man in the next half century.[75]

The key to the success of Edward's visit was perceived to be the way in which the prince projected himself as one of the people, reaching out to all levels of society – at least white society:

What makes the Prince of Wales ... so popular is the readiness to show himself to the people as simply one of themselves ... interested in what interested them and, above all, anxious to make friends with the lowly and the obscure.[76]

Over the next few days Edward visited the Keswick Hospital, where maimed soldiers were being retrained for civilian jobs, and the Exhibition Building to meet women who had been war workers. He also visited Adelaide University, where he was awarded an honorary doctorate, as he had been in Sydney and Melbourne.

After five days the royal party left Port Adelaide on the *Renown*, which had sailed back from Albany in Western Australia, for the voyage to Tasmania. Arriving in the magnificent harbour at Hobart on the morning of Tuesday 20 July, the prince went first to a large shed in the port where he met returned soldiers, many of whom had been severely wounded during the war.[77] There were too many of them to shake each hand so he walked up and down the lines saying hello. Edward was told of the very high commitment of Tasmanians during the war and that fifteen locals had been awarded the Victoria Cross.[78]

At an early lunch at Tasmania's beautiful Government House, which overlooked the harbour, a very tired Prince Edward had a sore throat and was only able to speak briefly in a hoarse voice. However, later that afternoon he was still able to impress the local newspapers with his horseriding ability:

The prince went to Elwick, where three horses were placed at his disposal. He rode Drawing in two six furlong sprints against Captain Leigh on Bogalus, and won both events. He then safely negotiated two flights of hurdles in the straight.

Jockeys expressed the opinion that the prince did not have much to learn about horseriding.[79]

The following day the royal party journeyed to Launceston on Tasmania's narrow-gauge rail track, which was very slow and took over ten hours. For the first time on the Australian tour everyone travelling with the prince, including local government ministers and the press, stayed under the same roof, in the magnificent Anzac Hotel in Brisbane Street, which the prince's staff said was the most comfortable accommodation yet on the tour. Early the next morning Edward was confronted with a huge crowd when he left the hotel, including some returned diggers who invited him to join them in a game of two-up. The prince was apparently familiar with the game from his encounters with Australian troops during the war and knew how to lay two pennies on a matchbox then spin them in the air and try to land both 'heads' upwards. *The Daily Telegraph* described Launceston as a 'pretty little city', whose

> 25,000 inhabitants looked its best in the brief sunshine of a cold winter day . . . The streets and buildings are gaily decorated with bunting and greenery and the crowds gathered beside the barricades cheer the prince energetically whenever he appears.[80]

After visiting Launceston's Cataract Gorge the party returned to the hotel, where the prince refused to dine privately, insisting instead on going down to the dining room. Louis Mountbatten said that it was to be with one of the women they had met:

> It had been arranged the HRH and staff should dine privately in their dining room, but for practically the first time HRH

not only volunteered to go down into the general dining room for dinner, but insisted on it. Shrewd guesses were made by the staff as to which of the ministers wives, or possible waitresses, attraction was at the bottom of it, but to quite honest there were no signs that they had guessed right during dinner.[81]

On Thursday 22 July, the royal party went south to Hobart, arriving around six in the evening to board the *Renown*, which left that night for Sydney. Three days later they reached Sydney Harbour and after landing drove the length of the city along streets 'thickly lined with enthusiastic crowds' to Central Station to catch the train to Brisbane for the tour of Queensland, the last state they were to visit.

After travelling on narrow-gauge trains from Western Australia to South Australia and in Tasmania, the royals were happy to be on the more comfortable standard gauge and in the luxurious royal carriage of the New South Wales railways, which had first been used by Edward's mother and father when they had visited Australia in 1901. The railway line took them more than 650 kilometres to the Queensland border, where at the town of Wallangarra they had to change trains back to the narrow gauge of Queensland's railways. As the prince walked across the red carpet from the platform on the western side of the station to board the train on the eastern side, the crowd was the quietest they had experienced. The Brisbane *Courier-Mail* reported that everyone was so intimidated by the formalities of receiving the prince 'that not a single cheer was raised'.[82]

During the 250-kilometre overnight train journey to Brisbane, an organiser had come into the saloon car and asked if the Boy Scouts could the next day present the prince with a koala. There was a lot of discussion by the royal party before a vote was taken. Admiral Halsey strongly argued against taking the creature, on the grounds that it would die due to the change in climate and he did not want it on the *Renown*. However, the party overwhelmingly voted to accept the gift. So the next morning at Brisbane's Parliament House a young girl and her brother handed it over to Prince Edward. It spent the entire day crawling around urinating and defecating, leaving a foul smell. Mountbatten described the koala:

> In general appearance it certainly bore a striking resemblance to an ordinary teddy bear . . . the face however, was the most ridiculous; it reminded one vaguely of a Jews face with a hooked nose and had the stupidest possible expression, with a pair of tiny eyes set rather close together.[83]

Late in the day the royal party were relieved to learn that the little girl who had given the gift was sobbing at the loss of her pet and they were gracefully able to give the koala back.

The Courier-Mail headlined the prince's visit to the city 'Empire Unity and Democracy', and went on most enthusiastically:

> The British Empire is the world's greatest insurance for the future safety of democracy. The Prince of Wales, who has spoken throughout Australia, with evident sincerity, has held up to the very highest ideals of Empire . . . the idea of the overseas dominions as distant lands, each carving out its own destiny, is folly. There are theorists and disruptionists who would break the magnetic grip of empire, but as Mr Hughes very truly said in his speech at Bendigo, on Saturday night, 'the division of Empire would mean death to Australia'. It would be the end of our freedom and our democracy. Australia took

part in the Great War and had a brilliant snare in the victory achieved by the Allies, as the Prince of Wales has said in truly eloquent language in different parts of the Commonwealth. It played that part because civilisation had to be saved from destruction, because the great principle of right had been availed by the spirit of military despotism and because the safety of Australia depended on the great issue.[84]

At the weekend Prince Edward and his entourage visited a large farm south of Brisbane, Coochin Coochin (Aboriginal for 'many black swans'), owned by the Bell family, prominent farmers in the district. Edward was entertained there by the three attractive Bell daughters, Eileen, Enid and Una, riding and partying. Louis Mountbatten said that the after-dinner party lasted till 1 am, when they finally retired 'battered and bruised far more from the dancing than from the riding'.[85] Edward was scheduled to visit other farms in the area but did not go because he had 'found the Bell girls more to his liking and did not want to leave them'.[86]

The following week the royals returned to New South Wales. By now the prince was complaining of being 'absolutely worn out'. 'Thank God it's all over bar the shouting now as I really don't think I can carry on much longer.'[87] Back in Sydney they went off to the races at Randwick and 'had a very bad day, losing vast sums of money between them'.[88]

Finally, late on the morning of Thursday 29 July, Prince Edward's Australian tour came to an end. As the *Renown* got underway he went up to the bridge to wave goodbye to the crowds lining the shores, and to the large number of boats that followed the ship out of Sydney Harbour. Little did any of those waving goodbye so enthusiastically know that hidden below the decks of the *Renown* were five young women. According to Mountbatten, the girls included two of the three Bell daughters from Brisbane:

> The Flag Lieutenant went on to Man-O'-War Steps and picked up a party consisting of . . . Eileen and Dolly [Enid] Bell. They arrived on board about half past eleven, just before H.R.H. arrived . . . The 'pieces' were put under cover while the ship proceeded out, and H.R.H. . . . went to the 'special bridge'; to wave to the crowds . . . after lunch everybody moved up to the reception deck and danced . . . about half past three . . . the party broke up and retired to various rooms for the afternoon . . . the Weigalls [South Australian governor Sir William Weigall and his wife, Lady Grace], having to catch a train, had to leave by picket boat at a quarter to three, leaving the young ladies on board unchaperoned . . . The party were eventually taken off by the *Australia's* picket boat at 5 o'clock . . . And so ends the account of H.R.H.'s tour of Australia.[89]

The *Renown* sailed back to England via Suva, British Samoa, Honolulu, Acapulco, the Panama Canal, Trinidad, British Guiana, Grenada, St Lucia and finally reached Plymouth on 11 October 1920. Prince Edward had been away for seven months. His trip had been an outstanding and unqualified success at cementing relations between Australia and Britain. In Australia newspapers pointed out that the unity between the countries had been 'incontestably demonstrated' in the Great War and

> by the enthusiastic reception everywhere accorded the Prince of Wales on his ambassadorial tour of the dominions. The tour was a triumphal procession . . . It was an important mission and wholly successful [with] the imperial spirit of the people being much stimulated.[90]

Even the royal-sceptic Australian prime minister Billy Hughes effused about the prince at the end of the tour:

> When first you came amongst us we welcomed you as a prince who is one day to be our king; but we part from you as a dear friend who has won over our affections and whom we love. Your visit has provoked demonstrations that in their spontaneous enthusiasm are unique in our history. The Australian people see in all that our gracious empire stands for, the deathless spirit of liberty, of progress, that distinguishes it from other Empires, ancient and modern. Come back to us prince, as soon as you can and as often as you can.[91]

Assessments in England were equally positive. When Prince Edward was officially welcomed home by the City of London Corporation at the Guildhall, British prime minister David Lloyd George proposed a toast to the prince. He hinted that the reaction following the war created a necessity for keeping Britain and the dominions together and said the prince 'had strengthened the invisible ties of empire'. 'The occasion,' he said, had 'demanded a man for the emergency, and the Prince of Wales was the man.'[92]

10

AUSTRALIA AND THE ABDICATION

> There would be outspoken hostility to His Majesty's wife
> becoming queen, while any proposal that she should become
> consort and not queen . . . would not be approved by my
> [Australian] government.

IN 1927, THE NATIONAL parliament building in the new
capital of Canberra was finally finished. The Australian
government wanted Crown Prince Edward to open the
new building. His tour of Australia seven years before
had been such an outstanding success that Prime Minister
Stanley Bruce asked that he be invited to return. However,
King George V insisted on sending instead his second son,
31-year-old Prince Albert ('Bertie'), the Duke of York and
Cornwall. King George had opened the first Australian
parliament in 1901 when he was the Duke of York and
Cornwall, and he thought it appropriate that his son who
held the same title now should do the honours; in any
event, Prince Edward was losing interest in demanding

royal engagements and was unenthusiastic about the prospect of another visit to Australia.[1]

It was clear that King George would have his way but Bruce was 'openly appalled' at the decision to send Albert, whose nervousness and stammer were well known in official circles.[2] Prince Bertie had been shy and nervous from an early age, spoke with a stammer and 'was easily frightened and somewhat prone to tears'. His biographer, Sir John Wheeler-Bennett, who also suffered from a stammer, described 'the infuriating inhibitions and frustrations, the bitter humiliation and anguish of the spirit; the orgies of self-pity; and the utter exhaustion, mental and physical' that Bertie's speech impediment caused.[3] It did not help that every time he tried to address his father, the irascible king would bark, 'Get it out!' before turning away in dismissal.

As a boy Bertie had been 'completely outshone' by the 'extraordinary and magnetic charm' of his brother Edward.[4] While Edward strolled through life's challenges with panache, Bertie struggled. He suffered from gastric problems and knock-knees, which required splints. He was also a poor scholar and when he joined his older brother at Osborne Naval College, he was regularly bottom of the class of the seventy-odd students in his year. In the navy, he was so timid about speaking that he was dismissed as simple.[5]

Despite the inauspicious start to Bertie's naval career, he received praise during World War I for having seen action and 'stuck to his gun' at the Battle of Jutland in 1916. At the end of the war he chose to transfer to the Royal Air Force, but soon afterwards his father decided Bertie should follow Edward to Cambridge, where he spent a few terms in 1919.[6] The next year he was made the Duke of York and began spending more time at Sandringham and Balmoral Castle where, as an accomplished horseman and a good shot, he enjoyed riding and hunting.

At a society party in the late summer of 1920, Bertie met the woman who would become the love of his life and his greatest supporter, and would later be best known as the queen mother. Aristocrat Lady Elizabeth Bowes-Lyon was twenty years old when she met Bertie. She was the ninth of ten children and had been brought up with her three sisters and six brothers, and scores of servants, on the family estate of Glamis Castle in Forfarshire, north of Dundee in Scotland. Unlike her seemingly unimpressive prince, young Elizabeth was charming and quick to impress those around her. An admirer of Elizabeth, Lord Gorell, said of her in a letter to Lady Cynthia Asquith: 'in the simplest and most unconscious way she was all conquering'.[7] She was by nature unpunctual, a characteristic that normally offended King George V, but he told his son how much he approved of his choice of wife when they married.

Elizabeth had not had an entirely sheltered childhood. During World War I, Glamis Castle had been used as a military convalescent hospital, so as a young girl she was exposed to the great suffering and endurance of the severely wounded soldiers who were sent there. Among the Australians she met as a teenager was Second Lieutenant Rupert Dent from the Sydney suburb of Stanmore, who had been wounded in the right shoulder by German machine-gun fire on the Somme in 1918. While convalescing at Glamis, Dent would join eighteen-year-old Elizabeth on long country walks and the two became close friends. For many years after the war they corresponded and when she visited Australia in 1927 with Bertie, Elizabeth invited Dent and his wife, who by then had a young daughter they'd named Elizabeth, to Sydney's Government House.[8]

After two years of hesitation, Elizabeth Bowes-Lyon became engaged to Bertie, and they married on 26 April 1923 in what was believed to have been her personal choice rather than an arranged marriage. For the rest of his life she was a great source of comfort and stability to her nervous, stuttering husband, particularly after he was forced to take the Crown following his brother Edward's abdication in 1936.

Three years into the marriage, on 21 April 1926, the royal couple had their first child, Princess Elizabeth – 'Lilibet' to the family – and less than a year later, in early 1927, the Duke of York and his new duchess were sent to Australia by King George. Neither relished the thought of half a year away from England when their baby daughter was only eight months old and they were just about to move to a new home in Piccadilly near Hyde Park Corner.[9] Bertie was also reluctant to go because of his lack of confidence about being able to speak clearly without stammering. For a time he pleaded with his father that he could not face the ordeal, but his protests were overruled and he finally gave in.

Before leaving London for Australia, the duke went to see Lionel Logue, an elocution teacher who came from Adelaide in South Australia and had opened a speech therapy practice in London in 1926:

> Many efforts had been made throughout his life to remedy his defect, but without success. It was decided that, before he left for Australia one final effort should be made . . . Among those consulted was Mr Lionel Logue – appropriately enough a young Australian – who had come to England a few months before with a reputation for handling difficult speech . . . For months the duke and Mr Logue spent an hour or two practically every day in a concentrated effort to attain normal speech.[10]

When the royal couple left Great Britain on 6 January 1927, the duchess wrote in her diary that she was 'very miserable' at leaving behind baby Elizabeth.[11] They sailed on the HMS

Renown, just as Edward had seven years before on his Australian tour. Travelling via Jamaica, the Panama Canal and the Pacific, they reached New Zealand on 22 February and during the next few weeks visited New Zealand's north island. Elizabeth became ill while they were there, so Bertie completed their overland tour of the south island on his own, before rejoining his wife on the *Renown*, which had sailed south to meet him.

The duke and duchess left Dunedin on 22 March and arrived in Sydney four days later. Their appearance on the harbour in glorious sunshine was described as impressive and spectacular by local newspapers, as they were greeted by what is believed to be the first gathering in Australia of more than a million people. When they landed at Farm Cove they were given a 'tumultuous welcome' by the crowds of people along the shoreline.[12] A hundred thousand people also lined the streets outside the Town Hall to greet the royal couple as they attended a state reception there, waiting patiently for three hours to see the visitors again when they emerged later.[13]

Twelve large British Crossley cars had been especially fitted out and shipped to Australia so that the duke and duchess could be driven around each Australian city they were to visit – Sydney, Brisbane, Hobart, Melbourne and Adelaide. Six of the cars were seven-seater tourers, four were enclosed limousines and two were landaulettes, which had an open front and closed cabin at the rear. The Crossley landaulette used by the duke and duchess was painted maroon, had matching leather upholstery and was fitted with a cigar lighter, dictaphone, cushions and footrests. Its spotlight and side lamps meant it was readily distinguished at night as their vehicle.[14]

In Sydney the couple attended a civic reception where 10,000 invited guests paraded past them, hosted a garden party, which was marred by rain, lunched with World War I veterans and visited repatriation and military hospitals, where they talked with severely disabled soldiers from the war. At Sydney Cricket Ground they saw a massive school-children's display. The 15,000 schoolchildren performed 'picturesque maypole dances . . . flag drill . . . physical exercises, marching displays and singing'.[15]

On 4 April, and in dismal rain, more than 4000 people turned up to wave the royal couple goodbye at Sydney's Central Station as they boarded the royal train to Queensland. They arrived in Brisbane to be greeted by another wildly enthusiastic crowd. The local press asserted that the support for the duchess and duke equalled that for Edward in 1920, and Bertie's parents, King George V and Queen Mary, when they had come to Queensland in 1901:

> There was the same splendid loyalty of the people, the same enthusiastic desire to extend a magnificent welcome to the royal visitors, the same love of British traditions, and the same unbounded confidence in the democratic trend of Empire as a safeguard of national liberty.[16]

In Brisbane, the duke and duchess took part in a procession through the city, attended a march of World War I veterans and a parade of Girl Guides and Boy Scouts, visited the Queensland state parliament and the University of Queensland, and witnessed thousands more schoolchildren taking part in a choreographed display for them at the Brisbane Exhibition Ground. On 9 April they went by train to a private property in Beaudesert, ninety kilometres south of Brisbane, for a quiet weekend.

When they left the city, a satisfied local press claimed Queenslanders had shown they were as loyal to the Crown as anyone in Australia:

From the time they stepped on Queensland's soil early on Tuesday morning until they rested last evening after an arduous day their royal highnesses, the Duke and Duchess of York, have had an opportunity of realising that Queensland, like the rest of the Commonwealth of Australia, is loyal to the core.[17]

—

Their next stop was Hobart, where the duke and duchess found the whole city 'illuminated by gas light and lanterns, making a magnificent spectacle', and large crowds lining the streets to give the royals a 'spontaneous, heartfelt, and sincere welcome'.[18] Among Hobart's decorations were four large arches, one seventeen metres high and mounted with a three-metre-tall floral crown that bore the words 'The Citizens Greet You'.

During their three-day visit, which included a short trip to Launceston, the duke and duchess went to the Queen's Domain (named after Victoria) where thousands of Sunday School children sang the especially composed 'Ode of Welcome' to them, attended a civic reception at Government House, a grand ball at Hobart Town Hall and laid the foundation stone for a new cathedral.

On 20 April they crossed the Bass Strait on the *Renown* and arrived the following day at Melbourne's St Kilda Pier. During a hectic eight days in Victoria, the duke and duchess attended a reception for 10,000 invited guests at the Exhibition Building, as well as the last session of the national parliament before it moved to Canberra. The royal couple was in Melbourne for the Anzac Day service on 25 April and visited the Caulfield Repatriation Hospital to see severely disabled diggers returned from the war.

Three days later they left on the rail journey to Adelaide, where they arrived to a crowd of about 150,000 people.[19]

The biggest event they saw in the South Australian capital was a giant display at the Adelaide showground staged by hundreds of schoolchildren:

> Never before had such a display been seen in Adelaide, and the crowd at the oval was unprecedented. It is estimated that more than 12,000 persons witnessed the display, and that another 15,000 lined King William street, from the Government House gates. The girls were dressed in white, with red, white, and blue hoods alternating and the boys in white gymnastic costumes. The display comprised a formation of the map of Australia, with the word 'welcome' and an outline of the Union Jack.[20]

On the couple's last day in South Australia the duke went on a private kangaroo hunt before he and Elizabeth left for Canberra.

At the time, 1927, the Australian capital was very small:

> a collection of isolated buildings scattered across the plains around Parliament House. There were a few hotels and hostels, a smattering of residential homes and a small number of government buildings. These were widely separated, loosely joined by roads that seemed to begin and end nowhere. Although a massive afforestation program was underway, there were few mature trees. There was little public transport and only a small number of privately owned cars, buses and trucks.[21]

Barely 6000 people lived there, and many of those who attended the parliamentary opening on 9 May had travelled from Sydney and Melbourne for the event. The ceremony took place at the top of the front steps of the new building and was broadcast on radio throughout New South Wales,

Victoria, Queensland and South Australia to an audience of around a million people.

The duke and duchess were first welcomed by a fanfare of bugles played by eight Royal Marines, and a 21-gun salute. The duke reviewed the guard of honour and the duchess was given a bouquet of flowers by a four-year-old local girl, Gwen Pinner. Dame Nellie Melba – Helen Porter Mitchell (Melba was a shortened version of her home town Melbourne) – then sang 'God Save the King' and the crowd and the Canberra Philharmonic Society followed with a spirited repeat of the first verse. At the time Melba was an international star in the major opera houses of Europe and America, and just three weeks before had become the first Australian to appear on the cover of *Time* magazine.

The formal proceedings began with short speeches from Prime Minister Stanley Bruce and the Duke of York. The duke's difficulty with speaking was widely known and everyone in the audience anxiously waited to see if he could manage. According to the press, and to everyone's relief, he successfully struggled through the speech, which was delivered in 'hesitant style but with crystal-clear enunciation'.[22] Some reports suggested his wife was every bit as nervous as he was:

Inside the House, as the duke began his reply, the duchess was obviously nervous. Her arms hung straight down, and her fingers convulsively closed and opened. In the first sentence the duke halted. He paused every few words, but there was apparently no stutter. After the first few sentences he spoke smoothly and audibly, and the duchess, in obvious relief, crossed her arms and regained her nerve. Plainly the duchess shares all the duke's anxieties, and mothers him through the troubles of speechmaking. Her eyelids fluttered during every long pause, her throat contracted whenever his nervousness showed, and her face flushed along with his when he seemed momentarily embarrassed.[23]

After the speeches the duke turned and led the party to the large doors of the parliament, which he unlocked with a gold key. The party then followed him across King's Hall and unveiled a statue of his father, King George V. Once the official proceedings were finished, guests went to nearby York Park, where the duke reviewed 2000 troops and witnessed a fly-past of biplanes of the Royal Australian Air Force. Tragically, during the various air squadrons' manoeuvres overhead, the plane of Flying Officer Francis Charles Ewen crashed, and he died later that night.

The next day the duke and duchess took the train back to Melbourne, where they were 'farewelled enthusiastically by the public' as they boarded the *Renown* for the voyage to Perth, their last port of call.[24] It took six days' sailing through rough weather in the Great Australian Bight before 'early rising sightseers at Cottesloe ... looked over the Indian Ocean' on a bright and sunny morning and 'saw the magnificent battlecruiser *Renown* approach the Western shores'.[25]

The royal couple were welcomed with the same enthusiasm they had encountered in other Australian cities, greeted all the way along the twenty-two kilometres from Fremantle to Perth by not only the people of Perth but 'thousands of state schoolchildren [who] exercised their lungs in exultant vociferation, and waved countless flags'.[26]

While in Perth, the duke and duchess were taken eighty kilometres south by train to visit the Fairbridge Farm School at Pinjarra, the first of many that had been set up by British churches and charities to take thousands of England's poorest children from the 'waif and pauper'

King George III was an enthusiastic student of science and took a great interest in the British settlement of Australia. He authorised the establishment of the convict colony, involved himself in many of the details of the First Fleet, read the reports sent back from New South Wales and agreed to the dispatch of emergency relief supplies to Sydney in 1789.

On Friday 1 December 1854, rebel Australian gold miners at Ballarat raised the Southern Cross flag for the first time. Before dawn two days later, the diggers' threat to the authority of the British Crown was brutally crushed when troops and police attacked the Eureka stockade, killing twenty-two, wounding scores and rounding up and arresting more than a hundred others.

Twenty-three-year-old Prince Alfred, the fourth child and second son of Queen Victoria, was the first member of the British royal family to visit Australia. He came for a five-month tour in 1867.

His tour nearly ended in tragedy when Alfred narrowly survived an assassination attempt at a picnic in Sydney in 1868. 'Good God, I am shot . . . my back is broken,' he cried.

Queen Victoria was increasingly revered and became a towering figure in Australia during her long reign, although she never visited the place and showed little interest in it.

Victoria's eighteen-year-old son Prince Albert was the first direct heir to the throne to visit Australia when he toured with his younger brother George (later King George V) in 1881.

A public holiday was called and the nation stirred with excitement as troops sailed from Sydney's Circular Quay to fight in the Sudan in 1885. Australians rushed to fight in Britain's Empire wars, including the Crimea, New Zealand's Maori Wars, the Boer Wars, the Boxer Rebellion and of course both World Wars.

The Duke of York (later King George V) officially opened Australia's first national parliament in Melbourne's Exhibition Hall on 9 May 1901. Tom Roberts' painting of the occasion is more than 5 metres across and took four years to complete. Known as the 'big picture', it features detailed portraits of 269 people, including the duke and duchess, the governor-general and MPs.

King George V (second from left) inspecting Australian troops at bayonet practice in France during World War I. Australia pledged to defend the British Empire 'to her last man and her last shilling'.

Edward, the Prince of Wales (later King Edward VIII) surrounded by massive and enthusiastic crowds outside Sydney Town Hall in 1920. His tour was to help rekindle the spirit of the Empire and to thank Australians for the sacrifices they'd made during the Great War. At the time he was one of the world's first superstars and the most popular figure Australia had ever seen.

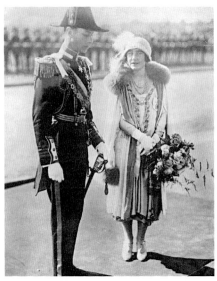

The Duke of York (later King George VI) and the duchess (later better known as the queen mother) at the opening of Canberra's new parliament in 1927. To everyone's relief the duke managed to control his stutter and successfully deliver his speech 'in hesitant style' but 'with crystal clear enunciation'.

Australia's high commissioner to London, Stanley Bruce (right), urged his good friend Stanley Baldwin, the prime minister of Britain, to be firm with King Edward VIII and deny his wish to marry twice-divorced Mrs Simpson.

Australia's most ardent monarchist, Prime Minister Robert Menzies, with Winston Churchill in London in 1941. Menzies had committed Australia to join World War II: 'Great Britain has declared war ... as a result, Australia is also at war.'

The Australian Girl Guides provided most of the ingredients for Princess Elizabeth and Philip's three-metre tall wedding cake. There was still war-time rationing in Britain so seven large crates of ingredients were sent for the cake on the P&O liner SS *Stratheden* three months before the wedding.

Members of the British and European royal families at Buckingham Palace after the marriage of Elizabeth and Philip on 20 November 1947, including King George VI and Elizabeth, later the queen mother (second from the left of Philip); and Queen Mary (standing behind the bride and groom), the widow of King George V.

Rockdale Town Hall in Sydney during the Coronation on 2 June 1953. All over Australia large crowds gathered to celebrate the ceremony, which was broadcast from London live on the radio.

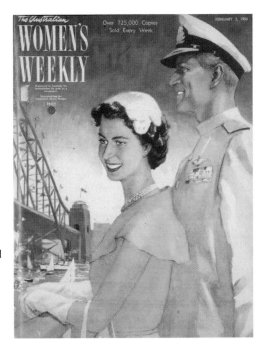

The queen and the Duke of Edinburgh as portrayed by the *Australian Women's Weekly* on their arrival in Sydney at the start of the spectacular 1954 royal tour, the first by a reigning monarch.

Part of a huge crowd at Melbourne Cricket Ground who came to see the queen and Duke of Edinburgh. It is estimated that 70 per cent of the population turned out to see the queen during her 1954 visit.

Australian Prime
Minister Menzies with
the queen in 1963,
delivering Robert Frost's
line 'I did but see her
passing by, and yet I will
love her till I die.'

Princess Margaret
was said to 'eat
anything at
all – but please
make sure there
is a gin and tonic
and a packet
of American
cigarettes waiting
for her'.

The queen at the official opening of the Sydney Opera House in 1973 on what is regarded as the last of the grand royal tours. As the years passed crowds became smaller as Australians increasingly followed the royal family's visits on television in the comfort of their own homes.

Not a John Cleese funny walk. Margaret Whitlam and her husband, Prime Minister Gough Whitlam, greet Queen Elizabeth at the opening of the Opera House.

Charles in the surf at a Perth beach in 1979 with local girl Jane Priest, who said
years later that the encounter had been set up to make Charles appear 'more
accessible'.

The growing rift between Prince Charles and Princess Diana became increasingly apparent on their later visits. Diana knew that the Australian public preferred her, complaining that Charles was jealous and 'took it out on me'.

Princess Diana on Terrigal Beach in New South Wales in 1988. She became, and remains, one of the most popular royals to visit Australia.

Australian Prime Minister Paul Keating was branded by the press as the 'Lizard of Oz' when he put his hand on the queen's back to guide her along a line of guests at an official function in 1992.

The closest Australia ever got to ditching the British monarchy and becoming a republic was when the issue went to a referendum in 1999. Former prime ministers and old political foes Gough Whitlam and Malcolm Fraser joined forces to support the referendum.

After watching an Aboriginal cultural performance in 2002, the Duke of Edinburgh reportedly asked, 'Do you still throw spears at each other?' Over the years fewer people came to regard Prince Philip's gaffes as the innocent comments of an old duffer and more began to feel that they revealed deep-seated racial and chauvinist prejudices.

Prince William with Aboriginal women in Sydney's inner-city suburb of Redfern in 2010. His friendly, relaxed and engaging manner made him instantly popular in Australia.

Prince Charles and his second wife, Camilla, on a tour of Australia in 2012.

Prince Harry in Sydney in 2014 being embraced by a girl in the crowd outside the Opera House. His larrikin image and reports of under-age drinking and marijuana smoking did little to dent his popularity with Australians.

classes to Australia with the promise of giving them a better life in Australia. Only a few of the children were orphans, who were from extremely poor and broken families, and most would never see their parents again.

The school at Pinjarra had been set up in 1913; later, other Fairbridge schools were opened in Canada, Rhodesia (Zimbabwe) and Molong in New South Wales. Over the years, the British royal family established a long-standing connection with Fairbridge: seven years after the visit of the duke and duchess, Bertie's older brother Edward launched a big fundraising campaign in England for Fairbridge with a personal donation of £1000. In 1948 Queen Elizabeth II donated £2000 from her wedding presents, and in the 1950s her uncle, the Duke of Gloucester, after serving as governor-general in Australia, became chairman of the Fairbridge Society.

On this trip, the duke and duchess had specifically requested to visit the school, which housed nearly 200 children migrants. *The Geraldton Guardian* explained that

[many of the children] . . . have parents in England, who possibly through straitened circumstances, have been forced to part – at least temporarily – with their children. The Farm School is surrounded by 3100 acres, and although Their Royal Highnesses did not walk over that area, they certainly saw over the greater part of it, so intense was their interest. Following the inspection of the settlement, the royal car was requisitioned and two car loads set off for a tour of the developed country.[27]

They inspected the buildings and working conditions of the 'youthful migrants from the Motherland' and the farm, which included a vegetable garden, a dairy herd, sheep, poultry, pigs, and an oat crop. The duke planted two oak trees 'by enthusiastic cheers of the thoroughly delighted children'.[28] *The Geraldton Guardian* said, 'It had been the day of their lives.'[29]

In their remaining four days in Perth, the duke and duchess witnessed a parade of 5000 schoolchildren at Kings Park, a garden party at Government House and a gathering of over 4000 nurses and members of the RSL, to whom, as a 'brother Digger' in the Great War, the duke expressed his spirit of comradeship.[30]

—

On 23 May the duke and duchess headed home on the *Renown*, sailing via the British-controlled ports of Mauritius, Suez, Malta and Gibraltar. Their trip to Australia had been another success. Prince Bertie had acquitted himself with more aplomb than anyone had expected, but it was the duchess who had truly won over the young country:

> The duchess has captured all hearts. Throughout the tour her charm has cast its spell upon the popular imagination, and in each city and state visited she has left behind her adoring multitudes to tell of how she smiled upon them. The people . . . were not proof against her fresh winsomeness, and capitulated without the slightest show of resistance. A charmingly demure figure, standing by the side of the duke, she smiled happily in response to the smiles and salutes of the people who passed four deep in slow procession before them at the public receptions.[31]

When the couple left Australia they took with them thousands of toys they had been given for baby Elizabeth. The presents weighed nearly three tonnes and included live animals and birds, not least thirty parrots, which made the *Renown* resemble a zoo:

A wireless from the *Renown* says that a floating zoo, though a trifle exaggerated, might serve as a description of the vessel. At present there are so many gifts of animals and birds made, not only to the Duke and Duchess of York, but also to the officers that the problem of dealing effectively with them is likely to become acute.[32]

There was also bedroom furniture for a dolls house made from local timber given by children of Tasmania, a giant doll from the Brownies in Launceston and a leather-bound bible with mounted silver kangaroos from the Tasmanian Bible Society. From New South Wales, little Elizabeth was given a toy gold and silver tea set engraved with an emu and kangaroo from the children of Cobar, a furry bear from Bombala and a linen embroidered frock from the women of Bathurst. From farmer's children in Western Australia she was given a drawing room suite made from local timbers. From the Melbourne Arts and Crafts Society she was given a Noah's ark filled with carved wooden animals and birds, and from the Women of Victoria, a gold and silver porridge bowl and spoon. Queensland children gave a large white velvet rabbit with pink satin ears and a decorated book of fairytales. The gifts from South Australia included children's playing blocks, a large silver plate and a tiny case of silk handkerchiefs.

There were so many toys, said *The Western Mail*, that when the royal couple reached London:

the town house of the Duke and Duchess of York, in Piccadilly, London [looks] almost like a museum. The larger pieces are placed in a roomy hall, whilst the quaint, carved curios and silver articles find a place in the many old cabinets belonging to the Duchess. Princess Elizabeth is allowed to play with some of the charming gifts sent home to her, but as yet she is too young for most of them, and these have been packed away until she can better appreciate them.[33]

—

In Britain, meanwhile, problems with Crown Prince Edward were coming to light. In the six years after the war, the prince had visited forty-five countries and travelled almost a quarter of a million kilometres. Since 1915, when he had first gone to France during the war, he had spent less than a third of his time in Britain. However, by 1927, and now thirty-two years old, he was confiding to his private secretary, Godfrey Thomas, and others who were close to him that he was tiring already of his role:

> It's just the chronic state of being Prince of Wales. I'm just so heartily and genuinely fed up. It's just so nerve-racking and distracting sometimes . . . that I could really go mad, and that wouldn't be suitable would it? I can put up with a certain amount of contact with officials and newspapers on official trips, when one is obviously on the job. It's when they get in on my personal life and trips that I want to pull out a gun and kill . . . I've got a lot older lately and don't look for excitement the way I used to. And I believe I'm more serious and conscientious over the less artificial side of my stunting than I was. But I have to go through too many artificial 'bulls'. I suppose some of it is inevitable, but I still rebel against it and I find it tricky.[34]

He was also being pressured to consider marriage and produce an heir. Traditionally, British monarchs would choose a spouse from one of the European royal families. This avenue was now closed, because of World War I and its outcome – Britain's prime minister David Lloyd George had advised Edward as early as 1920 that the country would no longer tolerate the king marrying a foreign princess.[35]

Despite the expectations of him, Edward was in no hurry, as he pointed out to his cousin Louis Mountbatten in the year he turned thirty:

> I'm getting quite an old bachelor now and a more confirmed one each year . . . tho' I'll have to take the fatal plunge one of these days, tho' I'll put it off as long as I can, cos' it'll destroy me.[36]

As the 1930s opened, Edward was a popular figure in Britain and the empire, but his excessive behaviour in private was increasingly concerning the palace and British officialdom. King George was appalled by his son's affairs and character, saying of his eldest son, 'After I am dead, the boy will ruin himself within twelve months.'[37] Yet there was still little public knowledge of any of this, and no scandalous reporting in the newspapers. Then, in January 1931, Edward met a wealthy American woman called Wallis Simpson. They were first introduced at Burrough Court in Leicestershire, a hunting lodge popular among gentry and the royal family. Though still in touch with Freda Dudley Ward, by now Edward was having an affair with Lady Thelma Furness, the daughter of an American diplomat, and at the time she and her husband were living at Burrough Court. Described as exquisitely pretty, glossy, elegant, good-natured and relentlessly frivolous, Lady Furness had been divorced once, and when Edward met her was on her second marriage, to Viscount Marmaduke Furness.

Thelma had invited her friend Wallis Simpson to stay one weekend, along with Prince Edward. At first the prince was apparently not much impressed by Wallis, but, according to Louis Mountbatten, within a few weeks they had become very close. In later years Edward always insisted that he did not have sex with Mrs Simpson until they were married in 1937, but in this he was contradicted by a number of former staff, who said they'd seen the couple in bed together shortly after they met. Alan Lascelles, who served for many years as Edward's assistant private secretary, said he would find it as easy to believe in the innocence of their relationship as in 'a herd of unicorns grazing in Hyde Park and a school of mermaids swimming in the Serpentine'.[38] Much later Mountbatten said that it was after the two of them went together to bed that '[Edward] lost all sense of reason'.[39]

Wallis Simpson was born in 1896 in Pennsylvania into a well-to-do family and aged twenty married US naval pilot Earl Winfield Spencer. During and after the war he had a number of overseas postings, and she and her husband were often apart, though she joined him for part of his tour of duty to China. By 1925 they were both back in America but living separately, and in 1927 they divorced. By the time her first marriage was dissolved, Wallis was involved with Ernest Simpson, an American-born shipping executive, who subsequently renounced his US citizenship to become a Briton, and divorced his wife to marry Wallis in 1928 and live with her in London.

Much to the consternation of British officialdom, the relationship between Wallis Simpson and Edward flourished and by the beginning of 1934 she was his mistress. In November 1934 Edward added his lover to the list of guests invited to a party at Buckingham Palace to celebrate the Duke of Kent's wedding. An enraged King George scratched his son's friend off the list, but Edward brought her anyway and introduced her to his mother.

By 1935 Mrs Simpson had become an embarrassment within the palace, but the affair was far from being a public scandal and only a handful of people in the British Isles – or

Australia – had heard of her. There remained a question mark over Edward's suitability for the kingship, but these doubts were discussed only among a close-knit group; the issues of his character and behaviour, and the existence of his mistress Mrs Simpson, only became a public crisis when King George V died on 20 January 1936.

The king was a heavy smoker and had been ill for some time with lung disease. He had taken to his bed a week or so before his death, lapsing in and out of consciousness. The London *Times* reported that just before he died he had asked his secretary,

> 'How is the empire?' An unusual phrase in that form, and the secretary said: 'All is well, sir, with the empire', and the king gave him a smile and relapsed once more into unconsciousness.[40]

There was an outpouring of grief in Australia for the loss of the king. The *Australian Women's Weekly* published a full-page painting of George on their front cover, with the headline 'World Mourns Our King', and inside described the 'poignant grief at the midnight announcement':

Empire Shares Royal Grief

> The heart of our mighty empire goes out to the royal family in its great grief. He was a king above men, a man above kings. The whole world mourns . . . On Edward, the new king, now devolves the duty of carrying on the high standard set by his beloved father.[41]

The initial response throughout the empire to the popular prince becoming King Edward VIII was overwhelmingly positive. Only three days after King George's death, Prime

Minister Stanley Baldwin told the House of Commons that Edward was perfectly qualified for the role of king:

> King Edward VIII brings to the altar of public service a personality richly endowed with the experience of public affairs, with the fruits of travel and immense good will. He has the secrets of youth in the prime of age. He has a wider and more intimate knowledge of all classes of his subjects . . . than any of his predecessors.[42]

The Australian newspapers were equally enthusiastic, pointing out that Edward had seen more of the empire than anyone else:

> Probably no King of England has ever ascended the throne better equipped for high office than His Majesty King Edward VIII, who commenced his reign on Tuesday 21 January . . . A man of good common sense, and experience beyond a lot of ordinary citizens in public matters, he has visited practically every important part of his far flung dominions and met people of various lands under his sway.[43]

The Sydney Morning Herald said:

> The new king has already found his way into the hearts of his people in a way that none of his predecessors have been able to accomplish . . . On his visits to all parts of the empire the prince was received with expressions of utmost loyalty, devotion and affection, and in no part more cordially and enthusiastically than when he visited Australia.[44]

Clive Wigram, who had been the private secretary to King George V, wrote to Lord Gowrie, the new governor-general to Australia, to reassure him of Edward's suitability:

No king could have a better start than King Edward. He is well known and the whole empire is solidly behind him. He is keenly interested in social problems and the working classes.[45]

Some of the Australian newspapers went even further:

Freed from any of the hidebound conventions of the past, he is able to get far closer to the spirit of democracy than any other Prince of Wales before him. He is able to live the fine, free life of an ordinary citizen and by that means he has earned for himself and the Crown a far more genuine affection and respect than any of his predecessors. In fact, it may be said of him that he is the chief instrument in the democratisation of the British monarchy.[46]

However, a number of those close to Edward continued to harbour grave concerns. Two weeks after Edward's ascension to the throne, Godfrey Thomas, who was Edward's private secretary until 1936, wrote prophetically in his diary:

[It is] my conviction that [Edward] is not fitted to be king and that his reign will end in disaster. Increased responsibility may work a miracle but I don't think he will last very long. One could prop up a façade for the Prince of Wales – not so easy for a king.[47]

—

Australia was to play a substantial role in Edward's abdication. Although British newspapers continually suppressed rumours of the king's social life, by November 1936 Australian newspapers, along with those in America and Canada, were giving one story some prominence: that the new king intended to marry Wallis Simpson, who was in the process of divorcing her second husband.

It was one thing for the king of England to have a mistress, and one who had already been married twice before, but it was altogether a different matter for him to marry her. At the time, the Australian high commissioner to London was Stanley Bruce. Bruce had become a close friend and confidant of British Prime Minister Baldwin, and in what rapidly unravelled into a constitutional crisis, Bruce believed Baldwin was being 'insufficiently firm' in confronting the issue of the king and Mrs Simpson.

On Sunday 15 November Bruce had lunch with Baldwin. The following day he set out in a letter the course he thought Baldwin should follow:

> There is no denying that there is sufficient evidence before you to show you that there is a possibility that the king may be contemplating marrying the woman. Being in such a position I suggest as prime minister you are compelled to put the question specifically to the king as to whether he has any such intention. If the answer was that he had such an intention then I think you would have to advise the king of what the consequences should be, e.g. that the people of this country and of the dominions would not accept this woman as queen and would demonstrate against both her and the king himself, that the House of Commons would probably take drastic action with regards to the civic list; that because of the perils both to the throne and the empire the king's conduct has created, there would be a demand for his abdication that he would find impossible to resist. In these circumstances you would have to tell him that unless he was prepared to abandon any ideas of marriage with the woman, you would be unable to continue as his adviser and would tender the resignation of the government.[48]

On the day he sent this letter, 16 November, the king summoned Prime Minister Baldwin and told him he was determined to marry Mrs Simpson. When Baldwin responded by telling the king that the people would never accept her as queen, Edward threatened to abdicate. Nine days later, on 25 November, Edward met with Baldwin again. This time he proposed that he be permitted a morganatic marriage, whereby Mrs Simpson would become his wife but his titles and privileges would not be passed on to her, or to any children they may have.

Prime Minister Baldwin consulted his cabinet and the leaders of the opposition parties, all of whom expressed opposition both to Mrs Simpson becoming queen and the idea of a morganatic marriage. Baldwin then told King Edward that he would also consult the dominions, as, he said, he was obliged to do.

South Africa, New Zealand and Canada were less emphatic than Australia, but none would endorse the proposal of the marriage. New Zealand hoped some 'arrangement might be possible' to avert abdication; South Africa suggested abdication was 'the lesser of two evils'; and Canada hoped the king would make the correct decision.[49] There was an interesting difference in public opinion between men and women in Canada. A sidewalk poll in Ottawa showed that 65 per cent of men said the king should be able to marry as he pleased, but 75 per cent of women thought the king should renounce Mrs Simpson.[50]

Australia remained implacable and put the final nail in the coffin. The prime minister, Joseph Lyons, cabled Baldwin to reiterate his view that Mrs Simpson becoming queen was out of the question, and so was the idea of a morganatic marriage:

There would be outspoken hostility to His Majesty's wife becoming queen, while any proposal that she should become consort and not queen ... would not be approved by my government.[51]

Five days later, on 10 December, King Edward VIII abdicated. Lyons expressed regret in a nationwide radio broadcast:

I feel sure that I am voicing the sentiments of every Australian when I express the most profound regret at the step which His Majesty King Edward has taken. We must all wish most heartily that he had acted otherwise.[52]

The following day Lyons told a packed parliament in Canberra that the Australian government had been consulted during the events of the past weeks, and explained that he had been in secret negotiations with Baldwin:

I ... communicated my view with Mr Baldwin, offering my personal view (since at that time the whole matter was highly secret and confidential), that the proposed marriage, if it had led to Mrs Simpson becoming queen, would provoke wide-spread condemnation, and that the alternative proposal or something in the nature of a specially sanctioned morganatic marriage would run counter to the best popular conceptions of the royal family.[53]

Lyons also told the parliament that Baldwin had conveyed the advice to King Edward. Lyons was supported in parliament by John Curtin, who was by now the opposition leader. Curtin began his speech on the matter by stressing the importance of the issue to the Australian people:

It would be idle to say that this is not a day of supreme importance to the people of Australia and the British Empire . . . We
are faced with the fact that the king abdicated because he
desires to marry Mrs. Simpson and in marrying her sought
that the law in respect of the marriage of the king should be
so altered that the wife would not be queen, and that any
children which should be born from that marriage would not
come into the first line of succession . . . I quite agree that the
course he contemplated was one which this parliament would
not support.

Lyons then asked the parliament to support passing a law
to bring into effect the king's abdication:

Any alteration to the law affecting the succession to the
throne . . . is a concern to every British dominion as well as
the UK. For that reason I am submitting to the house a resolution . . . that this house approves the legislation which has
already been introduced into the parliament of the UK giving
effect to the king's abdication.

Curtin said how sorry he was and stressed the popularity
of Edward:

I regret very much that His Majesty should have relinquished
the throne . . . He has made himself probably the most prominent and conspicuous symbol of the unity of the British
people. He has travelled throughout every part of the dominions. He knew the people of his dominions probably better
than anybody.[54]

The Australian newspapers reflected the sadness at the loss
of the monarch who had been such a popular prince:

Sorrow, occasioned by the circumstances which have brought about the abdication of King Edward VIII, will be felt by the 450 million subjects of the empire as no monarch commanded more affection and popularity throughout the realm which he reigned for so short a period. The people of the empire have followed with affectionate interest the former king's career – as a normal boy at school; as a slender and somewhat shy young man; as a youthful Galahad who sprang up the steps of the War Office and demanded to share in the trials and hardships of his fellow-countrymen; as a soldier who insisted on bearing his share of the burden of war; as a veteran beloved by his war comrades, and realising the true meaning of his affinity with them; as a reformer passionately desirous of improving the state of his less fortunate subjects; as a democrat, virile and independent in thought and action, and modest and sympathetic in character; as an ambassador of the empire; as the son of a great father; and finally, as a king-emperor. The former king's sunny personality, charm of manner, tact, and handsome appearance alone might have created for him some of the popularity which he enjoys, but his war record enthroned him as the national idol. The fact that he visited practically every territory which is part of the British Empire, and came into personal contact with his people, leaving the same spirit of unquenchable loyalty, helped further to entrench him deeply in the heart of the people. Wherever he has been, King Edward VIII knew no social differences, no racial divisions and no creeds. Whether he held court with ceremonial, wandered in the slum areas of London, played the part of a rancher, chased kangaroos with Australian stockmen, visited the poor homes of the Clyde side, held grave converse with veteran Hindu or dignified Chinese, whatever the role assigned to him by life he remained always the same smiling, deeply interested young man.[55]

Shortly after announcing his abdication, King Edward left England and joined Mrs Simpson in France, where she had fled at the height of the crisis.

At 11.30 am on 11 December 1936, the day after Edward had signed the abdication papers, his younger brother, Prince Albert Frederick Arthur George, was sworn in as King George VI at St James's Palace in London, just days before his forty-first birthday.

The press in Australia were quick to enthuse loyally about the new monarch:

> Everybody, in their hearts, is saluting the new king. We praise him. We love him. With a fervour hundred fold greater than we should have felt had he succeeded in due season, we hail the king who, when the bottom of our world seemed to be falling out, sustained the succession, and reminded us the moment he showed himself to the people, how much greater is the monarchy than the monarch.[56]

They pointed out that Australia's fidelity was to the monarchy rather than to a particular monarch:

> 1936 will be remarkable in history as the year of the three kings. The death of George V brought Edward VIII to the throne and Edward's recent abdication gave the succession to George VI. The dramatic circumstances of the abdication are too recent to call for discussion. Suffice it to say that this unexampled occurrence has not weakened, in Australia or elsewhere, sincere loyalty to the king or reverence for all that he represents. It has, however, demonstrated the superiority of the monarchy over the monarch.[57]

Although Edward had been possibly the most popular royal family member to have visited Australia, the public quickly embraced King George VI; and in spite of the crisis that had beset the Windsors for the first months of Edward VIII's ill-fated reign, it seemed little long-term damage had been done to the ties between Australia and the British monarchy.

Less than three years after the abdication, Australia's loyalty to the Crown was again demonstrated when the nation followed Britain into a second, catastrophic world war.

II

WORLD WAR II

Fellow Australians, it is my melancholy duty to inform you officially that in consequence of persistence by Germany in her invasion of Poland, Great Britain has declared war upon her and that, as a result, Australia is also at war.

IN SEPTEMBER 1939, THREE years after the constitutional crisis caused by Edward's abdication, Germany invaded Poland. France and Britain insisted Germany withdraw, and when their ultimatum was ignored by Adolf Hitler, both countries declared war. World War II was to cause a shift in Australian foreign policy from being focused almost solely on Great Britain to looking to the United States for strategic support. Nonetheless, by the end of the war, and in the years that followed, the relationship between the Australian people and the British monarchy continued to be as strong as ever.

At 11.15 am on Sunday 3 September, British prime minister Neville Chamberlain announced on BBC radio:

This morning the British ambassador in Berlin handed the German government a final note stating that, unless we heard from them by eleven o'clock that they were prepared at once to withdraw their troops from Poland, a state of war would exist between us. I have to tell you now that no such undertaking has been received, and that consequently this country is at war with Germany.[1]

Shortly after this announcement a speech by King George VI was broadcast, calling on all the empire's dominions to join the war effort:

In this grave hour, perhaps the most fateful in our history, I send to every household of my peoples, both at home and overseas, this message, spoken with the same depth of feeling for each one of you as if I were able to cross your threshold and speak to you myself . . . for we are called, with our allies, to meet the challenge of a principle which, if it were to prevail, would be fatal to any civilised order in the world.[2]

That evening at 9.15 pm in Australia, Australian prime minister Robert Menzies committed Australia to the war declared by Chamberlain, broadcasting the announcements on every radio station:

Fellow Australians, it is my melancholy duty to inform you officially that in consequence of persistence by Germany in her invasion of Poland, Great Britain has declared war upon her and that, as a result, Australia is also at war. No harder task can fall to the lot of a democratic leader than to make such an announcement. Great Britain and France, with the cooperation of the British dominions, have struggled to avoid this tragedy . . . I know that, in spite of the emotions we are all feeling, you will show that Australia is ready to see it through.[3]

Menzies had been prime minister for only five months when war broke out, having been voted by his colleagues to replace Joseph Lyons, who had died of a heart attack in April 1939. Menzies was born in 1894 in the tiny township of Jeparit in Victoria, the fourth of five children and the son of a storekeeper and lay preacher. After local schooling he showed himself as a brilliant scholar at the University of Melbourne, from where he graduated in law and became a barrister in 1918. At thirty-four years of age he entered the Victorian parliament, six years later switching to federal parliament in the safe conservative Melbourne constituency of Kooyong, a seat he held for the next thirty-two years. In August 1938, while he was Australia's attorney-general, Menzies went to Germany and was struck by Hitler's strenuous efforts to reverse the oppressive terms of the Versailles treaty. In the months after his return to Australia, Menzies strongly supported the appeasement policies of the Chamberlain government towards Hitler, which he hoped would prevent Europe from falling back into war.

Despite this, during his speech to Australia on 3 September, Menzies made it clear that Australia's following Britain was unquestionable, stating, 'There can be no doubt that where Great Britain stands there stand the people of the entire British world.' The next day he sent a telegram to Chamberlain:

> Your broadcast message moved Australia deeply. We ourselves have proclaimed a state of war and I have broadcast on behalf of the Commonwealth government that we stand for Great Britain. We firmly believe we have right on our side and in that strength victory is sure.[4]

Between the inauguration of Australian federation in 1901 and the declaration of this war in 1939, there had been a number of essentially symbolic moves by Australia to try to shape its own destiny, but to a large extent the country remained dependent on Britain for both its military and the management of its international relations. This sense of dependence was underwritten by a feeling that the 'superior wisdom of Westminster and Whitehall permeated the Australian ruling orders', fed amply by memories of the Great War and, now, fears of Australian vulnerability in the war to come.[5] At the outbreak of the war, Australia had a tiny Department of External Affairs with 'half a dozen officers with little experience in international diplomacy' and no overseas diplomatic offices.[6] It totally depended on the British for international representation to other countries and for assessments of international events and any potential military threats to Australia.

When Menzies declared Australia at war with Germany, there were no loud voices of dissent. No one pointed out that since World War I, the 1931 Statute of Westminster had given parliaments in the dominions the right to make their own decisions, nor questioned whether simply because England had declared war, the whole empire must automatically be at war.

The Labor opposition had been delivered a fait accompli. Its leader John Curtin had called for the parliament to be consulted on whether Australia should go to war, but in the end Labor was forced to go along with Menzies for fear of being seen as disloyal to Great Britain. On 10 September and after a party caucus meeting, Curtin told the federal parliament that Labor would support the declaration:

In this crisis, facing the reality of war, the Labor Party . . . stands for the maintenance of Australia as an integral part of the British Commonwealth of Nations. Therefore the party will do all that is possible to safeguard Australia, and at the same time, having regard to its platform, will do its utmost to maintain the integrity of the British Commonwealth.[7]

The pro-Labor *Catholic Worker* newspaper was one of the few voices that did question Australia's unstinting loyalty to Britain. On the day before the declaration of war it editorialised that Australia

> must not participate in a European War simply because England is involved. This is not any deviation of loyalty to Great Britain. It is simply a statement that in these realistic days the loyalty of Australians is first of all to Australia.[8]

There was a decided lack of public excitement in Australia at the prospect of another war, in stark contrast to the reaction that had greeted the declaration of World War I in 1914. The country was totally unprepared. In 1939 its army consisted of only 3000 regular soldiers and about 80,000 reservists in the Civilian Military Force, who were ill-equipped and scarcely trained.[9] As well as few soldiers, the nation had a serious shortage of weapons and munitions and possessed practically no modern artillery, tanks, anti-aircraft guns or fighter or bomber planes capable of engaging a formidable enemy, and the Australian Navy had too few ships to thwart any serious invasion threat to Australia's shores.[10]

Britain wanted as many troops as Australia could provide. However, from the outset senior Australian Army chiefs of staff felt insecure about Japan's intentions, and recommended postponing any decision to send Australian troops to Europe till the end of 1939. At the time, Japan already occupied territories in Asia, and had done so for several decades.

Winston Churchill, the first lord of the admiralty in

Neville Chamberlain's government, assured Australia that Japan was not a threat. In an assessment in November 1939 of the military risk to Australia, Churchill said there was no sign of any hostile action or intent from Japan and there was unlikely to be as long as the Royal Navy was undefeated and the empire controlled Singapore. He reassured Menzies that in the event of Japan becoming a threat to Australia, Britain would come to the rescue:

> If the choice were presented of defending Australia against serious attack, or sacrificing British interests in the Mediterranean, our duty to Australia would take precedence.[11]

Armed with these assurances, but still nervous about leaving Australia's defences denuded, a divided Australian cabinet agreed in November 1939 to send a division of soldiers to Europe early the following year. The Menzies government also agreed to a British scheme to recruit and train Australian air crews for the Royal Air Force, which ended any realistic hope of Australia building up its own air defences.

From then on the bulk of Australia's military effort was directed to recruiting, training, equipping and reinforcing an expeditionary force for overseas service, rather than building up the defences of the Australian continent. Australia's vulnerability to the north was made greater by the diversion of British navy ships from the Indian and Pacific Oceans to the Mediterranean and the Atlantic, where there was a greater need for them.

In January 1940 a total of 13,000 soldiers from the Australian 6th Division began embarking Australian ships in Sydney to be escorted by British warships, including the HMS *Ramillies* for the voyage across the Indian Ocean for training in Palestine, before joining up with the British

Expeditionary Force in France. However, in May 1940 Winston Churchill became British prime minister and increasingly assumed command of the empire war effort. Then in June Germany overran France, so the Australians destined for Europe spent more than two years fighting in the North African campaign. By the end of 1940, almost 50,000 Australian soldiers were overseas, and almost 90 per cent of them were in Egypt and Palestine.[12] In December of that year Australians were involved in attacks on the Italian armies in the Western Desert, where they captured over 40,000 prisoners in Sidi Barrani and Bardia.

Around this time Prime Minister Menzies decided to travel to London to talk directly with Churchill, the war cabinet and the senior British defence chiefs about the war, including the 'alarming position in regard to the defence of Singapore'.[13] It had been Menzies' intention that Australia's interests be given more consideration, yet no Australian felt a greater responsibility to the British Empire than Menzies. He was one of the generation who still felt Britain was 'home' even for those who were destined to live in the far-flung British Empire, and he did more than any other politician to strengthen Australian ties with Britain and the royal family in the twentieth century.

Menzies left Sydney on 24 January 1941 on a Qantas flying boat and took two days to reach Darwin. Over the next four weeks he visited the Dutch East Indies (Indonesia), Singapore, Thailand, Burma, India, Baghdad, and Palestine and Cairo, where he met with Australian troops. He finally reached England on 20 February.

Menzies had visited Britain twice before in the 1930s and was enchanted by the country. On this visit as prime minister, he met with the king and the royal family, and with Churchill and many leading politicians and military elite. He was invited to attend several British war cabinet meetings. His speeches were regularly reported in *The Times* and *The Daily Telegraph*; in fact, he appeared almost more popular in Britain than he was in Australia. He stayed in the best suite at the Dorchester Hotel and his diary is peppered with references to parties, weekends, lunches and dinners with the aristocracy and assorted celebrities, including Noël Coward, David Lloyd George, John Maynard Keynes, Lady Astor, the Duke and Duchess of Kent, American special envoy W. Averell Harriman and Countess Margot Asquith.

In his diary Menzies described vividly his first encounter with Winston Churchill at the British prime minister's official country residence of Chequers, when Churchill appeared in a blue jumpsuit with a zip from the crotch to the collar:

> Winston enters wearing what is called a Siren Suit, a dull blue woolen overall, with a zip fastener up the front. 'As Worn', I believe, for the sudden alarm and retreat to the basement. As a form of pre-prandial costume it mystified me because he later appeared at dinner in the white shirt of convention and forgot all about air raids till 2 a.m.[14]

Menzies was nevertheless charmed by Churchill and seduced by his belief in the inevitability of an Allied victory:

> Churchill grows on me. He has an astonishing grasp on detail and by daily contact with the service headquarters knows of disposition and establishments quite accurately. But I still feel that . . . his real tyrant is the glittering phrase so attractive to his mind that facts may have to give way. But this is the defect of his quality . . . it becomes something much better when the conclusion is that you are going to win the war,

and that you are damned if anything is going to stand in your way. Churchill's course is set. There is no defeat in his heart.[15]

Although captivated by his host, Menzies also recorded some less flattering observations in his diary during his weekend at Chequers:

> What a tempestuous creature he is; pacing up and down the room, always as if about to dart out of it, and then suddenly returning. Oratorical, even in conversation. The master of the mordant phrase and yet, I would think, almost without real humour. Enjoys hatred.[16]

On another occasion he described Churchill's dominance and bullying over his ministerial colleagues and military chiefs: 'All Military and service heads look and sound like 6th form boys in the presence of the headmaster.'[17]

Immediately after the weekend at Chequers, Menzies went to Windsor Castle for dinner ('a trois') with King George VI and the queen. Menzies said King George 'showed no trace of stammer and speaks often loudly with a kind of excitement', while the queen 'looks older but as fascinating as ever'.[18] The following morning in the courtyard of Windsor Castle he had his photograph taken with various members of the royal family, including Princess Elizabeth, who was fourteen years old by now, and whom Menzies described as 'much smaller and shyer than I expected, but natural'.[19]

A true conservative, Menzies was more impressed with the monarchy and Churchill than he was with those in the British Labour Party who were members of Churchill's war cabinet. He felt the best of them was the Labour leader Clement Attlee, whom he said was 'amiable but otherwise a confused Sunday School superintendent' though he later conceded that Attlee was 'earnest, intelligent and upright'.[20]

I already weary of the Socialist Ministers. They are so busy abusing 'the old gang' for our unreadiness that they have forgotten their old bad policy of sanctions of Bows and Arrows. God save us from the doctrinal democrats.[21]

Menzies found King George VI was deeply admired in Britain for refusing to leave London during the Blitz. Day after day the shy, nervous king walked through the bombed ruins of London homes with the queen, talking to homeless survivors. The king also gained plaudits when Buckingham Palace itself was bombed, while he and the queen were in residence. George and Elizabeth could have moved to any number of safer places outside London, including Windsor, or Sandringham in Norfolk, but by staying in Buckingham Palace with their daughters, Princess Elizabeth and her younger sister Princess Margaret, the king appeared to be sharing the suffering of his subjects. Photographs published in Australian papers later in the war of a uniformed Princess Elizabeth changing a truck tyre and knitting garments for servicemen helped to promote an image of the royal family's contribution to the war effort.

Menzies wanted but failed to receive clear assurances that Britain would cut its commitment in the Mediterranean if Australia was being threatened by Japan. In his diary he expressed his frustration when these were not forthcoming: 'What does "cutting our losses in the Mediterranean and going to your assistance" mean? Nobody knows.'[22] Instead, he was fobbed off with what proved to be a serious underestimation of Japan's military capabilities. In a conversation about the defence of Singapore, Acting Vice Admiral Sir Tom Phillips told Menzies that the Royal Navy would be happy to attack the Japanese navy with a fleet only 60 per cent of the size of the enemy force. Menzies was also told that Singapore was being 'heavily fortified' with British air fighters and that based on what was known of the war in China, 'the Jap is a pretty poor airman'.[23]

In London Menzies also met with Charles de Gaulle, the leader of the Free French movement, whom Menzies dubbed:

> the reverse of the small voluble Frenchman of fiction or the music hall stage ... He is very tall, with sad features – a heavy nose and a weakish chin, but I think a good mouth.[24]

After two and a half months in England, having extended his initial stay by two weeks despite anxious warnings from his wife that political plots against him at home required his early return, the most significant outcome of Menzies' visit was his compliance in Australia's involvement in military campaigns in Greece and Crete. Churchill had been arguing for an Allied force to cross the Mediterranean from North Africa and block the German and Italian forces who were at the time taking the lower Balkans and Greece. He had persuaded the Australian prime minister to divert Australian troops from North Africa to Greece. Menzies cabled his cabinet colleagues in Australia to convince them to back the venture:

> The military arguments are fairly well balanced ... you will have in mind that the enterprise is risky ... Politically, the argument is, I think, strongly in favour of the undertaking ... A bold move into Greece might possibly bring Yugoslavia and Turkey in, with the result that a strong Balkan front could be established.[25]

He acknowledged that the shift of Australian troops to Greece would deplete the force in North Africa, but said he had been given assurances by senior British military officers that the venture was sound. Italy had invaded Greece the previous October but the local Greek army had been able to repel the attack and counterattack in March 1941. But on 6 April German troops opened a second front when they poured over the Greek border from the north and within a week forced the Allies into retreat. The Allied forces were outnumbered and lacked the air power of the enemy. The more experienced Australian 6th Division was sent to the front first, but the whole expedition collapsed within three weeks and before the 7th Division could be landed. The campaign was ill-planned and hampered by poor communications, a primitive road and rail system, difficult terrain and the overwhelming speed of the German advance.

Later it was said that Churchill's gambit had been 'wilder than Gallipoli'.[26] The occupation of the Thermopylae pass by Australian troops was merely a temporary delay in the retreat down to Athens. On the night of 24 April, and for the next five nights, more than 50,000 Allied troops were evacuated in ships off the southern Greek coast in what was an echo of Dunkirk the year before. Of the 17,000 Australians who landed in Greece, 320 were killed, 500 wounded and more than 2000 were taken prisoner. The New Zealand losses were similar: 300 were killed, 600 wounded and 1600 taken prisoner. Of the 22,000 British troops, 150 were killed, 100 wounded and 6500 taken prisoner.[27]

Churchill then ordered the defence of the island of Crete, which was overrun within ten days when the Germans had landed more than 22,000 paratroopers and gliders along the island's coast. 'Victory in Crete is essential at this turning point of the war,' said Churchill, and he had ordered, 'keep hurling in all aid you can'. After the overwhelming German victory, 3000 Australians were among the 15,000 Allied troops left behind in Crete to be taken prisoner by the Germans.[28]

Menzies was still in London at the end of April when he received the news of the disaster looming in Greece, and he blamed the military advice he received from Britain's generals Sir John Dill and Sir Archibald Wavell: 'I am afraid of a disaster and understand less why Dill and Wavell advised the Greek adventure had military merit.'[29]

He finally left England on 3 May. He flew first to Lisbon, where he met President Salazar ('almost a dictator') and attended a bullfight ('a spectacle of colour, swank and cruelty. Worth seeing once') before flying across the Atlantic via the Azores and Bermuda to America.[30] In Canada he met with Prime Minister Mackenzie King, who, Menzies believed, was even less popular in Canada than he himself was in Australia.[31] In Washington he met with senior US advisers and had his only ever meeting with President Franklin Roosevelt. The hour-long meeting was at Roosevelt's bedside as the president was ill with gastritis. Menzies commented that he 'looked older and more tired' but was able to engage in a 'vigorous discussion'.[32] Again, the Australian was unable to extract any concrete commitments from the Americans in the event of an attack by the Japanese; nonetheless, he felt they 'will not stand by and see Australia attacked'.[33]

Menzies arrived back in Australia on 24 May, returning, as his wife had warned, into political hostility. Within his own party there were rumblings that he had become arrogant and unpopular with the public, and, unable to shore up his position when he failed to persuade the Labor opposition to join a national united government, he resigned as leader of the United Australia Party on 28 August in favour of his coalition partner and deputy Arthur Fadden of the Country Party.[34] But after only forty days Fadden lost the support of two key independents in parliament and was also forced to resign.

On 7 October Labor's John Curtin became prime minister, and the day after being sworn into office he cabled Churchill to reassure him of Australia's ongoing commitment to the British Empire. A Labor government, he said, would 'cooperate fully in all matters associated with the welfare of the empire' and would 'play our part in bringing victory to the empire and our allies'.[35]

Almost immediately, however, Curtin was urging the British to relieve the Australian 9th Division who had been pinned down in the siege of Tobruk in North Africa. Both Menzies and Fadden had asked that the Australian soldiers be rested from the front, based on recommendations of the Australian war chiefs who were in North Africa at the time. The Australian 9th Division had been continually engaged on the front line for nearly four months in what were the toughest climatic conditions to be experienced by any Allied forces for such an extended period. Australia's most senior officer, General Thomas Blamey, reported that the men lost on average more than a stone (six kilograms) in weight.

Some of the Australians had been withdrawn, but Churchill had repeatedly tried to prevent the rest from being relieved. In a cable to Artie Fadden only a week before Fadden was replaced as prime minister, Churchill implied the withdrawal of the Australian troops would jeopardise the entire North African campaign:

> I still hope that you will reconsider your decision that the last two brigades [of the 9th Division] might be pulled out of Tobruk without reference to the impending operation by which we hope all will be relieved.[36]

A week later, Churchill tried the same tactic with Curtin, cabling that it would be 'greatly helped if the remaining

Australians could stay in Tobruk until the result of the approaching battle is decided'. Curtin, however, stuck with the views of his predecessors and with the recommendations of the Australian high command, and the Australian troops were finally withdrawn in mid-November 1941.

Only weeks after the relief of the Australian troops from Tobruk, on 7 December the Japanese attacked Pearl Harbor, which finally brought America into the war and dramatically heightened Australia's fear of invasion and anxiety about its lack of home defences.

Curtin announced that Australia had declared war against Japan at 11.30 am on 9 December 1941, less than eleven hours after President Franklin Roosevelt's declaration of war in a radio broadcast on 8 December:

> Men and women of Australia, we are at war with Japan. That has happened because, in the first instance, Japanese naval and air forces launched an unprovoked attack on British and United States territory; because our vital interests are imperiled and because the rights of free people in the whole Pacific are assailed. As a result, the Australian government this afternoon took the necessary steps which will mean that a state of war exists between Australia and Japan. Tomorrow, in common with the United Kingdom, the United States of America and the Netherlands East Indies governments, the Australian government will formally and solemnly declare the state of war it has striven so sincerely and strenuously to avoid.[37]

It was the first time in its history that Australia had declared war as a nation standing alone, the first time it had committed to conflict without following Great Britain's lead. On the same day, Curtin cabled the Australian high commissioner in London asking him to formally advise King

George VI of his actions, taken on advice of his Australian ministers.

At the same time as the attack on Pearl Harbor, the Japanese embarked on a series of seemingly unstoppable invasions of large parts of South-East Asia and the Pacific. Over the next six months their troops attacked southern China, Hong Kong, Malaysia, the Philippines, the Dutch East Indies (Indonesia), French Indochina (Vietnam, Laos, Cambodia), Thailand, Burma, Singapore, Papua New Guinea and large parts of the Pacific.

Two months before Pearl Harbor the British had sent two of their most powerful battleships, the *Prince of Wales* and the *Repulse*, to Singapore with the object of further deterring Japan.[38] Churchill had boasted to Roosevelt that the recently commissioned *Prince of Wales* could 'catch and kill any Japanese ship'.[39] Critically, however, the two great warships had no air cover, and on 10 December they were both sunk by Japanese planes dropping bombs and torpedoes. It was the first time battleships had been sunk from the air, and the attack left the Allies with no capital ships in the Indian and Pacific oceans except for the American vessels that had survived the bombing raid at Pearl Harbor and were now heading to California for repairs.

Singapore was now even more vulnerable, and an anxious Curtin was worried enough to write two days before Christmas to both Winston Churchill and Franklin Roosevelt, urging the two leaders, who were currently meeting in Washington, to send increased air support:

At this time of great crisis I desire to address you both . . . [on] a matter of more pressing importance. From all reports, it is very evident that in North Malaya, the Japanese have assumed control of our air and sea. The small British army there includes one Australian division . . . The army must be provided with air support, otherwise there will be a repetition of Greece and Crete, and Singapore will be grievously threatened.[40]

On Christmas Day, Churchill wrote back to Curtin saying that a plan was being devised for sending planes and tanks to Singapore but only when 'the situation in Libya permits'.[41] The Australian prime minister then composed a New Year message to the people of Australia that was published in *The Herald* and *The Weekly Times* on 27 December. It was an historic turning point. In it Curtin pointed out that if Australia continued to follow Britain in the war, the continent could fall to the enemy while Britain could hang on. He announced that Australia would therefore shift its focus to the Pacific – away from its traditional protector to its new ally, America, which in future would be Australia's 'keystone':

We refuse to accept the dictum that the Pacific struggle must be treated as a subordinate segment of the general conflict . . . Australia asks for a concerted plan . . . determined upon hurling Japan back . . . The Australian government, therefore, regards the Pacific struggle as primarily one in which the United States and Australia must have the fullest say in the direction of the democracies' fighting plan. Without any inhibitions of any kind I make it clear that Australia looks to America, free of any pangs as to our traditional links or kinship with the United Kingdom.[42]

We know the problems that the United Kingdom faces. We know the constant threat of invasion . . . but we know too, that Australia can go and Britain can still hold on. We are, therefore, determined that Australia shall not go, and we shall exert all our energies towards shaping a plan, with the United States as its keystone, which will give to our country some confidence of being able to hold out until the tide of battle swings against the enemy.[43]

The Japanese 25th Army had begun their sweep south-wards down the Malayan Peninsula on 8 December 1941. Although outnumbered by more than three to one by Allied troops, the Japanese were vastly superior in coordination and tactics, and they possessed better equipment, which included tanks and greater air-strike capacity. They were also more experienced – many of the Allied soldiers had never seen combat.

By the end of the first week in January, with a combination of speed and savagery, the Japanese had overrun British and Indian army resistance and controlled all of the northern Malay Peninsula. By mid-January they had reached the southern end of the peninsula and engaged the Australian troops for the first time.

On 27 January 1942 Sir Archibald Wavell, the commander of the Allied forces based in Java, authorised General Arthur Percival, the commander of the British Commonwealth's forces, to withdraw all the Allied forces to the island of Singapore, blowing up the bridge across the causeway that separated the island from Malaya as they retreated. A total of 50,000 Allied soldiers had been killed or captured in the short Malay campaign.

The Japanese began bombarding the city of Singapore using artillery from Johore as well as long-range bomber planes flying missions from bases in Indochina. Churchill ordered that Singapore should be held at all costs:

The whole island must be fought for until every single unit and every single strong point has been separately destroyed. The city of Singapore must be converted into a citadel and defended to the death. No surrender can be contemplated.[44]

At the end of the first week of February, Japanese troops were crossing the causeway in inflatable boats and outflanking the island's defenders. Within a week they had reached the outskirts of the city, which was also being heavily bombed by Japanese planes. On 14 February the Japanese took the Alexandra Barracks Hospital and, in a chilling demonstration of their brutality, killed more than 200 patients and hospital staff. The next morning General Arthur Percival met with his senior officers and decided to capitulate. Later the same afternoon they were ordered to the local Ford Motor factory, where Percival accepted terms of unconditional surrender from the Japanese General Tomoyuki Yamashita.

The Japanese had taken Singapore and nearly 100,000 Allied prisoners with relative ease. Over the next few years 9000 Allied prisoners of war would die in the hands of their brutal captors and as slave labourers on the construction of the Thai-Burma railway.

The fall of Singapore was of great significance in the war. It was the biggest and most humiliating defeat of the British Army. It was to be the end of the British Empire's historic dominance in the Far East. It was the end of the unquestioned British leadership of Australian troops, and the end of Australia's military ties to the mother country. Australians were now increasingly anxious that Japan would invade their country. First, the Japanese invaded Papua New Guinea, immediately to Australia's north; then, only four days after the surrender of Singapore, a large force of Japanese planes began bombing Darwin. One hundred and eighty-eight planes attacked Darwin on the first day of the attacks, dropping more bombs than were dropped on Pearl Harbor, sinking eight ships and killing 243 people, many of them civilians.[45]

For the next eighteen months, Japan bombed a total of fourteen targets on the north Australian coast, from Port

Hedland and Broome in Western Australia to Mossman and Townsville in Queensland. Curtin now called for the return of all Australian troops from North Africa and Europe for the defence of their own country, and he worked with the Americans to fortify Australia as a base for pushing back the Japanese.

The first 4500 American soldiers had sailed from San Francisco and arrived in Brisbane on 22 December 1941. Over the next four years almost one million Americans would pass through Australia on their way to fighting the Japanese further to the north.

On 13 March 1942 Curtin broadcast a radio message to America that illustrated the shift of Australian focus:

> With the growing assistance of the United States of America, we shall one day go out and drive the enemy from the positions from which he now menaces our security, challenges the lifelines of the British Empire, and endangers democracy in the Pacific and in the world.[46]

Australia had agreed with the United States that all the Australian troops in the Pacific War would fight under the control of American military command. Initially they were led by Air Force General George H. Brett, but soon he was replaced by General Douglas MacArthur, who had been commander of the US Army in the Philippines before the country had fallen to the Japanese in April 1942.

Australia's defence forces were placed under the command of MacArthur, who became commander of all the naval, military and air forces in the south-west Pacific. The most senior Australian officer, General Thomas Blamey, led the Australian land forces under MacArthur's overall command. Although Australia's land forces were able to defeat the Japanese at Milne Bay and on the Kokoda

Track, their significance then faded as US forces began to be brought in in greater numbers to the Pacific.[47] The first checks to the phenomenal Japanese advance were the battles of the Coral Sea, Midway and Guadalcanal. The Battle of the Coral Sea took place five months after Pearl Harbor between the Japanese and the combined American and Australian naval and air forces more than 2000 kilometres off the north-east coast of Australia. There was no clear winner, but the battle halted the Japanese advance in Asia and the Pacific, and meant that the two damaged aircraft carriers, *Shokaku* and *Zuikaku*, weren't available for the next crucial air and naval battle at Midway the following month.

The Battle of Midway between 3 and 7 June 1942 resulted in a decisive victory for the United States, which dramatically reduced Japanese naval dominance in the Pacific and its capacity for further naval offensives. Two months later, the two sides clashed again to gain control of the island of Guadalcanal. On 7 August the Allies began landing 60,000 troops, mainly American and Australian, with some from New Zealand and Britain, and in a bloody six months of desperate fighting, on the sea, land and in the air, more than 90 per cent of the 36,000 Japanese defenders were killed and 683 Japanese planes lost. The allies had over 7000 men killed and lost 615 planes.[48]

Guadalcanal marked the end of Japanese territorial expansion in Asia and the Pacific. It also heralded the end of the Allies as defenders and the beginning of the offensive that over the next three years saw the Japanese progressively rolled back through Asia and the Pacific. By June 1943, Curtin was able to declare Australia was at last 'out of danger'.[49]

—

Australia had a new strategic partner, but its love of the royal family remained strong, and the relationship was further cemented towards the end of the war by the announcement that for the first time a member of the royal family was to become the Australian governor-general. In late 1943 Curtin announced that the Duke of Gloucester was to replace Lord Gowrie, whose vice-regal term had been extended because of the war. The duke was the third son of King George V and the younger brother of Edward VIII and King George VI. He was no stranger to Australia, having visited in 1934, when he toured each state while attending the centenary celebrations in Victoria.

According to the press, there was much resistance within the Labor government to recommending a non-Australian for the position of governor-general. Many Labor members of parliament believed a precedent had been set back in 1930 when James Scullin's Labor government had resisted pressure from King George V by insisting on nominating the Australian Sir Isaac Isaacs to fill the position:

> The appointment of Gloucester as Governor-General of Australia will be the basis for keen discussion at the federal ALP conference in Sydney on December 13. Many delegates are likely to attack the government for having acquiesced in the recommendation of a former Ministry in suggesting appointment of an overseas person. It was mentioned in Labour [sic] circles yesterday that for several years this has been the policy of the party that an Australian-born resident be appointed to such positions. Agreement to appointment of the Duke of Gloucester, it was claimed, was not in accord with Labour [sic] policy.[50]

Some Labor members also pointed to the duke's well-known drinking problem. But Curtin and his supporters stuck to their guns, believing the appointment of a member of the royal family 'reaffirmed the supreme importance of the Crown as the centre and symbol of crown unity' in Australia.[51]

—

Prime Minister John Curtin was very different from his predecessor, Robert Menzies. Born in Creswick, Victoria, into a poor family, the son of an Irish prison warder, soldier and policeman, he was raised Roman Catholic and left school at thirteen to work on a local newspaper. He soon became active in the Australian Labor Party and the Victorian Socialist Party. At the outbreak of World War I he was secretary of the Timberworkers' Union and a campaigner against military conscription. In 1917 he married Elsie Needham and moved to Perth to become the local editor of the trade union newspaper *The Westralian Worker*. He first became the federal Labor MP for Fremantle in 1928 but was kept out of James Scullin's cabinet because of his heavy drinking, which plagued him for much of his career. Curtin lost his seat in the 1931 election but won it back in 1934 before becoming party leader the following year after promising his colleagues that he would quit drinking.[52]

Like many of his Labor colleagues, Curtin was a frugal man who dressed plainly. Previous Australian prime ministers such as Menzies and Stanley Bruce had trunks of clothes looked after by valets accompany them on overseas tours, including 'morning suits, full evening dress and court dress'.[53] Curtin famously packed his own suitcase, which he carried himself. His limited wardrobe was the subject of fairly extensive reporting in the Australian press:

His wardrobe appears to consist of a brown tweed suit, which he calls his 'heavy suit'; a neat blue suit with a thin white

pencil stripe, known as his 'Roosevelt suit'; a dark blue suit,
unrelieved by any pattern, very severe in cut, worn on formal
occasions . . . A pair of white duck trousers, extremely aged,
a bit short, worn at weekends and on sporting occasions. Two
hats, one blue and good, the other grey, and not so good.
Two overcoats, again one good, the other not so good. Two
pairs of shoes, the one black, the other brown. A dinner suit,
rather old-fashioned in cut, a faithful friend of many years.
Curtin never wears colored shirts, always white, with a stiff
collar-and plain ties, of which he is reported to have six
dark-coloured socks of the well-known variety that have red
lettering across the top.[54]

He was proud of his austere wardrobe and once joked at
a press conference that he was the 'worst dressed' person
present. When he visited the United States in April 1944
and attended an official dinner in Washington, he was
reportedly wearing the same blue suit he'd had on ever since
arriving in America.

After meeting President Roosevelt in South Carolina in
late April, Curtin described in a radio interview how far
Australia had shifted towards America and away from
Britain:

On behalf of the Australian people I expressed to the president the warm and lasting gratitude which is owed to the
people of the United States for the aid given in the preserva-
tion of our country from the aggression of Japan . . . So when
I am asked what I contemplate will be the future relations of
America and Australia I say that my country is comparatively
small; that it must look in the future for such agreements
and understandings that will safeguard it, not only against
aggression, but also against the inflictions of misery and
human degradation suffered during the economic depression

of fifteen years ago. Australia will look to the United States in the future, as it will look to the other great powers with the greater resources, to work out, internationally, the salvation of human beings.[55]

From the United States, Curtin flew to Britain to attend a meeting in May of prime ministers of the British Commonwealth to discuss 'a wide variety of important matters connected with the future conduct of the war and affecting the British Commonwealth', according to the press release from the Dominions Office. When he landed, Curtin told waiting reporters:

> The first thing is to express the unbounded admiration and gratitude of the people of Australia to the people of Britain for having stood alone in the ramparts of civilisation and holding the fort that is about to become the most unforgettable part of the proud story of this land. We Australians are grateful because holding the fort meant not only holding it for us, but for all the hopes of the future, and when I speak of Australians, I speak of seven million Britishers . . . The British Commonwealth can render a great service to civilisation by the development of the fullest co-operation between its members. From their experience as units in the greater unity, they can make a contribution to the wider circle in international co-operation.[56]

While he was in London, as the war in the Pacific finally seemed to be near to an end, the Australian press was able to report that, despite Australia's shifting allegiances:

> the British throne still stands, its value again wonderfully demonstrated, and its foundations still further strengthened. The people of Australia, in common with those of the other

self-governing dominions of the empire, have no less cause than their kinsmen in the mother country to rejoice over the stability and permanence of the British Crown.[57]

And on 24 May 1944, Empire Day, Curtin broadcast from London to once more emphasise that Australia was still committed to the British Empire:

Self-government is the predicate upon which responsible government is founded and Australians are completely free to govern themselves. Nothing can be done in Britain that will affect any law the Australian parliament chooses to pass. The Australian parliament is modelled upon the British parliament because Australians believe that it is right to have responsibility and authority vested in the people . . . I believe that there is a great hope and a great outlook for mankind. But ideas and ideals will not be realised without hard work and, possibly, not without a good deal of misunderstanding on the part of many who may honestly or maliciously mistake the aims and objectives of the British Empire. Let us all then – we who speak the same tongue – join with one voice in expressing our determination to make of our empire a shining example for all. For, in so doing, we make for millions of Britishers yet unborn a place in which justice and decency will replace those things which must become part of the dead past. Australia salutes her partners in the British Commonwealth and pledges herself to work for Empire Days of the future which will reflect milestones in the advance of mankind towards a better and happier way of life.[58]

—

In November 1944 Curtin had a heart attack. After a spell recovering in hospital he resumed his office in January 1945, but he was severely incapacitated by his failing health and it was his treasurer, Ben Chifley, at that time the most powerful minister after the prime minister, who announced the end of the war in Europe in May 1945. Two months later John Curtin died, and Chifley, the new prime minister, announced in a radio broadcast at 9.30 am on 15 August 1945 that with the Allies' subsequent victory in the Far East, World War II was finally over.

12

A ROYAL WEDDING AND
THE CORONATION

The queen's picture seems to look from every shop window
and red, white and blue hangs everywhere; at night there is
the dazzle of thousands of electric light bulbs. Such signs of
a faraway city's deep interest and widespread participation in
the coronation celebrations surely give a fair measure of the
meaning the throne has for Australia.

TWO YEARS AFTER THE end of World War II Australia
enjoyed the biggest wedding celebrations in its history,
when the heir to the British throne, Princess Elizabeth,
married a Greek-born prince, the son of a Dane, in London
in 1947.

Elizabeth was thirteen years old and Philip eighteen
when they met in 1939 at Dartmouth Naval College, which
Philip was attending at the time, over a game of croquet.
The young princess was with her parents and her younger

sister, Margaret, visiting the college from the royal steam yacht, the *Victoria and Albert*.[1]

Philip was born Philippos, Prince of Greece and Denmark, on the dining room table at the family home on the island of Corfu in Greece on 10 June 1921.[2] Philip's mother, Princess Alice of Battenberg, was the sister of Louis Mountbatten and a great-grandchild of Queen Victoria. Alice was English, though her father was German. She was married to Prince Andrew of Greece and Denmark, the fourth son of the Danish-born King George I of Greece, and Philip was their fifth child and only son.

At the time of his birth, Greece was in a state of political turmoil and the following year, after a disastrous war with Turkey, his uncle, King Constantine, was forced to abdicate. Shortly afterwards, his father, Prince Andrew, although an officer in the Greek Army, was arrested and accused of treason.[3] On the urging of Britain's King George V, mindful of the execution of the royal family in Russia four years before, Andrew was released. In December 1922, along with his family, eighteen-month-old Philip was rescued from Greece by the British Navy light cruiser the *Calypso* and taken to exile in France.

For twenty-five years Philip would wander stateless through a number of different countries, living on the generosity of wealthy relatives; it was not until he married Elizabeth in 1947 that he secured a stable home. Many years later he said he was brought up as a mixture of nationalities:

If anything, I've thought myself as Scandinavian, particularly Danish. We spoke English at home . . . The others learned Greek. I could understand a certain amount of it. But then the [conversation] would go into French. Then it went into German, on occasion, because we had German cousins. If you couldn't think of a word in one language, you tended to go into another.[4]

When he was nine years old, his family began to break up. All four sisters married within nine months of each other in 1930 and 1931, three of them to Germans with Nazi connections. Shortly afterwards, their mentally fragile mother entered a sanitarium in Switzerland, and their father went to Monte Carlo, where he lived with a mistress and became a heavy gambler.[5]

In 1933, aged twelve, Philip was sent to the elite Schule Schloss Salem boarding school in southern Germany, where the husband of one of his older sisters was headmaster. At the time Hitler had been in power for nine months and the Hitler Youth Movement had become a dominant influence in the school, although Philip appeared to be unimpressed with Nazism. The following year he was moved by British relatives to the newly opened Gordonstoun School on the north-east coast of Scotland. He embraced its discipline and harsh conditions, which included daily cold showers and an emphasis on outdoor activities and sport.[6]

In 1939, now eighteen years old and encouraged by his uncle Lord Louis Mountbatten, Philip joined the Royal Navy, enrolling at the officers' training college at Dartmouth after coming sixteenth out of thirty-four in the entrance exam.[7] His first posting was as a midshipman on the old World War I battleship the HMS *Ramillies*, and in 1940 Philip made his first trip to and from Australia when his ship formed part of a convoy taking Australian troops to fight alongside British soldiers in North Africa. Not a lot is recorded of his stay in Sydney. During his shore leave he attended a number of private parties, where guests included the daughter of the New South Wales governor Lord Wakehurst, the Honourable Henrietta Loder. He was also entertained by the consul-general for Greece, Dr E. C. Vrisakis, at the consul's official residence in Sydney's Darling Point, and attended the Greek Orthodox Church in Sydney with members of the local Greek community.

In 1942, by now signing his name as 'Philip, Prince of Greece', he was promoted to lieutenant, and two years later was assigned to the HMS *Whelp*, which sailed to the Far East via the Mediterranean for the final stages of the war against Japan. While on shore leave in Australia, in Sydney Philip met and became friends with society photographer Jo Fallon and his wife, Judy, who lived in Vaucluse. Fallon 'squired him around town, introducing him to the city's prettiest girls'.[8] On every trip he made friends with men and women with whom he would stay in contact for many decades, and visit whenever he came back to Australia.

After their first meeting, Philip and Princess Elizabeth had corresponded, and after the war he began to visit her. Elizabeth's governess, Marion 'Crawfie' Crawford later wrote that her royal charge did not take her eyes off Philip when they'd meet. Indeed, by the 1940s Philip was 'six feet tall, with intense blue eyes, chiselled features, and blond hair . . . an Adonis as well as athletic and engaging, exuding confidence and a touch of impudence'.[9] When he proposed marriage to her in 1946, Elizabeth accepted without hesitation.

But there was considerable opposition to their match. Philip lacked the name of a good family, was not British and didn't belong to the Church of England. Sir Alan Lascelles said many in the family and of the courtiers 'felt that he was rough, uneducated and would probably not be faithful'.[10] The palace may have had grounds for their concern. Prince Alexander of Yugoslavia, a cousin of Prince Philip, said that between the war and the official engagement in

1947, 'Blondes, brunettes and redhead charmers – Philip gallantly, and I think quite impartially, squired them all.'[11]

His good friend John Brabourne described how the royal family tried to block Philip's courtship of Elizabeth:

> They were bloody to him. We were at Balmoral that summer [1947, the year of the engagement] and they were absolutely bloody to him. They didn't like him, they didn't trust him, and it showed.[12]

In due course Philip overcame the hurdles. He adopted his English mother's maiden name of Mountbatten, abandoned his Greek and Danish royal titles, converted from the Greek Orthodox faith and was received into the Anglican Church by the Archbishop of Canterbury. King George VI finally gave consent to the marriage on condition that the formal engagement remained unannounced until Elizabeth reached twenty-one years of age.

But in moving closer to the bosom of the British royal family, Philip became more isolated from his own. In 1944 his father had died penniless of heart failure at Monte Carlo's Metropole Hotel in the arms of his mistress before Philip could see him, which left Philip with no significant inheritance and was a further liability in his attempts to prove his worthiness as a groom to the future queen. Nor were his surviving family members an asset. All four sisters had married German men, and one had married a Nazi colonel who had been attached to Himmler's personal staff. When Philip finally married Elizabeth, none of his sisters were invited to the wedding.

A year before the wedding, Elizabeth seemed already to have come of age and impressed with her natural charm and grace. At a party given in February 1946 to celebrate the end of the war, it was observed: 'she opens with a very easy and cosy joke or remark . . . [She] danced every dance thoroughly enjoying herself'.[13] Her cousin, Patricia Mountbatten, said '[She] would not have been a difficult person to love. She was beautiful, amusing and gay.'[14]

—

From the date of the announcement of the couple's engagement on 9 July 1947 until the wedding on 20 November, the subject dominated the Australian newspapers, and hundreds of articles were published covering its every aspect, including the fact that Philip had 'not a drop of Greek blood in his veins':

> Australia has already met and approved the tall, blond, handsome young officer of the Royal Navy, who was born in Corfu in 1921 as Prince Philip of Greece, and is now Lieutenant Philip Mountbatten, a naturalised British subject. He visited this country several times during the war, enjoyed Sydney's surfing, picnics at the zoo, horse-back riding, and shooting . . . He earned lasting popularity because of his natural manner, sense of humour, personal charm and dignity. The only son of Prince Andrew of Greece and Denmark . . . A British naval landing party saved him and his father from Greek revolutionaries when he was a year old. Taken to England as a baby and in the home of his famous uncle, Admiral Lord Mountbatten, brought up (now Viceroy of India); his life has been completely British ever since. He has not a drop of Greek blood in his veins, has spent no more than fifteen months of his life in Greece, and cannot even speak the language.[15]

The *Australian Women's Weekly* correspondent Mary Coles wrote enthusiastically of the prince, whom she had met in Melbourne only two years before:

> From a strictly feminine point of view Princess Elizabeth is the luckiest girl in the world . . . He was a dashing debonair naval lieutenant with a disconcerting wit and ability to toss off Australian slang in a superbly English voice . . . He is tall, slimly built, and has the bluest eyes I have ever seen. The blue eyes danced with mischief . . . as he stood and surveyed the scene.[16]

The wedding ceremony in London brought two million people onto the streets to watch the procession to Westminster Abbey. Winston Churchill described the day as 'a flash of colour on the hard road we have to travel'. The princess wore a silk satin dress studded with pearl and crystal, designed by Norman Hartnell, and arrived with King George VI in the blue, black and gold trim four-horse-drawn Irish State Coach. It was followed by a number of other horse-drawn carriages carrying the royal family members and the eight bridesmaids, who included Princess Margaret. Prince Philip left Kensington Palace in a coach with his best man, the Marquess of Milford Haven, David Mountbatten. On the morning of the wedding King George VI made Philip the Duke of Edinburgh.[17]

Australia was involved in the wedding, which was broadcast live across the nation via the radio. The Australian Girl Guides had played a big role by providing most of the ingredients for the couple's giant wedding cake. There was still wartime rationing in Britain and many of the ingredients would have been difficult to obtain there. Sent in seven large crates on the P&O liner SS *Stratheden* three months before the wedding, the shipment included fifty-six pounds of icing sugar, seventy pounds of castor sugar, fifty pounds of plain flour, six tins of powdered milk, six pounds of ground cinnamon, mixed spices, six bottles of lemon essence, one tin of almond meal, sixty pounds of sultanas, ten pounds of lemon peel, fifteen pounds of seeded raisins, ten pounds of crystallised cherries, twelve pounds of currants, seven pounds of self-raising flour, one bottle of best Australian brandy, twenty pounds of brown sugar, ten pounds of almond kernels, twelve dozen eggs and thirty pounds of butter. The rest of the ingredients were provided by New Zealand (butter), Canada (flour), Jamaica (rum), South Africa (brandy) and Barbados (sugar). The final cake was of four tiers and stood almost three metres tall and nearly 1.3 metres across, with camellias and white roses on the top. One of the tiers of the cake was sent back to the Australian Girl Guides to thank them.[18]

The director of the music for the wedding was Australian organist and master of the Westminster Abbey choristers Dr William Neil McKie, who would also direct the music at the coronation in 1953.

The royal couple received over 10,000 telegrams of congratulations and more than 2500 wedding gifts from Australia. However, Prime Minister Ben Chifley was widely criticised for the official wedding gifts he sent on behalf of the country: 'two finely engraved silver dessert dishes and silver salvers each decorated with an Australian wattle motif', which were thought to be 'mean and paltry'.[19]

To send an insignificant wedding gift is extremely humiliating to the great majority of Australians, with whom our prime minister seems to be completely out of touch. If Mr Chifley is against royalty – and he seems to be, from his speeches and from his refusal to attend the wedding ceremony – it would be better if we sent no present at all. A paltry present merely belittles our great country. Australia is not a poor country and to send a shabby gift to our future queen is unpardonable. A gift to royalty is something symbolical – something that goes to strengthen the ties that bind us.[20]

Chifley was criticised for 'disloyalty' for not attending the wedding as the other dominion prime ministers did. He said he did not believe that the wedding alone was enough to justify the expensive visit. In explaining his absence, Chifley's office was, however, careful not to be disrespectful:

> It can be said on the strongest authority that Mr Chifley will not go to London only for the wedding, and at this stage [there is] no reason for empire talks. Mr Chifley's reluctance to attend the wedding, is known, it arises wholly from his own austere mode of living and does not in the slightest degree reflect a lack of satisfaction that it is to take place.[21]

A number of old friends of Philip from his time in Australia during World War II were invited and went to London for the ceremony, including Jo and Judy Fallon. Another Australian friend who was invited was Sue Other-Gee, but she was unable to make it. 'It is too bad,' she told Sydney's *Daily Mirror*, 'but I simply cannot go. Philip and I were good friends when he was in Sydney.'[22] Years later it would be claimed that Philip and Sue Other-Gee had been lovers before, and even after, his marriage.[23]

The wedding on 20 November was celebrated across the country and was front-page news in all the newspapers:

CELEBRATIONS IN AUSTRALIA

Bells and Flags for Royal Wedding

Cities and towns throughout Australia echoed to the peal of bells, yesterday and last night, as the Commonwealth joined in empire-wide celebration over the wedding of Princess Elizabeth and the Duke of Edinburgh. In hundreds of thousands of homes, the radio broadcast from Westminster Abbey brought listeners every detail of the ceremony.[24]

Around Australia 'ships and ferries were to sound their sirens and all bell towers [were] to synchronise their ringing from 8 am to 9 pm'.[25] On Sydney Harbour the ships were decked with royal flags, the Harbour Bridge was floodlit, and around the city the schools were closed. Hotels and restaurants were 'thronged', 'hostesses invited guests to radio listening parties'; and more than 1000 guests attended a special ball at the Trocadero, the famous dance and concert hall. In Melbourne the Stock Exchange halted trading while members stood and sang 'God Save the King'.

Wedding fever gripped Brisbane too, where the city buildings had been 'gaily decorated', and there was a rush on cafes for private celebration parties. In Adelaide shops closed early and churches held special services where 'Praise My Soul, the King of Heaven' was sung, as it was at the wedding ceremony in Westminster Abbey. In Canberra the parliament was adjourned early so members could listen to the radio broadcast, and the British high commissioner hosted a cocktail party for all the foreign diplomats.

Australian newspapers covered the wedding in vivid detail, with descriptions of the celebratory scenes in London:

Huge crowds thronged every available point along the wedding procession route. Reuters estimated that an hour before the wedding two million people packed the route and its approaches. Many had waited in bitter cold since early yesterday afternoon. Every window along the route was packed with people who had paid up to £25 for standing room.

The early drizzle, and cold, grey, November sky gave way to milder weather as the great day wore on. The sun did not come out, but by 11 a.m. the temperature had risen to the equivalent of a warm, spring day.

There was a brilliant scene in the abbey, where more than 2000 guests stood hushed as the princess gave her responses in a quiet, confident, but rather hurried, voice. The bridegroom spoke in a firm, resonant voice.

This radio-picture [front-page image of the couple smiling and waving from the Irish State Coach] of the royal bride and bridegroom returning to the palace after their marriage was received in Sydney early this morning. Normally, the radio-picture service operating from London has its terminal in Melbourne, but, because of the importance of the occasion, the Overseas Telecommunications Commission this morning arranged, as an experiment, to intercept this radio-picture in Sydney.[26]

After the wedding, Elizabeth and Philip went to live in Clarence House, next to Green Park and a stone's throw from Buckingham Palace. It was the first home Philip could call his own.

—

King George VI had planned to visit Australia in March 1949 but the tour was cancelled because of his failing health. He was then scheduled to visit Canada in September 1951 but became too unwell to go: a malignant tumour had been found on his left lung and the lung had to be removed. A few months later, in January 1952, representing her ailing father, Princess Elizabeth set out with Prince Philip on a five-month tour of Commonwealth countries, including Australia, New Zealand and Kenya.

Australians were enormously excited at the prospect of finally seeing for themselves the princess that they had read so much about in newspapers and magazines, heard about on the radio and seen on newsreels in cinemas. All the major towns and cities began planning decorations and parades. In Adelaide the local organising committee announced 'elaborate plans for the decorations' with 'many coloured features' for the royal visit:[27]

> The various states will be depicted in different coloured flowers and the route of the royal visitors' travel in South Australia will be outlined. The flowers for this display will be produced by the City Corporation and the Botanic Garden. Members of the Floral Decorations sub-committee would be responsible for the section adjacent to Government House, and floral societies had been allotted sections further east on Northern Terrace . . . Streamers and pendants would be continued on each side of the roadways along North Terrace, East Terrace and Rundle Street, and then along King William Street . . . With the arrival in Australia of the Duke of Edinburgh and Princess Elizabeth only a month away, the organising of functions and decorations are in full swing. The day of the royal arrival in Sydney (April 1) will be proclaimed a holiday.[28]

However, after all the preparations, the eagerly awaited tour was abruptly cancelled. On 6 February, while the couple was still in Kenya on the first leg, King George VI died.

The telegraphed news of his death first reached Elizabeth's private secretary, Martin Charteris, via a local newsflash, while the royal party was at Kenya's Sagana fishing lodge, having just left the Treetops Hotel where they had been staying on the night the king had died. Charteris telephoned Philip's private secretary, the Australian Michael Parker, who woke the prince from a nap to tell him the news.[29] Parker said later that Philip reacted as though 'he had been hit by a thunderbolt' but had the presence of mind to take

Elizabeth for a walk in the grounds to break the news to her. She was now the queen of England.

The couple immediately made arrangements to fly home, first in a small aircraft from nearby Nanyuki to Entebbe in Uganda, where a larger plane was waiting to take them to England. The departure from Entebbe was delayed several hours after a storm broke and then, during the flight, Elizabeth realised she did not have a suitable mourning outfit, so a message was sent ahead for one to be waiting in London. As soon the plane landed and it was brought aboard, she changed into the appropriate black attire and was met by the late king's brother, the Duke of Gloucester, and Prime Minister Winston Churchill.

When the news of King George VI's death reached Australia, the country was plunged into mourning. Flags were flown at half-mast and shops bordered photos of the king in black or black and mauve, or put up black or crepe paper in their windows. The events that had been planned for the visit had to be cancelled; all those people who had spent months preparing for the tour were bitterly disappointed. Charmian Williams was a thirteen-year-old at Sydney Girls High School, and for months had been practising 'The Wheat Dance' in the nearby Sydney Showgrounds, which was to be performed for the royal couple. 'We started as wheat seeds,' she said,

> then grew our green foliage, and finally out of our costumes sprouted the golden wheat. Green and gold, but it was really awful! Thank goodness our performance did not go ahead.[30]

—

The coronation of Queen Elizabeth II at Westminster Abbey in June 1953 caused the same 'emotions of loyalty, of happiness, of warm human affection' in Australia as in

Britain. At her coronation Elizabeth was named queen of Australia (along with six other Commonwealth countries); *The Sydney Morning Herald* wrote of 'sharing a common heritage and a common allegiance ... [and a] feeling of pride [that] she is the first British Monarch to be specifically designated Queen of Australia'.[31]

A large number of Australians went to London for the event: 7000 were given places in the procession and 250 dignitaries were given seats in Westminster Abbey to watch the coronation. Elizabeth chose her regnal name as Elizabeth, and the House of Windsor continued to be the royal house, despite Prince Philip's surname of Mountbatten.

One of those inside the abbey was Harold Holt, who was then the Australian Minister for Immigration – at a time when postwar migration from Britain was reaching a peak. Leaving Sydney on the afternoon of 9 May he and his wife, Zara, took fourteen days to fly to London, enjoying stops in Darwin, Jakarta, Bangkok, Rangoon, Calcutta, Delhi, Karachi, Bahrain, Beirut and Rome on the way.

The day before the coronation, Holt described in his diary a reception at Buckingham Palace, where he and the others who were attending were introduced to the queen and Prince Philip. Holt was particularly impressed by Philip:

> We all had drinks together afterwards, and this gave me my first chance to have my first talk with the duke. He looks just as good and talks just as intelligently as his picture would suggest ... the really impressive boy was [Philip] whose appearance and personality even in that galaxy of talent seemed overpowering.[32]

The next day, Tuesday 2 June, was Coronation Day. Holt described how they had to be at Westminster Abbey by

7.30 am – even though the service did not start till 11 am – and they would not be out before 3.30 pm:

> Woken at 5.30 a.m. Came down, and with a solid breakfast of bacon and eggs and a packet of sandwiches for the long session ahead of us at the Abbey.[33]

Holt said that he lost the argument with his wife about what he would wear: 'Zara had prevailed on me to wear full evening dress . . . after a long struggle in which I'd fought for greater comfort in a morning suit.'[34] He was especially interested in the toilet arrangements for the eight hours the invited guests were kept in the abbey:

> Special provision had been made of 'conveniences'. The peers were seated exactly opposite us on the ground floor level, and I had wondered what all the moment was in their ranks before the ceremony started until I realised what it was all about. As time went on, it became obvious that most people were waiting as long as they could before they moved but with every intention of moving there and back again just in time to avoid missing the first of the various royal processions. The result was that, at one time, half the occupants of the abbey appeared to have made a mass exodus. I thought they were carrying the class distinctions too far when I saw one of the doors marked 'peeresses' and the other marked 'ladies'; these were right opposite the door marked 'gentlemen' in a narrower corridor where queues had lined up on both sides. 'A very French arrangement' an elderly peeress muttered, who was rubbing shoulders with me as we stood in our respective queues. The sandwiches were munched both before the ceremony began and after it was over.[35]

Another Australian in the abbey that day was Albert David Reid, a Country Party senator in the federal parliament. He had won nomination to attend the coronation and although he was midway through an election campaign he travelled to London for the ceremony with his wife, Jessie. On 12 April the couple flew from Sydney on a Convair, changing to a Skymaster in Adelaide and overnighting in Perth. They then boarded the SS *Orion* and sailed via Ceylon and Cairo to Naples. From Naples they travelled by train to Rome and Zurich, where they boarded another plane for the flight for London.

On the day of the coronation the Reids were told they must leave their hotel at 6.30 am to be at the abbey on time, and were given a packed lunch to take into the church with them. In her diary Jessie Reid described how once they were in the abbey the chairs they were allocated 'were made of silver oak, upholstered with royal blue velvet and gold braid with the Queen's monogram E II R in one corner of the back of the chair'. Jessie said they were later able to purchase their coronation chairs and bring them back to Australia.[36]

Meanwhile, on the other side of the world, the towns and cities of Australia had been decorated and extravagant celebrations organised to mark the event. In Melbourne there were enormous traffic jams as large numbers of people turned out to be part of the festivities and watch a fireworks display:

Thousands of people in cars invaded the city to see Coronation decorations. It took cars more than twenty minutes to travel half a mile in Bourke Street. The city was brightly lit tonight. Nearly every store in Melbourne was decorated with flags and photos of the queen and the royal family. More than 80,000 people attended a fireworks display in St Kilda to celebrate the coronation. Newspaper offices were swamped with reports tonight of flying saucers. The 'saucers' were searchlights from the St Kilda display.[37]

Yvonne Fix remembered the chaotic scenes when she was taken as a ten-year-old to enjoy the celebrations in Melbourne.[38] She said that she didn't really want to go but her mother insisted she couldn't miss the opportunity. Once they reached the city, Yvonne said the city had gone crazy:

> Shops had closed all their doors and trams and vehicles were banned. There were brass bands on every street corner blaring out tunes and people dancing, or trying to wherever there was space enough to move. Paper party whistles and funny hats and shouting and singing and seas of people – Melbourne had gone mad. The walk from Flinders Street station to Bourke Street along Swanston Street was lined with vendors selling memorabilia of royalty; flags – Union Jack and Australian – were being sold or given out and koalas and kangaroos with union jack vests, photos of Elizabeth and Philip as a couple embedded on tin badges with safety pin fasteners, mugs emblazoned with the royals, baby Prince Charles, album photos of royals right back to Queen Victoria, and unfolding royal family photos with Queen Mary and all the relatives on both sides were there to buy.[39]

She described the crowd in Bourke Street as out of control: 'People and bodies were moving in all directions by now creating a whirlpool of human sea sucking us down into the vortex.' As her mother helped push her way out, Yvonne heard 'a scream and a crash and a shout' as someone was pushed through a giant Myer department store window and onto the display set up inside. A number of bands on the streets kept playing and the noise was horrific. Her mother likened it to the day in 1945 'when the war ended with Japan and our soldiers came home and there were celebrations in the streets then too'.

Months before the event, the premier of South Australia, Thomas Playford, announced on local radio that Adelaide would celebrate the coronation with a grand parade involving the air force, navy and army, and a 'monster fireworks display, band concerts, several special sporting fixtures and church services'.[40]

In Brisbane the impending coronation had an effect on women's fashion in the city:

> Queen Elizabeth II's coronation will have a great influence on the fashion world. Many women will wear styles combining attributes of the Elizabethan era of dressing. Most designers have named their new creations after some part of the coronation ceremony.[41]

At the mining city of Broken Hill, more than 1100 kilometres west of Sydney, the celebrations were reportedly the largest in decades:

> Broken Hill went gay last night and thousands flocked Argent Street to celebrate the coronation of Queen Elizabeth. It was the gayest scene for more than twenty years. The crowd was in a marvellous carnival mood and entered into the spirit of the occasion. Young and old walked arm-in-arm down flag bedecked streets which were lit by the glow of a thousand coloured lights. In the streets couples were dancing and singing and groups were showered with confetti and streamers.[42]

In Western Australia the city of Perth was 'transformed':

In Perth, physically so remote, the coronation has caused a transformation. The queen's picture seems to look from every shop window and red, white and blue hangs everywhere; at night there is the dazzle of thousands of electric light bulbs. Such signs of a faraway city's deep interest and widespread participation in the coronation celebrations surely give a fair measure of the meaning the throne has for Australia.[43]

In Canberra, contingents of navy, air force and army personnel were sent from Victoria, New South Wales and Queensland for the celebration, which lasted six days. Parliament House was decorated with red and green plants and was floodlit at night. The green was on the House of Representatives side of parliament and the red on the Senate side, which both used the same colours as the British House of Commons and House of Lords. On the morning of the coronation, every worker was given the morning off to attend a 'levee' in Kings Hall hosted by the governor-general, Sir William Slim, and thirty-six jet fighter aircraft flew overhead while 3000 local schoolchildren joined a parade. Later that evening a banquet was held for 400 dignitaries and the following night was the Coronation Ball.

After the lavish and joyous festivities to commemorate Elizabeth's wedding and coronation, the queen was already an extremely popular figure in Australia. But she would become even more so the following year, when Australians from all around the country clamoured to see her on the biggest and most spectacular royal tour yet.

13

THE 1954 TOUR

1954. The year of the Queen and the Duke brought us our most delightful time ever. The magic of the fabulous royal tour lingers still – so persistently that all Australia wants to know the thrill again.

FINALLY, FIVE YEARS AFTER the cancellation of King George VI's promised trip in 1949, and two years after Princess Elizabeth and Prince Philip's proposed visit had also been abandoned, in February 1954 Australia hosted a reigning British monarch for the first time, in what was to be the grandest of all the royal tours. Its scale was immense and each stage took months to organise. The queen would visit every state and territory apart from the Northern Territory, she would go to seventy country towns, make around 100 speeches and travel 3000 kilometres by road. The tour would last eight weeks and during that time it was estimated that 75 per cent of the population would catch a glimpse of the monarch and her husband.

On 23 November 1953 Queen Elizabeth and Prince Philip left London, and their five-year-old son, Prince Charles, and three-year-old daughter, Princess Anne, whom they would not see for six months. They flew from a cold and foggy England on a Boeing Stratocruiser and landed the next morning in sunny Bermuda, where they transferred to the SS *Gothic* for the voyage through the Panama Canal to New Zealand and Australia. The first-class, 14,426-tonne passenger liner had originally been chartered from the Shaw, Savill and Albion Steamship Company for a proposed Canadian tour by King George VI in 1952, but was now put to good use for this royal visit.

After leaving Bermuda the *Gothic* sailed across the Pacific Ocean and reached Auckland Harbour two days before Christmas. For the next four weeks they toured New Zealand's north and south islands, visiting Wellington, Nelson, Christchurch, Canterbury and Dunedin before reboarding the ship on 30 January for the voyage across the Tasman Sea. They arrived in Sydney on Wednesday 3 February on a perfect summer morning and anchored at Athol Wharf, near Taronga Park Zoo.

At the time of the queen's arrival, Australia's population was around nine million but growing rapidly, bolstered by a government-subsidised migration program targeted largely at British settlers. Despite postwar economic prosperity, it was still a very conservative place. A 'white Australia' immigration policy limited settlers to those coming from Europe, and women were encouraged to stay at home in the increasingly sprawling suburbs, raise children and care for their husbands. The conservative Robert Menzies was once again prime minister, having been re-elected in 1949, and the country had stood firmly behind the United States since the beginning of the Cold War in 1947.

To welcome the queen and Prince Philip, police estimated that one and a half million people crammed into all
the available spots on the foreshores from Sydney Heads to
the Harbour Bridge, and along the route the queen would
drive when she landed; and that 60,000 had slept out on
the city's footpaths in order to secure a better view of the
couple.[1] The BBC reported that Sydney was 'wonderful,
terrific . . . just like London . . . before the coronation';[2]
and excited local media claimed:

> the heartfelt loyalty of a country that has often been described
> as in some senses more English than England herself, found
> full expression. Elizabeth II is something more than a queen.
> She is certainly the most famous, the most eminent, and the
> best-loved woman now living. Her unbounded popularity is
> in part a tribute to her own natural charm. She has a radiant
> quality of which even her photographs make one aware, and
> an unfailing tact that excites the liveliest admiration, in every
> situation in which tact can save the face of an embarrassed
> official or tongue-tied functionary at a royal reception.[3]

The newspapers and women's magazines gave the visit
enormous prominence. The first television network did not
launch in Australia until September 1956, but practically
every move of the royal couple was broadcast in 'newsreels' and shown in cinemas both in Australia and back in
Britain. Each leg of the tour was recorded on Australian
Broadcasting Commission (ABC) radio, much of it 'live',
starting with a running commentary of the *Gothic* arriving
through Sydney Heads. Every night the ABC broadcast a
highlights package of each day's events. In addition, more
than 100 photographers and journalists from the government's Australian News and Information Bureau were
officially associated with the visit, which was seen as an

opportunity to promote Australia to the rest of the world in the postwar period.

The official welcoming party, including Governor-General Sir William Slim, Prime Minister Menzies and New South Wales Labor premier Joe Cahill, were taken by barge to the *Gothic* to greet the queen. Arguments about positions in the limelight dogged the tour from the start. Politicians at both the state and federal level hoped to shore themselves up by being connected with the tour; in fact, as *The Bulletin* pointed out on the day the queen arrived, all principles were abandoned in the quest to be part of the program:

> Not socialism, nor anarchical principles, nor professed contempt for the flag or the throne . . . will prevent the surliest demagogue, the sourest iconoclast from rushing to catch a glimpse of the royal couple or to bow the knee on the crimson carpet if he gets the chance.[4]

Premier Cahill especially was determined to be at every event possible to welcome the queen. He was from the inner Sydney working-class suburb of Redfern and had worked as a fitter in the railway workshops before being elected to the state parliament in 1925. He was premier of New South Wales from 1952 to 1959, and during the royal visit took any opportunity to be photographed with the queen, as well as endeavouring to be at her side during every event in the state. Loch Townsend, a cameraman who filmed much of the tour for the cinema newsreels, complained: 'it was impossible to take a shot of the queen in New South Wales without a small burly man somewhere in the frame'.[5]

The queen and Prince Philip finally landed at Farm Cove around 10.30 am on 3 February, brought in on a launch amid the noise of boat sirens, foghorns, cheering crowds, as well as six Royal Australian Air Force Mustangs and six Vampire jets flying over in a royal salute. After the welcoming ceremony, the couple left in the third of seventeen cars that were carrying various officials on the drive along packed and cheering streets through the city. Accompanied by mounted guards, the procession moved almost at a walking pace.

A special fleet of cars and a team of trained drivers had been sent out from England for the tour. The queen travelled in a Daimler, which had been specially built for her father's 1949 tour that had never taken place. The landaulette was almost seven metres long and had a roof at the rear that could be lowered so the couple could be seen more easily.

The first stop for the procession that morning was at the Cenotaph in Martin Place, where the queen laid a wreath in honour of the Australians killed in both world wars. In her first speech of the tour she praised Sydney for becoming 'famous throughout the world', having been established more than 150 years before by 'Arthur Phillip and his small band of Englishmen'. No reference was made in this or any other speeches on the tour to the fact that most of the first settlers were from England's unwanted criminal classes and had been sent out forcibly as prisoners of the Crown.

At lunchtime the queen was taken to Government House. It was a hot summer's day and, in scenes that would be repeated throughout Australia over coming weeks, more than 2000 people were treated by ambulance officers and more than sixty taken to hospital after fainting in the heat.

That evening more than a million people stayed on Sydney's streets to watch a giant fireworks display. The press captured the excitement:

The royal progress through Australia could not have begun more auspiciously than it did yesterday in Sydney. Everybody seems to have agreed that the scenes in the famous harbour and in the great city which surrounds it were wholly unprecedented. This is natural enough, after all. The event which had summoned such vast and enthusiastic crowds to the proud capital of our senior state was itself without precedent. For the first time in Australian history, a reigning monarch of Britain and of the British peoples set foot on these shores.[6]

The queen's visit had been eagerly anticipated for months and to make sure those who might meet her knew how to conduct themselves, the government had published a small booklet titled 'The Royal Visit and You', which was sold at local newsagents for a shilling a copy. The two pages on dress codes suggested 'short afternoon frocks' were appropriate for women at garden parties and that it was acceptable for dinner jackets to be worn by men at balls if they did not own white tie and tails.[7]

What women should wear during the tour occupied a great deal of space in newspapers and women's magazines for months before and during the visit: the media played an integral part in the tour and most promotional and commemorative material focused on presenting the young queen as both a glorious representation of a timeless institution and a role model for women.[8] A month before the royal couple arrived in Australia, the Brisbane *Courier-Mail* featured an article titled 'Intensive Planning for Royal Visit Frocks':

The first job in 1954 for several Brisbane women is to plan a royal visit wardrobe. In less than five weeks they'll be flying to Canberra for the first exciting moments of Australia's great occasion. The queen opens parliament and senators and federal members and their wives are presented . . . Lady Fadden, wife of the treasurer, won't have a chance to plan her Canberra wardrobe until the end of the month. 'I'll have to have alternate outfits for most occasions,' she said. 'The weather could be freezing or quite hot! But I'll buy everything in Brisbane – and will be happy with any colour except pink and, of course, black.'[9]

The royal visit caused a boom in the sale of women's fashion jewellery:

> Sydney women will spend on self-adornment more than four times the amount the state government will expend on royal tour decorations. Businessmen say they will spend at least £400,000 on women's jewellery alone. In addition, they will spend an estimated £125,000 on furs and £70,000 on frocks.[10]

Prime Minister Menzies was all for this dressing up. 'There is nothing snobbish about wearing conventional garments,' he said.

> When we meet our queen, let us wear our best. She won't complain at what we wear, but she will be pleased to know that we are wearing our best.[11]

The royals kept to a packed itinerary on the first few days. On the second morning tens of thousands of people packed Macquarie Street to see the queen arrive to open the new session of the New South Wales parliament. She then hosted a lunch for more than 100 women's organisations at the Trocadero. Philip had gone separately for lunch at Sydney University but was delayed as hundreds of enthusiastic spectators ran alongside and in front of his car. In the evening the couple attended the first of many official banquets and an estimated 20,000 people crowded round the venue to watch them arrive.

An important formality undertaken by the couple in Sydney and every other city they visited were 'investitures', the bestowing of knighthoods and other honours. Australia did not have its own system of honours until the 1970s, so until then the ultimate social recognition was being awarded a British imperial knighthood or other title. Normally, Australians would travel to Buckingham Palace in London to receive the awards but on this visit the queen was able to bestow the awards in person.

The third day of the tour, Friday 5 February, saw the first of the giant displays by schoolchildren that would be performed for the royals in almost every town and city over the next two months. In Sydney, more than 150,000 children gathered in Centennial Park, the Sydney Showground and the Sydney Cricket Ground, and formed a giant map of Australia and words of welcome for the queen. Most of them had spent months rehearsing and would have been waiting for many hours, only to see the queen drive past their display, gone in a matter of seconds. Years later Denise Young recalled:

I was nine at the time, and the whole school had to go, on the most boiling hot Sydney day . . . Way, way, way away from our school to dance for the queen. My memories are not nice. It was far too hot; there was no shade in the middle of whatever sports ground it was; my icy cold water, which Mum had sent me off with, soon became boiling hot but was quickly drunk. No further drinks were supplied. The queen sped past in a far too fast manner – we only glimpsed her. It was a horrible, horrible day![12]

Next, Elizabeth and Philip were presented to an assembly of ex-servicemen and women in Sydney's Domain, before going in the afternoon to visit the repatriation military hospital at Concord. On the ten-kilometre drive to the hospital, the cars were repeatedly stopped by the crowds that had burst through the roadside barriers.

On the evening of Friday 5 February, the pair attended the Lord Mayor's Ball at Sydney Town Hall. The local media took a highly critical view of any sign of disrespect for the royals and when Sydney communist alderman Tom Wright declared he was not going to wear a dinner suit to the ball because he didn't own one, the Sydney *Sun* thundered: 'Red to Wear Lounge Suit at Royal Ball'.[13] In the end, after a tiring day, the queen and prince stayed at the dance only an hour, but their brief appearance did not reduce the enthusiasm of the huge crowd that had turned up to catch a glimpse of Elizabeth in her gown:

> The queen was a glittering figure in a magnificent beltless gown of parchment satin cut on princess lines. She wore a new diamond tiara, necklace and chandelier earrings, and carried a bouquet of cattleya orchids specially flown from Queensland . . . Throwing restraint to the winds, the crowds swept in on the royal car, showering the queen with confetti and at times even throwing flags into the car.[14]

The next day, their first Saturday in Sydney, included a trip to the Randwick horseraces, a quick visit to see some cricket at the nearby Sydney Cricket Ground and a trip to Bondi Beach to watch a surf carnival. The queen enjoyed the surf carnival so much they stayed forty-five minutes longer than scheduled.[15]

That night they attended a gala event, which included John Antill's famous musical composition *Corroboree* performed as a ballet by the Arts Council Ballet – only the performers were not Aboriginal people. The dance was choreographed by American dancer Beth Dean and the dancers were white with blackened faces, including Dean, who played the lead role of an Aboriginal boy being initiated into manhood. At the time, it was not thought offensive. Indeed, the reviews of the dance were typically very positive, with one, Eunice Gardner, writing in the *Columnist* that 'with amazing sensitivity Beth Dean has crept inside the skin of our aborigine: she knows his mind, his spirit, his beliefs, his customs and his art of dancing'.[16]

On Sunday Elizabeth and Philip attended the St Andrew's Cathedral Anglican church service; then spent thirty-six hours without official appointments, resting at Government House. This day of rest became customary and after 1954 was always built into the couple's visit while they were in Australia.

Two days later the rigorous schedule resumed when the queen and Philip boarded the royal train for the journey to New South Wales's second-largest city, Newcastle, north of Sydney. The beautiful royal carriage was the one that the queen's grandfather, King George V, and her father, King George VI, had used on their respective Australian tours. It was fastidiously polished and cared for in Sydney's railway workshops at Eveleigh and, apart from rare trips by other visiting royals, and occasionally by the governor-general, was hardly ever taken out of the sheds. For the queen's trip north, the train was hauled by the pride of the railways, the giant C38 locomotive, designed and built in Australia, and famous for being able to reach 100 miles (160 kilometres) an hour.

A public holiday had been called in Newcastle for the queen and Prince Philip's visit, and tens of thousands turned out to cheer them. In their three and a half hours in the city the couple drove about fifteen kilometres around the thronged streets, witnessed another huge children's exhibition, were presented to an assembly of ex-servicemen and visited the giant BHP steelworks. Among the officials to welcome the couple was Joe Cahill, and by the time he greeted them there, the local press had had enough:

> The New South Wales premier, Mr Cahill, is making a complete and unpopular fool of himself by dogging the queen's footsteps, and grabbing the limelight wherever he can . . . Since greeting her aboard the *Gothic* last Wednesday, Mr Cahill has bobbed up in front of Her Majesty whenever he can. Mr Cahill greeted the Queen at the royal banquet from which the prime minister was rudely excluded. Mr Cahill welcomed the Queen at Randwick . . . many people expected to see the Queen's self-appointed Uncle Joe shooting in on a surf ski at Bondi . . . It was that man again who saw her off to Newcastle today . . . then he will whiz quietly away by road . . . in time to spruce himself up before the queen sees his welcoming smile [at Newcastle]. He will also be at Bathurst, Lithgow, Katoomba and Wagga.[17]

The next stop for the royals was Lismore, 700 kilometres north of Sydney. It was pouring with rain there and much of the flood-prone area was under water. They stayed at the Gollan Hotel, where they were served a forty-dish buffet dinner. The following morning the population of barely 18,000 local residents swelled to an estimated 50,000, who had turned out to watch the Lismore parade, after which the queen and prince were introduced to three-year-old quadruplets from Bellingen, 250 kilometres to the south.

In the afternoon the couple were flown 700 kilometres to the west to the regional city of Dubbo. In another whirlwind trip, in less than two hours they saw a display of agricultural products, demonstrations of wood chopping, whip cracking, tree felling, and sheep shearing. They attended another civic reception and an assembly of ex-service personnel, where they honoured a local who had posthumously been awarded the Victoria Cross.

Finally, after 'a quick run around 12,000 children at the oval', they flew back to Sydney that evening.[18] Elizabeth and Philip had travelled more than 1600 kilometres and been standing for more than twenty of the previous thirty-two hours, but, according to the Minister in Charge of the Royal Tour, Eric J. Harrison, Elizabeth

> returned from her first country tour fresh and happy. She showed no sign of fatigue or strain, and the queen's medical advisers considered that the royal tour programme had in no way impaired her excellent health.[19]

The following morning she and Philip were taken by train to Wollongong, 85 kilometres south of Sydney. Waiting on the suburban Oatley railway station with his classmates from Oatley West Public School was seven-year-old Ian McNamara to wave as her majesty went past. McNamara, who later became famous as a national radio presenter, said that when the train whizzed past they all cheered and waved their flags madly, but it was all over so quickly most of them didn't actually catch sight of the queen.[20]

After Wollongong the royals were flown over the Blue Mountains to the central-western town of Bathurst, where they were greeted by a crowd of 60,000 people. People had travelled for hundreds of kilometres, with many sleeping in the city's central park in the hope of gaining a good vantage point. There to greet them, again, was Premier Cahill, who had travelled up from Sydney the previous day. In Bathurst the queen was introduced to Elizabeth Chifley, who had been widowed three years before in June 1951 when the former prime minister Ben Chifley passed away.

Among the tens of thousands lining the queen's route to wave flags were about 200 British migrant children from the Fairbridge Farm School situated ninety kilometres further west, near the country town of Molong. It was one of more than twenty child migrant schools in Australia and aimed to take children from the slums of England before 'they had acquired the vices of professional pauperism' to train 'boys to be farmers, and girls for farmer's wives'.[21]

From Bathurst, travelling back over the Blue Mountains to Sydney, the royal train stopped briefly at the coalmining and industrial town of Lithgow, where the streets were decorated with some of the largest arches yet seen on the tour, and at the Blue Mountains tourist spot Echo Point and Katoomba. As the train came into the western suburbs of Sydney there were not enough police to stop huge, hysterical crowds from surging on to the tracks, behind and in front of the royal train, which was several times forced to stop.[22]

The following morning, Saturday 13 February, the queen and Prince Philip were flown 400 kilometres from Sydney to Wagga Wagga, where around 110,000 people had turned up from across the state's south-west on yet another very hot day. The royals spent two hours witnessing more wood chopping, shearing and a huge demonstration by 14,000 children at the town's showground. John Johnstone remembers being able to get a good look at Elizabeth:

I was so close to the queen's car that I could have touched the car or even shaken hands with the queen . . . I was only five to six years old and my father was a teacher at Wagga Wagga High School. He had the responsibility of organising a large number of schoolchildren from all parts of the Irrigation

Area (Griffith, Leeton and other schools). I was very lucky to be standing with my father at the front as the queen drove past waving to all the schoolchildren.[23]

It was at Wagga that the queen and Prince Philip finally met their first Australian Aboriginal family: Joe Timbery, his wife and three children gave a demonstration of boomerang throwing. Joe was not from Wagga but had been brought in from La Perouse in Sydney especially for the royal visit. Aboriginal people were largely excluded from the growing affluence of postwar Australia. Most had lost their lands, were alienated from their traditional way of life, were unemployed and lived in poverty on the fringes and outside of white society. Many were not eligible for the dole or other social security payments and some state laws controlled where they lived, where they could move and who they could marry. For decades from the late 1800s, many of their children were forcibly taken from their mothers to be placed in institutional care. Later, Elizabeth and Philip watched several Aboriginal performances in north-east Queensland and South Australia, but those occasions were the only times the couple met Australian Aboriginal people as a group: at no point on the tour were they given the opportunity to visit any townships or missions to see how Indigenous Australians lived.

After watching the Timberys, the queen and Prince Philip were flown to the national capital, Canberra, where they were met by Governor-General Sir William Slim, Prime Minister Robert Menzies, federal opposition leader Clive Evatt and a host of other dignitaries and national parliamentarians. Canberra was still a small city but, with a population of 30,000 by now, much bigger than at the time of previous royal visits.

The queen and Prince Philip stayed in the official

vice-regal residence at Yarralumla, a grand house that had been built for Australia's first governor-general after the nation was inaugurated in 1901. In addition to the usual parades and events, the most important part of the visit was the opening of the federal parliament. It was followed by a state banquet, which had created tensions among some Labor members of parliament, who refused to wear formal evening suits. Leading South Australian left-wing MP Clyde Cameron insisted on wearing a lounge suit, even though his wife wore a long evening gown and a tiara.

> It was impossible to dissuade [her]. She felt she was just as good as the Liberal women, and I had to agree on that point, so we didn't have an argument about it.[24]

However, Cameron was less charitable about his colleagues, including Gough Whitlam, who would later become prime minister, for wearing white tie and tails. According to Cameron, Whitlam and the others who dressed formally were 'parading around like peacocks on heat'.[25]

Prime Minister Menzies made sure that the national banquet was a night of grandeur. He brought in to Canberra the top chefs of Australia; the food included decorative boars' heads, sixteen hams, twenty turkeys, and caviar and salmon flown in especially from Scotland. The government also gave permission for six cock pheasants to be shot in Tasmania outside the normal hunting season. At the banquet the queen delivered a speech that was broadcast live on radio by the ABC and reported extensively in the media in Britain. She began by thanking Australians for their loyalty to the British Crown:

> In the short time during which we have been with you we have seen much that has interested and encouraged us and we

have come to know something of the warm-hearted loyalty of Australians in cities, towns and country districts.[26]

She then gave Australia's immigration program a boost:

This country offers wonderful opportunities for men and women, capital and industry from the old world, and to those in the UK who seek a wider scope for the talent and resources, Australia may be seen as the Promised Land.[27]

In Canberra the queen unveiled a new national memorial to the Americans who had died fighting north of Australia during World War II. Her gesture had great significance because it was a reminder of the shift that had occurred in the Australian alliance from Britain to America, and an acknowledgement that it did not signify any diminution in the affection Australians held towards the royal family. As *The Sydney Morning Herald* reported the day after the ceremony, 'Those that have said that this country's bonds with Britain and the throne are loosening have been confounded.'[28]

As usual, thousands of children were at the parade at Manuka Oval on another extremely hot day, where one in every twenty of the 16,000 children present had to be treated by ambulance officers. Some of the youngsters who had travelled into Canberra from faraway towns and farms had been out of bed since 3 am – twelve hours before the scheduled start of the display.[29]

After three days in Canberra, the couple and their entourage returned to Sydney, where, on their last day in the city, 18 February, the party were taken across the Harbour Bridge to St Leonards Park in North Sydney for a short drive past an estimated 48,000 cheering schoolchildren. Again, it was a very hot day and most of the children had been waiting for many hours; 250 'collapsed in the blazing sun'.[30]

In the afternoon 8000 guests attended a garden party at Government House. According to *The Sydney Morning Herald* the refreshment tents were late opening, and in the absence of shade the garden was 'like the Simpson Desert' and 'ambulance workers struggled to clear the fallen into a discreet corner of the verandah'.[31] The queen, however, who did not join the guests outdoors until around 4 pm, appeared as 'cool as a tinkle of ice in a glass'.[32]

Late the next afternoon, Elizabeth and Philip left Circular Quay to board the *Gothic,* and an estimated three quarters of a million people crowded the wharf and the harbour foreshores to wave goodbye.[33] There were reports of women and children weeping and men admitting that they felt 'a lump in their throat as the band played "Auld Lang Syne"'. The sound of the *Gothic*'s engines as it pulled away from the wharf 'was unheard in the thunder of cheers, the screaming and hooting whistles and sirens from all around the harbour'.[34]

Two days later it sailed up the Derwent River to Hobart, where the smaller crowds preferred to clap rather than cheer: 'a sound seldom heard before on the Australian tour'.[35] However, later in the day they became more excited, and despite Hobart's population of around 90,000, the crowd that came to town to welcome Elizabeth and Philip was an estimated 150,000:

Thousands of people, overawed in the morning, made up for their shyness on Saturday evening. As the queen and the Duke of Edinburgh emerged from the state reception at the City Hall they were greeted with deafening cheers from a crowd which had waited patiently for more than an hour. As the royal party made its way back to Government House by way of Elizabeth

Street, people in their thousands, reserve thrown to the wind, raced along the pavements in an effort to keep abreast. Many turned into side streets and sprinted to vantage points farther along the route to catch yet another glimpse.[36]

The newspapers reported that the locals in Tasmania took the visit every bit as seriously as those of the mainland:

Hobart women are paying anything from £50 upwards for outfits to wear to just one function during the royal visit. The rush to buy new wardrobes has reached its peak, and most fashion stores report that they have been doing much more business than usual since Christmas. Many buyers for leading firms are visiting the mainland this weekend to replenish their stocks after the rush.[37]

During the four-day visit the queen and Prince Philip attended the 150th anniversary celebrations of the first British settlement on the island, displays by schoolchildren, investitures of knighthoods, assemblies of ex-service men and women, the official opening of the state parliament, and a garden party in the grounds of Hobart's grand Government House. They also visited the north-west of the state, which reminded the queen of the countryside of England, and Wynyard, Deloraine and Launceston, on a 'history-making tour for the north-west of Tasmania'.[38]

Wendy Burbury remembers being part of a performance of hoop dancing at York Park in Launceston as a grade nine student at Methodist Ladies' College, Launceston:

We performed in the centre of the oval with white hoops and wearing white tennis dresses. The queen and duke drove round the perimeter of the oval where groups from all the schools in Northern Tasmania were gathered.[39]

At the end of the Tasmanian tour, 12,000 children from all over the state performed in a Launceston park, and an estimated 70,000 people lined the streets to wave and cheer as the royals were driven to the airport for their flight over the Bass Strait to Melbourne, where thousands of people had packed the small Essendon airport to greet the royals:

> Joy, suspense, and the deepest feeling stirred the hearts of 4000 people at Melbourne airport when the royal couple arrived yesterday. Joy . . . In the mighty shout that went up when the royal plane taxied to a stop. Suspense . . . in the silence – a great silence – as the engines stopped . . . as Mr R. J. Butler, of Australian National Airlines, walked up the thirteen red carpeted steps of the gangway to open the plane door . . . and for another ninety long seconds as 4000 watched the open door. Then mad joy as the royal couple suddenly appeared at the open doorway and walked down the steps to the tarmac.[40]

The crowds in the city of Melbourne were even larger than those in Sydney and 'the greatest cries in the crowd were from women'.[41] Along the route from the airport 'every home had rallied to spread bunting across its frontage' and hundreds of thousands of people packed the streets to cheer.[42] In the evening of the first day an estimated half a million people packed the banks of Melbourne's Yarra River for a carnival. Nine hundred people were treated during the day and in the evening by ambulance officials, mainly after fainting.

Thursday 25 February, the first full day in Melbourne, was probably the biggest day of the entire Australian tour. The royal schedule included the official opening of the state parliament, an assembly of ex-service personnel at the Melbourne Cricket Ground and a ball at Government

House in the evening. At the Melbourne Cricket Ground the 17,000 children who were to stage a demonstration began arriving at 7 am, having spent months rehearsing their display. By the time Queen Elizabeth and Prince Philip arrived at around 2.15 pm, the crowd had built up to more than 75,000 and the nearly 100 ambulance officers were busy treating those who had been overcome by the heat.

The following day the couple flew 425 kilometres across the South Australian border to Mount Gambier, where the locals had been given more than a year to plan and rehearse for a visit that lasted from around 12.45 pm till a little after 2.30 pm.

Back in Melbourne, the royals joined a crowd of more than 70,000 at the Flemington races, and later were taken to Kooyong for the tennis, where Australian champions Lew Hoad and Ken Rosewall were playing.

The following week they boarded the Victorian Railways royal train for a tour of the upland region east of Melbourne. However, shortly before leaving, it was decided to cancel stops at Castlemaine and Maryborough because a handful of cases of polio had been recently reported there. Local protests about the cancellations were so passionate that in the end the royal train did stop at both towns, but neither Queen Elizabeth nor Prince Philip left their carriage, and the speeches of welcome by the local mayors were passed to them through the train window in their written form.

That weekend the royal couple had a break. Leaving the train at Warburton, they were driven to spend the rest of the weekend at the O'Shannassy Lodge owned by the Melbourne Board of Works on the foothills of the Yarra Ranges. To ensure a 'genuine' bush experience, the nearest dam had been stocked with fish, and koalas imported from elsewhere in the state and placed in trees near the house.

Over the weekend the media were expected to respect

the royal couple's privacy. Before the tour started the reporters covering the visit had been given instructions in the Commonwealth government's *Central Planning Guide*, which included the edict that 'Her Majesty and HRH must never be given cause for embarrassment', 'the dignity of any official ceremony must never be impaired by the activities of photographers' and 'when rest periods occur, the relaxation of Her Majesty and HRH must be strictly respected'. But these were more conservative times, and even without these rules the media was naturally far less intrusive than it would later become. Throughout the entire 1954 tour, no photographs appeared in the press of the queen or Prince Philip eating or drinking, even while attending official banquets or state dinners. The only coverage during the weekend the couple spent near Warburton was when they attended a Sunday morning service at St Andrew's Presbyterian church, where that day only local regular worshippers were allowed.

After five weeks of gruelling schedules, the queen was still reported to be in 'splendid heath and spirits', although many of the press were said to be very tired.[43]

The Victorian media had no qualms at congratulating the state on being the best host:

Victoria – that is you, me, the chap over the road – can take a bow for being Australia's outstanding host state to the queen. This is not just my view – it is shared by most of the British and Australian correspondents who have travelled around with Her Majesty in the fifty-seven days of her tour . . . Generally, we should feel proud of our fourteen glorious days. Our crowds I think, were the biggest the Queen saw, and they were surely the most expressive, the warmest and best behaved. In the Victorian tour we correspondents noticed a change coming over Her Majesty. She acquired a new eagerness for her official engagements. She laughed more, and she lost much of the near nervousness which marked her early days in Sydney.[44]

—

The next stop was Brisbane. It was an extremely hot day in the city when the plane landed at 2.15 pm on Tuesday 9 March. Thousands of people had slept in local parks to get a glimpse of the queen and prince on the drive from Eagle Farm Airport into the city. Many broke the roadside barriers and 'ran in the wake of the royal car' to the Exhibition Ground, where 50,000 more were waiting for the civic reception.[45] The local Queensland press, too, had eagerly awaited the arrival:

> Her Majesty, Queen Elizabeth II, and the Duke of Edinburgh, will arrive in Brisbane on Tuesday, March 9. No reigning sovereign has ever before been to Australia, and the queen's visit to Queensland is the greatest event in the state's history. Thirty-two cars; three Land Rovers, and two vans will make up the royal tour car fleet for Queensland. Brisbane's display for the Queen would be second to none in Australia, the premier, Mr [Vince] Gair said. He said there had been an 'outstanding, spontaneous, and enthusiastic response' by most city firms and organisations to appeals for light and colour throughout the royal progress.[46]

On their first evening in Brisbane, the royals were treated to a city adorned with illuminated decorations that the travelling press corps voted the best in Australia:[47]

> As daylight fades, the state's first city becomes a glittering fairyland of twinkling, multi-coloured lights. Dwarfing everything in its magnificence is the Story Bridge across the

Brisbane River. When the lights go on, the bridge looks like a scene from a Walt Disney cartoon as the beams of thousands of car lamps glow against the brightness which reflects the shining faces of Queenslanders as they watch their queen pass.[48]

Wherever the queen appeared, and however hot the weather was, she was impeccably dressed and looked as cool as ice. She was travelling with her own hairdresser and wore over 100 different dresses that were taken care of by a sewing maid and three ladies-in-waiting, who each had their own maids. Every day they would be given detailed information about the conditions they could expect the following day so that the most appropriate dress and footwear could be chosen.

The queen and Prince Philip left the Brisbane Lord Mayor's Ball early because first thing the next morning they would begin a week-long tour of the vast north of Queensland. From Brisbane they flew 350 kilometres to their first stop at Bundaberg, where the local population of 30,000 had increased to more than 100,000 people. Many people had travelled from as far west as Mount Isa, and a group of twenty-two Aboriginal people had been sponsored to travel from the Northern Territory. Lyn Staunton remembers being one of thousands of schoolchildren who went to cheer the queen at Bundaberg Showground. She says that she was later given a piece of the royal blue carpet the queen had walked on, which she used for many years as a saddlecloth on her pony.[49]

In Townsville, the queen and the duke were treated for the first time to a dance performed by Aboriginal people. The next stop was Rockhampton, which they visited shortly after heavy rains had put a third of the city's homes under water and many of the streets were still covered in mud.

Plagues of flies and mosquitoes were only partially under control after giant clouds of disinfectant had been sprayed into the air.[50]

After travelling more than 4000 kilometres, the couple ended their Queensland tour on 15 March when they returned to Brisbane and then flew 1500 kilometres south-west to Broken Hill on the way to Adelaide. Now in the heart of Australia, the steaming humidity and mosquitoes of the tropical Queensland coast were replaced by the dry heat, flies and dust of the outback. At Broken Hill they were greeted by thousands of people who had travelled hundreds of kilometres from remote farms and from Brewarrina, Wilcannia, Tibooburra and Silverton. After only two hours, which included a drive round the city, visiting the giant Broken Hill zinc, silver and copper mines and the Royal Flying Doctor Service headquarters, they were off again for the flight of 500 kilometres to Adelaide. Despite the briefness of the stopover, the local newspapers said the trip would never be forgotten by the town:

> Yesterday nearly 50,000 people were charmed by the gracious-ness of our queen and the manliness and friendliness of the Duke of Edinburgh . . . from the time when the royal couple arrived by plane from their hectic touring in Queensland until they left again for Adelaide they made their stay, in our city as pleasant and exciting as possible for everyone and who converged on the city from the outback and nearby districts now feel more composed over the queen's health . . . The queen did more to consolidate the strength of the monarchy than all the patriotic speeches rolled into one . . . It was a day never to be forgotten.[51]

The largest crowd in Adelaide's history, upwards of 300,000 and believed to be close to half a million, turned out to welcome the queen and Prince Philip when they arrived in the South Australian capital on Friday 19 March. Alan Paterson was one of hundreds of schoolboy army cadets who lined the route from the airport into the city of Adelaide. He recalled a hot summer's day and wearing 'cast-off uniforms, badly fitting, heavy, prickly wool, as the Army would not issue lightweight summer uniforms to cadets at the time'. In addition to the heavy uniforms, each boy carried a .303 rifle, and a cadet standing near Alan soon fainted.[52]

The next day the queen visited Whyalla, where the royal couple watched Aboriginal dancing by the local desert people. At Port Lincoln, 600 kilometres from Adelaide on the western side of the Spencer Gulf, 900 children formed a map of the Eyre Peninsula before they transmogrified into a giant fan, with the boys in white forming the ribs and the girls in pink forming the panels – both combining to represent the colours of the local wildflowers.

On Monday 22 March, after a restful Sunday, the queen stayed in Adelaide while the duke flew to Koolymilka near Woomera to inspect the secret guided missile site being developed there by British and American scientists. During the visit Philip was taken to a rocket launching site and was allowed to operate the controls of a pilotless aircraft.

On the couple's final night in South Australia, nearly 70,000 people attended an open-air concert on Adelaide's River Torrens to listen to a choir, band and symphony orchestra. The next morning, a huge crowd, 'mainly women and children, had tears in their eyes, and some wept openly' as they lined the roads to the airport to farewell the royal couple.[53]

—

The Western Australian leg of the 1954 tour was very nearly cancelled. Five weeks before it was due to begin, the queen had shaken hands with a woman from Western Australia who shortly afterwards had become sick with symptoms of polio. After assessing the situation, the Western Australian health authorities maintained the outbreak could become another epidemic.

Polio had first been diagnosed in Australia in the late 1800s, and by the 1930s the authorities were aware of thousands of cases. From 1944 to 1954 nearly 17,000 were reported, with more than 1000 deaths. Outbreaks of polio usually occurred in summer, and they instilled huge fear in communities, often causing public hysteria. Swimming pools, theatres and cinemas were closed and large gatherings such as those that were inevitable with the royal visit were shunned.[54]

After intense discussions between tour organisers and Australian officials while the queen was still in South Australia, Prime Minister Menzies flew to Adelaide to meet with the couple. The following day it was announced that the tour of the west would still go ahead but with some important modifications. While in Perth, the queen, the duke, members of the royal household and British press representatives would live aboard the *Gothic*, which had sailed to Western Australia and was berthed at Fremantle. All events and functions that would have been held indoors were cancelled. Meals eaten onshore by the royal couple and members of their household would be prepared using food flown in from Adelaide and made on board the *Gothic*. Shaking hands would be banned, and the queen would not accept bouquets.[55]

The Western Australian premier Albert Hawke felt the measures too strict and accused Menzies of 'unnecessary interference' in an issue that could have easily been addressed by the state government.[56] Almost everyone seemed to have overlooked the fact that the queen and Prince Philip had been inoculated against polio while they were in Canberra.

Sue White was fourteen at the time and remembers being part of the choir at Perth's Presbyterian Ladies' College that was to sing for the queen and Prince Philip:

> We had been practising for months – various songs – I think 'Our Country' was one – and were all looking forward to taking part in the very large combined schools choir which was scheduled to sing in front of the royals at a huge children's parade . . . Anyway along came the polio epidemic and everything was cancelled! You can imagine our disappointment![57]

The queen and Prince Philip landed at Kalgoorlie, Western Australia, on 26 March. The welcome was muted:

> Not a single cheer arose from the sparse crowd as the queen stepped from the plane at Kalgoorlie yesterday afternoon to set foot on West Australian soil for the first time. In the crowd there were 197 adults and 29 children . . . The coolness of their reception contrasted with the warmth of the weather, as the thermometer read ninety-three degrees. The ice of shyness was melted by the spontaneous warmth of the children's reception at the Kalgoorlie oval, and the queen warmed in response.[58]

At the welcome the state governor, Sir Charles Gairdner, bowed rather than shook the queen's hand. The couple was then driven through the twin town of Boulder where over 3000 local schoolchildren staged a display. Once again,

> there were no handshakes, no bouquets, no contact of any kind between royalty and the public. People presented to the royal couple had to stand a yard away.[59]

From Kalgoorlie the royal party flew to Perth, arriving at dusk. An estimated 100,000 people, 'many children in pyjamas and dressing gowns' in 'an unbroken line' either side of the Canning Highway, cheered and waved flags as the royals drove back to the port at Fremantle to board the *Gothic* for the night. The following day one paper reported that 'members of the queen's party are jokingly referring to themselves as "the untouchables".'[60]

During their stay in Perth the queen and the duke visited the Perth war memorial, attended a civic reception, a parade of ex-servicemen and women and a garden party in the grounds of Parliament House. On Monday 29 March they watched hundreds of children from the Boy Scouts, Girl Guides and other youth organisations in a torch-lit procession outside Government House on Adelaide Terrace. Later the same evening the royals were taken to see horse-trotting races at Gloucester Park. Margie Ward was nine years old when she was brought into Perth to see the queen:

> I grew up on a farm at Yerecoin, about 150 kilometres north east of Perth and attended a small primary school. As far as I remember we were taken to Kings Park by our parents. I had a special white dress and flag for the occasion and stood in front so had a great view of the queen and Prince Philip and to this day am convinced she looked, smiled and waved just to me. A wonderfully 'out of the world' experience for a little country girl – there was no TV in those days![61]

The next day, the queen and the Duke of Edinburgh met up with British child migrants from the Pinjarra Fairbridge Farm School, just as the queen's father had almost thirty years before. This time the children had been invited to Perth to form a guard of honour for the royals:

A very special treat that will be remembered by 200 boys and girls from Fairbridge Farm School on the royal visit days of Tuesday and Wednesday, March 30 and 31. These children, who left relatives and friends in England to make their way to a new kind of life in Australia, have been given the coveted honour of forming a guard for their queen. As her majesty will not have time to see the farm school at Pinjarra for herself, the state director of the royal tour has invited the young farm colonists to come to Perth. They have been given the exclusive right of lining the driveway in Government House on both sides on the morning the royal party leaves by car and plane for Busselton. With the boys neat in grey drill uniforms and girls looking like the Australian sun-baked scene itself in yellow blouses and brown tunics, it should present her majesty with a very pleasing sight.[62]

As well as Perth, in the west the couple's tour included visits to Busselton, Albany, Northam and York. Finally, after attending one last civic reception at Fremantle, the queen and the Duke of Edinburgh were officially fare-welled from Australia by Governor-General Sir William Slim, Prime Minister Menzies and the leader of the opposition, H. V. Evatt, who had flown across from Canberra in a DC-4 aircraft for the occasion.

After leaving Western Australia, the queen and Prince Philip sailed north to the Red Sea and through the Suez Canal to the Mediterranean island of Malta, where they were reunited with Prince Charles and Princess Anne, who had been brought out to meet their parents on the recently commissioned motor yacht *Britannia*. As the Australian trip had progressed, Charles and Anne had spoken to their parents by radiotelephone, and had received news of their journeys in regular letters sent to the queen mother. Just as Elizabeth and Margaret had followed their parents' travels on maps, Prince Charles had drawn his mother and father's route on a globe in his nursery.[63]

The 1954 tour was an unforgettable experience for everyone involved. At the end of the year, one Australian paper summed up the spark and glamour people felt the queen and Prince Philip had brought with them to the country:

> 1954. The year of the Queen and the Duke brought us our most delightful time ever. The magic of the fabulous royal tour lingers still – so persistently that all Australia wants to know the thrill again.[64]

14

ELIZABETH, THE LATER YEARS

I did but see her passing by, and yet I love her till I die.

THE QUEEN HAS VISITED Australia fifteen times since the spectacular 1954 tour, and in more than sixty years on the throne her popularity among Australians has remained high. Many believe it is the main reason why the British monarchy remains Australia's head of state and the country has not become a republic.

Queen Elizabeth's second trip south was in 1963 with Prince Philip to celebrate the fiftieth anniversary of the founding of Canberra. The pace of the 1963 tour was planned to be less onerous than that of its grinding predecessor: the itinerary was more informal and the queen and duke were given a number of entirely free days between engagements, as well as seven days to spend at sea in the royal yacht, *Britannia*.[1]

The queen travelled to Australia on the *Britannia* for seven of her next nine visits over the following twenty-five years.[2]

The *Britannia* was the best known and the last of eighty-three royal yachts used by British monarchs since Charles II in 1660. It was built between 1952 and 1953 at Clydebank in Scotland. At 126 metres long and weighing more than 5000 tonnes, it was the size of a small ocean liner and more than half the size of some of the passenger liners that at that time were taking migrants from Britain to Australia. It had the capacity for 250 passengers, though it rarely carried a fraction of that number, and was crewed by 271 officers and staff, who serviced its series of majestic rooms, which had all the formality and grandeur of a palace. As a security measure it also carried a platoon of Royal Marines.

The yacht became a regular sight in the harbours of Australia's state capitals when the queen was visiting. By all accounts, the queen thoroughly enjoyed sailing on the *Britannia* and was always active as the yacht sailed the open seas. A typical day for her ran something like this:

07.30: Her Majesty the Queen is woken by her personal maid with morning tea, which has milk and no sugar. The maid fills the Queen's bath and checks temperature with thermometer.

08.30: the Queen takes breakfast in the Sun Lounge.

09.15: the Queen works in her sitting room with her Private Secretary. Boxes of official documents arrive daily from various government departments.

11.00: coffee break and a chance for the Queen to view the chart in the Sun Lounge showing *Britannia's* position and distance travelled overnight.

11.30: back to work on the official papers until lunchtime.

13.00: the Queen and members of the Royal Family gather in the State Dining Room for a buffet lunch.

14.30: the Queen spends the afternoon working on private correspondence.

17.00: afternoon tea is taken in the Sun Lounge. It would often be wafer-thin cucumber and smoked salmon sandwiches, pastries and cakes, served with tea in the finest bone china cups.

18.00: Her Majesty meets with her Dresser to discuss jewellery and dress requirements for that evening.

19.00: the Queen dresses for dinner in her bedroom.

19.30: the Royal Family gathers for drinks in the anteroom. They are joined by the Admiral of the Yacht and senior members of the Royal Household before moving through to the State Dining Room.

20.00: dinner is served. The Queen sits on the port side of the dining table and uses a small bell to signal when a course has to be cleared way. Younger Royal children would eat separately until they are fully aware of the correct protocol.

21.30: the Royal Family retire to the Drawing Room for coffee, liqueurs and the Queen's favourite chocolate mints. The rest of the evening may be spent playing cards, doing jigsaw puzzles or just enjoying conversation. Sometimes a film would be shown in the Dining Room.

23.00: the Queen retires to bed and everybody follows suit. As is Royal custom, no one goes to bed until Her Majesty retires. It was sometimes the case that Her Majesty would work on urgent documents in her cabin late into the night.[3]

On their way to Australia in January 1963, the queen and the Duke of Edinburgh spent twelve days visiting New Zealand, calling at the Bay of Islands, Auckland and Wellington, where the queen officially opened the New Zealand parliament.

To begin their Australian tour they flew from New Zealand in a chartered Qantas Boeing 707 to Canberra. Some thirty years later in 1992, the use of a specially chartered airliner to ferry the queen into and around the country would raise eyebrows, but in the 1960s deference to the monarchy had not yet wavered sufficiently for anyone to question it.

The royal party arrived at Fairbairn Air Force Base on the afternoon of 18 February, where they were met by the governor-general Lord De L'Isle and Prime Minister Robert Menzies. The royals had been invited to Australia by Prime Minister Menzies, who was in the fourteenth year of his second term as prime minister – a term that would last for seventeen years. Menzies was a staunch and lifelong supporter of the monarchy, having once boasted that he was 'British to his bootstraps'. It turned out he and Elizabeth both shared a love of making home movies, and some of the earliest footage of Princess Elizabeth was taken by Menzies himself.[4]

During her five-week tour the queen, with Philip, visited all six states and many of the remote parts of the continent she had not seen in 1954. The 1960s saw the beginning of social and political upheaval in Australia, just as it did in Great Britain and the United States. Young people began to challenge the traditional values of their parents' generation, the women's movement gathered momentum, Aboriginal people were finally recognised as citizens and given the vote, and street protests became widespread, including against Australia's involvement in the Vietnam War. In this changed environment royal tours attracted less attention than previously.

In the Northern Territory the couple went to Alice Springs, Tennant Creek, Katherine and Darwin. In the far north-west of Western Australia they visited Kununurra and Broome in the Kimberley, more than 2000 kilometres north of Perth. In Broome the crowds were bolstered by the temporary release of twenty-four prisoners from the local jail who, under the watch of an 'unarmed warder', were given paper flags and lined up outside the jail to wave at the queen and duke as they drove past.[5]

After the Kimberley they stopped off at the Pilbara, then Geraldton, before reaching Perth, where they joined the fiftieth anniversary celebrations of the University of Western Australia. After this they visited South Australia, Tasmania, Queensland, New South Wales and the Australian Capital Territory.

The most formal part of this trip was the commemoration of the fiftieth anniversary of the founding of Canberra. Menzies had authorised a great deal of spending to make the city look its best, including the cost of a massive transplant of flowers to adorn the roadsides which the queen's motorcade would pass.[6] He was keen to ensure that the visit would have all the ceremony of a traditional English royal pageant:

> Officer Cadets from the three services paraded before the queen and the Duke of Edinburgh in a colourful demonstration. All the pomp and pageantry of the combined services were observed as the cadets marched their colours past the queen. About 10,000 spectators cheered and clapped loudly as the royal car drove on to the oval. The queen wore a lime green ensemble and blonde mink stole. The duke wore the uniform of field marshal of the Australian Army.[7]

During the anniversary celebrations the prime minister made one of the most memorable comments of all the royal tours of Australia. In his speech in King's Hall, where 600 guests were gathered, Menzies quoted the Elizabethan poet Thomas Ford when he asked the queen to

> remember in this country of yours . . . that every man, woman and child who even sees you . . . will remember it

in the words of the old seventeenth-century poet who wrote those famous words, 'I did but see he passing by, and yet I love her till I die'.[8]

At this, the queen, who was sitting to the side and behind Menzies, smiled slightly but appeared momentarily a little uncomfortable. Australians were divided on Menzies' words: some thought they accurately reflected Australian sentiment towards the queen at the time; others squirmed with embarrassment. Sir William Heseltine, a West Australian who served as the queen's private secretary from 1986 to 1990, said later, 'It was one of the very few occasions I think Sir Robert misjudged his audience. And I can remember that there was a frisson of embarrassment and this was perhaps reflected on the queen's own look on that occasion.'

A fortnight later, the queen announced that Menzies would be made a knight. She bestowed on him the Order of the Thistle, one of the highest honours, which meant Menzies would now be Sir Robert. It was and remains the only time such a rank has been awarded to an Australian, and two years later the queen bestowed on Menzies an even rarer title – Lord Warden of the Cinque Ports and Constable of Dover Castle.

The royal couple left Australia from Sydney on the afternoon of 27 March, with about 2000 people braving heavy rain to catch a glimpse of the queen. According to press reports, when she saw the crowd she decided against being driven from the terminal; instead she 'raised a small black umbrella and walked 300 yards in driving rain' to the plane.[9]

———

In 1970 the queen and the Duke of Edinburgh returned to Australia to celebrate the 200th anniversary of Captain

James Cook's discovery of the east coast. With them this time were their twenty-one-year-old son Prince Charles and, for her first visit, nineteen-year-old Princess Anne. The younger sons of the queen and Prince Philip, ten-year-old Prince Andrew and six-year-old Prince Edward, remained behind in England. Prince Charles had visited Australia twice already: he had spent two terms at Timbertop, the annex of Geelong Grammar School, in 1966, and had attended on behalf of the queen the memorial service for Prime Minister Harold Holt in December 1967.

The highlight of this visit was on 29 April when the queen and Prince Philip were taken to the southern side of Botany Bay to watch a re-enactment of Cook's landing. The event was one of the first major outdoor broadcasts on ABC national television, although it was in black and white – colour broadcasting in Australia was still five years away. At Kurnell, 20,000 people witnessed the re-enactment – many arriving at daybreak so they could see the whole thing, as Captain Cook (played by schoolteacher Don Reid)

> came ashore in a long boat and met the resistance of the Aborigines with a volley of musket fire. The New South Wales premier [Robert Askin] said after the ceremony that the Aborigines who had made some resistance to Cook's landing had suffered from their contacts with European culture.[10]

Later that evening the royal couple watched a huge fireworks display over Sydney from the deck of the *Britannia*, which was moored at Kirribilli.

As with the earlier tours the queen and Prince Philip visited Canberra. Emily Booker was fourteen years old when they arrived in Canberra. The Canberra Lakes Pony Club had been approached to ask its young members to ride their horses over to greet the royals on their way to Government House in Yarralumla:

> I was fourteen years old at the time and I had thought my younger sister, who was then six, might like to come along too. So I pulled her up behind me on the horse. I didn't put the saddle on because it's more comfortable doubling on horse-back without. When we reached Dunrossil Drive we lined up and waited . . . eventually the cars stopped and the queen and Prince Philip got out and walked over to the riders. The queen sailed past my sister and I, but I was excited when Prince Philip stopped to pat my horse. He looked up and seeing two of us said, 'Is that your brother or sister up there behind you?' and then asked, 'Don't you have a saddle?' I told him it was my sister and explained the best way to be comfortable when dinking on horseback. He seemed satisfied with the response and headed off in the queen's wake.[11]

—

Just three years later, the royal couple were back on what was regarded as the last of Elizabeth II's great tours, when she was invited to open the Sydney Opera House in 1973. The spectacular opera house, with its soaring white roof and shell-shaped sails atop a red granite platform, had taken sixteen years to build and had been mired in controversy – from its revolutionary design to the eventual resignation of its genius architect, Jørn Utzon, seven years before the building was finished.

Seats for the official opening by the queen were limited to 15,000 guests, but tens of thousands more flocked to the opera house to try to catch a glimpse of the event. Local newspapers reported how boats and ferries filled the harbour to make it a spectacular occasion:

> Conceived in dream, delivered in controversy and bathed in uncertainty, the Sydney Opera House was opened on Saturday in a blaze of what some would call grandeur and others ballyhoo but which few would deny was spectacular.[12]

Again, wherever the royal party travelled in Australia the crowds were huge, but this was the last time they were quite so big. Almost every household had access to a television by the early 1970s, and people were increasingly able to watch such visits from the comfort of their own homes.

By the early 1970s Australia was in the throes of more radical social change that would alter its relationship with Britain. Economically and socially, Australia was continuing to create closer relations with the rest of the world, a process that accelerated after Britain joined the European Common Market in 1973. In late 1972 Gough Whitlam's progressive Labor government was elected, and it moved to make Australia more independent of Britain: in 1974 the High Court of Australia replaced the British Privy Council as the highest court of appeal and the Whitlam government introduced Australia's own national anthem, 'Advance Australia Fair'. Until then 'God Save the Queen' had been Australia's anthem and was regularly sung at public events, including in cinemas and theatres before a performance, when the audience was expected to stand and sing. The new anthem was chosen after a nationwide opinion survey was conducted by the Australian Bureau of Statistics of 60,000 people, who were given three choices: 'Song of Australia', written in 1859 by South Australian Caroline Carleton, 'Waltzing Matilda' and 'Advance Australia Fair', written by Peter Dodds McCormick and first performed in 1878. In January 1976 the Fraser government reinstated 'God Save the Queen' for royal, vice-regal, defence and loyal toast occasions, but in a plebiscite held the following year voters favoured 'Advance Australia Fair' over other options, including 'God Save the Queen'. It was not until 1984 that Governor-General Sir Ninian Stephen ended any ambiguity by proclaiming 'Advance Australia Fair' as Australia's anthem.

During Whitlam's short term in office, he also introduced a new national system of awards for outstanding civic duty – the Order of Australia, which replaced the system of British imperial honours that had been bestowed on Australians by the queen on the recommendation of national or state governments. The new honour, which was established on 14 February 1975, was based broadly on the Order of Canada. The Order of Australia differs from the imperial honours system in that final decisions relating to awards are made by the Council for the Order of Australia, rather than by the politicians. This is to help ensure that the awards system is merit-based and apolitical.

The changes made to Australia's national symbols reflected the Whitlam government's vision of a confident, independent Australia. Whitlam sought to abandon what he saw as colonial relics, and replace them with distinctively Australian symbols. All these changes were in keeping with a maturing Australia wanting to shape its own identity – but they did not yet appear to reduce the ongoing affection for and popularity of the British royals.

Despite being a staunch republican, Whitlam, like many Labor leaders before and since, saw great political value in the reflected popularity of the queen and the royal visits. In February 1974 he invited the queen to Canberra to open a new session of the national parliament, and did not shy away from taking part in the pomp and ceremony of the couple's fifth trip together to Australia in a little under twenty years.[13]

In Canberra the queen experienced one of the first political demonstrations to have taken place in all her visits to Australia. A group of Aboriginal people had the year before established a tent 'embassy' on the lawns in front of Canberra's Parliament House and were protesting for the right to own and take control of their traditional lands. When the queen arrived with Prince Philip at the parliament she was 'jeered, booed and called names' by 'noisy Aboriginal demonstrators', who held banners that read 'British Imperialists Out' and 'Solidarity with Blacks of Australia'.

> Chanting Aboriginal demonstrators drowned out the applause for the queen as she arrived on schedule to open federal parliament yesterday. As the queen stepped out of her black rolls-royce she was greeted by the prime minister Mr Whitlam and Mrs Whitlam, and a fanfare from the Royal Military [band]. The demonstrators booed as the fanfare was played and gave a clenched fist salute during the playing of the national anthem.[14]

The 1974 tour was to be the queen's shortest, lasting only two days. She had flown into Canberra on 27 February, 'noticeably sunburnt' after a short tour of Papua New Guinea, and the next day, when she opened the Australian parliament, there was a general election in the United Kingdom. In the election Edward Heath's conservative government won 297 seats and Harold Wilson's Labour Party 301, but a problem emerged when Heath would not immediately resign as he tried to negotiate a coalition with the minor parties to reach a majority. The queen had to return to London. By then Heath had found he could not lock in the small Liberal Party, and so five days after the election, she called on Wilson to form a minority government.

—

In November 1975, the governor-general Sir John Kerr, Queen Elizabeth's representative in Australia, dismissed the Whitlam government to break the political deadlock that had been caused by the refusal of the Senate to pass supply bills required by Whitlam's Labor government. Kerr installed the opposition leader, Malcolm Fraser, as the caretaker prime minister and ordered a national election. In the poll that followed on 13 December 1975, Fraser's conservative party coalition was easily elected to government.

Kerr's actions in sacking a democratically elected government remains one of Australia's most controversial constitutional events. Kerr later claimed he had the queen's backing because Buckingham Palace had known of and supported his actions. However, the palace denied they'd had advance notice from Kerr as to what he was about to do, and stated that they disagreed with his actions. Sir William Heseltine, at the time the Queen's assistant private secretary, was following the constitutional crisis in Australia very closely. He later said that Kerr had not told the queen of his intentions, nor had he sought her advice or given any 'clue to any of us at the palace what was in his mind'. Years later when he was interviewed about the Whitlam sacking, Heseltine said that early in the morning of 11 November 1975, he had been woken by a phone call in his apartment in St James's Palace. It was around 2 am and on the line was Sir John Kerr's official secretary, Sir David Smith.

> He was ringing to tell me the governor-general had just dismissed the prime minister. I said, 'What did you say?' He then told me and I had the rather delicate decision . . . whether I was going to wake the queen and tell her . . . I thought, 'Well, there is no possible advantage in doing that'.

Heseltine knew the queen would usually listen to the news at 8 am, so he decided to get to his office early to be ready to inform her of the sacking before she heard it on the radio.

> It was by this time about five to eight so we got the queen on the telephone and said, 'Can we come up and tell you about the dramatic events that have been happening overnight in Australia?' . . . She was interested and concerned but, as I had felt, there wasn't anything she could do about it.

Heseltine, who moved back to Western Australia when he retired, thought Kerr had acted too soon:

> I always thought if he could somehow have just held the line for a little bit longer that a political solution would have emerged rather than the drastic step that he took.[15]

—

Sixteen months later, in March 1977, the queen and Duke of Edinburgh were back in Australia again at the invitation of conservative prime minister Malcolm Fraser for the queen's Silver Jubilee celebrations. This time they stayed for three weeks, and again they visited every state. In Queensland the queen opened a sports stadium named after her in a southern Brisbane suburb. In New South Wales she opened new council buildings in Tamworth and an art gallery in Newcastle. In Melbourne she launched the Jubilee Art Acquisition at the National Gallery of Victoria. As part of the commemoration a special fifty-cent Australian Silver Jubilee coin was minted and put into circulation.

By the early 1980s interest in royal tours in Australia was, however, declining: their relative frequency meant they had become more routine to most Australians. Helen Kebby, a primary school teacher in Sydney's inner-city suburbs, took her Waterloo class out on to Botany Road to see the queen driving past to Sydney airport in 1977. She remembered as a little girl more than twenty years before the thrill of being taken on a bus by her mother from her home town of Eden on the New South Wales south coast on a 500-kilometre round trip to Canberra to see Her Majesty. But her pupils were far less excited: when the fleet of cars drove past the school and the children waved, only one or two were sure that they had even caught sight of her. 'Not much of a queen, miss,' said one boy. 'She didn't even have a crown.'[16]

The days of the long tours were also over. In May 1980 the queen and Prince Philip stayed three days when she opened Australia's new High Court building in Canberra and briefly visited Melbourne and Sydney. In September 1981 she officially opened the Commonwealth Heads of Government Meeting in Melbourne. CHOGM, as it became known, had first been held in 1971 to replace the Commonwealth Prime Ministers' conferences, which had previously always been held in London, reflecting the centralisation of power then in the British Commonwealth office. After CHOGM the royals accepted an invitation from Malcolm Fraser's government to extend their stay so as to briefly visit Victoria, Tasmania, Western Australia and South Australia.

In 1982 the queen and Prince Philip accepted another invitation from Fraser – this time to open the Commonwealth Games in Brisbane. The royal couple stayed in Australia for a week, which gave them time to briefly visit Sydney, where the queen opened a new hospital at Mount Druitt, and Canberra to open the new National Gallery there.

In 1986 the queen returned to Australia for a ceremony at Government House in Canberra, where she signed the *Australia Act*. The new law, simultaneously passed in the

UK parliament, removed the possibility of Britain passing any law that could affect Australia. The *Australia Act* was mainly symbolic because more than fifty years before, in 1931, the *Statute of Westminster* had effectively removed the power of Britain to unilaterally pass legislation in Australia and other Commonwealth countries; however, there remained a legal technical possibility that Westminster could still pass laws affecting individual Australian states, which the new act annulled.

During the visit the queen officiated at a number of events in different states, including Victoria, South Australia and New South Wales, where the popular Labor premier Neville Wran had been in office for a decade. Although a founding member of the Australian Republican Movement, Wran was another politician who was fascinated with the enduring popularity of the British royal family, and he happily welcomed them back to New South Wales whenever they visited.

The trend towards shorter and more modest tours was broken in 1988 when Queen Elizabeth came on a month-long visit for Australia's bicentenary commemorations of the arrival of the First Fleet. This trip took in all the states and territories apart from the Northern Territory, and its high point was the official opening of the new national Parliament House in Canberra on 9 May.

The queen's equerry on this royal tour was an Australian army officer, Lieutenant Colonel Geoffrey Hay. The role of the queen's equerry in the twentieth century was not much different from years before: to support the queen in her official duties and private life, and be responsible for the planning of her daily program. The equerry was always chosen from the armed forces, with each service taking its turn to provide an officer. In the early tours of Australia, the royals had brought out equerries with them from England, but after 1954 Australia appointed one for the duration of each tour. Hay said that he didn't know exactly why he had been chosen but quickly began learning as much as he could about the job from previous Australian equerries as there was no 'resident expert' within the Australian army or in the Department of Prime Minister to explain his duties.[17] He was told he must stay close enough to the queen to respond to any enquiry or problem, but not too close as to be in the way. His duties included providing advice on protocol, announcing visitors and guests at formal audiences and carrying petty cash – as the royals do not carry cash. He had to be ready for all contingencies, including providing the queen with money to place in a collection tray during a church service. On one occasion in Sydney he was called at short notice to join the Duke of Edinburgh, who wanted to buy twelve Akubra hats but didn't have any money to pay for them.

Hay's luggage for the queen's 1988 tour included a summer service dress, winter service dress, safari suit, patrol blues, mess dress, dinner suit, khaki cap, blue cap, Sam Browne belt, a sword with a leather scabbard, a ceremonial sword with a silver scabbard, ceremonial waist sash, ceremonial waist belt and slings, aiguillette, Royal Cypher and Crown (gold and silver) badges of rank, shoulder cords, white kid gloves, leather gloves, medals, miniatures and ribbons, mess boots and braces. Hay said to be safe he had to pack two of everything as well as smart casual clothing for off-duty and informal outings with palace staff.

Soon after being notified of his appointment, and four months before the tour, Hay was sent with a team from Buckingham Palace on a reconnaissance of all the places the queen would visit when she was in the country. Every part of the program was planned down to the minute, including the exact length of time it took to travel from one destination on the itinerary to the next; the composition of welcoming parties; the number of dignitaries to be formally introduced to the royal couple; the proposed number of speeches and their duration; and the proposed seating plans. Hay had to be perfectly versed in every detail of the queen's schedule, particularly to ensure that she and her entourage arrived and departed each location promptly.

In early April 1988 he and a small team of Australian officials flew on a Royal Australian Air Force VIP Boeing 707 to London to bring the royal party to Australia. The Boeing had been paid for by the Australian government and fitted out with special accommodation for the queen and Prince Philip and the approximately forty officials who would accompany them on their tour. Hay spent three nights at Buckingham Palace and one at Windsor Castle, where he met the queen, the Duke of Edinburgh and the staff who would accompany them. Among the staff were the mistress of the robes, the lady-in-waiting, the queen's doctor, the duke's private secretary, the senior palace press secretary, the master of the household, three specially assigned police officers, the duke's valet, the queen's page and two maids, a footman and deputy footman and a number of staff from the royal yacht *Britannia*.[18] The *Britannia* had already left Britain and would meet up with the royal tour later in Brisbane.

The plane carrying the royals landed in Perth on 19 April at 5 pm. The party was met by the governor-general, Sir Ninian Stephen, and Labor prime minister Bob Hawke and their wives, who had flown from Canberra for the welcome. The prime minister's wife, Hazel, attracted criticism for not wearing a hat.

Bob Hawke's Labor government had been in power since 11 March 1983. Australia was now a nation much more confident about its own identity and its place in the world. Within five years public opinion polls would show for the first time that a majority of the population wanted to become a republic.

After a day's rest at a private farm thirty kilometres from Perth, the official 1988 royal tour started on Thursday 21 April with a number of receptions, which were followed by a garden party at Government House for 5000 invited guests and a state dinner in the evening. The guest list for these official events was compiled by the protocol department of the state government in consultation with the prime minister's office and the palace. Great care was taken to ensure 'unsuitable' people were not invited.

The following morning the party flew 400 kilometres north in a smaller Australian government plane to the coastal town of Geraldton, which the queen proclaimed a city. At lunchtime they flew 900 more kilometres across the desert to the east to the goldmining city of Kalgoorlie, where thousands of children put on a parade in much the same way they had for the queen in 1954. They then flew 600 kilometres back to Perth for a quiet, private dinner. Over the next two days the couple attended a number of events in Perth. Philip presented Duke of Edinburgh Awards to thirty recipients and the queen delivered a lecture to 900 people at the University of Western Australia.

On Sunday the royal couple flew more than 4000 kilometres to Hobart, arriving in time for a dinner at Government House. The next day was Anzac Day. Prince Philip went to the dawn memorial service and later in the morning the queen took the salute at the Anzac Day march-past. After two days of events and a state dinner with 700 guests at Government House, the royals flew to Burnie, where they attended a reception for 700, and Launceston, where they visited a school of nursing before walking through the city centre.

On Wednesday 27 April the queen and Prince Philip flew to Melbourne, where they undertook the now familiar round of official functions, including a state reception for 500 guests on the promenade deck of the grand old Sydney ferry the SS *South Steyne*. The next day they travelled on one of the last rides on a royal train to Geelong, the first time either the queen or the duke had visited the city. Then the royal party flew 2000 kilometres from Melbourne to Longreach in remote western Queensland to officially open the Stockman's Hall of Fame. The next evening they flew south to Brisbane where they met up with their youngest son, Prince Edward, who had flown out from London on a commercial Qantas flight. The main event in Brisbane was the official opening of the Brisbane World Expo '88, which was the biggest bicentennial event in Australia in 1988 and over the next six months attracted more than fifteen million visitors. *The Canberra Times* described the opening:

> The queen opened Expo, a task she obviously enjoyed, in hot, fine steamy weather. She recalled the world exposition at the Crystal Palace in 1851 as the first of its kind. 'It featured the telegraph and the sewing machine,' she said, and in a rare display of humour, she won the crowd with a one-liner. 'I know you people like to call this the Sunshine State,' she said. 'I prefer to call it by its real name, Queensland.'[19]

In Brisbane the family boarded the *Britannia*, waiting in Moreton Bay to take them to Sydney. According to Geoffrey Hay, the whole atmosphere changed as soon as they were on the yacht. The queen, he said, became instantly more relaxed and at ease. So too was Prince Philip, who, Hay said, often walked around the decks barefoot when the yacht was at sea.

In Sydney the *Britannia* moored at Circular Quay and the royals were taken by barge to open the redeveloped Darling Harbour parklands, a centrepiece of Sydney's celebrations.

The last big event was in Canberra – the opening of the new parliament building. Hay remembers arriving at Fairbairn Air Force Base and for once leaving the queen's side to walk into the dense crowds, where his wife, Caroline, was waiting with their eight-year-old son, Adam, and six-year-old daughter, Emma, whom he hadn't seen since he had flown off to London more than a month before. The queen opened the new Parliament House on 9 May 1988.

—

By the early 1990s there was growing support around the nation for Australia to become a republic, which coincided with, and was no doubt fed by, a decline in enthusiasm for the British royal family. At the time a succession of scandals in Britain caused by the behaviour of various members of the family had helped sap some of the blind faith Australians had in the monarchy.

In 1992, the year the queen later described as her 'annus horribilis', a number of events rocked the monarchy to its foundations, and, like anything concerning the royal family, they were extensively reported in the Australian media. In March, the palace announced that Prince Andrew and his wife, the Duchess of York (popularly known as Fergie), were to divorce, after months of speculation about their marriage. The following month the news broke that Princess Anne was also to divorce her husband, Captain Mark Phillips.

In June, *Diana, Her True Story* by journalist Andrew Morton was published and its controversial revelations were minutely examined by the Australian press. At the time Prince Charles and Diana, the Princess of Wales had been married for eleven years and had two sons – the second-in-line to the throne, Prince William, and his younger brother, Prince Harry. It was by now well known that Charles and Diana were estranged, but Morton's book confirmed rumours of Charles's long-running affair with Camilla Parker Bowles, and the lack of support Diana had received from Charles and the royal family over the previous decade, having been thrust into the glare of the world and scrutinised relentlessly by the global media.

In November 1992, a fire seriously damaged much of Windsor Castle. When British prime minister John Major suggested that taxpayers' money would be used to repair the damage, there was a strongly expressed adverse public reaction and Major was forced to make arrangements for several royal estates to be opened to tourists when not being used by the royal family as a way of defraying the cost of restoring the castle.

When the queen visited Australia in February 1992, there were already signs of a backlash in public opinion. From time to time over the years the expense of royal tours had been raised, but now the press was pointing it out more frequently and more critically. In 1992 the Australian press wanted to know why the queen needed to fly out on a specially fitted Boeing jumbo jet at a cost of more than a million dollars rather than using a commercial airliner.

The queen, said by some to be the world's richest woman, will travel in extraordinary style to Australia later this month – and the Australian taxpayer will pick up the tab. The Australian government has chartered a Qantas jumbo jet to fly the queen and her entourage to Australia. The bill? A cool $1.1 million, according to reliable sources. The jumbo jet is capable of carrying 400 people but the queen, the Duke of Edinburgh and their retinue of twenty-eight people will have the aircraft to themselves. The huge jet is being converted to royal style especially for the flight. The queen and the duke will have their own bedroom, lounge and other conveniences fitted for their journey. Because Qantas will use the plane for ordinary scheduled flights for fare-paying passengers while the queen is in Australia, it will be stripped of the royal fittings in the interim. Everything will be refitted for the return journey. It will be the first time Australia has been so extravagant. On previous visits, the queen has come to Australia on the royal yacht *Britannia*, or been flown by the RAAF.[20]

It was during this 1992 tour that the strongly pro-republic prime minister Paul Keating caused a stir by touching the queen. Keating would have been very well aware of protocol when hosting Her Majesty – that the only time she should be touched was if she offered a handshake – but while he was introducing her to a line of dignitaries, he placed his hand on the middle of her back to guide her along the line. Australian and British newspapers criticised Keating as well as his Dutch-born wife, Annita, who refused to curtsy when she was introduced to the queen. The UK *Daily Mail* claimed the Keatings had made 'a gauche show of skimping the traditional courtesies' and called the prime minister 'the oaf of Oz'.[21] The *Sun* newspaper branded him the 'Lizard of Oz'.[22] The mischievous Keating would have been well aware that forty years before, his old friend and political ally Sydney's Labor lord mayor Pat Hills had attracted similar criticism when he had put his hand under the queen's elbow, believing he was helping her upstairs in her long dress in Sydney during the 1954 tour.

Before leaving Australia, the queen made it clear that she believed the question of Australia becoming a republic was entirely a matter for its citizens to decide, and she did not visit Australia for the remainder of the 1990s while Australia debated the issue.

In March 2000, four months after the 1999 referendum, in which Australians voted 'No' to becoming a republic, the queen returned with Prince Philip for the thirteenth time. When they visited again in 2002, she was seventy-five and her husband eighty. There was no doubt she remained popular – as the result of the referendum proved – but questions were being asked as to how many more tours she could undertake at her age. She came again in 2006; and her most recent, and perhaps her last, visit was with Prince Philip, by then ninety years old, in October 2011. The nine-day visit was her sixteenth trip in nearly sixty years.

—

The queen's interest in Australia, and her many visits over the past sixty years, have encouraged other members of the royal family to tour the country as well. Following her first tour with Prince Philip, there have been more than 50 tours by other members of the British royal family to Australia.

The first other member to visit after 1954 was the queen's widowed mother, Queen Elizabeth the Queen Mother, who came in 1958 to attend the British Empire Service League Conference in Canberra. She returned in 1966 to open the Adelaide Festival of Arts, and on this tour she spent a weekend with her seventeen-year-old grandson Prince Charles, who was then at Timbertop school.

Charles and his siblings, Anne, Andrew and Edward, have also visited the country several times. Princess Anne has returned eight times since her first trip in 1970, including in 2009 when she attended a memorial service for the victims of the terrible bushfires in Victoria:

Everywhere one treads on the hills and in the valleys of the bushfires there are stories. Princess Anne discovered that yesterday when she drove into blackened Wandong aboard the Victorian governor's dusty limousine. After a couple of intense hours, the princess royal left half-apologetically, maybe even moved by the experience. 'I hope we haven't interrupted too much,' she told a small group outside the Wandong relief centre.[23]

Prince Andrew first toured in 1988 with his then wife, the Duchess of York, 'Fergie', and returned in 2005 for a private visit, when he provoked controversy for refusing a security screening at Melbourne airport:

'There was a bit of consternation on both sides,' one source said. 'Managers and security were called and it was suggested to the prince that he sit down in the next room and think about it for a while. He was told he would not be allowed to board the flight unless he agreed to be screened because it was the law. Eventually he reluctantly agreed.'[24]

The youngest of the queen's children, Prince Edward, visited Australia for the first time in March 1994 as chairman of the Duke of Edinburgh's International Award Association that had been set up by his father in 1956. He was back in 2006 to announce the winners of the Commonwealth Writers' Prize and again in 2014 to commemorate more than fifty years of the Duke of Edinburgh's Awards in Australia.

15

PRINCE PHILIP

Do you still throw spears at each other?

WHEN PHILIP MADE HIS first visit to Australia in April 1940, as a midshipman on HMS *Ramillies*, a local newspaper reported that the 'Prince of Greece and cousin of the Duchess of Kent' had been on leave in Sydney and made a few 'trips around the city incognito'.[1]

Two years later, Philip met and became friends with Australian Michael Parker, who was a navy sub-lieutenant as Philip was, and part of the same Royal Navy flotilla.[2] Parker was born in 1920 in Melbourne and was educated at the city's Xavier College. He had wanted to follow in the footsteps of his father, Captain C. A. Parker of the Royal Australian Navy, but to avoid any accusations of nepotism he instead went to England and joined the Royal Navy.[3] During the war when Philip was on the HMS *Whelp*, Parker was on the HMS *Wessex*, and both ships were sent to the Pacific for action against the Japanese, who were by then being driven back by the Allies through the Pacific.

The two young men spent time together on leave in Australia in 1945, when Parker took Philip around Melbourne. He showed the prince a good time; he was said to have been 'adept at organizing parties, and assorted extravaganzas'.[4] At the time the prince kept his whereabouts when he was in Melbourne or Sydney close to his chest, no doubt wanting the freedom afforded by some level of anonymity:

> Prince Philip was welcomed by the Sydney Greek community during yesterday's service at the Greek Orthodox Cathedral of St Sophia . . . Prince Philip, of Greece, a first cousin of King George of Greece, and of the Duchess of Kent, has arrived in Melbourne. The Greek Consulate was not advised of his arrival, and knows nothing of his whereabouts. The consular authorities believe that the prince is staying incognito for the time being. He is serving as an officer with the British Fleet in the Pacific.[5]

After the war, and shortly after he married Princess Elizabeth in 1947, Philip invited Parker to become equerry-in-waiting to the royal couple, and the following year he appointed Parker as his private secretary.

In 1949 the prince resumed active service in the navy when he was made first lieutenant and second-in-command on the destroyer HMS *Chequers*. He was based in Malta, and the queen would visit him there for weeks at a time. However, in July 1951, when it became clear that King George VI was very unwell, he took leave from the navy to return to London. He knew that he was ending his military career, having enjoyed so much being in his own command: he called those months 'the happiest of my sailor life' and said later:

I thought I was going to have a career in the Navy but . . . there was no choice . . . You have to make compromises. That's life. I accepted it. I tried to make the best of it.[6]

King George VI was said to have liked Michael Parker, taking him out shooting and introducing him to the ways of the court, and Parker became a highly valued member of the palace staff as well as Philip's close friend. It was Parker who woke Philip in Sagana Lodge, Kenya, in February 1952 so he could tell Princess Elizabeth that her father had died. In all the years Philip and Parker were together, the prince and his Australian mate had a reputation for enjoying themselves. Together they formed part of what was known as the Thursday Club, which met in a private room of Wheeler's Restaurant in Old Compton Street in London's Soho on Thursdays for often very long lunches. Others who joined the lunches included Peter Ustinov, David Niven, Iain Macleod and Francis Bacon. Parker later denied as 'absolute rubbish' the suggestion of drunkenness and womanising at the lunches.[7]

After the grand tour to Australia in 1954 with his wife, Prince Philip's next visit was in 1956 to open the Olympic Games in Melbourne. They were the first Olympic Games to be held in the southern hemisphere and helped launch the postwar reputation of Australia as one of the world's most successful sporting nations. Australia won thirteen gold medals, eight silver medals and fourteen bronze medals (only two countries won more: the Soviet Union and America), and many Australian athletes starred in front of their home crowd. Eighteen-year-old 'Golden Girl' Betty Cuthbert won three gold medals on the track; swimmer Dawn Fraser achieved two gold medals for the 100-metres freestyle and the 4 × 100 metres freestyle relay; athlete Shirley Strickland won gold in the 80-metres hurdles and for the 4 × 100 metres relay; and seventeen-year-old wonder boy swimmer Murray Rose became the youngest athlete to win three gold medals.

Philip, who arrived in Melbourne to open the games resplendent in the white uniform of the 'Admiral of the Fleet', was, according to the Australian press, every bit as popular as he had been in his role as the dashing prince to Queen Elizabeth on his visit to Australia two years before:

> Women – even matrons – go into raptures at a glimpse of him, and worldly-wise men come up with outpourings of superlatives. The duke just smiles – an intimate, embracing smile. People by the thousand wait for hours in broiling heat or chilling rain just for a nod, a hand wave, a smile from this, the most publicised man on earth today. He satisfies them, friendly, all with a 10 second appearance and they are happy.[8]

Huge crowds turned out to see the prince in Melbourne and Sydney, which, according to the *Australian Women's Weekly*, was immersed in 'crowds, flags, tickertape and cheers'.[9]

After the games, the prince and his entourage continued what would be a four-month-long cruise on the royal yacht *Britannia*, and parts of the trip were to prove controversial. After the *Britannia*'s commission two years before, the duke was taking it on its first long journey, with a crew of 257. He had with him a few close male friends, including of course Parker, as well as a new Aston Martin Lagonda car for their use on shore. When the *Britannia* reached Gibraltar, where the queen joined her husband for a tour of Portugal, the newspapers were full of stories about Parker's wife, Eileen, suing him for divorce, at a time when divorce was still socially controversial, and Parker was obliged to stay discreetly aboard the yacht. Though the queen and

Prince Philip supported him and wished him to stay in their service, a year later, when he was still being pursued by journalists, he was seen to have no choice but to finally resign his post as the duke's private secretary.

As soon as the cruise began, the press was questioning why the prince was to be away from his wife and two young children for so long and whether there was a rift between the couple.[10] On the way back from Australia the *Baltimore Sun* in the United States published the first story exploring this possibility, under the headline: 'Report. Queen, Duke in Rift Over Party Girl'. The paper's UK correspondent claimed that the Duke of Edinburgh was romantically involved with an unnamed woman, whom he met on regular basis in the London West End apartment of a society photographer.[11] According to Parker, who was still with the duke when the story broke, Philip was 'incandescent' about it; 'very, very angry'. The queen was equally upset and, against the monarchy's customary principle of never responding to such gossip, the palace issued a 'complete denial' that there was any rift between the queen and the duke.[12]

Over the years plenty of other newspaper stories were published around the world about royal 'scandals' that involved the Duke of Edinburgh. On different occasions he has been accused of having affairs with Princess Alexandra of Kent, Susan Barrantes – who was the mother of Sarah, the Duchess of York – the film actresses Merle Oberon and Zsa Zsa Gabor, and a number of women Philip knew in Australia. In 1972 the Paris newspaper *France Dimanche* calculated that in the previous fifteen years there had been seventy-three reports of the queen having divorced Philip.[13] However, there has never been any verifiable evidence or corroboration from those he has supposedly had affairs with, and it is unlikely he could have carried on these relationships without someone eventually coming forward with evidence.

—

The next time Prince Philip was back in Australia was six years later in 1962, at the invitation of Prime Minister Robert Menzies, to open the British Empire and Commonwealth Games in Perth. Originally known as the British Empire Games, the first competition was held in Hamilton, Canada in 1930 and hosted competitors from eleven British Empire countries. By the time of the 1962 games in Perth, their name had been changed to the British Empire and Commonwealth Games; and eventually in 1978, for the games in Edmonton, Canada, the words 'British' and 'Empire' were dropped and they became known, as they are today, as the Commonwealth Games.

The week before arriving, Philip became embroiled in a public spat with Australian farmers. Philip realised when his wife became queen that he must find his own niche, and in the decades that followed he dedicated himself to more than 800 charities, including those that focused on sport, education, the environment and wildlife conservation. In 1961 he became the president of the World Wildlife Fund, and prior to leaving London in 1962 he addressed a banquet they were holding, and in the blunt language that would make him famous, criticised Australian graziers who were killing kangaroos to protect grazing land:

> Just imagine a group of vandals going around the world every year and taking down all the works of two or three great masters and carefully wrecking them.[14]

The farmers were quick to attack the prince's comments as 'misguided' and 'distressing', and pledged to expose him to the 'true state of affairs regarding the danger of excessive kangaroo numbers'. Fortunately for Philip their anger did not last, and when he arrived in Australia two weeks later on a regular Qantas flight, he was warmly welcomed with 'Perth cheers' and 'in brilliant sunshine' to open the games.[15]

Three years later, in February 1965, the prince was invited to Australia to open the Royal Australian Mint in Canberra. In February 1966, Australia introduced its own decimal currency, moving to dollars and cents and dropping Australian pounds, shillings and pence that had been pegged in value to British sterling. Despite Australia's adopting its own currency, the queen's portrait remained for many years on all Australian notes and coins, and is still on the $5 note and all coins.

The Duke of Edinburgh was back again for a short stay in Sydney in May 1967. He was given a tour of the construction works of the Sydney Opera House, which had reached the stage where the giant 'shelled' roof was being installed. But the principal reason for this visit was to allow him to participate in the planning of the 1968 Commonwealth Study Conference, which was to take place in Melbourne. The duke had first come up with the idea during a visit to Canada in 1954:

I had asked to visit some of the new and developing industries in Canada's far north . . . Two things struck me. The great majority of these developments were 'single-industry' enterprises, and in most cases the towns associated with the industries were 'company towns'. This is not typical for an industrialised country, but it had the effect of drawing my attention to one of the basic problems faced by industrial communities. While a company in control of an industrial enterprise has to be based on a system of managerial and technical qualifications, the town in which all the workers and the management have to live needs to be managed by some democratic system involving all the inhabitants as citizens.[16]

The duke went on to say that he thought the Commonwealth Study Conferences could organise regular discussions involving all the 'professional, military, academic, parliamentary and scientific activity' within the British Commonwealth.[17] Since 1956 these conferences have been held every six years.

When Philip arrived in Australia in 1968 to open the Duke of Edinburgh's Commonwealth Study Conference, a local paper rather unkindly reported his presence was 'merely a device to give him something to do'.[18] The paper also noted that a generation had passed since the prince had come to Australia during World War II and 'it showed' on the face of the now 47-year-old duke.[19]

The stories became less and less deferential: in June 1970 *The Canberra Times* ran a short profile of him at forty-nine, describing him as 'unwrinkled, lean and far from mellowing':

'He is far more irritable now and he certainly drops far more bricks, apparently more deliberately than ever before,' a Buckingham Palace source close to Prince Philip said.

The piece concluded with what appeared to be a typically wry, unguarded remark of Philip's:

[he] touched off a flurry of abdication speculation when he said there was no truth in a rumour the queen might step down in favour of Prince Charles, but added, 'Of course, the idea has its advantages'.[20]

In 1971 he returned to take part in the fiftieth anniversary celebrations of the Royal Australian Air Force. Two
years later he was back as president of the Australian
Conservation Foundation when he visited Lake Pedder in
Tasmania. At the time, conservationists were protesting
Tasmanian government plans to dam Lake Pedder in the
state's south-west, and, in a breach of the convention that
royalty does not become involved in political matters, Prince
Philip wrote to Prime Minister Gough Whitlam protesting
that 'the Tasmanian government simply does not understand the point of conservation'.[21] The protests were in vain.
The Tasmanian government's Hydro-Electric Commission
was given permission to dam the Gordon River and flood
the valleys of the Serpentine and upper Huon rivers. More
than 240 square kilometres of Tasmania's wilderness
were drowned and the original lake is now twenty metres
underwater.[22]

Just seven months later, in October 1973, the duke
returned for the opening of the Sydney Opera House, and
in the nine years that followed he made five more trips.
During his 1982 tour he formally launched the Dunhill
International Indoor Showjumping Competition and,
as president of the International Equestrian Federation,
accepted a cheque from Dunhill, the cigarette company,
in the days when tobacco companies were big sponsors
of sport, to establish a fund to raise money for equestrian
tournaments.

In May 1986, he accepted an invitation to visit Australia
from the Queensland premier, Joh Bjelke-Petersen, to officially open the new Gateway Bridge, which had been built
over the Brisbane River. The problem was that the bridge
had already been officially opened the previous January,
when more than 200,000 people had walked across
it before it was opened for cars. Local politician Peter

Beattie accused the premier of 'insulting Prince Philip and the whole royal family' by inviting the duke to this second ceremony before a state election later in the year.[23] Philip appeared unabashed at the opening ceremony, but 'left dignitaries at the official launch red-faced' when he finished his speech:

> Now it's quite evident to everybody that it doesn't seem entirely appropriate to open it because it appears to be in use. So I now declare the bridge more open than usual.[24]

—

As the years rolled on, the prince made a number of statements or acted in certain ways that in earlier times may have been dismissed as badly judged but now began to be perceived as simply in bad taste. His critics came to regard Prince Philip's gaffes not as the comments of a harmless old duffer but more indicative of someone with deep-seated racial and chauvinist prejudices.

In 1989 he offended many when he agreed to attend the funeral of Japan's Emperor Hirohito in Tokyo. The Australian prime minister, Bob Hawke, had decided not to go to the funeral after a number of critical headlines and newspaper editorials, and quickly, because of the Japanese atrocities committed in the emperor's name during World War II and the barbarous treatment of Allied prisoners of war, Australian soldiers joined British veterans in condemning the duke's proposed trip. Bruce Ruxton, the president of the Victorian Returned Services League of Australia, characterised Philip's going to Hirohito's funeral as 'like going to the funeral of the devil'.[25]

The duke's more extreme gaffes were all widely reported in the Australian media. In 1986 he told British exchange students in Beijing that 'If you stay here much longer, you'll all be slitty-eyed,' and announced to a World Wildlife Fund meeting, 'If it has four legs and it's not a chair, if it's got two wings and it flies but is not an aeroplane, and if it swims and it's not a submarine, the Cantonese will eat it.' In 1984 he reportedly told a gift-bearing Masai in Kenya, 'You are a woman, aren't you?' In 1992 when he was accompanying Queen Elizabeth to the Sydney sesqui-centenary celebrations, he declined an invitation to pat a koala, saying, 'Oh no, I might catch some ghastly disease.'[26] On stress counselling provided to soldiers who experience trauma in war zones he said in 1995, 'We didn't have coun-sellors rushing around every time somebody let off a gun. You just got on with it!'[27] And when tighter gun laws were being discussed in Britain following the terrible shooting massacre in Dunblane in Scotland the following year, he reacted to the proposal for a ban on firearms by saying, 'If a cricketer suddenly decided to go into a school and batter a lot of people to death with a cricket bat, are you going to ban cricket bats?'[28]

In 2002 in Cairns in Far North Queensland, the queen and the Duke of Edinburgh watched a performance of the Aboriginal Tjapukai dance group and after the show, while the royal couple talked to the dancers, Philip report-edly asked Aboriginal leader Ivan Brim, 'Do you still throw spears at each other?'[29] And later that year he managed to offend travellers everywhere when he told the Aircraft Research Association that air travel comfort had improved, 'provided you don't travel in something called economy class, which sounds ghastly'.[30]

The prince was again embroiled in controversy, though indirectly, in Australia in 2015 when Prime Minister Tony Abbott misjudged the Australian public mood and announced that the prince would be made a knight of Australia. The awarding of knights and dames had been abandoned in Australia almost forty years before by the Whitlam Labor government, but, following Abbott's election in 2013, he controversially reintroduced them into the Australian system in 2014, and his first two recipients were the outgoing governor-general, Quentin Bryce, and the incoming governor-general, Peter Cosgrove. Then, to an overwhelmingly negative response, the following year he decided to offer a knighthood to Prince Philip.

It was not as if Philip needed another award. Not only had he already been made a Companion of the Order of Australia in 1988 but, as the British press were quick to point out, it was odd that Australia should add a knighthood to the list of Philip's titles that was 'already longer than his arm'.[31] He also has titles, awards, honours and medals from more than 100 countries, including a Collar of the Royal Family Order of Saints George and Constantine with Swords and the Order of the Phoenix from Greece, a Knight of the Order of the Elephant from Denmark, a Knight Grand Cross of the Order of the Condor of the Andes from Bolivia, the Grand Cordon of the Supreme Order of the Chrysanthemum from Japan, a Knight Grand Cross with Chain of the Order of the Queen of Sheba from Ethiopia, a Collar of the Order of the Aztec Eagle from Mexico, a Member Special Class of the Order of Muhammad from Morocco and the Grand Cordon of the National Order of the Leopard from Zaire.

Even though the offer of the knighthood was not Philip's fault, he was attacked by some in the Australian media for his various 'cringe-worthy gaffes' which made him an especially unworthy recipient of the award. The media also pummelled Abbott: the knighthood, according to the newspaper headlines, was 'a joke', 'ludicrous', an 'embarrassment', a 'time warp decision' and 'a throwback to another era'.

It seems Abbott had originally wanted to make the queen

a dame but Buckingham Palace had politely declined and suggested he give a knighthood to Philip instead, meaning Abbott found himself in a position where it would have been impolite to refuse. However, his decision was so unpopular it provoked a move by parliamentary colleagues to try to ditch him as prime minister. Abbott survived the challenge, which he later described as a 'near-death experience'.

—

Prince Philip has visited Australia twenty-three times, more than any other member of British royalty. He has remained involved in a number of organisations that are active in Australia, including the Duke of Edinburgh's Awards, which he established in 1956 as a way to motivate teenagers 'to become involved in a balanced program of voluntary self-development activities' and which have been popular with thousands of Australian boys and girls for more than half a century.

The role of queen's consort cannot be an easy one. Philip is expected to play a role but what exactly is it? There is no manual about how to do the job and little from the past to provide a guide. The only remotely similar case was Prince Albert, husband of Queen Victoria, but he died in 1861, leaving his widowed wife to reign for the next forty years. Elizabeth II's role was mapped out from her ascension to the throne, but Philip has been forced to invent his own duties under the scrutiny of courtiers. So what do Australians think of him? As someone who has stood loyally at the queen's side and has done the best he can in a difficult position? Or as a man who became outdated and out-of-touch? Or maybe a bit of both?

16

MARGARET

The princess would eat anything at all – but please make sure
there was a gin and tonic and a packet of American cigarettes
waiting for her.

ONE OF THE LAST of the queen's immediate family to visit
Australia was her younger sister, Princess Margaret, who
made her first trip in 1972.

Margaret was born in 1930 and had a happy childhood
and a 'close and affectionate relationship' with her older
sister.[1] When she was twenty-three and, according to one
of her biographers, 'a beautiful young woman with an
eighteen-inch waist' and 'vivid blue eyes', she fell in love
with RAF Group Commander Peter Townsend. She had
first met Townsend when she was a teenager and he was
an equerry to her father, King George VI.[2] Townsend, an
RAF pilot who had fought in the Battle of Britain and had
a distinguished war record, was sixteen years Margaret's
senior and married with two children when they first met.

In 1953 their relationship was exposed after they were photographed at the coronation of Queen Elizabeth, and a journalist noticed Margaret removing a piece of fluff from Townsend's jacket.

When Townsend told the queen's private secretary, Sir Alan 'Tommy' Lascelles, of his desire to marry the young princess, the old-school courtier was apparently outraged and told Townsend, 'You must be either mad or bad.'[3] But that year Townsend divorced his wife and proposed to Margaret, who accepted. While Elizabeth did not want to stand in the way of Margaret's happiness, there was overwhelming public and political opposition to the princess marrying a divorcee, and shortly after the coronation, to discourage the relationship, and on Lascelles' advice, Townsend was 'transferred' to work for the British government in Brussels.

As had been the case in 1936 when King Edward VIII had wanted to marry Wallis Simpson, the British cabinet, led in 1953 by the conservative, seventy-nine-year-old Winston Churchill, refused to approve the royal marriage to a divorcee. Neither would the Church of England agree to recognise it unless Margaret renounced her rights to the throne.[4] The British press also attacked the idea, saying that the union was 'unthinkable' and 'would fly in the face of royal and Christian tradition', stating what was already being widely reported across Europe and the United States.

The dominions, including Australia, were consulted, as they had been in 1936 and, according to Winston Churchill, their prime ministers, including Australia's Robert Menzies, were also 'unanimously' against the marriage.[5]

Finally, after two years of press speculation and hostile stories, in October 1955 Princess Margaret announced she would not marry Townsend. In her statement she included a reference to her obligations to Commonwealth countries:

I would like it to be known that I have decided not to marry Group Captain Peter Townsend. I have been aware that, subject to my renouncing my rights to succession, it might have been possible for me to contract a civil marriage. But mindful of the church's teachings that Christian marriage is indissoluble, and conscious of my duty to the Commonwealth, I have resolved to put these considerations before others. I have reached the decision entirely alone, and in doing so I have been strengthened by the unfailing support and devotion of Group Captain Townsend.[6]

Margaret was said to have been devastated by the break-up, and afterwards was regularly seen in London's West End at fashionable clubs and restaurants. She was a heavy smoker and increasingly a heavy drinker. In 1960, and shortly after hearing that Peter Townsend had proposed to a Belgian girlfriend half his age, Margaret married 29-year-old fashionable photographer and filmmaker Antony Armstrong-Jones. The announcement came as a surprise and provoked rumours that she was 'on the rebound'.[7]

The couple's marriage on 6 May 1960 in Westminster Abbey was the first royal wedding to be broadcast on TV. Her marriage to Armstrong-Jones, who was given the title of Lord Snowdon shortly before the wedding, widened Margaret's social circle to take in show-business personalities and a number of bohemian characters. But by the mid-1960s the marriage was on the slide: Lord Snowdon was by nature promiscuous – in the words of a friend of his, 'If it moves, he'll have it' – and both had affairs.[8] It was later reported in the Australian press that in 1967 the queen had tried to patch things up between the two. When it failed she is reported to have told them to each go their own way, but to be discreet about it.[9]

By 1970, when Margaret was forty years old, the marriage

was 'damaged beyond repair'.[10] To many, she was a tragic figure who had been denied the opportunity to marry the man she loved and had been eclipsed by her elder sister, who had become a very popular queen. But not everyone had sympathy for the princess, including aristocrat Lady Cynthia Gladwyn, who in a diary that was published years later said that Princess Margaret had wanted it both ways:

> Princess Margaret seems to have fallen between two stools. She wants to convey that she is very much the princess, but at the same time she is not prepared to stick to the rules if they bore or annoy her, such as being polite to people. She is quick, bright in repartee, wanting to be amused, all the more so if it is at someone else's expense. This is the most disagreeable side of her character.[11]

On Margaret's first visit to Australia in 1972, she was accompanied by Lord Snowdon. She was to officially open the new international airport on the Seychelles in the Indian Ocean and had agreed to add a trip to Western Australia afterwards. It would help make up for the queen not having been able to visit the west coast on her visit to Australia two years before, and for the west missing out on several other previous royal visits.

'Margaret and Tony to See Australia at Last', headlined the *Australian Women's Weekly* on 11 October 1972:

> The Snowdons are reported to be looking forward to their ten-day stay in Western Australia. Their itinerary is planned to enable them to see much of the country as well as its industrial and mining development.

The *Weekly*, which ran more royal stories than any other magazine or paper in Australia, reported that

Australians will meet a happy couple in the Snowdons. The year 1972 has been a particularly harmonious one for them – no rumors of a marriage rift; no nasty party incidents as when Tony threw the wine over the other feller's shirt front: no brushes with photographers.[12]

The article continued:

Although Princess Margaret carries out her royal visits abroad so well there has been criticism at times and the controversies are remembered long after the glow has worn off. One palace adviser admitted that they breathe a sigh of relief when Princess Margaret returns . . . 'You never quite know what she will do next,' he said.[13]

The *Weekly* also reported that in order to ensure her sister's tour ran 'smoothly', the queen had asked their cousin, the Hon. Mrs John Wills, to accompany Margaret:

She is to the royal family what most people understand as the dependable one – the relative who can be trusted to see that things go well. Mrs Wills not only knows all the ropes, she is a perfectionist. It is a measure of how much the queen desires the Snowdons' tour to go smoothly that she suggested they be accompanied by Mrs Wills.[14]

The *Weekly* described, too, how Margaret made the most of her appearance:

She may never again have that neat waist and dainty figure, but in staying plump she reminds every one of the queen mother. Her smile, her complexion, her beautiful blue eyes, and her ever-soignee hair give her distinction and warmth and there is now no trace of imperiousness.[15]

Arriving in Perth on the night of Saturday 7 October at the beginning of a ten-day tour, the royal couple were officially greeted by the Australian governor-general, Sir Paul Hasluck, and his wife, Lady Alexandra. Normally the prime minister would have been part of the official welcome but Prime Minister Billy McMahon was at the start of a federal election campaign, which two months later saw him lose to Labor's Gough Whitlam.

On Sunday the royal couple attended a garden party at Perth's Government House, which included 6000 Girl Guides and Brownies 'who stormed steep banks in Government House gardens . . . today to give the royal visitors, Princess Margaret and Lord Snowdon, a rousing farewell after the presentation'.[16]

After the weekend in Perth the royal party travelled thousands of kilometres through the vastness of Western Australia and saw Albany on the south coast, the great goldmining centres of Kalgoorlie and Coolgardie in the eastern desert and Fitzroy Crossing in the Kimberley, more than 2500 kilometres north of Perth.

To the relief of everyone, the tour ended at the Top End of Australia without any public embarrassments, and on 17 October Margaret left to return to England from Darwin, without her husband – Lord Snowdon flew first to Sydney on 'private business'.[17]

Her next visit to Australia was three years later in October 1975 to commemorate the twenty-fifth anniversary of the formation of the Women's Royal Australian Army Corps in Canberra; it also included visits to Sydney and Melbourne. The official invitation from the Australian government had been addressed to both the princess and Lord Snowdon, but by 1975 the relationship between the two was poisonous – they were barely speaking to each other – and Margaret was adamant that she wanted to go alone. But the Australian High Commission had asked the palace if both Margaret and Snowdon were available to make the trip, and the palace had written back: 'Her Majesty is glad to approve that Princess Margaret and Lord Snowdon should be invited to visit Australia.'[18] So the Australian government had invited them both.

On hearing that her husband had been invited, Margaret summoned her private secretary, Lord Napier, and asked if Snowdon intended to accept. Napier said that he wasn't certain but thought Snowdon would. At that, Princess Margaret ordered Napier to go to her husband and tell him that if he insisted on going ahead, she would cancel her trip. Lord Napier duly presented himself at Lord Snowdon's office and told him what Princess Margaret had said. Snowdon asked Napier if it was correct that they had both been invited, and when this was confirmed, Snowdon insisted he was entitled to go. However, in the end he withdrew, citing 'professional commitments'.[19]

There was a flurry of local media interest for the trip, even though Australia was in the grip of the serious political crisis that saw the dismissal of the Whitlam government by Sir John Kerr only eight days after Margaret had left to go home to England.

The *Australian Women's Weekly* this time described Margaret as 'possibly the most provocative and controversial' of all the royals: 'Her sharp wit, her outspokenness, her temper, her weight problems, her marriage with Lord Snowdon have, all her life, made round-the-world headlines.'[20]

The magazine opined that it was better Princess Margaret had come to Australia by herself:

The tour is, in fact, so very special that it marks the beginning of a new life for the princess . . . It is fairly well accepted that the Snowdons are happier apart than together and now that their daughter Lady Sarah Armstrong-Jones is at boarding school, friends close to Margaret are delighted that she is taking . . . the trip to Australia.[21]

The *Weekly* also mentioned Margaret's dietary preferences, having been told by a palace spokesperson that 'the princess would eat anything at all – but please make sure there was a gin and tonic and a packet of American cigarettes waiting for her'.[22]

Margaret arrived at Sydney Airport at 6 am on 22 October. Waiting with the welcoming committee of senior New South Wales and national leaders was the princess's Australian equerry, army officer Major Stephen Gower.[23] Vietnam War veteran Gower said that he could only guess at why he was appointed to the job:

> I had no idea as to why I had been nominated. I was a Vietnam veteran, had recently done well as an artillery battery commander and . . . had attended the year-long staff college course where the system looks over your performance very carefully . . . Perhaps it was because I'd previously been an honorary aide-de-camp to the governor of Queensland . . . and presumably could be counted on to know the ropes after the apprenticeship.[24]

He said he had little idea of what an equerry did and was far from bowled over at the offer of the job:

> What was an equerry? I had some ideas from seeing the queen pass by in her Rolls-Royce during the 1954 and 1963 visits. There was a bloke looking resplendent in uniform and gold braid in the front seat . . . I think I surprised the director by responding that I wasn't really enthusiastic about such an appointment . . . My protest was in vain. He briskly told me

I'd been nominated and that was that, and I'd best get on with it.

For the duration of the appointment, Gower was attached to the Australian prime minister's department and given a set of files dealing with the previous royal tours and the 'various applicable protocols'. There were also briefing notes on the princess provided by Buckingham Palace.

Gower was on hand in Sydney to meet the princess, whom he said looked tired after her long flight, which was understandable since this was well before the days of beds on commercial aircraft, even in first class. After being introduced to an array of New South Wales and federal officials the princess was whisked on to a Royal Australian Air Force 'VIP' plane for the short flight to Canberra. In Canberra she was given four hours' rest before her first commitment, an official lunch at Government House. Gower said the short break gave him a little time to get to know the officials travelling with the princess, including Lord Napier and her lady-in-waiting and good friend Lady Glenconner, whom he described as 'an elegant and striking woman'. Born Lady Anne Coke, Lady Glenconner had been a maid-of-honour at Queen Elizabeth's coronation. Her father was the fifth Earl of Leicester and her mother Lady Elizabeth Mary Yorke, daughter of Charles Yorke, eighth Earl of Hardwicke. Gower said Lord Napier and Lady Glenconner were good company and that he was able to work well with them.

Margaret's lunch was with Prime Minister Gough Whitlam and the leader of the opposition, Malcolm Fraser, and their wives. It could not have been a relaxed meal because the parliament was by then deadlocked; within three weeks Whitlam would be sacked by the governor-general and replaced by Fraser.

After lunch Princess Margaret was taken to the popular

Canberra vantage spot of Mount Ainslie and then to the Australian War Memorial to lay a wreath in honour of those who had died in war. On the way back to Government House, the royal party was surprised to see hundreds of Girl Guides and Brownies on the side of the road waving as the princess drove past. The press was highly critical of Margaret because her entourage failed to stop and meet some of the girls:

> Her visit to the Australian War Memorial was reduced from the programmed fifty minutes to seven, and she then arrived at the Regatta Point pavilion about forty minutes ahead of schedule . . . Guides and Brownies who had made the effort to be at Regatta Point to greet Princess Margaret when she was due to arrive at 4.20 pm . . . They were unhappy because long before many of them arrived the princess had been and gone.[25]

But Gower said the criticism of the princess was unfair. She had not ignored the girls; she didn't know they were going to be there:

> They all appeared excited and charming, but what on earth were they doing there? There had been no mention of them during the detailed planning and no event was listed on the program. I was told subsequently that Girl Guide officials thought it would be a good idea to line the girls up on the bridge. A well-meaning gesture backfired badly and caused a media storm.[26]

The next leg of the tour in Melbourne went more smoothly. According to Gower, Margaret was seen 'at her charming best' and 'obviously at ease at functions and events she attended'. Over the next two days she attended a lord mayoral reception, visited a disabled children's home, attended a state dinner and a performance of the Australian Ballet, made a visit to the Royal Botanic Gardens and took a trip in the pouring rain to Moonee Valley racecourse for the running of the Cox Plate. During the tour Gower explained that one of his roles was to ensure 'a steady supply of gin and tonics and cigarettes – which she smoked using a long white holder'.

Back in Sydney on the last leg of the tour, the royal party stayed at Government House with the governor, Sir Roden Cutler, and his wife. Cutler was a popular war hero in Australia. He had lost a leg during World War II and won a Victoria Cross. After the war he served as an Australian diplomat, and he and his wife became known for their extreme observance of protocol. Gower later recounted how he had been invited by the princess to join her for a swim in the pool but had been confronted by Lady Cutler when she caught him coming down the official staircase dressed in a tracksuit. 'What on earth are you doing?' asked Lady Cutler, who expected everyone to use the servants' stairs unless accompanying the princess. When Gower explained the princess was waiting for him at the pool, apparently both Lady Cutler and her husband hurriedly changed into their swimmers and joined them.

Gower described Margaret as 'bright, vivacious and witty', and was impressed by her conscientious performance of royal duties. He said that every day was crammed with engagements – 'a seemingly never-ending line of dignitaries' and 'always a crowd of others wanting to meet her'. As an example of her stamina, Gower described a typical day on the tour: he and others gave the princess a thirty-minute briefing after breakfast before driving out to Parramatta in Sydney's west for a visit to the old Government House. This was followed by a 'splendid luncheon with the National

Trust accompanied by an excellent selection of wine'. At 2.30 pm, the princess visited a Barnardo's home for deserted wives at Granville, where, he said, she appeared 'genuinely interested' and 'empathised with the women' even though there were no media to capture the event'. After Barnardo's they were driven across to the north shore of Sydney for 'billy' tea and scones with Girl Guides at Turramurra. At 4.30 pm they were back at Government House, but there was no time for a refreshing swim, because at 5.30 pm Margaret had to attend a reception for members of the Women's Royal Australian Army Corps in the Government House ballroom. Then, after a light dinner in her room of scrambled eggs and smoked salmon (something she was partial to), it was off to the Sydney Opera House for a concert by internationally renowned pianist Rudolf Serkin. Gower said that after meeting the opera house hierarchy, the princess was seated prominently for all to see in the royal box. 'It had been a long day,' he said, 'and I can't speak for the princess – but I found it hard to stay awake.'

Margaret enjoyed parts of the Sydney visit but not others. She liked the Australian Ballet performance of *The Two Pigeons* but did not want to visit lifesavers at the famous Bondi Beach in Sydney. She insisted she had the wrong sort of shoes for walking on the sand, but Lady Glenconner was carrying a flat pair of shoes in her bag and Margaret was forced, albeit reluctantly, to go on the beach.

At the end of the twelve-day tour, Margaret jetted off on 3 November to Mustique in the Caribbean, where she often holidayed; in 1959 Lady Glenconner's husband, Colin Tennant, to whom Margaret had been romantically connected after she'd broken off with Captain Townsend, had bought the princess a ten-acre plot on the island as a wedding gift, and a decade later had built her a five-bedroom villa on it. In a biography of Margaret, its author describes how:

By the late '70s Mustique was a glittering meeting place, the most exclusive island in the Caribbean . . . it boasted dozens of million-dollar holiday homes, owned by businessmen and stars such as Mick Jagger, David Bowie and Billy Joel. The hub of island life was Colin Tennant's hotel, the Cotton House, and life on Mustique was like a very grand Scottish house party.[27]

When Margaret finally returned to London she told friends that she'd 'hated' the Australian tour. Among her complaints were the small crowds that came out to greet her and the fact that the traffic lights had been left on rather than being fixed on green for her when she was being driven around Melbourne and Sydney.[28]

—

Princess Margaret's third visit to Australia was unplanned and only happened as a result of a medical emergency. Late in 1977 she agreed to represent the queen at the celebrations of independence of the tiny Pacific state of Tuvalu. Formerly part of the British protectorate of the Gilbert and Ellice islands, Tuvalu, with a population of barely 10,000 people, is a small collection of islands and coral reefs about halfway between Hawaii and Australia. It was hardly well suited to host a member of the British royal family. Described as being 'much the same size as a typical English village', the only official accommodation was in the British Government House, which had one spare bedroom but no hot water or air conditioning.

The princess's private secretary, Lord Napier, reported that such accommodation was completely inappropriate, so the New Zealand government agreed to offer its navy ship HMNZS *Otago*, which had plenty of accommodation, for the princess while she was in Tuvalu. The New Zealanders would provide transportation to and from the island on their Air Force Hercules transport aircraft and their generosity went as far as flying in a royal car for the princess from Fiji, 1100 kilometres to the south.

Among the other international dignitaries attending the independence celebrations was the Australian Minister for Foreign Affairs, forty-year-old Andrew Peacock, who had travelled from Fiji on the Hercules to Tuvalu with Princess Margaret, and other British officials. According to Hugh Cortazzi, an under-secretary with the British Foreign Office, Peacock began chatting up Princess Margaret even before they got there: 'My main memory was the way Andrew Peacock flirted with the princess before we ever got to Tuvalu. I found him arrogant and conceited.'[29]

John Snodgrass, head of the Pacific Territories Department of the British Foreign Office, also remembered Andrew Peacock, who he knew had a reputation for being a 'ladies' man': Snodgrass said that on arriving at Tuvalu, Peacock had quickly targeted one of the American delegates:

> He attached himself at the outset to the attractive lady representing the Americans. When the time came to present the farewell gifts, the Tuvaluans evidently assumed she was Peacock's wife. To their embarrassment and to many of the guests', the gifts to the Australians were presented to them when they were sitting together. I do not know what happened to the gift for the American representative.[30]

The night before the independence ceremony, Margaret dined with Peacock on the Australian warship anchored near the *Otago*. In the early hours of the following morning, back on the *Otago*, she rang Lord Napier's cabin, saying she was very ill. It was reported in the Australian press that the *Otago*'s doctor recommended she go immediately to Sydney for treatment and Lord Napier had to take her place at the ceremony that day while arrangements were made to fly the princess to Australia:[31]

> Princess Margaret became ill with a fever aboard a New Zealand war ship today while she was attending independence celebrations of Tuvalu in the South Pacific. The 48-year-old princess, who was to represent her sister the queen at the island's independence ceremony, was taken ill during the night, a spokesman aboard the frigate *Otago* said.[32]

Margaret did not go ashore for any of the celebrations on Sunday but stayed on board the *Otago*. The following day she left Tuvalu on the Hercules aircraft on the nine-hour flight to Sydney. Peacock, who was supposed to leave for the United States after the independence celebrations, instead travelled with her to Australia.

The Australian press described the illness that had made it impossible for the princess to stay for the celebrations:

> She complained of breathing problems and a high temperature, and the ship's doctor, Dr Peter Robinson, diagnosed an acute febrile upper respiratory illness. She had a temperature of 40 degrees (105 degrees F) and was being treated with antibiotics.[33]

She was, they said, 'quite obviously incapable of carrying out the remainder of her engagements on Tuvalu and her visit to Fiji also has been cancelled'.[34] The press also duly reported concern, including the queen's, about Margaret's health:

The queen is deeply concerned about Princess Margaret's continuing ill health, a close friend of the royal family said after the princess had run a high temperature and had to be airlifted from Tuvalu to Sydney at the beginning of a long royal tour. The queen has always been anxious about Princess Margaret, who is far from robust, but now she is more worried than ever that the strain of a royal tour is too much for the princess. As we all know, the queen can take the most gruelling royal tour in her stride, but the princess hasn't that kind of stamina.[35]

But no amount of sympathetic reporting could scotch the rumours about the relationship between Margaret and Andrew Peacock, which were fuelled by the princess's private secretary when he told the press later in the week in Sydney that 'talk of romance' between the princess and the Australian foreign minister was 'absurd'.

Lord Napier . . . lashed out at 'scurrilous and inflammatory gossip' when answering questions at a press conference on Friday, shortly before the princess left Sydney . . . Lord Napier, obviously angered by the rumours, said there was no romantic involvement and that Mr Peacock had merely been fulfilling an official role. He said Princess Margaret and Mr Peacock had been good friends for some time and he commended Mr Peacock for breaking his journey to the US.[36]

When Peacock was asked about his relationship with Margaret some months later by the *Australian Women's Weekly*, he insisted, 'she's a friend'.[37] Years later the London *Daily Telegraph* reported that:

Viral pneumonia was the official reason given, but it was said privately that she got rather drunk on board with the

Australian foreign minister, Andrew Peacock, and was in no fit state to come ashore.[38]

And the Tuvaluan prime minister, Ionatana Ionatana, was reported to have complained years later that Margaret had indeed overindulged: 'We understand she had a good time on the ship with Andrew Peacock without ever making it ashore to the celebrations.'[39]

The X-rays at Sydney's Royal Prince Alfred Hospital showed nothing untoward, and Princess Margaret went back to stay at Government House in Sydney. But not for long. She found she simply couldn't bear staying with the Cutlers. She complained that whenever she came down the front stairs, both Sir Roden and Lady Cutler would be standing rigidly to attention at the bottom of the banister but facing away from the princess. As Margaret reached the ground they would turn around, the governor would give a courtly bow and Lady Cutler would curtsy. The Cutlers also continued to insist that Lady Glenconner use the back stairs like the other servants unless she was accompanying the princess somewhere.

The princess took such a dislike to the Cutlers that she asked Lord Napier to phone the British ambassador in Japan, Sir Michael Wilford, to ask if Margaret's party could come to Japan earlier than had been originally scheduled.[40]

—

Margaret spent much of the rest of her life out of the public eye, afflicted with ill health and increased disability. She had begun smoking at fifteen and was a heavy smoker throughout her adult life. In 1985 she had her left lung removed, as her father, King George VI, had thirty years before – he too had been a heavy smoker. She quit smoking in 1989 but remained a heavy drinker. In 1993 she was admitted to hospital with pneumonia and in 1998 had a stroke while holidaying in Mustique. In 1999 she suffered severe scalding in a bathroom accident, which left her with difficulty when walking and largely restricted her to a wheelchair. In January 2001 she suffered a further stroke, which left her with impaired vision and paralysis on her left side. She died the following year aged seventy-one.

17

PRINCE CHARLES,
PRINCE OF WALES

Prince Charles will be the next governor-general of
Australia . . . There will be an official announcement soon.

PRINCE CHARLES HAS VISITED Australia fourteen times,
more than any other member of the royal family except
Queen Elizabeth and Prince Philip. For many years he
has done his best to win the affection of Australians and
wanted badly to become the country's governor-general.
Yet Australians have not warmed to him the way they
have to his grandmother, the queen mother; his mother,
the queen; his first wife, the Princess of Wales; or his sons,
William and Harry and he has never quite managed to
overcome the awkward aloofness that has been interpreted
by some as snooty and condescending.

Charles was born in 1948 and had what most today
would regard as an old-fashioned, even Edwardian

upbringing. Many Australians well remember the news-reel footage of the reunion with the queen after she and Prince Philip returned from their tour of Australia in 1954. Three-year-old Princess Anne and five-year-old Prince Charles were taken to Malta to meet their parents as they sailed home to England via the Suez Canal. The newsreels captured the moment when little Charles ran excitedly to his mother, whom he had not seen for six months. Rather than grab and cuddle him, she thrust out her hand for him to shake.

Charles attended preparatory school at Hill House in west London for eight months before going to Cheam School in Hampshire, and then, five years later, to secondary school at Gordonstoun in Scotland. Prince Philip's time at the school, which he believed had shaped him positively, led him to believe it would do the same for his son. But, according to letters later made public, the queen mother counselled against the decision:

> In May 1961, when Charles was twelve, [the queen mother] wrote to the queen: 'I suppose he will be taking his entrance exam for Eton soon. I do hope he passes because it might be the ideal school for one of his character and temperament.' She added: 'All your friends' sons are at Eton, and it is so important to be able to grow up with people you will be with later in life. And so nice and so important when boys are growing up that you and Philip can see him during school days and keep in touch with what is happening. He would be terribly cut off and lonely in the far north.'[1]

Gordonstoun promoted physical toughness with an emphasis on the outdoors and plenty of sport, including sailing and mountaineering. But Charles was far more sensitive than his father, and these were activities he did not relish. Not only that, but he was bullied there. He quickly grew to loathe the place, describing it as 'A prison sentence. Colditz in kilts.'[2] According to his biographer Jonathan Dimbleby, the boys at the school smoked, drank, talked sex, traded pornographic magazines and pilfered from local shops as a matter of course. This, to a sheltered young boy who wanted at that time in his life only to do the right thing, was horribly unfamiliar to him. Yet his father did not see it, and he wrote his son bracing letters of admonition, urging him to be strong and resourceful.

In early 1966 Charles was given a break from Gordonstoun and went to Australia for two terms, as 'a tall, slim, rosy-cheeked' seventeen-year-old, to attend the Timbertop campus of Geelong Grammar School, one of Australia's most exclusive private schools.[3] The palace made it clear that Charles would not be undertaking any official engagements while he was in Australia and 'requested that the prince's visit should be treated as a private one and that he should be allowed the same freedom from public attention as any other school boy'.

According to an *Australian Women's Weekly* article published in 1981, it was hoped Timbertop might achieve what Gordonstoun had failed to:

What Prince Philip had in mind for his son was for him to be a confident fellow, a little aloof, as became his royal heritage, yet friendly, a good mixer, with an air of command, a dashing young man with a subtle wit and, of course, a touch of his own arrogance. Prince Charles had yet to show any of these qualities. He was shy, grave and punctilious, a nice little boy with his hair falling into his eyes, but he wasn't tough. The queen worried about him. Prince Charles made no intimate friends his own age while he was at Gordonstoun, and he wasn't at all interested in girls.[4]

Charles appeared to enjoy Timbertop more than Gordonstoun; his acting equerry when he was there, David Checketts, famously said, 'I took him out there a boy and brought back a man.'[5] In May 1966 his grandmother took him with her to the Snowy Mountains for a few days when she was in Australia. The queen mother was reported as saying, 'Prince Charles likes school in Australia but he gets a little homesick.' According to *The Canberra Times*, 'She enjoyed her tour but particularly enjoyed seeing her grandson.'[6]

After leaving Timbertop and returning to Gordonstoun to finish his final year there, Charles made his first official visit to Australia when he attended the funeral of the Australian prime minister Harold Holt at Melbourne's St Paul's Cathedral on 22 December 1967. But his first full-length tour came in March 1970 when he visited with the queen, Prince Philip and Princess Anne to participate in the commemoration of the discovery of the east coast of Australia by Captain James Cook 200 years before.

Three months before his next visit in 1974, Charles gave a long interview to the *Australian Women's Weekly*. He had grown up since finishing school, but had not yet adopted many of the causes he was to later espouse. In the interview he was defensive:

> It's a fallacy that I don't mix, or don't mix enough, with other people in different walks of life. You may think I don't show any signs of benefiting from it. That's a different matter. That's one thing about this job, you do meet people. I don't go off and spend a month in the house of somebody in a walk of life quite different from mine, and mix in that sense, but that's got nothing to do with being royal: that goes for hundreds of thousands of people in all walks of life.[7]

He also complained that being a royal was a liability in Australia:

> As a matter of fact, having a title, and being a member of the upper classes as often as not militates against you in this country today. In Australia you certainly have to fend for yourself. Australia got me over my shyness. I was fairly shy when I was younger.

He denied that he would be restricted to marrying someone from the British aristocracy but confessed it was likely his future wife would be from his own class:

> There's no essential reason why I shouldn't. I'd be perfectly free to. What would make it unlikely would be accidental, not essential. Whatever your place in life, when you marry, you're forming a partnership which you hope will last, say, fifty years. I certainly hope so . . . I've been brought up in a close-knit happy family, and family life means more to me than anything else. So I'd want to marry somebody who had interests which I understood and could share. Then look at it from the woman's point of view. A woman not only marries a man: she marries into a way of life, a job, into a life where she's got a contribution to make.

Charles added that it was important that his future wife had some knowledge of the realities of being queen, perhaps ironic given his choice of bride seven years later as naive twenty-year-old Lady Diana Spencer, with whom he had almost nothing in common:

> She's got to have some knowledge of it, some sense of it, or she wouldn't have a clue about whether she's going to like it, and if she didn't have a clue, it would be risky for her,

wouldn't it? If I'm deciding whom I want to live with for fifty years, well, that's the last decision in which I want my head to be ruled entirely by my heart. It's nothing to do with class; it's to do with compatibility.

When he arrived at Canberra's Fairbairn Air Force Base in October 1974 to begin his eighteen-day visit, he was greeted by a small crowd of about 400 people who had braved the cool and windy weather to welcome him.[8] He was welcomed by the governor-general, Sir John Kerr, and the acting prime minister, Rex Connor, in the absence of Prime Minister Gough Whitlam, who was overseas, making him the first Australian prime minister to be away at the time of the arrival of a member of the royal family.

One of his first duties was to open the Anglo-Australian Telescope at Siding Spring, in the remote north-west of New South Wales. The large telescope, which was described as looking 'like a giant ice-cream', had been designed to allow for higher quality astronomical observations from the southern hemisphere and was capable of penetrating the southern skies by more than a billion light years.

It was later claimed that it was on this tour that Charles first discussed with the incumbent governor-general, Sir John Kerr, the possibility of becoming Australia's governor-general at some future date. It was, says Dimbleby, 'a proposal seriously considered in the light of the lengthy time the prince was likely to wait before becoming king'.[9] According to Commander Michael Parker, who had been private secretary to Prince Philip, 'the idea behind the appointment was for him to put a foot on the ladder of monarchy, for being the future king and start learning the trade'.[10]

During this trip, Charles admitted he would be interested in becoming the next Australian governor-general, 'if it was desirable'. However, in an interview from Canberra's Government House that was televised nationally on all of the four stations existing in Australia at the time, he played down the matter.[11] 'That is not the sort of thing that I can discuss,' he said. 'It would be for the prime minister, Mr Whitlam, to discuss the matter with the queen.'[12] When asked if he would accept the position, he replied by saying that he was not sure if he would enjoy being the governor-general but 'would be delighted to consider it'.[13]

The idea of Charles being a possible future governor-general came with the news that he was considering buying land in Australia. Wearing a dandelion in his button-hole and speaking at an impromptu press conference beside the White Swan Reservoir in Ballarat in Victoria, *The Canberra Times* said the prince thought

> buying land in Australia was a lovely idea . . . he had been thinking of buying land in Australia since he attended Geelong Grammar School . . . but economically speaking it is very difficult at the moment.[14]

It has been claimed that Kerr and Prince Charles discussed the matter of Charles's being made governor-general again in September 1975 when they stayed at the same hotel in Port Moresby for the Papua New Guinea independence celebrations, just two months before the governor-general dismissed Gough Whitlam as prime minister.[15] And less than a year later, in August 1976, the *Australian Women's Weekly* confidently predicted the still unmarried prince would be Australia's next governor-general and that an announcement of the appointment was imminent. The magazine was happy to give the story prominence as its circulation always jumped when it broke a royal story:

338

Prince Charles will be the next governor-general of Australia . . . There will be an official announcement soon . . . but you can be certain he would only accept the governor-generalship only if everyone was happy with it . . . His combined knowledge and self-proclaimed affection for Australia must surely make the queen's charismatic son a popular choice for the governor-generalship. In England they see Prince Charles term as governor-general as dissolving political problems like snowflakes.[16]

The *Women's Weekly* went on to quote 'one of the close circle of friends who have known him since his Timbertop days', who said, 'The prince has a great love of Australia and to be governor-general of the country he knows so well will fulfill his wish to return to serve Australia.'[17]

The London *Times* also thought Charles would be a good choice and would be able to bring stability to the office following Kerr's overtly political move in dismissing Whitlam the year before:

It is exclusively for the Australian people . . . to consider if such an appointment sometime in the future would strengthen the Australian monarchy and serve their purpose in restoring impartiality to Government House . . . If it were found that any governor-general henceforth would always face such political decisions as Sir John Kerr did, obviously the prince could not be asked to serve. If on the other hand he were seen in Australia as capable of taking the governor-general out of politics, and so restoring smoothness in Australia's democracy, there is no other task for him in Britain which could be considered to have priority.[18]

It was known that the conservative prime minister, Malcolm Fraser, favoured Prince Charles for the position and tried unsuccessfully several times during his seven years in office to bring about the appointment. However, there was a widespread lack of enthusiasm in Australia for the idea, and in November 1976 the government was forced to announce it 'was not likely to replace the Governor-General Sir John Kerr with Prince Charles'.[19] When Sir John Kerr resigned his post in July 1977, cutting short his five-year term with effect from that December, he was instead succeeded by Sir Zelman Cowen, a distinguished law professor and someone who was seen as apolitical. Prime Minister Malcolm Fraser said on the press release about Kerr's stepping down:

> He feels that the events of 1975 and the association of his office with issues of state which arose at that time evoked partisan feelings in the Australian community which have now substantially subsided but which nevertheless left feelings which might be resolved more quickly if he now makes way for a successor.

Prince Charles was back in Australia for the fifth time that November, as patron of the Queen's Silver Jubilee Appeal for Young Australians, which would raise money to make awards to individuals or organisations in each state and territory. Prime Minister Fraser described the awards as being

> to assist in the widest possible variety of projects and causes involving young people . . . to offer new hope and opportunity for young men and women who might not otherwise have the chance to develop their talents to full capacity. Above all, it will help our young nation realise our potential, our vast capacity which as yet has been barely tapped. I have no doubt that the trust will be a fitting tribute to the first twenty-five years' reign of the queen.[20]

For the visit the palace and the governor-general worked hard at promoting 29-year-old Charles as having a special connection with youth:

> In Canberra, the governor-general and Lady Kerr would be hosts at a barbecue lunch at Government House to which representative groups of young citizens in the capital would be invited. In Sydney, Melbourne and Brisbane, the Premier of each State would hold a reception to which young people were to be invited.[21]

The *Australian Women's Weekly* helped promote the image of a youthful and accessible prince by publishing a story shortly before the start of the tour suggesting Charles was

> the prince with the common touch! He will be in Australia next month and meeting people – especially the young – will be his main aim throughout the tour. He is known as 'Charlie Wales' to his friends, 'Charlie Chester' (Earl of Chester is one of his titles) when he is crowd shy, occasionally 'Charles the Clown Prince' (a name which irritates him). He is Charles, Prince of Wales. Next month he will be in Australia as Patron of the Queen's Silver Jubilee Appeal for Young Australians Charles.[22]

His itinerary had been planned to allow him to meet as many young people as possible. In Brisbane he attended the Young Queenslanders Exhibition. In Sydney he went to a reception of young sports stars and to a Little Athletics carnival. He also launched the Australian Broadcasting Commission's Silver Jubilee pop album, attended a youth musical and cultural evening in Adelaide; and in Alice Springs he met young people involved with Festival Week.

In Sydney, Charles stayed at the private home of Harry M. Miller in Sydney's prosperous Centennial Park. Miller was a colourful entrepreneur and entertainment promoter who had been appointed chairman of the Australian Silver Jubilee Appeal by Prime Minister Fraser. (Five years later he was jailed for fraud and served ten months in prison.) According to Miller, like Princess Margaret, Charles could not stand staying with the governor, Sir Roden Cutler:

> The reason Prince Charles spent so much time at my house during his stay was because he couldn't stand NSW Government House. Apparently none of the royals like it because it had more protocol and stuffiness than Buckingham Palace. As a single man, Charles had his own set of unique problems while staying there, namely difficulty in sneaking in young women late at night, because sitting up waiting for him, fully dressed in pinstripe splendor was the Governor, Sir Roden Cutler. In the end, Charles had to order Cutler to bed, and not wait up for him any longer.[23]

Miller said Charles brought women back to his home at night:

> He had a lot of fun during that visit – and I mean fun – and he even used my house at Centennial Park to entertain a handful of young women, including his friend Lady Dale 'Kanga' Tryon and the very pretty daughter of a well-known NSW politician, whose name I best not reveal.[24]

Dale Elizabeth Harper, or 'Kanga' as she became known, had been born into a rich Melbourne family in 1948. Already a well-known socialite, she moved to England when she was twenty-one to be the London social correspondent for the *Australian Women's Weekly* and was soon known as 'a colourful figure in royal circles'.[25] In 1973 she married Baron Tryon, who was a member of Prince Charles's social set. Kanga and the prince became good friends and reputedly lovers. She said Charles had given her her nickname, and he once famously said of her that she 'was the only woman that really understood me'.[26] In her forties Kanga suffered from uterine cancer and while in a rehabilitation clinic in 1996 she fell from a window and shattered her spine – she later claimed she was pushed. She died aged forty-nine the following year, only three months after the death of Princess Diana.

Six months after the Silver Jubilee Appeal, in May 1978, Charles was in Australia again briefly, for the funeral of Sir Robert Menzies, who had died at the age of eighty-three. Menzies had been Australian prime minister twice for a total of nineteen years between 1939 and 1966, and had been the British monarchy's strongest supporter in Australia in modern times. Charles arrived on a special Royal Air Force DC-10 with former British prime ministers Harold Wilson and Alec Douglas-Home as well as other senior British politicians and officials, and was gone in forty-eight hours, staying only for the funeral.

—

When the prince arrived in Canberra at the start of his next visit in 1979, only 100 people turned out to greet him. *The Canberra Times* suggested that Australians saw more of the royals than most of the British public and were growing tired of so many visits.

The queen's family are frequent visitors to Australia. Indeed it is quite possible that Australians see more of them than many people in Britain who do not find themselves on the royal tour circuit. Besides, the frequency of visits by one or other of the family has the comfortable acceptance of friends dropping in.[27]

Not that the prince was involved in many exciting, crowd-pulling spectacles. His 1979 itinerary included the inauguration of the Googong Water Supply Project, the opening of an agricultural research station museum and the planting of a tree in Western Australia, receiving representatives of the Royal Australian Armoured Corps, attending the anniversary celebrations of the Australian Academy of Science, and laying a wreath at the Canberra War Memorial.

But this tour is remembered well for one incident: a bikini-clad woman lunging at the prince and kissing him in the early morning surf at Cottesloe Beach in Perth. Pictures of the 26-year-old local Perth model Jane Priest leaping out of the surf to hug the prince flashed around the world, brought Priest instant notoriety and helped give the 'somewhat stodgy Charles something of an image makeover'.[28]

Jane Priest's kiss appeared to have been a spontaneous gesture by the young model, but years later she was reported as saying that the event had been set up. Interviewed by the UK *Evening Standard* in 2005, she implied the stunt was the idea of Charles's staff:

> My meeting with Charles on the beach wasn't my suggestion, it was theirs. It was a PR thing to try and make Charles more accessible. It was a set-up photograph of the Prince of Wales meeting an Australian native.[29]

She also said that the stunt did not go according to plan:

> but he threw a spanner in the works. When he saw me he dived into the water, so I thought I'd follow him in, but as

I went in, he got out. So I followed him out, hair ruined, make-up ruined, and I felt like such an idiot. I actually went and put my hands on his chest to give him a kiss and Charles said: 'No, I can't touch you, I can't touch you.'

After making the front page of just about every newspaper in the Western world, Priest said she did not regret that she'd failed to make a more favourable impression on the future king. 'This was a five minutes of fame thing. I was never going to be Queen Jane, let me tell you. Apart from anything else my background wasn't clean enough.'

—

There was far greater public interest in Charles and the royals when he visited Australia again in April 1981. Two months earlier, his engagement to Diana Spencer had been announced in London and Charles had suddenly become a much more exciting and romantic figure:

When the prince from a real-life romantic fairytale lands in town, nobody likes it better than the young-at-heart. On his latest visit to Sydney, Prince Charles took on a new magic. Lady Di was on his and everyone else's mind and people turned out in droves to cheer the royal bridegroom-to-be.[30]

Prince Charles is believed to have first met the then sixteen-year-old Diana in late 1977 when he was dating her older sister, Lady Sarah. He took a serious interest in Diana as a potential bride during the summer of 1980, when they were guests at a country weekend, where she watched him play polo. Later the same year Charles invited Diana to Balmoral and she met his family, who were impressed by her.

In September 1980, *The Canberra Times* ran an article headlined 'Way "is Clear" for Charles to Marry'. In it,

London gossip columnist Nigel Dempster was quoted as saying that Charles's choice of girlfriend had been approved by two married female friends of his, Lady Dale 'Kanga' Tryon and Camilla Parker Bowles. According to Dempster, they

> had told the prince that he must find an unblemished girl with an understanding of the life she would have to lead. 'No future Queen of England can afford a past,' Dempster said in the *Daily Mail* . . . 'an intimate tells me this may be his last chance, he'd be a fool to pass it up. She's ideal.'[31]

The couple regularly saw each other in London, and in February 1981 the prince proposed marriage and Lady Diana accepted. Diana later said that immediately after she had accepted Charles's offer of marriage he 'ran upstairs and rang his mother'.[32] The engagement was kept a secret for a few weeks, and was finally announced on 24 February 1981.

Australian lawyer Richard Spencer was thirty years old and working in London when the engagement was announced. At the time his girlfriend worked at Buckingham Palace and each night after work he would drive to the palace, through the gates, park in the forecourt and enter via the Privy Purse door to wait for her in the queen's waiting room.

> It was the day of the announcement of Charles and Diana Spencer's engagement and I arrived at the palace gates as usual. A large crowd had gathered to celebrate the good news. There was extra security and they didn't recognise the car with the kangaroo sticker on the back. 'Your name, sir?' I gave my name: Richard Spencer, and the crowd murmurs 'Spencer!' and wondered what the connection was between this Spencer and

Diana Spencer. I was cleared to enter, park the car and take my usual seat in the queen's waiting room. This day, unusually, there are three people at the other end of the room to whom I nodded on entering. They were excitedly talking about the announcement and how thrilled her majesty was about the news. After a short time, being British, they felt the need to introduce themselves. 'I'm Sir – and this is Lord and Lady –.' I replied in an unambiguously Australian accent, 'Very nice to meet you. My name is Richard Spencer.' Silence, as their astonished faces display a desperate need to know who this Spencer is and where does he fit in? Possibly a long-lost relative from the colonies? But being British they can't ask the obvious question. My girlfriend enters and we depart. If they had asked I would have explained that 'Yes, I do have a sister Diana – she lives on the Central Coast of New South Wales.'[33]

At the time of the engagement, there were questions as to why Charles had chosen Diana over all the other young aristocratic young women he might have been interested in. One reason was that Diana was very much still a virgin, which remained even then an important issue for the fiancée of the heir to the British throne. As Diana's uncle Lord Fermoy put it:

Diana, I can assure you, has never had a lover . . . she really doesn't have any blemishes . . . all this I know to be true. Diana is indeed the rose without a thorn.[34]

Years later Diana confirmed her virginity was a critical factor: 'He'd found the virgin, the sacrificial lamb.'[35]

During the prince's 1981 Australian visit, the local media focused on the forthcoming wedding. But during the tour the prince again discussed with Prime Minister Fraser the possibility of becoming governor-general – a position

Charles still coveted. Fraser said the prince had made it clear to him that he wanted to be 'more involved in a permanent way with Australians from different walks of life'. When asked specifically about the possibility of giving Charles the governor-general's job, Fraser told *The Canberra Times* that he still felt Charles was suitable. 'He [Prince Charles], one day God willing, will be monarch, King of Australia – with the warmth and affection overwhelmingly of the Australian people.'[36]

But Australians remained unsure about the proposal. *The Canberra Times* published an editorial that tried to cover both sides of the argument:

> First, the benefits. There can be no objection to Australia being involved in job-training and it has been suggested that it would be of some value to a future king to serve an apprenticeship as governor-general . . . A second benefit concerns the job rather than the person who fills it. It has been suggested before that there would be merit in Australia offering the job of governor-general not only to Australians but also to other people in Commonwealth countries. Provided the person invited has the necessary qualifications for the high office it would be of some significance in international understanding if, on occasions, he or she could be drawn from another Commonwealth country. Prince Charles would again fit into this category.[37]

The newspaper also argued that the appointment had become more problematic since the sacking of the Whitlam government by Governor-General Sir John Kerr:

> The drawbacks to nominating Prince Charles reflect rather on the Australian Constitution and its interpretation than on the man himself. It must be acknowledged that the position of governor-general since 1975 has been a delicate one . . . the

prime minister, Mr Fraser, would not do Australia or the monarchy a service by putting Prince Charles into a position where he just might have to make a political decision. The normal royal practice, as was pointed out repeatedly at the time of the Whitlam dismissal, was that the queen would have relied on the advice of her ministers. But it has now been demonstrated that things can be vastly different in Australia. If, in similar circumstances, Prince Charles as governor-general followed British practice he would certainly alienate those in the Australian electorate who felt he should use the reserve powers of the governor-general.

It was highly unlikely that the prince would ever be acceptable as Australia's governor-general unless the proposition was supported by both sides of politics. Unfortunately for Charles, the Labor opposition leader, Bill Hayden, would not endorse the idea. Hayden said that Prince Charles was 'indisputably a popular public figure' and a 'good representative of what the royal family has been about', but went on:

> there is no reason why Australians should have a cultural cringe or any form of inferiority about their place in the world . . . There had not been an outside appointment to the post for more than twelve years . . . It's more important for us to believe, to have the confidence . . . that Australians can do these jobs . . . We shouldn't defer to other countries or the leaders of other countries no matter how much respect we indisputably have for Prince Charles as a person.[38]

Hayden insisted he was not playing politics, 'just good old-fashioned Australian nationalism: I'm an Australian nationalist from way back . . . There's nothing that comes before us that we can't handle as Australians.'

The prince's ambitions suffered a further setback two months after he returned to England: an opinion poll published in the Melbourne *Age* in June 1981 revealed that 70 per cent of people of voting age said they would prefer an Australian for governor-general. Only 24 per cent said they wanted Prince Charles. For a while Prime Minister Fraser battled on. However, within weeks he could see that he would not be able to muster enough support, and he let it be known that he was 'no longer pursuing the possibility' of Charles's appointment to the post.[39]

Charles's tour of Australia in 1981 was his last as a single man. Later in the year he married Princess Di, and on his next visits he would be completely overshadowed and upstaged by his young wife, who proved almost from the very start to be far more popular with Australians than her prince.

18

THE PRINCE AND DIANA,
PRINCESS OF WALES

> The first day . . . in Alice Springs. It was hot, I was jet-lagged,
> being sick. I was too thin. The whole world was focusing on
> me every day. I was in the front of the papers . . . I learned to
> be a royal . . . in one week. I was thrown in the deep end . . .
> Nobody ever helped me.

AUSTRALIANS INSTANTLY WARMED TO Princess Diana,
who would become – and remains – one of the most
popular royals ever to visit Australia. She made only three
official trips – in 1983, 1985 and 1988 – spending a total
of just seven weeks in the country, yet her impact was
huge.[1]

Diana was born on 1 July 1961 into a family of British
nobility, the youngest daughter of Edward John Spencer,
Viscount Althorp, and the Honourable Frances Shand
Kydd. Her family had a number of connections with the

British royal family: her father had been an equerry to both King George VI and Queen Elizabeth II; and her maternal grandmother, Lady Fermoy, was a close friend and lady-in-waiting to the queen mother. On the death of Diana's paternal grandfather, Albert Spencer, her father became the eighth Earl Spencer, and at fourteen years of age Diana became Lady Diana Spencer. At the same time she moved with her family from Park House on the Sandringham estate to the sixteenth-century ancestral home at Althorp.

Diana was educated at the exclusive private schools of Riddlesworth Hall in Norfolk and West Heath Girls' School in Sevenoaks in Kent. She was a very poor student and failed all her O-level examinations twice. In 1977, at sixteen years of age, she briefly attended Institut Alpin Videmanette, an expensive finishing school in Rougemont in Switzerland, where she reportedly enjoyed singing, sport and ballet dancing.

Shortly after Charles proposed to Diana, she made her first trip to Australia with her mother and stepfather on a private visit to their sheep station near Yass, north of Canberra. While the press besieged the farm, Diana and her mother went off together to a rented beach house at Mollymook, 200 kilometres south of Sydney. Diana spent her time swimming and surfing on the beautiful beach, not daring to accompany her mother shopping in case she was recognised. Her stay in Mollymook was, she recalled later, 'the last time I ever walked alone'.[2] The owner of the beach house where Diana stayed, Margie Nyholm, said that Diana's attempts at avoiding recognition were comical.

She used to wear a towelling beach coat and scarf with big black glasses. It was so obvious that she was trying to be incognito that she stuck out like dogs' balls.[3]

While she was away, Diana said she heard nothing from her fiancé.

> I pined for him but he never rang me up. I thought that very strange and whenever I rang he was out and he never rang me back. I thought 'OK' but I was just being generous – 'he is being very busy, this that and the other'.[4]

When she arrived back in England she recalled that flowers were delivered to her:

> I came back from Australia, somebody knocks on my door – someone from his office with a bunch of flowers and I knew that they hadn't come from Charles because there was no note. It was just someone being very tactful in his office.[5]

Diana said that right from the start of her relationship with Charles, she was aware there was 'someone else around' and that well before her wedding day she had discovered it was Charles's former girlfriend Camilla Parker Bowles.[6] Camilla and Charles had met and dated in the early 1970s, but in 1973 Camilla had married Royal Horse Guards officer Andrew Parker Bowles. They had two children, Tom in 1974 and Laura in 1978. However, by the late 1970s Charles was again discreetly seeing Camilla, and did so right up to his wedding day. Diana suspected this was the case and complained of Charles's 'lies and deceit', which included his sending Camilla flowers when she was ill. Diana also claimed later that she heard Charles on the telephone telling Camilla that 'whatever happens, I will always love you'.[7]

She said that shortly before the wedding she had told her sisters that she didn't want to go through with it:

So I went upstairs, had lunch with my sisters who were there and said: 'I can't marry him. I can't do this, this is absolutely unbelievable.' They were wonderful and said: 'Well, bad luck, Dutch, your face is on the tea towels so you're too late to chicken out.' So we made light of it.[8]

Many years later it was claimed that Charles too had confided in a close friend the night before the marriage that he wanted to pull out, but felt it was too late.[9]

Diana insisted she was suffering from the eating disorder bulimia before the wedding. She told Andrew Morton she had a 'very bad fit of bulimia the night before . . . I was as sick as a parrot that night.' As an indication of her sickness, she claimed that when she was measured for her wedding dress she was 29 inches (73 centimetres) around the waist but that had been reduced to 23½ inches (60 centimetres) on her wedding day.[10]

The advent of television meant the wedding was enjoyed by many more people than had witnessed the marriage of Princess Elizabeth and Prince Philip in 1947. The ceremony took place at St Paul's Cathedral on Wednesday 29 July 1981 in front of 3500 invited guests and was watched by a global audience estimated at 750 million viewers. The wedding attracted the highest Australian television audience for one broadcast to that time.[11]

Afterwards the newlyweds spent a few days at Broadlands, the Hampshire estate of Charles's late uncle Lord Louis Mountbatten, and then flew to Gibraltar to board the *Britannia* for a cruise of the Mediterranean. There were 277 officers and crew on the yacht, and every night there were black-tie dinners in the boardroom with selected senior officers. This meant, said Diana, 'there was never any time on our own'.[12] Charles had also brought aboard seven books written by South African philosopher

Laurens van der Post, which 'we had to analyse over lunch every day'. Di said that her bulimia became 'absolutely appalling . . . rife' and that she was vomiting up her food four times a day on the yacht.[13]

After returning to England, the couple went to stay with the royal family at Balmoral Castle in Scotland, where Diana claimed Charles paid more attention to his family than he did to her:

> He was in awe of his Mama, intimidated by his father and I was always the third person in the room. It was never, 'Darling, would you like a drink?' It was always, 'Mummy, would you like a drink?', 'Granny, would you like a drink?', 'Diana, would you like a drink?' Fine, no problem. But I had to be told that was normal because I always thought it was the wife first – stupid thought![14]

In March 1983 Princess Diana and Prince Charles made their first trip to Australia. On this tour, Charles and Diana brought with them their nine-month-old baby, William. It was the first time a royal infant had accompanied his or her parents on a royal tour. Princess Diana said that the idea of bringing baby William to Australia had come from the Australian prime minister Malcolm Fraser:

> The person who never got any credit was Malcolm Fraser who was the prime minister [although not by the time the tour took place]. He wrote to us out of the blue. All ready to leave William. I accepted that as part of the duty; albeit it wasn't going to be easy. He wrote to me and said: 'It seems to me that you being such a young family would like to bring your child out?' and Charles said: 'What do you think about this?' and I said: 'Oh, it would be absolutely wonderful.'[15]

She also denied there had been any argument with the queen about taking her son: 'It was always reputed that I had an argument with the queen about the decision. We never even asked her. We just did it.'[16]

Diana immediately struck a chord with the public. Even before the tour had begun, the *Australian Women's Weekly* was in raptures about her:

> In the short time she has been in the public eye, Diana's unaffected charm has won her many hearts. But she is only twenty and there's much to be learnt about the finer points of royalty . . . The Princess of Wales continues to charm the world with her outgoing manner. She is a 'giver' with a naturalness that is one of her most endearing qualities.[17]

Shortly after arriving, Charles and Diana had a photo session with baby William before the child was taken by his nanny Barbara Barnes on a jet to a Woomargama sheep and cattle property in southern New South Wales, the homestead that was used as a base for the couple during their visit. William remained there for the rest of the tour, reputedly taking his first steps there, and his parents phoned nine times over the next four weeks to check on him when they weren't with him.

The tour began in Alice Springs, known as the 'red centre' of the Australian continent. The small remote town with a population of 16,000 people had never been visited by anyone from the royal family before. In the normally dry desert town, the prince and princess stayed at the humble Gap Motor Hotel because the short heavy-rain season had flooded the route to the recently completed multi-million-dollar Crown Casino hotel on the other side of the Todd River. As they had with the young Queen Elizabeth thirty years before, the Australian media focused on every aspect of the young princess, including her clothing:

The dress-conscious princess, who arrived in fashionable turquoise on Sunday, wore a soft buttercup yellow yesterday, again with the accent on the neckline. Sunday's was with a petalled broad collar, yesterday's a feminine version of the trendy wing-collar and bow-tie. Once past the interesting necklines, the dresses are simplicity itself.[18]

The local press were also quick to pick up on Diana's nervousness:

In Alice Springs she had been shy and hesitant, seemingly thinking that Prince Charles was the one who should receive all the adulation; she was awkward on a dais and her nervousness was reflected in little mannerisms like brushing her hair out of her eyes which, of course, kept falling because she consistently lowered her head to talk to the small children she relates to so well, covering her shyness.[19]

Diana later complained that she'd had no guidance as to how she should conduct herself on this first trip away:

The first day . . . in Alice Springs. It was hot, I was jet-lagged, being sick. I was too thin. The whole world was focusing on me every day. I was in the front of the papers . . . I learned to be a royal in inverted commas in one week. I was thrown in the deep end . . . Nobody ever helped me *at all*. They'd be there to criticise me, but never there to say 'Well done'.[20]

On the second day the couple visited the School of the Air, where more than 100 children living on cattle stations spread over nearly a million square kilometres were being schooled by radio in each of their homes. During a question-and-answer session, Diana was asked, 'Does Prince William have a favourite toy?' and she answered, 'He loves his koala bear.' All the questions had first been submitted to Buckingham Palace, which had rejected some, including: 'Do you sleep in a double bed?'[21]

At the end of the first week the local media were reporting that Diana was quickly learning the ropes and gaining confidence, and the travelling British media noted how Diana had already begun to overshadow her husband:

> It dawned on the prince fairly quickly that the crowds who turned out to see them were more interested in a tall glamorous blonde and her frocks than a worthy but dull heir to a thousand-year-old British institution. The prince had never seen his role as that of a superstar, while his wife undoubtedly did. In the outside world, her presence electrified crowds but merely made her husband gloomy. 'I might just as well stay in the car,' he said. She was an instant smash hit . . . she just behaved as herself. And the crowd loved her for it. She was great at small talk, she was great with kids and older people and she never once complained about the appalling weather except in a jokey fashion. Diana-mania had well and truly started.[22]

Diana said the crowds were bigger than she or Charles had ever seen, and it didn't take long for her to realise that most of the people were struggling to see her rather than Charles:

> The crowds were just something to be believed. My husband had never seen crowds like it and I sure as hell hadn't . . . Everybody said when we were in the car, 'Oh, we're on the wrong side, we want to see her, we don't want to see him,' and that's all we could hear when we went down these crowds and obviously he wasn't used to that, and nor was I.[23]

By the end of the tour, it was clear it was Diana who was looking more relaxed and less strained:

> She walked and talked confidently, took the lead in civic meet-the-people walks and paid attention to the offerings of massed schoolchildren on sports ovals, from choirs and bands to dance and gymnastics. There was still some hesitancy at the beginning of the second week of the tour. Sydney appeared to be slightly overwhelming and [driving around] the circuits of the 43,000 children on the oval at Newcastle something of a physical strain. But somewhere in that second week she got her second wind. The very full Hobart program had a slightly slower pace and gave the princess time to catch her breath. In South Australia Prince Charles . . . introduced his princess with a new confidence, but it was in Perth that third week that the princess went solo for the first time. The crowds at Fremantle Hospital . . . lost nothing in enthusiasm and it was apparent that Princess Diana was not only confident but enjoying herself. She continued to show her independence from then on, even when in the company of her prince . . . By the time she got to Brisbane . . . she was the one who looked relaxed . . . The Prince looked as if these were rather straining the limits of friendship and of duty.[24]

Later, she complained that Charles was resentful of her greater popularity. 'He took it out on me,' she said. 'He was jealous and I couldn't explain that I didn't ask for it.' She added that the tour had been a 'make or break', during which time she'd had to grow up:

> When I came back from our six week tour I was a different person. I was more grown-up, more mature, but not anything like the process I was going to go through in the next four to five years.[25]

During the visit, there was yet more talk in the Australian press that Charles would be interested in replacing Sir Ninian Stephen, who was to retire in 1989, as governor-general. However, Labor's Bob Hawke, a staunch republican, had replaced Malcolm Fraser as prime minister in 1983 and quickly vetoed the idea. According to Jonathan Dimbleby, the prince remained bitter about the rejection. During a television interview with Dimbleby years later, in June 1994, Charles said that he had let it be known to the Hawke government that he would like to represent the queen in Australia. 'What are you supposed to do,' Prince Charles complained, 'when you are prepared to do something to help and are told you are not wanted?'[26]

—

After the couple's first sensational tour of Australia, Diana tried to settle down as a member of the royal family. But she did not enjoy the best of relationships with her mother-in-law, complaining that after becoming engaged to Charles, 'I was a threat, wasn't I?' She also claimed the queen saw her bulimia 'as the *cause* of her marriage problems and not a symptom'.[27]

She said Charles had a 'very tricky' relationship with his father and that Prince Philip 'intimidated' his son. Diana said Philip longed to be asked for advice, 'instead of Charles giving advice'.[28] She described the queen mother as 'grim and stilted' and 'anti me', but she admired Princess Anne and they got on well. However, she added, 'I keep out of her way [and] when she is there I don't rattle her cage and she never rattled mine.'[29] She felt sorry for Prince Andrew, who was dismissed as 'an idiot' but was really 'very shrewd and astute'.

Andrew was very happy to sit in front of the television all day watching cartoons and videos because he is not a goer.

He doesn't like taking exercise – he loves his golf and it's rather touching. But he gets crushed by his family the whole time . . . but actually there's a lot more there that hasn't arisen yet.[30]

The couple returned to Australia two years later in 1985 in Charles's ninth and Diana's second official visit. By now the princess had become so popular in Australia and the rest of the world that she completely outshone Prince Charles and the rest of the royal family wherever she went. Writing in *The Canberra Times* in October 1985, royal watcher Nigel Dempster said that in the decade before Diana, 'the once glamorous' British monarchy had been in serious decline. The queen and Prince Philip were both showing 'visible signs of staleness'; Princess Margaret and Princess Anne were both unpopular; and there was 'mounting concern over the lacklustre showing of the heir apparent', Prince Charles. What had saved the monarchy from further decline, according to Dempster, was 'the advent of Lady Diana Spencer into its stuffy midst':

It is a metamorphosis . . . Thanks to Diana, still only twenty-four, the ancient throne of England has received publicity beyond the dreams of any ad agency. Her picture, more often than not these days without that of her husband, smiles out from the covers of millions of magazines. She is more famous than Britain's greatest export of the 1960s, the Beatles. Quite startlingly, she has become in the space of four years better known than her mother-in-law, Her Britannic Majesty, Queen Elizabeth II . . . Diana . . . is the best thing to have happened to the fusty first family . . . Diana is dismantling the cobwebs of court. Gone is formal dress on practically every occasion, to be replaced by hip-hugging jeans, leg warmers in winter and casual clothes that are the norm of Oxford Street . . . [She] sashays around the vastness of Windsor Castle or Sandringham as she listens to a Walkman tape player blaring pop music . . . Among the members of the royal family the chant is no longer, 'God Save The Queen,' rather, 'Thank God for Diana'. She's keeping them all in their jobs – and they know it.[31]

He also claimed that Diana had saved Charles's reputation:

Where Prince Charles was treated once as a slightly ludicrous figure for his shyness, his stiffness and lack of ease, he is envied now for the beauty who shares his life and his bed and has borne him two sons, the elder a future king. The more senior members of the family are now able to relax, a luxury they could not permit themselves while Charles wallowed in a sea of indecision, unable to find a bride, suitable or otherwise.

The couple's visit in 1985 was to commemorate the 150th anniversary of the state of Victoria and was notable for its informality and for the relaxed atmosphere Diana created around her. The tour was jointly announced by Australian prime minister Bob Hawke and Victorian premier John Cain. Both were republicans and headed Labor governments; nonetheless, they expressed 'delight' that the couple had agreed to come to Australia.[32]

While the prince and princess were in Victoria they were taken to Flemington Racecourse to watch Australia's biggest horserace, the Melbourne Cup. Held the first Tuesday in November each year, the race attracts crowds of more than 100,000 people. Race day is a public holiday in Victoria and an opportunity for women to wear the latest spring fashions. The locals at the 1985 race were hoping Diana would dazzle them with her outfit, but she created widespread disappointment among Melbourne's society matrons:

The matrons of Melbourne were miffed. They were all in new dresses, hats and bags for the Cup. Princess Diana was not. 'She looks nice . . . but a new outfit would have been marvellous,' pealed the belle in the wildly floral fez. Princess Diana wore what she wore in Florence and at Ascot – a straight black skirt, white hip-hugging jacket with a black collar and white silk camisole. Her hat was black and white, and her shoes were black. 'Didn't she know,' they hissed waspishly, 'that this is the Cup' and that Melbourne wanted, nay deserved, more. Fancy wearing the same outfit three times![33]

There was further disappointment for the upper echelons of Melbourne society. At a big state reception in Melbourne's National Gallery of Victoria, the guest list was notable not for the people invited but for those who were not, as, said *The Canberra Times*, 'the belles of society were excluded'.[34] Labor Premier Cain had insisted on citizens from all walks of life being invited and the list was dominated by workers, trade union officials, young people and people from different ethnic backgrounds.

—

Charles and Diana made their third and final official tour to Australia together early in 1988, when the couple were invited to join in the Australian bicentennial celebrations. Diana again electrified the crowds. In addition to the Sydney celebrations they visited South Australia and Darwin, where they met different Aboriginal community leaders and were shown traditional bush medicines.

By now the plight of the marriage was clear to everyone, and the Australian and world media were regularly publishing images to illustrate the obvious tension between the couple. Charles later admitted that the relationship had 'irretrievably broken down' by 1986, but it was not until December 1992 that the British prime minister, John Major, announced their separation in parliament.[35] It had been the queen's hope that this legal separation would stop the couple's feuding, but the rift between them ran too deep, and in 1996 and following a number of sensational media revelations that damaged both the prince and Diana, the couple divorced amid bitter recriminations.

A factor in the marriage breakdown was Charles's relationship with Camilla Parker Bowles. After the separation and divorce, Diana attracted far more sympathy from the Australian public than her ex-husband, even after it was revealed some years later that she had also had an affair, with former army officer James Hewitt, which had lasted five years. Charles and Camilla were demonised in the press, particularly after the publication of an extremely explicit taped telephone conversation between the two. The night-time call on Charles's car phone to Camilla had taken place on the night of 18 December 1989 and had been intercepted on a scanner. The transcript of the six-minute conversation was first published by the Australian women's magazine *New Idea* in January 1993, a month after Charles and Diana had separated. It was later published in newspapers and magazines in Germany, America, Ireland, Switzerland and Italy, before, finally, English newspapers also published it.

It is difficult to imagine a more damaging conversation, during which Charles said he wanted to be Camilla's tampon:

Camilla: Mmmm. You're awfully good feeling your way along.
Charles: Oh stop! I want to feel my way along you, all over you and up and down you and in and out . . .
Camilla: Oh!

Charles: Particularly in and out!

Camilla: Oh. That's just what I need at the moment.

Charles: Is it?

Camilla: I know it would revive me. I can't bear a Sunday night without you . . .

Charles: What about me? The trouble is I need you several times a week.

Camilla: Mmmm, so do I. I need you all the week. All the time.

Charles: Oh. God. I'll just live inside your trousers or something. It would be much easier!

Camilla: (laughing) What are you going to turn into, a pair of knickers?

(Both laugh)

Camilla: Oh, you're going to come back as a pair of knickers.

Charles: Or, God forbid, a Tampax. Just my luck! (Laughs)

Camilla: You are a complete idiot. (Laughs) Oh, what a wonderful idea.

—

Charles made a visit to Australia by himself in 1994. It was to be a low-key trip during which he would try to restore his image following the breakdown of his marriage. Before the tour Australian newspapers published a public opinion poll that showed Diana had an approval rating of 47 per cent in Australia and Charles only 17 per cent. A decade earlier and in the early days of his marriage, Charles had been the most popular member of the royal family with an approval rating of 50 per cent.[36] Now, he had a lot on his plate:

London: Prince Charles heads to Australia on Sunday for his first royal tour in a milestone year which not only marks his twenty-fifth anniversary as Prince of Wales, but will also be a testing time to re-launch his battered public image . . . with

365

Prime Minister Paul Keating's plans for an Australian republic, and polls in Britain in favour of Charles being bypassed as king for his son Prince William, whether Charles ever gets to be head of state of Australia remains in doubt.[37]

Charles was coping with marriage breakdown and

a divorce which would be finalised by the end of the year. He has come clean on his father's domineering place in his life, Camilla saving him, and the world knowing of his adultery, he is beginning to speak out about the state of the royals – his approval rating is rock bottom while that of his wife is still very high.[38]

The prince flew from London on a regular Qantas flight, with an entourage of twelve staff. He was greeted by a small crowd of about 250 supporters waving the Australian flag, chanting 'God Save the Queen' and 'He's a Jolly Good Fellow'. The official welcoming party included the governor-general, Bill Hayden, the prime minister, Paul Keating, the New South Wales governor, Admiral Peter Sinclair AC, the New South Wales premier, John Fahey, and the federal opposition leader, John Hewson. Each man had with him his wife, and the press again noted that Annita Keating was the only woman who did not curtsy.

During the twelve-day tour Prince Charles visited Sydney, the New South Wales country town of Parkes, as well as Hobart, Queenstown and Strahan on the west coast of Tasmania, where he spoke passionately about the value of the environment. It was while he was in Tasmania that the Australian newspapers published British news reports that Charles had broken off his relationship with Camilla in an effort to reverse his plummeting popularity following his split from Diana:

Prince Charles, who is now reported to have ended his sensational affair with a British Army officer's wife, found himself dogged by the issue of marital strife in Tasmania yesterday. London newspapers reported at the weekend that the prince had ended his affair with Camilla Parker Bowles in a bid to regain the public esteem lost through the break-up of his marriage to Princess Diana. The Prince's relationship with Camilla Parker Bowles was commonly cited as a major cause of the royal marriage split. But in Launceston yesterday Prince Charles was confronted with the issue of divorce and its effect on the family during a visit to a youth theatre group.[39]

Several days later in Sydney on Australia Day, while delivering a speech in Darling Harbour, Prince Charles was shot at by a man brandishing a pistol. The two shots were blanks fired by an Australian university student, David Kang, who was protesting the treatment of Cambodian asylum seekers being held in detention camps in Australia. Kang was quickly overpowered and the press reported that Charles was unhurt and had not been shaken by the event:

He is unconcerned. He is not upset, and his major concern is the fact that what has otherwise been a marvellous day has been spoiled by that small incident. He felt in no danger and at no time did he believe that there was anything untoward occurring.[40]

Kang was found guilty of threatening unlawful violence and sentenced to 500 hours of community service. Years later he insisted that he didn't have any intention to hurt anyone.[41]

After returning to England, Prince Charles again complained in a TV interview that many Australians did not like him:

It's never very easy going there because there's always been, ever since I started going to Australia, a substantial minority of people who didn't like the idea of a monarchy because they say that it's foreign or something.[42]

—

In October 1996 Diana made a private visit to Australia – her last. She came to support the memorial fund for the Victor Chang Cardiac Research Institute, which had been established following the murder of the brilliant heart surgeon and cardiac researcher Victor Chang in 1991. At a giant fundraising ball in Sydney at which the institute raised more than $1 million, she exuded the same magic and charm she had brought to her earlier visits to Australia:

There was a huge crowd in front of the venue . . . and then the princess arrived. She had an incredible impact on people . . . Some burst into tears upon seeing her and others audibly gasped. She had chosen to wear a stunning electric blue over-the-shoulder dress as she had become known for wearing this style while in Australia.[43]

Ten months later, she was dead. Princess Diana was killed in the early hours of the morning on Sunday 31 August 1997 as a result of injuries sustained in a car crash in the Pont de l'Alma road tunnel in Paris. Her boyfriend, Dodi Fayed, and the driver of the Mercedes-Benz W140, Henri Paul, were pronounced dead at the scene; Diana's bodyguard, Trevor Rees-Jones, was the only survivor. A French investigation found the crash had been caused by Paul, who, having consumed alcohol and antidepressants, was driving at high speed and lost control of the car.

News of Diana's death reached Australia in the middle of Sunday morning local time, causing huge shock and an immediate and sustained outpouring of grief. Many thousands attended memorials and church services around the country, wrote letters, left flowers at the UK High Commission and consulate buildings or donated money to charities that had been supported by Diana. The televised coverage of her funeral became the most watched event on Australian TV, surpassing the record audiences for her wedding sixteen years before. A university study later revealed Australians were devastated by her death:

> The death of Princess Diana not only created a shared sense of mourning among Australians, it also had a much stronger impact on some people's physical and mental health, according to a new study. Research conducted jointly by Adelaide and Flinders universities in Australia reveals there was a dramatic increase in demand for support group and counselling services in the city of Adelaide, South Australia, in the weeks immediately following Diana Spencer's death. More than 50 per cent of services in metropolitan Adelaide that specialise in grief counselling experienced an increase in requests for help.[44]

According to the survey, many of the people providing the support services were emotionally unprepared for the intensity of the demand for counselling:

> Many of them felt that they were unprepared for the number of callers, that the people who worked in these organisations were emotionally unprepared, they were surprised at the impact Diana's death had had, and that the counsellors themselves – many of whom have suffered their own grief experiences – felt very drained as a result.

The royal family were slow to respond to the huge expression of sorrow by the public, and it took several days before the queen and the Duke of Edinburgh bowed to public pressure and left Balmoral in Scotland, where they were spending the summer, to join the mourners in London and to have the flags at Buckingham Palace flown at half-mast. Their failure to empathise with Diana's tragic demise provoked widespread criticism of the monarchy and is widely regarded as the queen's most serious misjudgment in her very long and otherwise extremely popular reign.

—

After Diana's death, Charles appointed PR specialist Mark Bolland to help refurbish his tattered public image. In 1999 Bolland was involved in the first social event – at London's Ritz Hotel – at which Charles and Camilla were publicly seen together. Over the next few years the PR campaign chipped away at public opinion, and while the resentment to Charles and Camilla took years to fade, eventually it almost entirely disappeared.

It was nearly a decade after the death of Diana before Charles came back to Australia. During a week-long visit in March 2005, he travelled to Perth, Alice Springs, Melbourne, Sydney and Canberra. During the eight-day visit, according to the Australian prime minister, John Howard, Charles would focus on three areas of great interest to the prince: the environment, sustainable fishing and urban regeneration. In Western Australia he visited a lobster fishery, a dry-land salinity plant in Perth and a sustainable demonstration home in Subiaco. In Alice Springs, where he had last been with his wife twenty years before, he visited the Royal Flying Doctor Service, a technology centre, an Indigenous art exhibition and a desert park. In Melbourne he went to the farmers markets, a primary school and a hockey and netball centre. In Sydney he saw a former gasworks that was being converted to a sustainable community and visited the cancer centre at the Royal Prince Alfred Hospital. He finished the tour in Canberra where he went to see a farm focusing on ecological sustainability.

Just before his visit, his engagement to Camilla was announced by Buckingham Palace, and a month after his return to England the two were married at Windsor Guildhall. It was the first time a British royal had been permitted to marry a divorcee, and the first royal marriage in a civil rather than a religious ceremony. It was also the first time a royal mistress had married her lover.

In November 2012, 64-year-old Prince Charles was invited to visit Australia with his second wife, the Duchess of Cornwall – with the blessing of the queen. For five days the couple represented the queen in Australia as part of the commemoration of her Diamond Jubilee year. They visited Longreach in Queensland, as well as Melbourne, Adelaide, Sydney, Tasmania and Canberra. While Charles proved to be an old hand at the endless media photo shoots, it was all new to Camilla, who was now the one to look ill-at-ease during the obligatory cuddling of koalas, stroking of wombats and shaking hands with strangers in the crowds.

Despite Charles's apparent resurrection in the eyes of the public, that year an opinion poll revealed that 81 per cent of respondents would prefer Prince William to leap-frog his father on the death of Queen Elizabeth and become king. The survey also showed that many more Australians said they would support Australia's becoming a republic if Charles became king, and fewer if William wore the crown.[45]

In the near half-century that Charles has been coming to Australia, it seems he has never really achieved the warm relationship with Australians that he sought and so hoped for, apart from the spike in his approval when he was with Princess Diana. After her death it would take the arrival of a new generation of royals before the popularity of the British monarchy was well and truly restored in Australia.

19

THE REPUBLIC OF AUSTRALIA

> I explained to Her Majesty that, notwithstanding the deep
> respect and warm affection felt towards her by the Australian
> people, there was a growing feeling that Australia should
> make the necessary constitutional changes to allow the
> appointment of an Australian head of state . . . The Australian
> government's view was that, if approved by the Australian
> people at a referendum, it would be appropriate for Australia
> to become a republic by the centenary of federation in 2001.

FROM THE EARLIEST DAYS of British settlement there have
been those who have called for the overthrow of the authority
of the British Crown and an independent Australia. In
1804 a group of mainly Irish convicts rebelled at Castle
Hill, west of Sydney, intending to march on Parramatta,
then Sydney Town, where they planned to capture a ship
and return to Ireland. On 5 March, at what became known
as the Battle of Vinegar Hill, the rebels were overrun by
the colonial forces. Nine of the convicts, including their

leader, Phillip Cunningham, were executed and hundreds more were flogged. From the 1830s local colonists began arguing for self-government and greater independence from British authority. In 1852 influential local politician the Reverend John Dunmore Lang argued for a republic in a book titled *Freedom and Independence for the Golden Lands of Australia*. By the 1880s and when the colonies began serious discussions about federation, a strong sense of an independent Australian identity was being articulated by political leaders, trade unionists, artists and writers.

The widespread pro-Australian, pro-republican, anti-British sentiment of the times was captured by Henry Lawson, who argued Australia should part with Britain.

> The only protection Australia needs is from the landlordism, the title-worship, the class distinctions and privileges, the oppression of the poor, the monarchy, and all the dust-covered customs that England has humped out of the Middle Ages where she properly belongs. Australia's progress has been marvellously fast, but not half fast enough for today. Once free, the spirit of independence or self-dependence will push her ahead 50 per cent faster.[1]

After federation in 1901 the push for an Australian republic abated, but throughout the twentieth century a significant minority always supported the idea of an Australian republic. Australia's bicentennial celebrations provided an opportunity for a modern and increasingly confident Australia to look ahead and to ask itself whether the time had finally come to move away from the monarchy and elect its own head of state.

In 1991 Labor prime minister Bob Hawke kicked the issue along by announcing at a press conference his belief that the coming of the republic was inevitable:

You know my position on the question of a republic. It is inevitable Australia will become a republic. It is a question of when. I think it is something in which political parties have to get a sense of the feeling of the community. It still would be something which for a lot of people would be hurtful but for an increasing number of the Australian population I think there is probably a feeling that Australia should in all its constitutional and legal apparatus be seen to be and in fact be totally independent.[2]

The idea of a republican Australia was popular with members of the Australian Labor Party, and at its national conference earlier that year the party unanimously voted to aim for Australia to become a republic by 1 January 2001, which would be the 100th anniversary of the inauguration of the nation.[3]

There was widespread opposition to the proposal from the conservative side of Australian politics. Many Australians still felt a deep attachment to Britain and the royal family and believed that the nation had been well served by the constitutional monarchy with the queen as its head of state. The leader of the federal parliamentary opposition, John Hewson, and the former conservative prime minister Malcolm Fraser both condemned the idea as unnecessary and 'divisive'.[4] Even Australia's first Aboriginal parliamentarian, conservative Queensland senator Neville Bonner, opposed the idea, saying that Australia had benefited from its ties with Britain, and:

If Australia became a republic we, the Aboriginal people, would be no better off because the changes that are needed to help us don't include republican status. I see no point.[5]

In July 1991, the Australian Republican Movement (ARM) was formed by a number of prominent Australians, including former New South Wales premier Neville Wran, editor and writer Donald Horne, Aboriginal leader and poet Faith Bandler, businessman and, later, politician Malcolm Turnbull, broadcaster Geraldine Doogue, David Hill (the author of this book), who was the managing director of the ABC at the time, fashion designer Jenny Kee, playwright David Williamson, journalist Mark Day and politician Franca Arena. The movement released a declaration, which had been drafted by another foundation member and its chairman, the well-known author Tom Keneally:

> We, as Australians, united in one indissoluble Common-
> wealth, affirm our allegiance to the nation and people of
> Australia. We assert that the freedom and unity of Australia
> must derive its strength from the will of the people. We
> believe that the harmonious development of the Australian
> community demands that the allegiance of Australians must
> be fixed wholly within and upon Australia and Australian
> institutions.[6]

John Howard, who was then in the parliamentary opposition, and later as prime minister became a key figure in the
republic debate, pointed out that most Australians felt a
close affinity with the British monarchy:

> Those people, who don't particularly care for the royal link,
> don't find their daily lives invaded with it. On the other hand,
> there are millions of Australians who hold the association
> very dear.[7]

Among the most vociferous opposition to the republican
push was the influential Returned Services League of
Australia (RSL). Its Victorian state president, Bruce Ruxton,
described the proposed republic as 'obscene':

> We are proud to be associated with the queen, who is our patron, and who, as this country's head of state, has never once put a foot wrong. Show me a politician with such a record.[8]

Shortly afterwards, RSL vice-president Ray De Vere said that the idea of a republic was 'against everything Australian servicemen and women have fought for'.[9] Helen Gow, the vice-president of the Royal Commonwealth Society, which had been founded in 1868 to be 'a network of individuals and organisations committed to improving the lives and prospects of Commonwealth citizens across the world', and then claimed to have 600 members, said that anyone who spoke ill of the queen and who pushed for a republic was guilty of 'sedition and/or treason'.[10]

Feelings were running high and the debate that raged between republicans and those who wished to maintain the status quo was often heated. On one occasion matters literally came to blows. When the issue was being debated live on the *Midday Show* on Channel Nine in July 1991, famous Australian rock singer and Vietnam War veteran Normie Rowe, arguing that Australia should keep the queen as its head of state, became upset when radio and TV presenter Ron Casey, arguing for the country to become a republic, made comments about Rowe's Vietnam War record. Rowe pushed Casey back into his chair, whereupon Casey leaped up and punched Rowe in the head before studio staff could separate the two men. Afterwards, Casey and Rowe were unrepentant, and Ray Martin, who had been moderating the debate, said, 'It underlines how divisive and how emotional and potentially violent this thing can be, this discussion of republicanism in Australia.' Channel Nine received more than 500 calls about the incident, with 70 per cent saying they were against Australia becoming a republic.

At the end of 1991 Paul Keating usurped his leader, Bob Hawke, and became Labor's new prime minister. Keating immediately embraced republicanism and pushed it high on the political agenda. Early the following year he broadened the debate to include a proposal for Australia to have its own flag without the Union Jack in the top corner.

> I suppose people around the world are entitled to say, 'We look at your flag – you've got the flag of another country in the corner. Are you a colony or are you a nation?'[11]

Persuading Australians to change their flag was even more of a challenge than persuading them to become a republic. Successive public opinion polls in Australia have revealed that support for changing the flag to rid it of the Union Jack has always been below the level of support for a republic.[12]

The RSL's national president at the time, Brigadier Alf Garland, accused Prime Minister Keating of being 'an Irish republican bigot'[13] and said RSL members would 'oppose to the bitter end' Keating's plans for the flag.[14] So incensed was the RSL that it declared republic supporters would be banned from entering RSL social clubs on Anzac Day.[15]

In February 1992, the queen and Prince Philip visited Australia for a week for the sesquicentenary celebrations for the declaration of the City of Sydney in 1842. During his welcome speech in the Great Hall at Parliament House, Prime Minister Keating congratulated the queen on the fortieth anniversary of her accession to the throne. He then told her that both Australia and Britain had experienced 'profound change' since her first visit to Australia in 1954, when many still saw Australia through 'imperial eyes', and that Britain had moved away from the former colonies towards Europe:

As our constitutional relationship has evolved, so have the circumstances of our economic and political lives. These days we must both face the necessities of a global economy and global change of often staggering speed and magnitude. Just as Great Britain some time ago sought to make her future secure in the European community, so Australia now vigorously seeks partnerships with countries in our own region. Our outlook is necessarily independent. That independence . . . is reflected in our growing sense of national purpose.[16]

Keating's blunt talking earned the rebuke of opposition leader John Hewson, who criticised Keating for taking the opportunity 'to give a tilt in favour of republicanism in front of the Queen'.[17] Keating further enraged monarchists a few days later when the incident came to light of him touching the queen's back as he was guiding her along a line of guests at a government reception.

In the Australian parliament the day afterwards, Keating accused Britain of abandoning Australia to the Japanese during World War II:

Britain was the country which decided not to defend the Malayan peninsula, not to worry about Singapore and not to give us our troops back to keep ourselves free from Japanese domination.[18]

Then, in an act that would help make sure the republican debate became even more bitter, and reduced the prospects of bipartisan support for it, he went on to accuse the conservative parliamentary opposition of having more respect for Britain than Australia:

If he [John Hewson] believes that I cannot say that this is a more independent country, that we're not tied to Britain's

379

coat tails . . . if he thinks that we ought to be basically into British boot-strapping, forelock tugging, and he calls that respect, it's not respect for this country.[19]

After more than a year of debate and discussions on the subject, in February 1992 a Saulwick *Age* newspaper poll revealed that of people questioned, 57 per cent now wanted Australia to become a republic. A month later, two of England's cricket team stormed out of an Australian hotel because they felt the queen was being insulted. All-rounder Ian Botham, who was playing his last tour, and opening batsman Graham Gooch walked out of a dinner on the eve of a World Cup cricket match when a local comedian, Gerry Connolly, joked that the queen was being privatised and sponsored by Foster's Beer. Botham later said he and Gooch didn't see the funny side and 'left their team-mates and a shocked audience in their wake': 'I'm there and I've got some poofter gay guy comes on stage in drag with a stuffed corgi under his arm and takes the piss out of the queen.'[20]

In the same month, Prime Minister Paul Keating further inflamed traditionalists when he told the Irish-Australian Chamber of Commerce on St Patrick's Day that the old Australian flag had to go.

I said a few things recently about the flag, but let me say this. We've got to be certain of who we are to take our place in the world, and we can't fly two symbols with our nation for much longer. A nation internally uncertain about its representational image is of course a nation uncertain about itself.[21]

In June 1992, a newly formed group, Australians for Constitutional Monarchy (ACM), held its first meeting, attended by 450 people, at Sydney's Town Hall. Prominent among its members was former ABC chair Professor Dame Leonie Kramer, judge (later High Court Justice) Michael Kirby and former Sydney lord mayor Doug Sutherland. The organisation would prove to be an effective opponent to the ARM in the national referendum held later in 1999. By now opponents to the republic were saying it would be more decent to wait until the end of the queen's reign to address the issue, but Keating pointed out that to wait until the reign of the queen finishes 'could be a very long time from now'.[22]

In March 1993, and in defiance of opinion polls, the Labor government was re-elected. During the year a number of conservative politicians indicated they would support, or at least not oppose, the republic. In April the Anglican archbishop of Sydney, Richard Henry 'Harry' Goodhew, expressed 'cautious support' for Australia becoming a republic, but the Anglican archbishop of Brisbane, Peter Hollingworth, warned that Keating's republican push risked dividing the nation.[23]

Later in the year former Labor Party leader Bill Hayden, who had been regarded as a supporter of an Australian republic but was now governor-general, completely changed his tune. In a national TV interview he broke with the convention that governors-general do not join in political debates when he said a republic would destabilise the Australian political system:

I will risk my arm by going further as governor-general, and say this: the present system works well. It allows us to have stable government in this country because the head of state is aware of the restraints under which he must function. They are understood all round and they have worked since federation quite effectively. If we move away from that and there is no restraint, then my apprehension would be that we could

go through periods – intense periods sometimes – of quite
unstable government.[24]

Among those who criticised Hayden was David Hill, who
said in a speech at the Australian National University that
it was outrageous that 'Bill Hayden, who is a committed
life-long republican, should suddenly see the light, having
taken the King's shilling'.[25] The parliamentary opposition responded by saying that Hill should be sacked
as the managing director of the ABC for attacking the
governor-general.[26]

In September 1993, while he was in the United Kingdom,
Prime Minister Keating was granted an audience with
Queen Elizabeth at Balmoral Castle. Afterwards he issued a
press release in which he said Australia planned to continue
to move towards becoming a republic and that the queen
had made it clear that the question was one for the people
of Australia to decide:

I explained to Her Majesty that, notwithstanding the deep
respect and warm affection felt towards her by the Australian
people, there was a growing feeling that Australia should
make the necessary constitutional changes to allow the
appointment of an Australian head of state. I said such a
move was seen as necessary to establish clearly Australia's
identity as an independent nation . . . The Australian government's view was that, if approved by the Australian people
at a referendum, it would be appropriate for Australia to
become a republic by the centenary of federation in 2001. I
told Her Majesty that, in such a situation, Australia would
remain a member of the Commonwealth of Nations, and
that the Australian people would warmly welcome visits to
Australia by Her Majesty as head of the Commonwealth and
as the Queen of the United Kingdom. Her Majesty authorised

me to say that she would, of course, act on the advice of her Australian ministers, as she always has, and on any decision made by the Australian people.[27]

The next day Keating was asked by a journalist when he thought a referendum about a republic might be held in Australia and he replied:

Well, that's again a matter for the Australian public and a matter for debate in Australia. And that debate has already started, it will obviously again revolve around the presentation of the report of the committee we've established and so no doubt in 1994 we'll see some, I think, you know, some real reflections by all concerned in Australia upon the merits of a republic and the modalities of such a change.[28]

The committee to which Keating was referring was the Republic Advisory Committee, which he'd established in April 1993. With Malcolm Turnbull as its chairman, it was to look at the constitutional and legal issues that would come about were Australia to become a republic.

The following month, with Keating back in Australia, the government changed the Oath of Allegiance sworn by people who were becoming Australian citizens. The old oath had required new Australians to

swear by almighty God that I will be faithful and bear true allegiance to Her Majesty Elizabeth the Second, Queen of Australia, her heirs and successors according to law, and that I will faithfully observe the laws of Australia and fulfil my duties as an Australian citizen.

The new oath dropped all reference to the queen:

> From this time forward (under God) I pledge my loyalty to
> Australia and its people, whose democratic beliefs I share,
> whose rights and liberties I respect, and whose laws I will
> uphold and obey.[29]

During Prince Charles's 1994 Australian visit, in a speech
in Sydney he too made it clear that the royal family believed
the question was entirely a local matter:

> The point I want to make here, and for everyone to be
> perfectly clear about, is that this is something which only
> you, the Australian people, can decide. Personally, I happen to
> think that it is the sign of a mature and self-confident nation
> to debate those issues and to use the democratic process to
> re-examine the way in which you want to face the future.[30]

Throughout the year the debate continued. In March the
new head of the ACM, Kerry Jones, who had taken over
as its executive director from Tony Abbott after he was
elected to federal parliament, called on Australian women
to join the fight to retain the queen as head of state. The
Labor government's attorney-general, Michael Lavarch,
responded by saying that the rules governing the monarchy
breached human rights, in that royal succession discrimi-
nated against women by favouring the oldest male child
over older female children, and the rule that the monarch
should be a member of the Church of England discrimi-
nated on religious grounds.

The conservative side of Australian politics was still
formally committed to a constitutional monarchy but,
increasingly, individual members were switching camps. In
July 1994 former prime minister Malcolm Fraser suggested
the republic was inevitable, citing the behaviour of the
heirs to the throne and the changing attitudes of younger

Australians.[31] A month later Senator Baden Teague became the first Liberal Party member to use the parliament to advocate a republic, saying that it was 'inappropriate' that Australia has as a head of state, 'a foreigner, a person who is not a citizen of Australia and who has prior allegiance to the United Kingdom'.[32]

But Australia's famous opera star, Dame Joan Sutherland, was opposed to the republic. Addressing a lunch for the ACM, she claimed that she was 'not particularly racist' but complained that Australians now had to make do with an Australian passport. Prior to 1967, Australian-issued passports had also carried the words 'British Passport' on the cover.

> I was brought up having a British passport and it upsets me that I don't have a British passport now . . . When I go to the [Australian] post office to be interviewed by a Chinese or an Indian – I'm not particularly racist – but I find it ludicrous, when I've had a passport for forty years.[33]

A *Sydney Morning Herald* Saulwick public opinion poll towards the end of 1994 showed that support for a republic had now reached 66 per cent, the highest recorded figure yet, with only 31 per cent opposed. In early 1995 John Howard became the leader of the conservative Liberal–National Party opposition in federal parliament. He argued that despite the passions surrounding the issue, neither Liberal nor Labor supporters 'were going to change their vote' over the issue. For some time he had also been disputing changing the Australian constitution, with the argument that 'if it works, don't fix it'.[34]

Throughout the 1990s the opinion polls consistently continued to show that a majority of people were pro-republic. From early in the decade the Australian media had begun to report extensively on the problems of the royal family, and the revelations were damaging to both sides; support for the royal family slumped. When Diana was killed in 1997, Australians were shocked and upset, and unimpressed by the royal family's apparent reluctance to join the widespread and public mourning. It seemed inevitable that Australia's growing impatience with the monarchy's stiff protocols and dissolute private lives could only damage the anti-republican movement.

In March 1996 John Howard became prime minister, sweeping Paul Keating's Labor government from office in an election landslide and one of the worst defeats of any government in Australian political history. Paul Keating quit as Labor leader a week later and in April 1996 stepped down from the parliament altogether.

Howard was an avowed monarchist but, despite his own opposition to a republic, he agreed to the constitutional convention that had been promised by his predecessor as Liberal leader, Alexander Downer, to discuss the issue once more and formally. And so, nearly two years after Howard's election to office, 152 delegates gathered in Old Parliament House in Canberra from 2 to 13 February 1998 to take part in the convention. Half had been elected in a voluntary postal vote; the other half had been appointed by the government.[35]

Like the constitutional conventions of a hundred years before that had led to the creation of the Australian nation, this 1998 convention was one of the most impressive gatherings of senior figures ever in Australia. The elected delegates taking part included many prominent campaigners for and against the republic, and the appointed delegates included representatives of the federal, state and territory parliaments.

The conference was chaired by former conservative National Party leader Ian Sinclair, and his deputy was Labor's Barry Jones. Delegates debated three issues: whether or not Australia should become a republic; which republic model should be put to the voters to consider against the current system of government; and in what time frame and under what circumstances might any change be considered.

At the end of the convention, a majority recommended that Australia proceed to a referendum to decide the question. By a vote of seventy-three to fifty-seven, with twenty-two abstentions, it was also proposed that the president of the new republic, who would replace the governor-general, would be appointed by a two-thirds majority of parliament, rather than being popularly elected.

This decision – for the president to be appointed by the parliament rather than elected by the people – was a disappointment to many supporters of a republic, and was a significant factor in the defeat of the motion put forth in the subsequent referendum. Many pro-republicans, including the ARM, did not want an elected president, believing that being popularly elected would give the president a mandate to actively participate in the political process. The ARM believed that an appointed president, on the other hand, would have no political powers other than to be the 'guardian' of the constitution.

At the convention, Clem Jones, the former lord mayor of Brisbane, formally moved for a directly elected president, supported by a left-wing independent parliamentarian from Melbourne, Phil Cleary. If Australia was to have a president, Cleary argued, it should be the choice of the people and not the choice of the politicians.

Now the best thing the conservative wing of the republican league can offer the people is an appointed president – a president palatable to both parties. Their justification is pure scaremongering – What are they frightened of? . . . Is it more that they fear giving up their power and loss of influence?[36]

However, said Malcolm Turnbull, a prominent ARM member,

> Mr Clem Jones has proposed a directly elected model that
> would give the president additional powers. We feel that a
> directly elected president should either have no powers – for
> example, as in Ireland – or be the chief executive of the
> nation, as in the case of the United States. We think the
> French arrangement, where executive power is shared in a
> very confused fashion between the president and the prime
> minister, is the worst of all options. So I would say that we
> either go to Dublin for a directly elected president or we go
> to Washington; the Paris option, for the reasons advanced by
> Mr [Bob] Carr, is not on.[37]

Finally, at the national referendum on 6 November 1999,
the question was put to the vote. Electors were asked to
vote whether the constitution should be altered

> to establish the Commonwealth of Australia as a republic
> with the queen and governor-general being replaced by a
> president appointed by a two-thirds majority of the members
> of the Commonwealth parliament.[38]

Despite the opinion polls having for almost a decade
indicated majority support for the republic, those pro-
republicans who had demanded a directly elected president
combined with the anti-republicans to defeat the proposal.
The 'Yes' vote was 45.13 per cent; 'No' was 54.87 per cent.
The constitution would not be changed and the Queen of
England would remain Australia's head of state.

—

After the referendum, the issue of a republic languished,
though the ARM has continued to try to keep it alive and

the move to a republic remains Labor Party policy. In 2004 the leader of the Labor Party, Mark Latham, tried to generate new interest when he released 'Labor's plan for an Australian republic'. In 2010, Labor prime minister Julia Gillard said that while she felt the status quo could not remain, and that as a country Australia needed to work its way through to an agreement on a model for the republic, she thought there would never be enough support to replace the monarchy as long as the queen was on the throne.

A *Sun-Herald*/Nielsen poll conducted two weeks before 2010's federal election showed that when asked straight out if Australia should become a republic, 48 per cent of the 1400 respondents were opposed to constitutional change (a rise of 8 per cent since 2008) while 44 per cent were in favour of change (a drop of 8 per cent since 2008). The poll results also showed that 31 per cent of respondents believed Australia should never become a republic, 29 per cent thought Australia should become a republic as soon as possible, and 34 per cent were of the view that Australia should become a republic only after Queen Elizabeth II's reign ends.

Backing for a republic was at its lowest level since 1994 – five years before Australia had held its referendum. And at the same time, federal opposition leader Tony Abbott said he doubted Australia would become a republic even after the death of the queen:

> This republican cause has been with us for a long time but the Australian people have demonstrated themselves to be remarkably attached to institutions that work. So while there may very well be further episodes of republicanism in this country, I am far from certain that at least in our lifetimes that there's likely to be any significant change.[39]

20

THE NEW GENERATION

> Prince George is being hailed as 'the republican slayer' in Australia, after a poll showed the lowest support for a republican movement in the country for thirty-five years.

IN THE EARLY TWENTY-FIRST century, a new generation of the royal family rose to prominence and re-energised the British monarchy, restoring its fortunes. The coming of age of Princes William and Harry, combined with another fairytale royal wedding and the births of Prince George and Princess Charlotte, have not only lifted the popularity of the British royal family in Australia and around the world, but have arguably further frustrated progress towards founding a republic in Australia.

Prince William visited Australia as an infant with his mother and father in 1983, but as adults it was the younger Prince Harry who first visited the continent, more than six years before his older brother. In September 2003, after leaving school, nineteen-year-old Harry spent three months working as a jackaroo on a ranch in outback Queensland, Tooloombilla Station, which was owned by a friend of the late Princess of Wales, and her husband, the son of a millionaire polo star.

Harry was born at St Mary's Hospital in London on 15 September 1984. He was educated at two preparatory schools before going to Eton College aged thirteen. His mother, Princess Diana, was determined to broaden her sons' education and world view, and took William and Harry when they were boys to shelters for the homeless and AIDS clinics. Diana once told a BBC interviewer that she wanted her sons to have an understanding of 'people's emotions, of people's insecurities, of people's distress, of their hopes and dreams'.[1] She was killed when Harry was twelve and William fifteen. At her funeral her brother Earl Spencer made an extraordinary speech. Addressing William and Harry directly, he said:

'And beyond that, on behalf of your mother and sisters, I pledge that we, your blood family, will do all we can to continue the imaginative and loving way in which you were steering these two exceptional young men so that their souls are not simply immersed by duty and tradition, but can sing openly as you planned.

'We fully respect the heritage into which they have both been born, and will always respect and encourage them in their royal role, but we, like you, recognise the need for them to experience as many different aspects of life as possible to arm them spiritually and emotionally for the years ahead. I know you would have expected nothing less from us.'

The Observer newspaper said:

The affections of the United Kingdom have clearly turned from their mother to the young princes, William and Harry, bypassing the Windsors. Whether this sea-change spells a republic in the years to come or merely the skipping of a generation, one thing is certain: the British monarchy will never be the same.[2]

Harry travelled to Australia in 2003 without other members of the royal family, but having been involved in several highly publicised incidents in England the year before – British newspapers had published stories of how he had consumed alcohol and smoked pot at a pub and at his father's country home – he was not without some form of escort:

> A team of twelve royal security officers . . . will be a few steps behind him, trying to keep tabs on the young prince whose healthy teenage appetite for a good time has seen him give his minders the slip more than once in the past to drink with friends and smoke marijuana.[3]

The Labor opposition baulked at the cost of security for what was essentially a private trip by the prince. Shadow Minister for Foreign Affairs Kevin Rudd said Labor would not have objected to paying for the tour if it was an official visit involving charity work,

> but if it is just a bit of a jaunt, I think maybe we should look carefully at the cost-sharing arrangements with the British government on this, because it's a lot of money. At the end of the day it's the British royal family, the queen is the head of Australia, the princes are not, and I think therefore we should be a bit more cautious about this.[4]

When Harry arrived in the country, he appeared over-whelmed by the press attention and threatened to go straight home if he was not 'left in peace'. However, soon afterwards a Clarence House spokeswoman insisted: 'Things have settled down. Harry appears to be fine now.'[5]

Harry was well received by the Australian people on the occasions he did appear in public: he visited Sydney's Taronga Zoo, played polo for young England against young Australia and watched England play Australia in the Rugby World Cup in Sydney.

Harry's continued controversial behaviour did little to reduce his popularity in Australia. In early 2005 the twenty-year-old attracted a torrent of criticism for attending a fancy-dress party in London dressed in a German Nazi uniform, which *The Times* suggested showed that he had fallen in with a 'dubious group of self-indulgent young men who are apparently content with a life of pointless privilege'.[6]

His next visit to Australia was a 'whirlwind' three-day trip in 2013 to attend the International Fleet Review, the centenary celebrations of the first entry into Sydney Harbour of the Royal Australian Navy's first fleet. Since his first visit, the 29-year-old prince had undergone officer training at Britain's Royal Military Academy, Sandhurst, served in a combat zone in Afghanistan, where he patrolled in hostile areas, qualified as a helicopter pilot and been promoted to the rank of captain.

Before he had even arrived, the Australian Monarchist League called on the government to commence negotiations with the palace on the possibility of Captain Wales, as he likes to be known, serving with a Branch of the Australian Defence Force (ADF):

It will not only strengthen bonds between the UK, Australia and the royal family, but lift the morale of Australian troops and bring international media attention to Australia – which would no doubt have an obvious effect on the ailing Australian tourism industry, and possibly even recruitment levels for the ADF.[7]

Harry again proved popular in a country, where, according to the UK *Mirror* newspaper, he was considered 'the wildest of the young royals'.[8] When he attended the fleet review in Sydney, which featured more than 40 warships, 16 tall ships and 8000 naval personnel from 19 nations, thousands of people crowded the shoreline to catch a glimpse of the prince, commonly described by the press as a 'playboy'.[9] There were screams from the crowd as Harry, wearing a white British army tropical dress uniform, chatted and shook hands with members of the public. One young girl described him as 'Gorgeous: I'm in love. He wears a uniform very well.' Another agreed, adding, 'We all love him in Australia. I remember when he was born.'[10]

During the visit, Prime Minister Tony Abbott made a speech for the prince at Kirribilli House during which he gently teased Harry about the republican issue:

> Prince Harry, I regret to say not every Australian is a monarchist. But today everyone feels like a monarchist. You grace us as your family has graced our nation from its beginning, as the crown is a symbol of our stability, continuity and decency in public life.[11]

Thirty-year-old Harry made a third trip to Australia in 2015 when he was attached for a month to the Australian army for outback military exercises in Western Australia and the Northern Territory. At the start of the tour large crowds of cheering well-wishers gathered to welcome him outside the Australian War Memorial in Canberra.[12] On the last day, the prince spent more than an hour among thousands of well-wishers who had turned out at Sydney Opera House to see him. While he was greeting the crowd he was grabbed by a blonde young woman, Victoria McRae. Wearing an Australian flag dress and carrying a sign that said, 'Marry Me Last Chance Prince Harry', she stole her kiss in a scene that was reminiscent of his father being embraced by Jane Priest in the surf in Western Australia thirty-six years before. McRae told the *Daily Mail*:

> I love the royals, I loved Princess Diana and the younger generation as well. I've met Kate and William . . . Probably Harry's my favourite now. I think he's a bit cheeky, he's a bit of a rebel in the royal family and he's got a wicked sense of humour. What's not to love?[13]

—

Harry's trips to Australia were popular, but visits by his older brother, William would prove to be even more so.

William was born in London on 21 June 1982. He attended nursery in London's Notting Hill and preparatory school at Ludgrove in Berkshire before going to Eton College from the age of thirteen, where in his last two years he studied geography, biology and history of art as A levels. Like his younger brother, he took a year off after school to travel, including a stint teaching children for several months in Chile. He subsequently went to St Andrews University in Scotland and became the first heir to the throne to earn a university degree. A 'gentlemen's agreement' was made by British newspaper editors with Buckingham Palace during William's time at the university that they would not publish photographs of the prince. St Andrews was also where he met his future wife, Kate Middleton.

After university William joined the British army, before switching in 2009 to the Royal Air Force, where he became a search-and-rescue pilot. That year it was claimed that both Prince William and Prince Harry had shown interest in the job of governor-general to Australia, just as their father had. While not confirming that either of the princes had ever actively sought the job, an adviser admitted that they would give it 'very serious consideration' if they were offered the post.[14] William had been brought up as a candidate two years before when a biography had raised his interest in the position, but when the prime minister at the time, John Howard, was asked about the possibility, he ruled it out:

> Although I remain a supporter of our current constitutional arrangements I do think the practice of having a person who is an Australian in every way and a long-term and permanent resident of this country is a practice I would not like to see altered . . . We have for a long time embraced the idea that the person who occupies that post should be in every way an Australian citizen.[15]

William did not visit Australia as an adult until 2010 when he was twenty-seven years old. His first tour of the country was a three-day visit to towns affected by the 'Black Saturday' bushfires in Victoria the previous year.[16] The hundreds of fires that ignited and raged across thousands of square kilometres on Saturday 7 February 2009 were the worst on record. A number of townships burned to the ground, with 173 people killed and over 400 injured.

There was heightened local interest in William's visit because of speculation at the time that he would soon propose marriage to Kate Middleton. After arriving at Sydney Airport shortly after midday on 19 January, he was whisked away for lunch with Governor-General Quentin Bryce and about twenty prominent young Australians, including singer Delta Goodrem, Australian cricketer Michael Clarke, rugby Wallabies skipper Rocky Elsom and Olympic gold-medal diving champion Matthew Mitcham.

After lunch William met with Aboriginal people in the inner Sydney suburb of Redfern. According to Aboriginal Land Councillor Rob Welsh,

> the prince should come with a truck too, because there are lots of people who want to give him gifts. 'I'm really impressed, his mother was fantastic and made him a bit of a grassroots kind of royal,' he explains. 'He's out there in the community, he's a royal trying to embrace the community, he's a good young man.' It is likely to be quite a welcome and will include a smoking ceremony.[17]

The Australian media described the prince's visit to the Aboriginal community as a clever move:

> The shrewd choice of visiting an Aboriginal community centre in Redfern – a deprived and sometimes dangerous part of Sydney – has melted the hearts of locals and helped the city fall in love with 'Prince Charming'.[18]

After a day in Sydney, the prince was off to Victoria, where the local media said 'he is indeed the prince of hearts in reaching out' to the families devastated by Victoria's Black Saturday bushfires:

> Prince William leapt from his motorcade as he arrived in the town [of Whittlesea] and without prompting rushed into the waiting crowd, spending minutes with those he knew had lost families and homes.[19]

Eighty-five-year-old Louise Murray had lost her grandson, his wife and their two children in the fires, and she was delighted the prince wore a yellow ribbon to remember those who had died. 'He shook my hand and asked me how I was,' Ms Murray said. 'I didn't have a chance for much conversation at all but it was lovely. I won't wash my hand for a week.'[20]

Local republican spokesperson Simon Bateman tried to dismiss the visit as nothing more than the 'cult of celebrity':

> I mean we had a lot of media when Paris Hilton was here too, so I am not sure what it [the trip] means. It doesn't really mean much in terms of how we live and are as Australians.

Bateman also criticised the Victorian premier, John Brumby, 'an avowed republican', over his planned meeting with Prince William. 'I think he [John Brumby] is playing pretty much the game of "How can I milk this and get popularity out of it?"' Bateman said.[21]

At the end of the tour the media described the visit as 'a resounding success'.[22] William had been an instant hit with Australians. Whomever he met, he appeared friendly, relaxed, engaging and genuinely interested in what they had to say. His manner was in contrast to that of his father, Prince Charles, who when meeting ordinary Australians as a young man had often been stiff, formal and even aloof.

The Australian declared the prince had 'won the hearts of Australians' with his relaxed, unpretentious and endearing manner.[23] Sydney's *Daily Telegraph* predicted the visit would 'cement Australia's deep admiration for the Windsors and put the republican issue on the back burner':

> William is a powerful weapon for the royals in Australia. You'd be happy to have a beer with him. He has a sense of

humour, applies himself to his work, loves sport and enjoys a night on the turps with his brother and his mates.[24]

The UK *Guardian* reported that the Australian media was celebrating William's triumph in converting Australians:

In the end the lure of celebrity proved just too much. The arrival of the diffident 27-year-old Old Etonian, who might conceivably one day become their monarch, provoked sneers in Australia before he touched down on Tuesday. But by last night he had been transformed from Willy the Wombat into – according to the [Melbourne] tabloid *Herald Sun* – a Dinkum Aussie Larrikin . . .

The paper noted William's part in thwarting the republican cause for now:

As he and his advisers flew back home last night – business class on a scheduled flight, not by private jet like some royals – they will undoubtedly feel buoyed up by success. They may even have been chortling gently that the pro-republican Melbourne *Age* noted yesterday, under the headline "All-round Good Egg William Snares Many with his Charm Offensive", that the prince "may have done more to set back the republican cause than anything since the 1999 referendum" – which, of course, the republicans narrowly lost.[25]

After returning to the United Kingdom, William proposed to Kate Middleton in October 2010, giving her the engagement ring that had belonged to his mother. Their wedding was planned for April 2011, but a month beforehand William made another short trip to Australia to comfort Queenslanders who had been devastated by Cyclone Yasi, a very powerful and destructive tropical cyclone that had hit the north Queensland coast earlier in the year.

In advance of the prince's arrival, Queensland Labor premier (and republican) Anna Bligh told the Queensland parliament she hoped the royal visit would boost her state's 'struggling tourist industry', which had been badly damaged by the cyclone. 'I do thank the prince for his decision to visit Australia,' she said.

> I hope that he sends the message back to his friends and colleagues in the UK that Queensland is open for business, and that while he's here he gets an opportunity to see that for himself.[26]

The 'disaster tour', as some British media dubbed it, also took in flood-damaged communities in south-east Queensland and north-western Victoria.[27] Again the prince proved extremely popular. The local Australian media compared him to his mother, and claimed William 'brings back the sunshine':

> Like mother, like son. As Prince William yesterday mingled with residents of cyclone and flood-ravaged communities in north Queensland, the same qualities that won Princess Diana such adoration around the world were strikingly clear. The unhesitating connection with ordinary people, the natural warmth, the shining smile, the willingness to reach out with a comforting hand on a shoulder. The future king charmed the thousands of Queenslanders who flocked from far and wide for a glimpse, a handshake, a few words and a welcome break from the task of rebuilding homes and lives shattered by the most powerful cyclone to hit Australia in a century.[28]

A month after returning to London, William married Catherine Elizabeth Middleton at Westminster Abbey on 29 April 2011. Kate, who would become almost as popular in Australia as her late mother-in-law, Princess Diana, was the first commoner to marry an heir to the British throne. She was born in Reading on 9 January 1982. Her mother and father were a flight attendant and flight dispatcher respectively, but in 1987 started a successful company selling party supplies and decorations. Kate went to nursery school in Amman, Jordan, for two and a half years when her parents were based there, before returning to England, where she attended private schools in Berkshire and Wiltshire. After William and Kate met at and finished university together, Kate was a guest at William's passing-out parade in 2006, which was the first high-profile public event where they were seen as a couple. Over the following months the couple holidayed together and Kate was invited to join the royal family on a number of private outings and at public events.

The wedding of Kate and William was a spectacularly grand, extravagant event that displayed all the pomp and ceremony of past British royal weddings. The Melbourne *Herald Sun* estimated it had cost more than A$30 million, including A$800,000 for flowers. Among the 1900 guests invited to the ceremony in Westminster Abbey were Australian governor-general Quentin Bryce and her husband, Michael, and Australian prime minister Julia Gillard and her partner, Tim Mathieson. Australian celebrities invited included Australian Olympic swimming champion Ian Thorpe. A record 77 per cent of Australians watched all or at least some of the ceremony on TV; it was broadcast on all four of the major free-to-air channels. At the same time a Morgan public opinion poll revealed that support for retaining the monarchy in Australia had surged to 55 per cent, up 7 per cent on the previous year and the highest polled figure since 1991. In contrast, only 34 per cent believed Australia should become a republic, down 8 per cent on the previous year.[29]

William and Kate's popularity in Australia soared after the wedding. A public opinion poll conducted in mid-2012 revealed that 81 per cent would prefer Prince William to become king on the death of Queen Elizabeth rather than his father, Prince Charles.[30] The *Australian Women's Weekly* deputy editor and royal correspondent Juliet Rieden said there was still strong support for the queen but that Kate and William had become more appealing to their readers as 'celebrities':

> There's interest in her [Queen Elizabeth]. She's not our first choice of cover, no, William and Kate, however, definitely, yes. When we did their wedding this year, we got a 56 per cent sales increase. The new generation are more interested in the celebrity of royalty than in the standing of the royalty as people who run the country.[31]

On 22 July 2013, the Duchess of Cambridge (Kate's new title) gave birth to the couple's first child, who was named George. The following year the royal family of three made their first trip together to Australia.

William, Kate and baby George arrived in Sydney on a beautiful autumn day in April, after eight days touring New Zealand. From their first day at the Sydney Opera House the royals attracted large and enthusiastic crowds, the like of which had not been seen in Australia for royal tours since Princess Diana had visited thirty years before.

They spent five days visiting the Blue Mountains, the Sydney Royal Easter Show, a children's hospice and a surf lifesaving display at Manly Beach, as well as squeezing in a visit with George to Taronga Zoo. After Sydney they flew to Brisbane for a reception at the Brisbane Convention Centre and an inspection of RAAF troops, before going to Uluru in Central Australia. Next they flew to Adelaide for two days where they saw a skateboarding display and attended a big civic reception. At the end of the ten-day tour, in Canberra they attended the annual Anzac Day ceremony.

Everywhere they went, tens of thousands of people came to catch a glimpse of them, clutching bouquets of flowers for Kate and toys for baby George:

> They came, they stopped, they chatted, they laughed and they conquered. Oh boy, did they conquer! The republican cause was set back at least another generation or two as the Duke and Duchess of Cambridge wowed thousands of adoring fans at Brisbane's South Bank on Saturday.[32]

There was hardly a word of complaint about the visit, or the cost, which as Australian online media site *Crikey* pointed out, would be met by Australian taxpayers:

> No expense has been spared. The royals will be accompanied by an entourage of eleven people, including Kate's hairdresser, three press officers, an orderly and a nanny. The group of fourteen will be ferried to and around Australia by special air force jets. So when they pop from Sydney to Brisbane for the day, an RAAF plane will take them there, wait, and bring them back again. The royals will not take any commercial flights, except for the flight back to London.
>
> Will and Co. will stay in official vice-regal mansions in Sydney and Canberra, and in commercial accommodation near Uluru. Official receptions have been organised around the country . . . The royals will tour four cities (Sydney, Brisbane,

Adelaide and Canberra) plus Uluru and the Blue Mountains from April 16. That means at least seven RAAF flights with a total flying time of sixteen hours. Based on estimates of the cost of chartering a RAAF jet, at $17,000 per hour of flying time, *Crikey* calculates the royal party's flights alone will cost the Australian taxpayer at least $272,000 . . . When British royals come on official visits the federal government pays for flights, accommodation, meals, phone calls, minibar bills, and even the presents the royals give out (which can cost $15,000). State governments cough up, too. Organising a day trip for a royal can cost $100,000 an hour. The British royals have been availing themselves of free Australian hospitality with enthusiasm. Since 2005 . . . ten British royals have visited: Queen Elizabeth, Prince Philip, Princess Anne, Prince Edward, Charles, Camilla, William, Harry, Kate and George. It's been estimated each trip cost between $350,000 and $1.8 million.[33]

The tour was another outstanding success. While the three were in Australia *The Sydney Morning Herald* published a Fairfax Nielsen poll that showed support for making Australia a republic was at its lowest level in more than thirty years. What was new about the poll was that the strongest support for continuing with the crowned monarch as Australia's head of state was among 18–24-year-olds (60 per cent), who previously were most likely to have supported a republican Australia.

Support for an Australian republic has slumped to its lowest level in more than three decades just as royal enthusiasm reaches fever pitch over the arrival of the Duke and Duchess of Cambridge, William and Kate. In a set-back for the long-struggling republican movement . . . more than half of all Australians now believe the switch to a republic is unnecessary.[34]

Much of the increased support for the British monarchy was attributed to baby George:

> Prince George is being hailed as 'the republican slayer' in Australia, after a poll showed the lowest support for a republican movement in the country for thirty-five years . . . The Royal baby, along with his famous parents, are thought to be largely responsible for this apparent shift in attitude towards the monarchy, as 51 per cent of Australians said switching to a republic is unnecessary.[35]

In July 2015 the christening of George's two-month-old baby sister, Princess Charlotte, dominated newspaper front pages and television news bulletins in Australia. And in April 2016 Australia Post celebrated the queen's ninetieth birthday by issuing a stamp of Her Majesty wearing a golden wattle diamond brooch, which the nation had given her during her famous first tour of Australia in 1954.

Astonishingly, Queen Elizabeth II has been on the throne for more than half of the nation's existence, and a significant proportion of the Australian public appear as devoted and attached to her and the British royal family as they ever have been.

The relationship between Australia and the royals has always been unlikely: the young, rebellious, egalitarian nation wed to an ancient symbol of power and social inequality. Even today an invitation to meet with royalty remains a pinnacle of social achievement and recognition to most Australians. Members of the royal family are often discussed and remembered with more affection than prominent Australians, and the failings and flaws of the royals are quickly overlooked, forgiven and forgotten.

What is the magic the royals hold over Australians? How have they enthralled us for well over two centuries as Australia has developed and grown away from its traditional ties with England? Perhaps it is the familiarity and comfort that comes from continuity and predictability. Maybe a feeling that the British monarchy provides Australia with some political stability we can't be trusted to provide for ourselves. Perhaps it has something to do with the thrill of the colour, pomp and ceremony of royal celebrations and the new breed of royal 'celebrity'. There is certainly no rational reason why an increasingly diverse, modern Australia needs to cling to this ancient aristocratic bloodline from the other side of the world to provide our head of state. But whatever the appeal, Australian interest in and appetite for the British royal family show no sign of ending soon.

NOTES

1. King George III

1   Cook, *Journal*, April 1770.

2   Ibid., 22 August 1770.

3   Lord Sydney to Treasury, letter, 18 August 1786, *Historical Records of New South Wales*, Vol. 1, Part 2, pp. 14–16.

4   Ibid.

5   Ibid.

6   20 April 1787, *Historical Records of New South Wales*, Vol. 1, Part 2, p. 81.

7   12 October 1786, *Historical Records of New South Wales*, Vol. 1, Part 2, p. 24.

8   Phillip's instructions, 25 April 1787, *Historical Records of New South Wales*, Vol. 1, Part 2, p. 89.

9   George Worgan, *Journal*, 27 January 1788.

10   Kohen, p. 76.

11   Phillip to Sydney, letter, 15 May 1788, *Historical Records of New South Wales*, Vol. 1, Part 2, p. 126.

12   Sydney to Admiralty, letter, 29 April 1789, *Historical Records of New South Wales*, Vol. 1, Part 2, p. 230.

13   Grenville to Admiralty, letter, 8 June 1789, *Historical Records of New South Wales*, Vol. 1, Part 2, p. 248.

14   Dundas to Phillip, letter, 15 June 1792, *Historical Records of New South Wales*, Vol. 1, Part 2, p. 622.
15   Sydney officers to King George III, letter, 14 June 1793, *Historical Records of New South Wales*, Vol. 1, Part 2, p. 344.

2. Fighting for and against the British Crown

1   Godfrey, p. 356.
2   Sunter.
3   Hotham to Bart, letter, 18 September 1854, Public Record Office of Victoria (VPRS).
4   Ibid.
5   Ibid.
6   *The Sydney Morning Herald*, 29 January 1855.
7   *The Ballarat Times*, 12 November 1854.
8   Sunter.
9   Hotham to Bart, letter, 18 November 1854, VPRS.
10   Carboni, p. 35.
11   Samaha, p. 450.
12   Rede to Colonial Secretary, letter, VPRS.
13   Kelly; and Rusden, as quoted in Sunter.
14   *The Age*, 5 December 1854.
15   Ibid., 11 December 1854.
16   *The Age*, 23 January 1855.
17   'The State Trials'.
18   *The Empire*, 24 February 1855.
19   *The Sydney Morning Herald*, 23 May 1854.
20   Gover.
21   Ibid.
22   *The Sydney Morning Herald*, 15 July 1854.
23   Ibid., 1 May 1911.
24   *The Mercury*, 17 September 1860.
25   *The Argus*, 22 August 1863.
26   Davidson.
27   Ibid.
28   *The Sydney Morning Herald*, 15 August, 1863.
29   *The Brisbane Courier*, 19 August 1863.
30   Davidson. *The Sydney Morning Herald*, 15 August 1863.
31   *The Argus*, 1 September 1863.

32   Davidson.
33   Glen, p. 91, cited in Davidson.

3. The First Australian Royal Tour

1   *Cornwall Chronicle*, 18 May 1867.
2   McKinlay, p. 3.
3   Ibid.
4   Ibid., p. 4.
5   'Otto, King of Greece', www.britannica.com/biography.
6   McKinlay, p. 4.
7   *Inquirer and Commercial News*, 17 July 1867.
8   *The Adelaide Observer*, 2 November 1867.
9   *The South Australian Register*, 2 November 1867.
10   McKinlay, p. 28.
11   Ibid., p. 33.
12   *The South Australian Register*, 2 November 1867.
13   McKinlay, p. 35.
14   *The South Australian Register*, 24 November 1867.
15   *Adelaide Advertiser*, 7 December 1867.
16   *The Sydney Morning Herald*, 22 November 1867
17   Ibid.
18   McKinlay, p. 55.
19   *The Age*, 12 November 1867.
20   McKinlay, p. 82.
21   *The Sydney Morning Herald*, 6 December 1867.
22   *The Argus*, 29 November 1867.
23   *Launceston Examiner*, 14 December 1867.
24   *Bendigo Advertiser*, 12 December 1867.
25   *The Australasian*, 21 December 1867.
26   Ibid.
27   *The Argus*, 24 December 1867.
28   *The South Australian Advertiser*, 27 December 1867
29   Ibid., 5 January 1868.
30   Ibid., 6 January 1868.
31   Callaway, pp. 103–9.
32   *The Age*, 6 January 1868.
33   Ibid.
34   Ibid., 5 January 1868.
35   *The Mercury*, 10 January 1868.

36   *The Cornwall Chronicle*, 15 January 1868.
37   Ibid.
38   Ibid.
39   McKinlay, p. 137.
40   Ibid.
41   *The Sydney Morning Herald*, 1 February 1868.
42   *The Brisbane Courier*, 24 January 1868.
43   Ibid.
44   *The Queensland Times*, 24 March 1868.
45   McKinlay, p. 155.
46   *The Queensland Times*, 24 March 1868.
47   Symons, pp. 64–5.
48   *The Sydney Morning Herald*, 13 March 1868.
49   Ibid.
50   Ibid., 15 July 1868.
51   *The Queensland Times*, 7 April 1868.
52   Ibid.
53   Knight.

4. For Queen and Country

1   *Goulburn Evening Penny Post*, 5 March 1885.
2   Ibid., 21 March 1885.
3   Australian War Memorial, 'Sudan (New South Wales
      Contingent), March–June 1885'.
4   McKenna, p. 127.
5   Ibid.
6   *The Argus*, 15 April 1885.
7   *The Australian Town and Country Journal*, 7 March 1885.
8   *The South Australian Weekly Chronicle*, 5 March 1885.
9   Ibid.
10   *Evening News*, 7 March 1885.
11   McKenna, p. 128.
12   *The South Australian Weekly Chronicle*, 5 March 1885.
13   *Geelong Advertiser*, 25 June 1885.
14   Australian War Memorial, 'Sudan (New South Wales
      Contingent), March–June 1885'.
15   *Australasian Sketcher with Pen and Pencil*, 12 July 1887.
16   *Gympie Times*, 23 June 1887.
17   *Australasian Sketcher with Pen and Pencil*, 12 July 1887.

18   Ibid.
19   *Gympie Times*, 23 June 1887.
20   *The South Australian Register*, 21 June 1887.
21   *Gympie Times*, 23 June 1887.
22   *The South Australian Register*, 21 June 1887.
23   *The West Australian*, 21 June 1887.
24   Ibid.
25   *Launceston Examiner*, 23 June 1887.
26   *The Shoalhaven Telegraph*, 29 June 1887.
27   *The West Australian*, 21 June 1887.
28   *Kapunda Herald*, 21 June 1887.
29   *The Sydney Morning Herald*, 4 June 1887.
30   Davies.
31   *The Sydney Morning Herald*, 16 June 1887.
32   Davies.

5. Two Princes in Australia

1   Feuchtwanger, pp. 222–3.
2   Dalton, Vol. 1, p. x.
3   Ibid.
4   *The Illustrated Australian News*, 1 June 1881.
5   *Bendigo Advertiser*, 19 October 1880.
6   Dalton, Vol. 1, p. 429.
7   Ibid., p. 467.
8   Ibid., p. 470.
9   Ibid., p. 451.
10   Ibid., p. 452.
11   Ibid., p. 454.
12   Ibid., p. 451.
13   Ibid., p. 465
14   Ibid., p. 470.
15   *The South Australian Advertiser*, 22 June 1881.
16   *Border Watch*, 18 June 1881.
17   Dalton, Vol. 1, p. 471.
18   Ibid., p. 470.
19   *The South Australian Advertiser*, 22 June 1881.
20   Dalton, Vol. 1, p. 481.
21   Ibid., p. 479.
22   *The South Australian Register*, 21 June 1881.

23   Ibid.
24   Dalton, Vol. 1, p. 488.
25   Ibid., p. 494.
26   Ibid., p. 495.
27   Ibid.
28   Ibid.
29   *The Argus*, 28 June 1881.
30   Dalton, Vol. 1, p. 498.
31   Ibid., p. 515.
32   *The Argus*, 30 June 1881.
33   Dalton, Vol. 1 p. 507.
34   Ibid., p. 512.
35   Ibid., p. 513.
36   Ibid., p. 515.
37   Ibid., p. 526.
38   Ibid.
39   Ibid., p. 529; *The Argus*, 6 August 1881.
40   *The Mercury*, 23 August 1882.
41   Dalton, Vol. 1, p. 551.
42   *Sydney Morning Herald*, 18 July 1882.
43   Dalton, Vol. 1, p. 567.
44   Ibid., p. 594.
45   Ibid., p. 597.
46   Ibid., p. 567.
47   Ibid., p. 582.
48   Ibid., p. 584.
49   Ibid., p. 609.
50   Ibid., p. 618.
51   *The Capricornian*, 27 August 1881.
52   *The Australian*, 27 August 1881.
53   Dalton, Vol. 1, p. 618.
54   Ibid., p. 625.
55   *The Australian Town and Country Journal*, 9 October 1886.
56   Ibid.
57   *The South Australian Register*, 3 March 1890.
58   *The Inquirer and Commercial News*, 7 October 1891.
59   Harrison, p. 237; Nicolson, p. 46.

6. The Creation of the Nation of Australia

1   *The Sydney Morning Herald*, 25 October 1889.
2   Ibid.
3   'Official Record of the Proceedings and Debates of the Australian Federation Conference, Melbourne 1890'.
4   Ibid.
5   *The Sydney Morning Herald*, 3 March 1891.
6   Ibid., 11 April 1891.
7   State Library of Western Australia, 'The Reluctant State'.
8   Ibid.
9   Deakin, p. 57.
10   *The Age*, 23 June 1897.
11   *The Empire*, 20 June 1897.
12   *The Wagga Wagga Express and Murrumbidgee District Advertiser*, 26 June 1897.
13   *The Sydney Morning Herald*, 22 June 1897.
14   *The Wagga Wagga Express and Murrumbidgee District Advertiser*, 22 June 1897.
15   *The South Australian Register*, 8 May 1897.
16   *Adelaide Observer*, 12 June 1897.
17   *The South Australian Register*, 1 July 1897 and 13 July 1897.
18   *Bendigo Advertiser*, 13 April 1897.
19   *Coburg Leader*, 26 June 1897.
20   *Healesville Guardian*, 25 June 1897.
21   *The Riverine Herald*, 23 June 1897.
22   *The West Australian*, 21 May 1897 and 25 May 1897.
23   Ibid., 22 June 1897.
24   *The Mercury*, 22 June 1897 and 25 June 1897.
25   *Ipswich Herald*, 24 June 1897.
26   *The Morning Bulletin*, 23 June 1897.
27   Deakin, p. 11.
28   *The Argus*, 4 June 1898.
29   *The Sydney Morning Herald*, 29 March 1898.
30   Ibid., 25 April 1898.
31   Ibid.
32   Garvin, Vol. 3, p. 557.

7. Australia after Victoria

1   Carroll, p. 34.
2   *The Sydney Morning Herald*, 5 October 1900.
3   *Launceston Examiner*, 17 July 1900.
4   *The Mercury*, 21 December 1900.
5   *The West Australian*, 2 January 1901
6   *Sunday Times*, 6 January 1901.
7   *The Clarence River Advocate*, 1 February 1901.
8   *Inquirer and Commercial News*, 24 January 1901.
9   *The Southern Mail* (Bowral), 25 January 1901.
10   *Camperdown Chronicle*, 27 April 1901.
11   *The Worker* (Wagga), 20 February 1901.
12   Ibid.
13   *Southern Argus*, 24 January 1901.
14   *The Sydney Morning Herald*, 24 January 1901.
15   *The South Australian Register*, 25 January 1901.
16   *The West Australian*, 29 January 1901.
17   *South Bourke and Mornington Journal* (Richmond), 30 January 1901.
18   *Coburg Leader*, 26 January 1901.
19   *South Bourke and Mornington Journal* (Richmond), 30 January 1901.
20   *The Methodist*, 9 January 1901.
21   *Bowral Free Press and Berrima District Intelligencer*, 26 January 1901.
22   *The Southern Mail* (Bowral), 25 January 1901.
23   *Jewish Herald*, 1 February 1901.
24   *The Mercury*, 28 January 1901.
25   *Western Star and Roma Advertiser*, 30 January 1901.
26   *The Northern Star* (Lismore), 30 January 1901.
27   *Launceston Examiner*, 16 February 1901.
28   The *Britannia* was 126 metres long.
29   *The Daily Telegraph*, 9 May 1901.
30   Ibid.
31   *The Albany Advertiser*, 23 April 1901.
32   Australian Dictionary of Biography, 'Byron, John Joseph (1863–1935)'.
33   *The Advertiser*, 9 July 1901.
34   *Border Watch*, 17 July 1901.

35   Australian War Memorial, 'Australia and the Boer War (1899–1902)'.

36   *The Argus*, 6 April 1901.

37   *The Daily Telegraph*, 9 May 1901.

38   Ibid., 10 May 1901.

39   'Opening of the First Parliament', Parliament of Australia.

40   *The Sydney Morning Herald*, 10 May 1901.

41   Maxwell, p. 82.

42   Museum of Victoria, 'Federation'.

43   Maxwell, p. 84; Roberts, Tom, *Opening of the First Parliament of the Commonwealth of Australia by H. R. H. The Duke of Cornwall and York (Later King George V), May 9, 1901*, 1903, oil on canvas.

44   Australian Parliament House, 'Tom Roberts' Big Picture'.

45   National Gallery of Australia, 'Federation: Australian Art & Society 1901–2001'.

46   *The Argus*, 10 May 1901.

47   *The Bulletin*, 18 May 1901.

48   *The Argus*, 10 May 1901.

49   *Daily Telegraph* (Launceston), 11 May 1901.

50   *The Sydney Mail and New South Wales Advertiser*, 25 May 1901.

51   Powerhouse Museum, 'Governor-General's railway carriage, 1901'.

52   *Warwick Examiner and Times*, 25 May 1901.

53   Maxwell, p. 104.

54   *Warwick Examiner and Times*, 25 May 1901.

55   *Mount Magnet Miner and Lennonville Leader*, 18 May 1901.

56   Ibid.

57   Ibid.

58   *Sydney Mail*, 9 June 1901.

59   *The Western Argus* (Kalgoorlie), 27 August 1901.

60   *Adelaide Observer*, 18 May 1901.

61   *The Naracoorte Herald*, 12 July 1901.

62   *The Clarence and Richmond Examiner* (Grafton), 6 August 1901.

63   Ibid.

64   *The Australasian*, 3 August 1901.

8. World War I

1   *The Argus*, 5 August 1914.
2   *Newcastle Morning Herald and Miners' Advocate*, 10 August 1914.
3   *The Australasian*, 3 October 1913.
4   *The Daily News* (Perth), 18 November 1914.
5   *Truth* (Melbourne), 26 December 1914.
6   Australian Army, 'WWI Gallipoli'.
7   British Pathé.
8   The British Monarchy, 'King George V's Message to Australian Troops'.
9   Australian War Memorial, 'Disaster at Fromelles'.
10   Australian War Memorial, 'Battle of Pozieres'.
11   Unofficial History of the Australian and New Zealand Armed Forces, 'Mouquet Farm'.
12   *Border Watch*, 21 July 1917.
13   *The Australasian*, 28 July 1917.
14   *The Queenslander*, 27 July 1917.
15   *The Mercury*, 19 July 1917.
16   National Archives of Australia, 'World War I Internment Camps'.
17   Migration Heritage Centre of New South Wales.
18   National Archives of Australia, 'World War I'.
19   ANZAC Day Commemoration Committee (Qld) Incorporated.
20   Booker, p. 162.
21   *The Daily Advertiser*, 19 July 1919.
22   *Horsham Times*, 19 September 1919.
23   Cannadine, p. 56.
24   *The Queenslander*, 6 October 1918.

9. Edward, Prince of Wales

1   Windsor, p. 132.
2   *The Mail* (Adelaide), 3 January 1920
3   Lady Lloyd George's diary, republished in Donaldson, p. 76.
4   Ibid.
5   Windsor, p. 151.
6   Booker, p. x.
7   Zeigler, *Edward VIII*, p. 120.
8   Donaldson, p. 13.

9   Edward to Freda Ward, letter, 18 November 1920.
Reproduced in Zeigler, *Edward VIII*, p. 95.

10   *The Mail* (Adelaide), 20 March 1920.

11   Ibid.

12   Ziegler, *Mountbatten Diaries*, p. 9.

13   Ibid., p. 10.

14   Ibid.

15   Ibid., p. 11.

16   Thomas papers, 25 December 1919. Reproduced in Zeigler, *Edward VIII*, p. 122.

17   Ziegler, *Edward VIII*, p. 19.

18   *The Mail* (Adelaide), 20 March 1920.

19   Ziegler, *Mountbatten Diaries*, p. 22.

20   Ziegler, *Edward VIII*, p. 126.

21   Halsey to Stamfordham, letter, 23 April 1920, RA GV O 1548A/15, reproduced in Zeigler, *Edward VIII*, p. 126.

22   Windsor, p. 154.

23   Ziegler, *Mountbatten Diaries*, p. 64.

24   Ibid.

25   Ibid.

26   Ibid., p. 65.

27   Ibid., p. 65.

28   Ziegler, *Edward VIII*, p. 181.

29   Ibid.

30   *The Advertiser* (Adelaide), 28 May 1920.

31   Windsor, p. 155.

32   Lionel Halsey to Sir Frederick and Lady Halsey, 14 June 1920.

33   *The Daily News* (Perth), 18 March 1920.

34   Ibid., 1 June 1920.

35   Ziegler, *Mountbatten Diaries*, p. 76.

36   Ibid., p. 77.

37   The Sunday Times (Sydney), 6 June 1920.

38   *The Maitland Mercury*, 16 June 1920.

39   Edward to Freda Ward, letter, 18–24 June 1920, State Library NSW.

40   Ibid.

41   Ibid.

42   *Table Talk*, Melbourne, 1 July 1920.

43   Edward to Freda Ward, letter, 18–24 June 1920, State Library NSW.
44   Ibid.
45   *Table Talk*, 13 May 1920.
46   Ziegler, *Mountbatten Diaries*, p. 83.
47   Ibid.
48   Ibid., p. 83.
49   Lascelles, p. 104.
50   Ibid., p. 110.
51   *The Queanbeyan Age*, 24 June 1920.
52   Ziegler, *Mountbatten Diaries*, p. 84.
53   *Singleton Argus*, 24 June 1920.
54   Ziegler, *Mountbatten Diaries*, p. 84.
55   Ibid., p. 86.
56   Ibid.
57   Edward to Freda Ward, letter, 18–24 June 1920, State Library NSW.
58   Ziegler, *Mountbatten Diaries*, p. 93
59   *The Sunday Times* (Perth), 7 July 1920
60   Oliver, p. 162.
61   Ziegler, *Mountbatten Diaries*, p. 95.
62   *Morning Bulletin*, 7 July 1920.
63   Ibid.
64   Ziegler, *Mountbatten Diaries*, p. 102.
65   Ibid., p. 103.
66   *The Kalgoorlie Miner*, 9 July 1920.
67   *The Register* (Adelaide), 10 July 1920.
68   Ziegler, *Mountbatten Diaries*, p. 105.
69   Edward to Freda Ward, letter, reproduced in Godfrey.
70   Ibid., p. 108.
71   *The Register* (Adelaide), 2 September 1920. The London *Daily Telegraph* had published the account originally in its 13 July issue. It was cabled to the *Register* and published on 2 September.
72   Ziegler, *Mountbatten Diaries*, p. 108.
73   Ibid.
74   Ibid., p. 109.
75   *The Mail* (Adelaide), 17 July 1920.
76   *The Chronicle* (Adelaide), 17 July 1920.
77   Ziegler, *Mountbatten Diaries*, p. 110.

78   *The Zeehan and Dundas Herald*, 21 July 1920.
79   Ibid.
80   *The Daily Telegraph*, 18 July 1920.
81   Ziegler, *Mountbatten Diaries*, p. 113.
82   *The Courier-Mail*, 27 July 1920.
83   Ziegler, *Mountbatten Diaries*, p. 116.
84   *The Courier-Mail*, 27 July 1920.
85   Ziegler, *Mountbatten Diaries*, p. 122.
86   Ibid.
87   Edward to Phillip Sassoon, in Zeigler, *Edward VIII*, p. 130.
88   Ziegler, *Mountbatten Diaries*, p. 136.
89   Ibid., p. 138.
90   *Maryborough Chronicle, Wide Bay and Burnett Advertiser*, 30 December 1920.
91   Zeigler, *Mountbatten Diaries*, p. 133.
92   *The Sydney Morning Herald*, 9 December 1920.

10. Australia and the Abdication
1   Bousfield and Toffoli, p. 51.
2   Donaldson, p. 36.
3   Farquhar, p. 294.
4   Donaldson, p. 9.
5   *Daily Mail*, 25 December 2010.
6   Donaldson, p. 18.
7   Ibid., p. 22.
8   *The Sydney Morning Herald*, 10 March 2013.
9   Bousfield and Toffoli, p. 51.
10   *Dubbo Liberal and Macquarie Advocate*, 5 February 1929.
11   Elizabeth's diary, 6 January 1927, quoted in Shawcross, p. 264.
12   *The Australasian*, 2 April 1927.
13   *The Argus*, 28 March 1927.
14   Vintage Motor Club, NSW.
15   *The Australasian*, 2 April 1927.
16   *The Courier-Mail*, 7 April 1927.
17   Ibid.
18   *The Mercury*, 16 April 1927.
19   *The Courier-Mail*, 2 May 1927.
20   Ibid., 4 May 1927.

21 National Archives of Australia, Parliament House, Canberra, 1927'.
22 *The Bulletin*, 12 May 1927.
23 *Daily Guardian* (Sydney), 10 May 1927.
24 *Launceston Examiner*, 12 May 1927.
25 *The Sunday Times* (Perth), 22 May 1927.
26 *The Register* (Adelaide), 19 May 1927.
27 *The Geraldton Guardian*, 24 May 1927.
28 *The Sunday Times*, 22 May 1927.
29 *The Geraldton Guardian*, 24 May 1927.
30 *The Northern Times* (Carnarvon), 28 May 1927.
31 *The Canberra Times*, 13 May 1927.
32 *The Morning Bulletin*, 16 May 1927.
33 *The Western Mail*, 3 November 1927.
34 15 April 1927, Thomas papers, quoted in Zeigler, p. 168.
35 Ziegler, *Edward VIII*, p. 173.
36 Ibid.
37 Ibid., p. 199.
38 Ibid., p. 231.
39 Ibid., p. 227.
40 *The Times* (London), 22 January 1936.
41 *Australian Women's Weekly*, 25 January 1936.
42 House of Commons, 23 January 1936.
43 *The Western Age* (Dubbo), 7 February 1936.
44 *The Sydney Morning Herald*, 22 January 1936.
45 19 February 1936, Royal Archives, GV P 1945/94.
46 *The Albury Banner and Wodonga Express*, 24 January 1936.
47 4 February 1936, Thomas papers, reproduced in Zeigler, *Edward*, p. 245.
48 Bruce to Baldwin, letter, 16 November 1936, National Archives of Australia M104/1 4.
49 Ziegler, *Edward VIII*, p. 306.
50 Ibid.
51 Lyons to Baldwin, telegram, 5 December 1936, Royal Archvies, KEVIII Ab Box 1/19.
52 National Archives of Australia, 'Stanley Melbourne Bruce'.
53 *Hansard*, 11 December 1936.
54 Ibid., 10 December 1936.
55 *The Mercury*, 11 December 1936.

56   *Maryborough Chronicle, Wide Bay and Burnett Advertiser*,
      30 December 1936.

57   *The Courier-Mail*, 31 December 1936.

11. World War II

1   BBC, 'On this day. 1939: Britain and France declare war on
      Germany'.

2   Royal Archives, 'Historic Royal Speeches and Writings, George VI'.

3   Australian War Memorial, 'Prime Minister Robert G Menzies:
      wartime broadcast'.

4   Australian Government Anzac website.

5   Freudenberg, p. 188.

6   Australian Bureau of Statistics, 'The Department of the
      Foreign Affairs – A Brief History'.

7   *Hansard*, 10 September 2015.

8   *Catholic Worker*, 2 September 1939.

9   Freudenberg, p. 209.

10   Day, p. 376.

11   Documents in Australian Foreign Policy (DAFP) 1937–1949,
      Vol. III, 17 November 1939.

12   Freudenberg, p. 240.

13   Advisory War Council Minute, 25 November 1940, DAFP
      Vol. IV, document 243.

14   Martin, *Menzies Diary*, 22 February 1941.

15   Ibid., 2 March 1941.

16   Ibid., 22 February 1941.

17   Ibid., 26 March 1941.

18   Ibid., 24 February 1941.

19   Ibid., 25 February 1941.

20   Ibid., 4 March 1941.

21   Ibid., 21 February 1941.

22   Ibid., 27 February 1941.

23   Ibid., 5 and 8 March 1941.

24   Ibid., 14 March 1941.

25   Menzies to Fadden, telegram, 25 February 1941, DAFP, Vol.
      IV, document 321.

26   Semmler, *Slessor War Diaries*, p. 267.

27   Freudenberg, p. 266.

28   Ibid., p. 273.

29   Martin, *Menzies Diary*, 23 April 1941.

30   Ibid., 5 May 1941.

31   Ibid., 10 May 1941.

32   Ibid.

33   Ibid., 12 May 1941.

34   National Archives of Australia, 'Robert Menzies: In Office'.

35   Curtin to Churchill, telegram, quoted in Day, p. 420.

36   Churchill to Fadden, telegram, DAFP, Vol. V, document 73.

37   Curtin, 'Japan enters Second World War'.

38   Freudenberg, p. 313

39   Ibid.

40   Curtin to Casey for Roosevelt and Churchill, message, 23 December 1941, DAFP, Vol. V, document 214.

41   Churchill to Curtin, letter, 25 December 1941, DAFP, Vol. V, document 231.

42   *The Herald* (Melbourne), 27 December 1941.

43   Ibid.

44   Churchill, *Hinge of Fate*, p. 45.

45   National Archives of Australia, 'The bombing of Darwin'.

46   Freudenberg, p. 393.

47   Australian War Memorial, 'The Australian Military Contribution to the Occupation of Japan'.

48   The Pacific War Online Encyclopedia, 'Guadalcanal'.

49   Freudenberg, p. 462.

50   *The Argus*, 17 November 1943.

51   Australian Dictionary of Biography, 'Gloucester, first Duke of (1900–1974)'.

52   Ibid., 'Curtin, John (1885–1945)'.

53   *Australian Women's Weekly*, 1 April 1944.

54   *The Barrier Miner*, 23 June 1942.

55   Curtin, *Diary of a Labour Man*, 26 April 1944.

56   *The Canberra Times*, 1 May 1944.

57   *The Advertiser* (Adelaide), 15 May 1945.

58   Curtin, *Diary of a Labour Man*, 24 May 1944.

12. A Royal Wedding and the Coronation

1   It has been suggested that the two met even earlier: in 1934 when Elizabeth was only eight years old, at the wedding of Philip's cousin, Princess Marina of Greece and Denmark, with Prince

George, Duke of Kent and Elizabeth's uncle. It is also thought they may have met again three years later in 1937: Brandreth, pp. 133–39; Lacey (*Majesty*), pp. 124–25; Pimlott, p. 86.

2   Judd, p. 50.

3   *The Independent*, 13 December 1992.

4   Ibid.

5   *Independent* (UK), 13 December 1992

6   Judd p.76

7   Ibid., p. 84.

8   *The Sydney Morning Herald*, 14 April 2006.

9   Smith, Sally Bedell, *Vanity Fair*, January 2012.

10   *The Daily Telegraph* (UK), 5 September 2004.

11   Ibid.

12   Ibid.

13   Smith, Sally Bedell, *Vanity Fair*, January 2012.

14   Ibid.

15   *The Sydney Morning Herald*, 11 July 1947.

16   *Australian Women's Weekly*, 26 July 1947.

17   At the same time he was also made Earl of Merioneth, and Baron Greenwich of Greenwich in the City of London.

18   'Princess Elizabeth's Wedding Cake', 'Guides Victoria Archives Links to Royalty'.

19   *The Morning Bulletin*, 31 October 1947.

20   *News* (Adelaide), 5 November 1947.

21   *The Courier-Mail*, 30 October 1947.

22   *Daily Mirror*, 6 November 1947.

23   *Daily Mail*, 4 September, 2004, *Daily Telegraph*, 5 September 2004, *Age*, 6 September 2004.

24   *The Sydney Morning Herald*, 21 November 1947.

25   Ibid., 20 November 1947

26   *The Sydney Morning Herald*, 21 November 1947.

27   *The Advertiser* (Adelaide), 9 January 1952.

28   The Mercury, 30 January 1952.

29   *Daily Mail*, 9 January 2012.

30   Interview with the author, 3 May 2015.

31   *The Sydney Morning Herald*, 2 June 1953.

32   Holt, *Coronation Diary*.

33   Ibid.

34   Ibid.

35   Ibid.
36   Diary of Jessie Reid, provided to the author by granddaughter
     Shona Gibson.
37   *The Mail* (Adelaide), 30 May 1953.
38   Interview with the author, 3 May 2015.
39   Ibid., 3 March 2015.
40   *The Chronicle* (Adelaide), 18 December 1952.
41   *The Northern Star* (Lismore), 4 June 1953.
42   *The Barrier Miner* (Broken Hill), 3 June 1953.
43   *The West Australian*, 2 June 1953.

13. The 1954 Tour

1   *The Sydney Morning Herald*, 3 February 1954.
2   Ibid., 2 February 1954.
3   *The Advertiser* (Adelaide), 4 February 1954.
4   *The Bulletin*, 3 February 1954.
5   Connors, 'Glittering Thread', p. 196.
6   *The Advertiser* (Adelaide), 4 February 1954.
7   Connors, 'Glittering Thread', p. 134.
8   Lowe, p. 2.
9   *The Courier-Mail*, 7 January 1954.
10   *The Daily Advertiser* (Wagga), 9 January 1954.
11   Ibid., 25 February 1954.
12   ABC Archives, 'Queen Elizabeth II Visits Australia', comment,
     21 April 2012.
13   *The Sun* (Sydney), 4 February 1954.
14   *The Sydney Morning Herald*, 6 February 1954.
15   Ibid., 7 February 1954.
16   Haskins, 'Beth Dean and the Transnational Circulation
     of Aboriginal Dance Culture: Gender, Authority and
     C. P. Mountford'.
17   *The News* (Adelaide), 11 February 1954.
18   Ibid.
19   Ibid.
20   Interview with the author, 3 May 2015.
21   Hill, *Forgotten Children*, p. 28.
22   *The Sydney Morning Herald*, 13 February 1954.
23   Information supplied to the author, May 2015.
24   Connors, 'Glittering Thread', p. 211.

25 Ibid.
26 *The Sydney Morning Herald*, 17 February 1954.
27 Australian News and Information Bureau, p. 15.
28 *The Sydney Morning Herald*, 17 February 1954.
29 *The Barrier Miner*, 22 February 1954
30 *Sydney Morning Herald*, 19 February 1954
31 *The Sydney Morning Herald*, 19 February 1954; Connors, 'Glittering Thread', p. 220.
32 Connors, 'Glittering Thread', p. 220.
33 *The Sydney Morning Herald*, 19 February 1954.
34 *Newcastle Morning Herald and Miners' Advocate*, 19 February 1954.
35 *The Townsville Daily Bulletin*, 23 February 1954.
36 *The Advocate* (Burnie), 22 February 1954.
37 *The Mercury* (Hobart), 6 February 1954.
38 *The Advocate* (Burnie), 23 February 1954.
39 Interview with the author, 3 May 2015.
40 *The Argus*, 25 February 1954.
41 Ibid.
42 Ibid.
43 Connors, 'Glittering Thread', p. 255.
44 *The Argus*, 4 April 1954.
45 Connors, 'Glittering Thread', p. 255.
46 *The Charleville Times*, 11 February 1954.
47 *The Courier-Mail*, 3 April 1954.
48 *Queensland Country Life*, 11 March 1954.
49 Interview with the author, 3 May 2015.
50 Connors, 'Glittering Thread', pp. 277–78
51 *The Barrier Miner*, 19 March 1954.
52 Interview with the author, 3 May 2015.
53 *The Illawarra Daily Mercury*, 27 May 1954.
54 National Museum of Australia, 'Polio: A Virulent and Incurable Disease'.
55 *Queensland Times*, 23 May 1954.
56 *The National Advocate* (Bathurst), 24 March 1954.
57 Interview with the author, 3 May 2015.
58 *Launceston Examiner*, 27 March 1954.
59 Ibid.
60 Ibid.

61 Interview with the author, 3 May 2015.
62 *The Western Mail*, 11 March 1954.
63 Smith, Sally Bedell, *Vanity Fair*, January 2012.
64 *The Argus*, 24 December 1954.

14. Elizabeth, the Later Years
1   *The Canberra Times*, 18 February 1963.
2   While it was the first time the queen had travelled to Australia on the *Britannia*, Prince Philip had used it when he opened the Olympic Games in Melbourne in 1956. The other trips were in 1970, 1974, 1977, 1981, 1982, 1986 and 1988.
3   Royal Yacht Britannia, 'A Day in the Life'.
4   National Archives of Australia, 'Prime Minister Robert G Menzies'.
5   *The Canberra Times*, 22 March 1963.
6   Ibid, 14 March 1963.
7   Ibid.
8   Ibid., 19 February 1963.
9   *The Canberra Times*, 28 March 1963.
10 Ibid., 30 April 1970.
11 Interview with the author, May 2015.
12 *The Canberra Times*, 22 October 1973.
13 The earlier tours were 1954, 1963, 1970 and 1973.
14 *The Canberra Times*, 1 March 1974.
15 *The West Australian*, 12 April 2011.
16 Notes supplied to the author by Helen Kebby.
17 Interview with the author, May 2015.
18 For information on each of these roles, see the British Monarchy, 'Royal Household departments'.
19 *The Canberra Times*, 1 May 1988.
20 Ibid., 4 February 1992.
21 *Daily Mail*, 6 March 1992.
22 *The Sun*, 6 March 1992.
23 *The Daily Telegraph*, 24 February 2009.
24 *The Sydney Morning Herald*, 2 October 2005.

15. Prince Philip
1   *The News* (Adelaide), 8 April 1940.
2   Judd, p. 103.

3   *The Telegraph* (UK), 2 January 2002.
4   Judd, p. 108.
5   *The Queensland Times*, 11 June 1945.
6   Smith, Sally Bedell, *Vanity Fair*, January 2012.
7   *The Telegraph* (UK), 2 January 2002.
8   *The Argus*, 26 November 1956.
9   *Australian Women's Weekly*, 12 December 1956.
10   Judd, p. 167.
11   *The Telegraph* (UK), 5 September 2004.
12   Ibid.
13   Judd, p. 168.
14   *The Canberra Times*, 9 November 1962.
15   Ibid., 22 November 1962.
16   Commonwealth Study Conference.
17   Ibid.
18   *The Canberra Times*, 17 May 1968.
19   Ibid.
20   Ibid., 11 June 1970.
21   *The Age*, 1 January 2004.
22   Brown, *Lake Pedder*.
23   *The Canberra Times*, 17 May 1986.
24   *The Courier-Mail*, 19 February 2009.
25   *Boston Globe*, 12 January 1989.
26   *The Sydney Morning Herald*, 26 January 2015.
27   *Mirror*, 10 July 2015.
28   *The Sydney Morning Herald*, 26 January 2015.
29   *The Telegraph* (UK), 2 March 2002.
30   Dampier, P. and Walton, A., p. 31.
31   *Daily Mirror*, 27 January 2015.

16. Margaret

1   Heald, p. 11.
2   Warwick, p. 138.
3   *Daily Mail*, 2 July 2007.
4   Warwick, p. 191.
5   Ibid.
6   Princess Margaret, 31 October 1955, quoted in Warwick, p. 205.
7   Heald, p. 114.

8   de Courcy, p. 102

9   *The Canberra Times*, 20 March 1974.

10   Heald, p. 174.

11   *The Diaries of Cynthia Gladwin*, republished in Heald, p. 155.

12   *Australian Women's Weekly*, 11 October 1972.

13   Ibid.

14   Ibid.

15   Ibid.

16   *The Canberra Times*, 9 October 1972.

17   Ibid., 18 October 1972.

18   Heald, p. 188.

19   Ibid., p. 189.

20   *Australian Women's Weekly*, 5 November 1975.

21   Ibid.

22   Ibid.

23   Gower later reached the rank of major general in the Australian army and was director of the Australian War Memorial. In 2002 he was made an Officer of the Order of Australia.

24   Interview with the author, March 2015.

25   *The Canberra Times*, 23 October 1975.

26   Ibid.

27   Aronson, *Princess Margaret: A Biography*, quoted in 'The Original Royal Rebel', *Express* (UK), 3 November 2013

28   Heald, p. 190

29   Ibid., p. 204.

30   Ibid.

31   *The Telegraph* (UK), 3 April 2012.

32   *The Canberra Times*, 1 October 1978

33   Ibid.

34   Ibid.

35   *Australian Women's Weekly*, 18 October 1978.

36   *The Sydney Morning Herald*, 8 October 1978.

37   *Australian Women's Weekly*, 28 March 1979.

38   *Daily Telegraph*, 6 December 2012.

39   Field, p. 436

40   Heald, p. 208.

17. Prince Charles, Prince of Wales

1   *Daily Mail* (UK), 2 February 2013.
2   *The Telegraph* (UK), 29 June 2014.
3   *The Canberra Times*, 31 January 1966.
4   Australian Women's Weekly, 29 July 1981.
5   *Daily Mail* (UK), 2 February 2013.
6   *The Canberra Times*, 6 May 1966.
7   *Australia Women's Weekly*, 4 July 1974.
8   *The Canberra Times*, 14 October 1974.
9   Dimbleby, p. 226.
10 Halliburton, p. 23.
11 Prince Charles appeared on television Channel 7, the ABC, Channel 9 and Channel 10 on 13 October 1974.
12 *The Canberra Times*, 30 October 1974.
13 Ibid.
14 Ibid., 29 October 1974.
15 Hocking, p. 312.
16 *Australian Women's Weekly*, 18 August 1976.
17 Ibid.
18 *The Times* (London), 23 July 1976; *The Canberra Times*, 27 July 1976.
19 Senator Reg Withers, Government Leader in the Senate, 11 November 1976.
20 Department of Prime Minister and Cabinet, PM Transcripts Closing of Jubilee Appeal, Prime Minister Malcolm Fraser. Media Release 4 July 1978.
21 *The Canberra Times*, 29 September 1977.
22 *Australian Women's Weekly*, 26 October 1977.
23 Miller, pp. 166–67.
24 Ibid.
25 *The Independent* (UK), 18 November 1997.
26 *Daily Mail*, 11 October 2008.
27 *The Canberra Times*, 25 March 1979.
28 *Evening Standard* (UK), 25 February 2005.
29 Ibid.
30 *Australian Women's Weekly*, 5 May 1981.
31 *The Canberra Times*, 19 September 1980.
32 Morton, *Diana*, p. 34.
33 Interview with the author, June 2015.

34   *The Canberra Times*, 29 July 1981.

35   Morton, *Diana*, p. 38.

36   *The Canberra Times*, 3 August 1981.

37   Ibid., 14 April 1981.

38   *The Canberra Times*, 27 February 1981.

39   *Christian Science Monitor*, 19 August 1981.

18. The Prince and Diana, Princess of Wales

1   She had also been in Australia for a family visit a few months
      before marrying Charles in 1981, and returned briefly on a
      private tour, after her divorce from Charles, in November 1996.

2   Bradford, *Diana*, p. 74.

3   *Milton Ulladulla Times*, 28 January 2014.

4   Morton, *Diana*, p. 34.

5   Ibid.

6   Ibid., p. 33.

7   Ibid., p 37.

8   Mayer, p. 135.

9   Ibid., p. 135.

10   Morton, *Diana*, p. 41.

11   *The Sydney Morning Herald*, 29 May 2000.

12   Morton, *Diana*, p. 42.

13   Ibid., p. 42.

14   Ibid., p 43.

15   Morton, *Diana*, p. 49.

16   Ibid., p. 50.

17   *Australian Women's Weekly*, 13 January 1982.

18   *The Canberra Times*, 22 March 1983.

19   *Canberra Times*, 24 April 1983.

20   Morton, *Diana*, p.68–69.

21   *People*, 4 April 1983.

22   *Daily Mirror* (UK), 30 August 2012.

23   Morton, *Diana*, p. 49.

24   *The Canberra Times*, 24 April 1983.

25   Morton, *Diana, Diana*, p. 49.

26   *The Sydney Morning Herald*, 15 February 2005.

27   Morton, *Diana*, p. 52.

28   Ibid., p.53.

29   Ibid., p. 54.

30   Ibid., p. 53.
31   *The Canberra Times*, 13 October 1985.
32   Ibid., 17 January 1985.
33   Ibid., 6 November 1985.
34   Ibid., 29 October 1985.
35   Dimbleby, p. 395.
36   *The Canberra Times*, 31 January 1994.
37   Ibid., 20 January 1994.
38   Ibid., 24 January 1994.
39   *The Canberra Times*, 21 January 1994
40   Ibid., 27 January 1994.
41   *The Age*, 6 February 2005.
42   *The Canberra Times*, 1 July 1994.
43   Blog, 'Hotly Spiced', 'Charlie and the Princess', 1 May 2012
44   Clark, University of Adelaide.
45   Australian Associated Press, 6 June 2012.

19. The Republic of Australia

1   Lawson, 'Australian Loyalty'.
2   Transcript of News Conference, Parliament House, 5 April
     1991.
3   Dawkins, 25 June 1991, quoted in Australian Parliament
     House, Background Paper 9, 1995–96.
4   *The Sydney Morning Herald*, 26 June 1991, quoted in ibid.
5   Ibid.
6   Ibid., 7 July 1991.
7   Australian Parliament House, Background Paper 9, 1995–96.
8   *The Australian*, 31 January 1992.
9   Australian Parliament House, Background Paper 9, 1995–96.
10   *The Sydney Morning Herald*, 9 July 1991.
11   *The Canberra Times*, 1 February 1992.
12   Trends in Australian Political Opinion, 1987– 2013, ANU,
     p. 50.
13   *The West Australian*, 14 May 1992, quoted in Australian
     Parliament House, Background Paper 9, 1995–96.
14   *The Australian*, 2 July 1992.
15   *The Sunday Telegraph*, 12 April 1992, quoted in Australian
     Parliament House, Background Paper 9, 1995–96.
16   *The Canberra Times*, 25 February 1992.

17   *Hansard*, 27 February 1992.
18   Ibid.
19   Ibid.
20   *The Sydney Morning Herald*, 27 September 2007.
21   Australian Parliament House, 'Background Paper 9, 1995–96', 17 March 1992.
22   Ibid., 7 April 1992.
23   Goodhew, *The Australian*, 30 April 1993; Hollingworth, *The Australian*, 18 June 1993, quoted in Australian Parliament House, Background Paper 9, 1995–96.
24   *The Australian*, 13 September 1993.
25   Ibid., 14 October 1993.
26   *The Canberra Times*, 1 November 1993.
27   *The Age*, 18 September 1993.
28   Transcript of interview with the Prime Minister, the Hon Paul Keating MP, Shelbourne Hotel, Dublin, Ireland Sunday 19 September, 1993.
29   'The Citizenship Ceremony'.
30   Speech, HRH the Prince of Wales, at the Australia Day Reception, Sydney.
31   *Canberra Times*, 25 July 1994.
32   Ibid., 30 August 1994.
33   Dame Joan Sutherland and Roy McKeen, 14 October 2010.
34   *The Australian*, 15 February 1992.
35   Of the seventy-six elected delegates, twenty were from New South Wales, sixteen from Victoria, thirteen from Queensland, nine from Western Australia, eight from South Australia, six from Tasmania and two from each of the Northern Territory and the Australian Capital Territory.
36   Australian Parliament House, Constitutional Convention, 2nd to 13th February 1998, transcript.
37   Ibid.
38   'Joint Select Committee on the Republic Referendum', *Hansard*.
39   *The Telegraph* (UK), 17 August 2010.

20. The New Generation

1   *People*, June 2015.
2   *The Observer* (UK), 7 September 1997.
3   *The Age*, 21 September 2003.

4   Australian Associated Press, 23 September 2003.
5   *The Age*, 29 September 2003.
6   Ibid, 14 January 2005.
7   Australian Monarchist League, April 2013.
8   *Mirror*, 23 September 2013.
9   *The Australian*, 23 September 2013.
10   *Daily Mirror*, 5 October 2013.
11   *The Guardian*, 5 October 2013.
12   *CBS News*, 6 April 2015.
13   *Daily Mail* (Australia), 7 May 2015.
14   *The Australian*, 24 November 2009.
15   *The Sydney Morning Herald*, 29 June 2007.
16   *ABC News*, 19 January 2010.
17   Ibid.
18   *The Telegraph*, 20 January 2010.
19   *The Courier-Mail*, 21 January 2010.
20   *ABC News*, 21 January 2010.
21   Ibid.
22   *The Telegraph* (UK), 20 January 2010.
23   Ibid.
24   Ibid.
25   *The Guardian*, 22 January 2010.
26   *ABC News*, 10 March 2011.
27   *The Sydney Morning Herald*, 19 March 2011.
28   *The Sunday Mail*, 20 March 2011.
29   Roy Morgan, 6 May 2011.
30   'The Australians' attitudes towards England and the Royal
     Family' survey, commissioned by Ancestry.com.au, May 2012,
     conducted by Pure Profile.
31   ABC TV, *7.30*, 17 October 2011.
32   *The Courier-Mail*, 13 April 2014.
33   *Crikey*, 6 March 2014.
34   *The Sydney Morning Herald*, 15 April 2014.
35   *Daily Mail* (Australia), 16 April 2014.

BIBLIOGRAPHY AND
FURTHER READING

Andrews, Allen. *The Follies of King Edward VII*. Lexington Avenue Press, London, 1975

Aronson, Theo. *Prince Eddy and the Homosexual Underworld*. Thistle Publishing, London, 2013

——, *Princess Margaret: A Biography*. Thistle Publishing, London, 2013

Asquith, Lady Cynthia. *Her Majesty the Queen, an entirely new and complete biography written with the approval of Her Majesty*. E. P. Dutton., New York, 1937

Australian News and Information Bureau, Department of the Interior, *Royal Visit to Australia of Her Majesty Queen Elizabeth II and His Royal Highness The Duke of Edinburgh, 1954*, Angus & Robertson, Sydney, 1954

Booker, M. *The Great Professional. A Study of W. M. Hughes*. McGraw-Hill, Sydney, 1980

Bousfield, Arthur and Toffoli, Garry. *The Queen Mother and Her Century: An Illustrated Biography of Queen Elizabeth the Queen Mother on Her 100th Birthday*. Dundurn Press, Toronto, 2000

Bradford, Sarah. *Diana*. Viking, London, 2006

——. *The Reluctant King: The Life and Reign of George V 1895–1952*. St Martin's Press, New York, 1990

Brandreth, Gyles. *Philip and Elizabeth Portrait of a Marriage*. Century, London, 2004

Brown, B., Kiernan, K. *Lake Pedder*. Wilderness Society, Hobart, 1985

Callaway, Anita. *Visual Ephemera: Theatrical art in nineteenth-century Australia, Sydney*. UNSW Press, Sydney, 2000

Cannadine, David. *George V*. Allen Lane, London, 2014

Carboni, Raffaello. *The Eureka Stockade Prince Albert Hotel, Bakery Hill, Ballaarat, Anniversary of the Burning of Bentley's Eureka Hotel, 1855*. Project Gutenberg, Australia

Carlyon, Les. *The Great War*, Pan MacMillan, Sydney, 2007

Carroll, Brian. *Australia's Governors-General: From Hopetoun to Jeffrey*. Rosenberg Publishing, Kenthurst, NSW, 2004

Churchill, Winston S. *The Hinge of Fate (The Second World War Volume IV)*. Houghton Mifflin Company, Boston, 1950

Collins, Gerald. *Patrick McMahon Glynn: A Founder of Australian Federation*. Melbourne University Press, Melbourne, 1965

Connors, Jane. *Royal Visits to Australia*. National Library of Australia, Canberra, 2015

Dalton, John N. *The Cruise of Her Majesty's Ship "Bacchante" 1879–1882" The Private Journals, Letters, and Note-books of Prince Albert Victor and Prince George of Wales, with additions by John N. Dalton*. Macmillan, London, 1888. Digitised 2007

Dampier, Phil and Walton, Ashley. *Prince Philip: Wise Words and Golden Gaffes*. Barzipan Publishing, Oxford, 2012

Day, David. *Curtin: A Life*. HarperCollins, Sydney, 1999

de Courcy, Anne. *Snowden: The Biography*. Weidenfeld & Nicolson, London, 2008

Deakin, Alfred. *The Federal Story: The Inner History of the Federal Cause (edited and with an introduction by John Andrew La Nauze)*. Melbourne University Press, Melbourne, 1963

Dimbleby, Jonathan. *Prince of Wales: A Biography*. Little, Brown, London, 1994

Donaldson, Frances. *King George VI and Queen Elizabeth*. Weidenfeld & Nicolson, London 1977

——. *Edward VIII*. Trinity, London, 1974

Evans, Gareth (ed.). *Labor and the Constitution, 1972–1975: Essays and Comments on the Constitutional Controversies of the Whitlam Years in Australian Government*, Heinemann, London, 1977.

Farquhar, Michael. *Behind Palace Doors: Five Centuries of Sex, Adventure, Vice, Treachery and Folly from Royal Britain*. Random House, London, 2011

Feuchtwanger, Edgar F. *Albert and Victoria: The Rise and Fall of the House of Saxe-Coburg-Gotha*. Hambledon Continuum, London, 2006

Field, M. *Swimming with Sharks*. Penguin, London, 2010

Freudenberg, Graham. *Churchill and Australia*. Pan MacMillan, Sydney, 2008

Garvin, J. L. *The Life of Sir Joseph Chamberlain*. MacMillan, London, 1934

Gladwin, Cynthia. Miles Jebb (ed.). *The Diaries of Cynthia Gladwyn*. Constable, London, 1995

Glen, F. *For Glory and a Farm*. Whatakane Historical Society, Whatakane, New Zealand, 1984

Godfrey, R. (ed.). *Letters from a Prince: Edward to Mrs. Freda Dudley Ward 1918–1921*. Little, Brown, London, 1998

Halliburton, Darlene. *The Kate Middleton Handbook*. Emereo Publishing, 2012

Harrison, Michael. *Clarence, the Life of H.R.H. The Duke of Clarence and Avondale 1864–1892*. Virgin Books, London, 1972

Heald, Tim. *Princess Margaret: A Life Unravelled*. Phoenix, London, 2008

Hill, David. *The Forgotten Children*. Random House, Sydney, 2007
——. *The Making of Australia*. Random House, Sydney, 2014

Hocking, Jenny. *Gough Whitlam: His Time*. Miegunyah Press, Melbourne, 2012

Holden, Anthony. *Prince Charles, A Biography*. Bantam Press, London, 1998

Irving, Helen (ed). *The Centenary Companion to Australian Federation*. Cambridge University Press, Cambridge, 1999

Judd, Denis. *Prince Philip, A Biography*. Michael Joseph, London, 1980

Kohen, J. L. 'First and Last People: Aboriginal Sydney', *in* J. Connell (ed.) *Sydney, The Emergence of a Global City*. Oxford University Press, Oxford, 2000

Lacey, Robert. *The Queen, A Life in Brief*. Duckworth & Co., London, 2012

——. *Majesty. Elizabeth II and the House of Windsor*, Little, Brown, London, 2002

Lascelles, Sir Alan. Hart-Davis, Hart (ed). *King's Counsellor: Abdication and War, the Diaries of Sir Alan Lascelles.* Orion Books, London, 2006

McKenna, Mark. *The Captive Republic: A History of Republicanism in Australia 1788–1996*, Press Syndicate of the University of Cambridge, Cambridge, 1996

McKinlay, Brian. *The First Royal Tour 1867–1868.* Rigby Limited, Sydney, 1970

Martin, A. W. and Hardy, Patsy (eds), *Dark and Hurrying Days, Menzies, 1941 Diary.* National Library of Australia, Canberra, 1993

Maxwell, William. *With the Ophir Round the Empire.* Cassell, London, 1901

Mayer, Catherine. *Charles, the Heart of a King.* W. H. Allen, London, 2015

Miller, Harry M. with Holder, P. *Confessions of a Not-so-secret Agent.* Hachette, Sydney, 2009

Morton, Andrew. *Diana: Her True Story.* Michael O'Mara, London, 1992

——. *Inside Buckingham Palace.* Summit Books, Philippines, 1991

Nicolson, Harold. *King George V.* TransAtlantic Publications, Philadelphia, 1952

Oliver, B. *War and Peace in Western Australia.* University of Western Australia Press, Perth, 1995

Pimlott, Ben. *The Queen: A Biography of Elizabeth II.* John Wiley, London, 1996

Samaha, Joel. *Criminal Law 11th Edition.* Cengage Learning, Boston, 2013

Schreuder, Deryck and Ward, Stuart. *Australia's Empire.* Oxford University Press, Oxford, 2001

Semmler, Clement (ed). *The War Diaries of Kenneth Slessor, Official Australian Correspondent 1940–1944.* University of Queensland Press, Brisbane, 1985

Shawcross, William. *Queen Elizabeth, The Queen Mother the Official Biography.* Macmillan, London, 2010

Symons, Michael. *One Continuous Picnic.* Melbourne University Press, Melbourne, 2007

Van Der Kiste, John. *Edward VII's Children.* Sutton, London, 1989

Warwick, Christopher. *Princess Margaret: A Life of Contrasts*. Andre Deutsch, London, 2003

Windsor, Edward Duke of Windsor. *A King's Story: The Memoirs of H.R.H. The Duke of Windsor K.G.* Prion Press, London, 1988

Ziegler, Philip (ed.). *The Diaries of Lord Louis Mountbatten 1920– 1922, Tours with the Prince of Wales*. William Collins, London, 1987

——. *King Edward VIII, the Official Biography*, Williams Collins, London, 1990

ONLINE ARTICLES AND RESOURCES

ABC Archives, http://www.abc.net.au/archives/

ABC News, http://www.abc.net.au/news/

ANZAC Day Commemoration Committee Incorporated, http://www.anzacday.org.au/history/ww1/

Australian Army, http://www.army.gov.au/

Australian Dictionary of Biography, http://adb.anu.edu.au/biography

Australian Government ANZAC website, http://www.anzacsite.gov.au/

Australian Monarchist League, http://www.monarchist.org.au

Australian Parliament House, http://www.aph.gov.au/

Australian Senate, http://exhibitions.senate.gov.au/

Australian War Memorial, https://www.awm.gov.au/atwar/boer/.

Biography Online, http://www.biographyonline.net

British Monarchy, see 'Royal Archives'

British Monarchy 'King George V's Message to Australian Troops', https://www.flickr.com/photos/britishmonarchy/

British Pathé, http://www.britishpathe.com/

'Citizenship Ceremony, The', http://www.immigrationcitizenship.com.au/citizenship-information/the-citizenship-ceremony

Clark, Dr Sheila, 'Impact of Di's Death Finally Revealed in Study', https://www.adelaide.edu.au/news/news157.html

Connors, Jane Holley. 'The Glittering Thread', thesis, University of Technology, Sydney, https://opus.lib.uts.edu.au/research/bitstream/handle/2100/249/02Whole.pdf?sequence=9

Curtin, John, 'Diary of a Labour Man 1917–1945'. John Curtin Prime Ministerial Library, 2008, http://john.curtin.edu.au/diary/

——, 'Japan enters Second World War', http://aso.gov.au/titles/radio/curtin-japan-second-world-war/clip1/

Dame Joan Sutherland and Aussie Jock Roy McKeen, 14 October 2010, https://independentaustralia.net/australia/australia-display/dame-joan-sutherland-and-aussie-jock,3083

Davidson, S. 'The First Significant Overseas War: Australians leave for the Waikato War in New Zealand in 1863', www.jcu.edu.au/aff/hisotry/articles/davidson.htm

Davies, Glenn, 31 July 2011, 'Independent Australia', https://independentaustralia.net/tag/glenn+davies

Department of Prime Minister and Cabinet, PM Transcripts, http://pmtranscripts.dpmc.gov.au/about.php

Digger History, http://www.diggerhistory.info/

Documents in Australian Foreign Policy (DAFP), http://dfat.gov.au/about-us/publications/historical-documents/Pages/historical-documents.aspx?OpenView

Gover, Elena. 'Australia and the Crimean War', http://www.australiarussia.com/AusCrimea

Hansard, House of Representatives, Australian Parliament, Canberra, http://www.aph.gov.au/parliamentary_business/hansard

Haskins V. 'Beth Dean and the Transnational Circulation of Aboriginal Dance Culture: Gender, Authority and C. P. Mountford', http://press.anu.edu.au/wp-content/uploads/2014/12/ch024.pdf

Independent Australia, https://independentaustralia.net/

Knight, J. D. 'Narrative of the Visit of His Royal Highness the Duke of Edinburgh to the Colony of Victoria, Australia', http://archive.org/stream/narrativeofvisit00knig/narrativeofvisit00knig_djvu.txt

Lawson, H. 'Australian Loyalty', 1887, http://www.telelib.com/words/authors/L/LawsonHenry/prose/republican/australianloyalty.html

Lowe, Michael. '1954: The Queen and Australia in the world', http://recollections.nma.gov.au/issues/vol_6_no_1/refereed_papers/

Migration Heritage Centre of New South Wales, http://www.migration-heritage.nsw.gov.au/exhibition/enemyathome/the-enemy-at-home/.

Museum of Victoria, 'Federation', http://museumvictoria.com.au/reb/history/federation/

National Archives of Australia, Parliament House, Canberra, 1927, http://naa.gov.au/

National Gallery of Australia, http://nga.gov.au/

National Library of Australia, http://trove.nla.gov.au/newspaper/

National Museum of Australia, http://www.nma.gov.au/

'Official Record of the Proceedings and Debates of the Australian Federation Conference, Melbourne 1890', http://adc.library.usyd. edu.au

Pacific War Online Encyclopedia, http://pwencycl.kgbudge.com/

Parliament of Australia, http://exhibitions.senate.gov.au/

Polls Roy Morgan, http://www.roymorgan.com/findings/

Power House Museum Powerhouse Museum, 'Governor-General's railway carriage, 1901', https://maas.museum/powerhouse-museum/

Royal Archives, http://www.royal.gov.uk/

Royal Yacht Britannia, http://www.royalyachtbritannia.co.uk/

Speech, HRH the Prince of Wales at Australia Day reception, Darling Harbour, Sydney, published on 26 January 1994, http://www. princeofwales.gov.uk/media/speeches/speech-hrh-the-prince-of-wales-the-australia-day-reception-darling-harbour-sydney

State Library of Western Australia, 'The Reluctant State', http://slwa. wa.gov.au/federation/fed/index.htm.

'State Trials, The', http://prov.vic.gov.au/whats-on/exhibitions/eureka-on-trial/the-state-trials

Sunter, Dr Anne Beggs. 'William Kelly, Life in Victoria, 1858', and Rusden, G.W., 'History of Australia, 1883', https://independen-taustralia.net/australia/

Vintage Motor Club, http://www.vmc.org.au/vmc-bulletin---articles-from-our-club-magazine

LIBRARY COLLECTIONS AND PAPERS, JOURNALS

Australian Parliament House, Background Paper 9, 1995–96, 'The Recent Republic Debate – A Chronology'. Carolyn Hide Consultant to the Law and Public Administration Group,

'Captain Cook's Journal during His First Voyage Round the World Made in H.M. Bark "Endeavour" 1768–71', Captain W. J. L. Wharton, R.N., F.R.S. Hydrographer of the Admiralty (ed.), digit-ised by Project Gutenberg Australia

Commonwealth Study Conference, Duke of Edinburgh's Study Conference, Commonwealth Record Volume 4, Issues 18 to 34

Godley, John Robert. *Extracts from a Journal of a Visit to New South Wales in 1853,* call number DSM/981.4/H, Mitchell Library, Sydney

'Guides Victorian Archives Links to Royalty, Royal Wedding Cake', printed in *Matilda,* September 1947

Historical Records of New South Wales (HRNSW), vol. 1, part 2, Bladen, F. M. and Murcott, Frank (eds), Government Printer, Sydney, 1892–1901

Holt, Harold, 'Personal Papers of Prime Minister Holt, Coronation Diary, 9 May to 23 July 1953', NAA: M2608.3, Series Number M2608, Control Symbol, 3 Barcode 3066375

Letter from Prince Edward to Freda Ward 18–24 June 1920 and 18 November 1920, State Library of New South Wales, SAFE / MLMSS 7765

Lionel Halsey to Sir Frederick and Lady Halsey, 14 June 1920, Micro-MS-0099, ATL, Hertfordshire Record Office

Public Record Office of Victoria (VPRS), 1085/P unit 8 no. 4, North Melbourne, Victoria

Reid, Jessie. 'Diary of Jessie Reid', provided to the author by granddaughter, Shona Gibson

Worgan, George. 'Journal, 27 January 1788', Library Council of NSW in association with the Library of Australian History, Sydney, 1978

LIST OF ILLUSTRATIONS

ACKNOWLEDGEMENTS

I FOUND WHEN I was researching this book that there is an abundance of historic material dealing with British royalty and Australia. In additional to a plethora of royal histories and biographies, all royal events have been extensively reported in Australian newspapers and magazines since the early nineteenth century; indeed, tours of Australia by royals have been given saturation local media coverage. Most colonial newspaper reports are now readily accessible on the National Library of Australia's 'Trove' website, which has made the task of researching more accessible than ever before. I was also fortunate to have access to a number of personal stories of ordinary Australians and their encounters with members of the British royal family. In May 2015 I was invited on to Ian McNamara's national ABC radio program *Australia All Over* to talk about Australia and the monarchy. As a result hundreds of listeners sent in fascinating and often humorous anecdotes, and several have been included in the book.

For help with the substantial research task involved in writing a book such as this I am indebted to the indefatigable Linda Atkinson, to whom this book is dedicated. I am also grateful to everyone at Random House and my publisher Nikki Christer for all the help, guidance and advice. My very special thanks go to editor Catherine Hill, who despite being a monarchist (I'm a republican) has helped make this book much better than it otherwise would have been.

INDEX